Rally 'Round the Flag

Rally 'Round the Flag

Chicago and the Civil War

Theodore J. Karamanski

Nelson-Hall Publishers/Chicago

Text Designer: Corasue Nicholas

Library of Congress Cataloging-in-Publication Data

Karamanski, Theodore J., 1953–
    Rally 'round the flag : Chicago and the Civil War / Theodore J.
Karamanski.
        p.   cm.
    Includes bibliographical references and index.
    ISBN 0-8304-1295-6
    1. Chicago (Ill.)—History—Civil War, 1861–1865.   I. Title.
F548.4K37   1993
977.3'1103—dc20   92-24197
                                                                    CIP

Manufactured in the United States of America

10   9   8   7   6   5   4   3   2   1

 TM The paper used in this book meets the
minimum requirements of American
National Standard for Information
Sciences—Permanence of Paper for
Printed Library Materials, ANSI
Z39.48-1984.

For My Son

CONTENTS

Acknowledgments

W hen I was a boy, the Civil War Centennial took place, and as a result the War Between the States was alive in my imagination. For hours I would pour over *American Heritage* books about the war's great battles and leaders. On Boy Scout outings to downtown Chicago, I enjoyed scrambling over the cannons in the Grand Army of the Republic Hall of the Chicago Public Library. Yet as a young historian I turned away from the war, attracted more by the drama of frontier history and the opportunities in the new field of historic preservation. It was Frederick Francis Cook's 1910 memoir *Bygone Days in Chicago* that drew me back to the Civil War and encouraged me to explore Chicago's role in the conflict. Cook's colorful account of Chicago during the 1860s lured me to the newspapers, letters, and memoirs that survived the Great Fire. In telling the story of the men and women of Civil War Chicago, I hope that I have preserved at least some of the intimacy and the excitement of the original sources.

The institutions who care for the records of Civil War Chicago made this project possible. At the Chicago Historical Society, Linda Evans and Archie Motley were always helpful and knowledgeable. The Newberry Library, the Illinois Historical Library, the Special Collections Departments at the Chicago Public Library, and the University of Chicago were also of considerable assistance. At the Cudahy Library of Loyola University, Lorna Newman was a wonderful help with interlibrary-loan requests.

My principle source of support and guidance in doing this project has been my wife and dearest colleague, Eileen M. McMahon. For four years she welcomed nineteenth century Chicagoans into our home and along on each vacation, never hinting that perhaps they had overstayed their welcome. Robert I. Girardi of the Chicago Civil War Roundtable helped me identify Southern sources. My colleagues at Loyola University, Timothy Gilfoyle, Harold Platt, and Patricia Mooney-Melvin, shared ideas, sources, and commiseration at various stages of the project. Department Chairman Joseph Gagliano smoothed the writing process with flexible scheduling, and Research Director Thomas Bennett helped bring closure to the effort with a summer grant and research stimulation funds for assembling the final manuscript. In all ways Loyola University (and the History Department, in particular) has been a supportive and congenial place to practice the craft of history.

Introduction

To step on the sidewalks of nineteenth-century Chicago was to become part of a bustling, no-holds-barred burg on the verge of greatness. A cow town knee deep in mud, the city burst at the seams with new people and new opportunities. "Would that I were able to suggest in prose the throb and urge and sting of my first days in Chicago," Theodore Dreiser wrote. For Dreiser, the city's personality "was a compound of hope and joy in existence, intense hope and intense joy." There was a supple quality to Chicago's clay that inspired architects, capitalists, and politicians to shape new and grand designs. The city's money was new, its institutions raw, and its prospects unlimited. From the mid-nineteenth century to the beginning of the twentieth, Chicago was the "wonder city" of the Western world. "I wish I could go to America," said Otto von Bismarck while in the midst of remaking the map of Europe, "if only to see that Chicago."[1]

The magical quality of Chicago was a product of its location and its people. Late twentieth-century complaints of Chicago as the blue-collar capital of the Rust Belt would seem incongruous to the city's nineteenth-century boosters. Chicago was "Queen of the Lakes," master of the American heartland, the fastest growing metropolis on the continent. Belching smoke stacks and noisy railroad yards were symbols of progress to be proudly displayed. The winters of the Great Lakes region were anticipated, not dreaded. The cold months slowed the pace of business, while entertainments heated up in a cycle of balls, shows, and concerts. Popular, inexpensive sports like ice-skating and sleigh rides increased whenever the mercury plunged. Indeed, the frost sealed the stench of the polluted river and froze the unyielding mud that generally mired Chicagoans.

The Civil War was a critical event in the maturation of this nineteenth-century city. Located a safe distance behind the lines and accessible to the armies via a superior network of railroads and waterways, Chicago was enriched by war contracts. It became, in Carl Sandburg's words, "hog butcher to the world" and was a vital Union supply center, ensuring its future industrial greatness. Even men were stockpiled in Chicago. Thousands of troops from northern Illinois, Michigan, and Wisconsin were trained at Camp Douglas on the city's South Side, a camp that became better known later as a prisoner-of-war detention center.

The Civil War divided Chicago not as severely as it divided the Union but in ways that were meaningful and lasting. The special tension that continues to exist between African-Americans and the descendants of the Irish in Chicago can be traced to the economic and partisan political clashes of the 1860s. While some Chicagoans risked their lives to win equality for all men, the city government acted to legally segregate the races. Although de jure segregation did not long endure in Chicago, the foundation was laid for a persistent de facto separation of the races.

Chicago during the Civil War continued its feverish growth. The city nearly tripled in population between 1860 and 1870, growing from 109,260 to 298,977, while it was also playing a major role in the most important conflict in American history. The intersection of these two events—Chicago's rise to urban maturity and the Civil War—make the years from 1860 to 1865 among the most crucial in the city's history. In telling that story I have steered clear of those events which relate solely to either Chicago history or Civil War military history. There are no detailed accounts of campaigns or battles or of city council debates or public works improvements. Those can be found elsewhere in great detail. This book focuses on those personalities and incidents that reflect how Chicagoans affected the struggle for the Union and how the war shaped the city.

Viewed through the lens of the Civil War, Chicago was a contradiction. Before 1860 the city was routinely denounced by Southerners as a "nigger lovin' town" and a "sink hole of abolitionism." Yet during the war Chicago was often described as a "hotbed" of antiwar dissent. The *Chicago Times,* one of the most popular newspapers, was actually suppressed for a time by order of the Union Army. On the other hand, Lincoln once said that Chicago was second only to Boston in urging an aggressive war. Long after Appomattox, Southerners remembered Chicago as "the bitterest city during the war."

The war produced the enlightened and efficient U.S. Sanitary Commission, and its Northwestern Division was headquartered in Chicago. The commission was sustained by the selflessness of hundreds of Chicago women, who provided wounded soldiers, hundreds of miles from home, with medical care. At the same time but across town, Southern prisoners died of disease by the thousands. While Chicago ministers passed out Bibles to the "boys in blue," the city became so overrun with prostitution that it earned the title "Wickedest city in America."

Only recently have historians examined the impact of the war on American cities. James M. Gallman's study of wartime Philadelphia revealed that war bought only short-term changes to that city's economy. Chicago saw some of the same "minor" economic adjustments found in Philadelphia. In both cities, for example, tailors turned to making uniforms, shoemakers made boots, and sailmakers made tents. But unlike Philadelphia, Chicago was forever transformed by the war. The processes which made it an industrial and meat packing center were accelerated. Industries such as iron making, railroad car construction, and food processing, only incipient before the war, were stimulated by government contracts. Unlike arms manufacturing, these industries were logical areas of economic expansion for Chicago and did not require postwar government spending to be sustained. Before the war Chicago's commercial economy had matured and was pregnant with opportunities for industrial expansion. The war did not cause industrialization in the city nor did it determine the direction of Chicago's production economy, but the conflict did fan the flames of industry and hurry the economic transformation.[2]

The close proximity of Chicago to the killing fields of Kentucky gave Civil War events an immediacy lacking in more recent wars. At the beginning of the war Chicago was a mere three hundred miles from the front. Throughout the conflict, soldiers at the front were seldom more than a two-day journey from the city. A close bond developed between Chicago and its volunteers during the first two years of the war. Chicagoans visited the troops in camp and rushed to the front after battles were fought. As early as 1862, this identification with the soldiers led many Chicagoans to urge a total war against the South. They wanted none of the "kid gloves business" of knightly warfare. They advocated a war of "conquest" against the South's civilians. This early conversion of the city's Republicans and War Democrats by war psychology in part accounted for the harsh conditions imposed upon rebel prisoners at Camp Douglas. The Chicago Board of Trade stoutly defended its harsh attitude toward all rebels as "a matter of necessity."[3]

Although many Chicago civilians, like the men at the front, supported the drift toward a "war of terror" against the South, the bonds between the battlefield and the city became weaker as the war progressed. The reality of combat was seldom depicted in the newspapers, and most Chicagoans seemed to have had little idea of how the war looked from the soldiers' perspective.

Chicago grew and changed a great deal during the war. For people on the home front it was those changes that dominated their experience of the war—not the combat, comradeship, and disease of military life. The prosperity of Civil War Chicago, the noisy cooperheadism of the *Chicago Times,* and the city's fear of the draft drove a wedge between soldiers and civilians. As historian Gerald Linderman has demonstrated, soldiers bitterly resented the war profiteers and the "cowardly" peace advocates. After the war several returning Illinois soldiers complained that the contribution of the ordinary soldier was unappreciated in Chicago. Although they returned victorious, the boys in blue were cheered more lustily when they went off to war than when they came marching home.[4]

Abraham Lincoln and Stephen Douglas both cast giant shadows over Chicago in the Civil War era. Douglas lost his bid to be the first Chicagoan elected president, yet on the eve of his death he rallied the Democrats of the city to the Union cause. Lincoln visited Chicago only once after his election, but his presence offstage exerted a powerful influence on politics of wartime Chicago. His most bitter critic, Wilbur F. Storey of the *Chicago Times,* was based in the city as were some of his staunchest allies. While it is too much to suggest, as Carl Sandburg did, that Storey's journalism drove John Wilkes Booth to assassinate Lincoln, the editor did as much to weaken Democratic support for the war in Chicago as Douglas had done to bolster it.

Chicago Republicans played a critical role in securing Lincoln the nomination. It is doubtful Lincoln would have been president had the convention been held in another city. By the time of the convention, Lincoln was for many in Chicago a symbol of the entire northwest region—rawboned, robust, and true to traditional values. As the war progressed he came to symbolize the nation's dogged determination to prevail. In this sense, Illinois became America. And in the wake of the Civil War, Lincoln became the focus for an idealism that seemed to be lost in the expanding commercial culture of late nineteenth-century Chicago.

Today Chicagoans are largely unaware of the physical reminders of the Civil War. Commuters rush past equestrian heroes frozen in bronze. The Victorian splendor of the Grand Army of the Republic Hall in the Cultural Center is known only to groups of restless school children and dedicated Civil War buffs. The most prominent testament of the war's economic impact, the Union Stockyards, is gone, and the giant railroad freight yards shrink every year. Yet the landscape of the city will not let the war be forgotten. We bicycle through parks named after Lincoln and Grant and drive down streets commemorating lesser heroes. Stephen Douglas's statue towers over the ghetto, which has emerged where Camp Douglas once stood. The "Little Giant" looks down on South Lake Shore Drive, where motorists speed past the poverty in cars with license plates that proclaim this to be the "Land of Lincoln."

Chicago is still the entrepôt of the heartland. In the bustle of trading pits and the tension of racially divided communities, the hand of the Civil War generation still rests on Chicago's shoulder. That ghostly generation offers no "lessons of the past" to guide the present, only the testament of ordinary men and women in an extraordinary time, a local perspective on a national tragedy.

1

⬦

THE
IRREPRESSIBLE
CANDIDATE

A plume of black smoke and red-hot sparks spewed from the stack of the engine as it hurtled across the prairie. Mileposts flew past in quick succession as the engineer eased open the throttle of the iron horse *Huron*. The fireman labored to keep the firebox aglow. With the air rushing past at gale force, the churning of the piston rods, and the clatter of iron wheels on steel rails, the fireman's shovel went unheard as it bit into the coal supply. Like veteran sailors with steady sea legs the two railroad men kept their balance as the *Huron* swayed from side to side as it streaked over side tracks. Engineer A. E. Bates pulled the rod that operated the whistle, releasing a jet of white smoke and an ear-numbing scream that pierced the early evening air. Bates blew the steam whistle two more times as the train streaked past a station so fast that two elderly men enjoying their pipes were nearly "frightened out of their wits." The engineer had no intention of slowing down. Instead, Bates opened the throttle more, and the train sped forward at nearly sixty miles per hour. The *Huron* was pulling a special train of the New York and Erie Railroad, and its passengers were in a hurry to reach Chicago.[1]

In the cars behind the speeding engine were delegates to the 1860 Republican National Convention. Thirty hours before, two hundred strong, they had left New York City. As the train made its westward journey it continued to pick up more delegates. Politicos from Albany, Cleveland, and Toledo flocked aboard. All were somberly dressed and looked not at all like the radicals their Democratic rivals accused them of being. The men (this group was all male) were mostly middle aged and wore black coats and vests, white shirts, and black hats. Their appearance was brightened only by their gold watch chains. Most had long curly hair and beards, and clutched a black cotton umbrella or a black wooden cane in one hand. In spite of their dress there would be no mistaking these men for mourners. Animated by their exhilarating journey, political high hopes, and more than a little alcohol, the men passed bottles of whiskey, flasks of brandy, and gin "cock-tail" jugs among them. Crude stories, bawdy songs, and poker games in the smoking car all belied the image of the Republicans as the "party of virtue."[2]

The festive atmosphere was elevated further whenever the train stopped at a depot, where it was greeted by banners, and bouquets from the local Republican clubs and bands that played "Hail Columbia" or "The Girl I Left Behind Me." As the train pulled out of the station with more passengers and freshened bottles, the throng would treat the delegates to three cheers for their favorite candidate. In most cases, the name that rang out was William H. Seward.

Seward was senator from New York and the unquestioned leader of the party nationally as well as in the Empire State. It was he who helped crystallize the young Republican party when, in a 1858 speech, he described America's "irrepressible conflict" between northern free labor and southern "slave power." The men aboard the train were believers in the "irrepressible conflict" and were confident in the nomination of the man who coined the phrase. Seward's supporters were going to Chicago, one of their number wrote, "to convey to the assembled wisdom an idea of their might and power." They boldly said they were unafraid of how the South would react to their candidate. The patience and willingness to negotiate which had headed off civil war and produced the Compromises of 1820 and 1850 had dissipated by 1860 in an acrimonious national debate over slavery. It is not that the men aboard the train were unequal to the task of compromise; rather, increasingly they felt that political compromise was incapable of settling the issue of slavery. In this regard the New York Republicans were not unlike many southern Democrats who were also inclined to regard the impending civil war as "irrepressible." Slavery's stalwarts insisted that their "peculiar institution" be guaranteed the right to grow along with the rest of America, while Republicans like Seward demanded that, like a malignant bacillus, slavery be contained where it was. The westbound locomotive was a metaphor for many American politicians in 1860—relentless, unswerving, and speeding toward the goal, assured that theirs was the right way.[3]

At 9:15 P.M. the train neared Chicago. Delegates eagerly peered out of the windows on the left side of the car for their first views of the city. The train sped out onto a trestle over Lake Michigan, and in no time the delegates found themselves one hundred yards from shore. The last light of day still glowed behind the city while over the lake the moon rose. Between the trestle and the shore was a basin dotted with small sailboats. Beyond it was park land and Chicago's most magnificent street, tree-lined Michigan Avenue. All the homes along the street were gaily illuminated. The stately marble facades of Terrace Row's three-story townhouses glittered like alabaster. The mansions of Park Row shone like beads of pearls strung out along the lake shore. In the park the Chicago Light Artillery deployed its batteries and fired salutes to the passing delegates. At the foot of Jackson Street rockets were launched, and the twilight sky was painted with explosions of red, white, and blue.[4]

Engineer Bates gradually slowed the long train as the yawning entrance of the Great Central Depot, brightly lit and festooned with Republican emblems, loomed ahead. As the *Huron* drew to a stop in a cloud of steam Bates looked at his watch and proudly noted he was half an hour ahead of schedule. Nonetheless, the Chicagoans were ready for them. Bands immediately struck up patriotic airs and reception committees hastily arranged themselves. The New Yorkers were formally met by a delegation of Chicagoans who hailed from New York. Similarly, the Ohio men were met by former Ohioans, and Massachusetts conventioneers were greeted by former Bay Staters. In a town like Chicago, which had so quickly risen to urban eminence, almost everyone was from somewhere else. The baggage was loaded onto a dray, and the reception committee escorted the visitors to their hotels.[5]

The delegates' brief view of the city that first evening impressed most of them and surprised the rest. Even those from New York were inclined to comment on the fine buildings, numerous shops, stately hotels, and bustling streets. Although Chicago in 1860 was less than thirty years old, it was already more than a frontier town. It had grown from a collection of rude huts huddled around Fort Dearborn in 1837 to a city of 108,000 people. It was still as raw, socially fluid, and alive with opportunity as the frontier, but metropolitan enough to yearn to be recognized as one of America's great cities. Indeed, there was an expansiveness in the way Chicagoans already viewed the world. No Chicago businessman would identify himself as being from "Chicago, Illinois." It was always simply "Chicago." The phenomenal town needed no further description or qualification. Editorial writers openly dreamed of the day when burgeoning Chicago would be the "great central commercial city of the North American continent." An 1856 city directory boasted that "its past growth had been miraculous. . . . Nothing . . . can apparently arrest or even check its onward progress." Those who scoffed at Chicago's civic pride were warned that "our city is one of the manifest destinies, and all the croaking in the world will not impede her march a single day."[6]

Youthful pride, geographical position, and human industry were responsible for the windy praise and remarkable growth of Chicago. Located on a flat wet prairie between the Great Lakes Basin and a tributary of the Mississippi River, Chicago sat astride America's two premier avenues of commerce. Although the completion of the Illinois and Michigan Canal in 1848 bankrupted the State of Illinois, it linked the two waterways and assured Chicago's position as the trade center of the West. In a few short years Chicago became the target of the lumber industry of Michigan and Wisconsin. "Miles of timber yards extend along one of the forks of the river," wrote an 1860 visitor to the city. "The harbor is choked with arriving timber vessels; timber trains snort over the prairie in every direction."[7]

Midwest agriculture also focused on Chicago at an early date. By 1854 the *Democratic Press* could with justice proclaim Chicago "The Greatest Primary Grain Port in the World." A year later direct grain shipments to Europe began. Giant grain elevators along the Chicago River dominated the skyline. Each behemoth was capable of handling thousands of tons of grain each day. Trains could be unloaded and a fleet of schooners supplied with their cargo in a matter of hours. Growing hand in hand with the grain trade was Chicago's meat-packing industry. The city's five packing houses vied for space with the lumber yards and grain elevators along the busy banks of the Chicago River.[8]

The great boomtown of the mid-nineteenth century was a magnet for people. The population of Chicago tripled between 1850 and 1860, with more than half of the newcomers coming from abroad. Ireland, the German states, Scandinavia, and Britain provided the bulk of the immigrants. Yet there were enough native-born Americans in Chicago to make up reception committees for every Republican delegation, including those from California and Oregon.

The central focus of the city of Chicago was Courthouse Square. The grassy enclosure was separated from the busy traffic on Washington and LaSalle streets by a wrought iron fence. At the center of the square sat the two-and-a-half story Italianate-style courthouse. Atop the structure was a cupola that held a great bell. The city was not yet so large that the courthouse bell could not be heard in every neighborhood. The bell's regular clang called children to dinner and husbands home from their jobs. Emergencies and celebrations always brought forth an energetic tolling of the bell. Towering over the city, the courthouse cupola was visible from most neighborhoods. Visitors were fond of climbing the long circular staircase that led to a balcony, where they could view the city below and the sand dunes of Michigan thirty miles away.[9]

From the cupola the three divisions of the city were also clearly discernible. Chicago's hundred thousand residents were separated by the forks of the Chicago River. The most populous section, which included the central business district, was called the South Division. Lake Street, the narrow, congested core of retail shopping, banking, and wholesale commerce, was crowded during the day with wagons, carriages, and drays of every description. Along its sidewalks society women hurried past grain merchants and gawkish woodsmen. Produce sellers hawked their fruits and vegetables in a sing-song pitch that was nearly drowned out by the clatter of horses' hoofs on the wood-block street. All the city's fine hotels were in the South Division, as were most of the business offices. Residences were scattered throughout the area, but the most fashionable place to build was along Michigan Avenue. To those who lived in the row houses or mansions that faced the lake it was known simply as "the Avenue." They viewed those with other addresses with pity and condescension.[10]

North of the Chicago River was an area some called "Nord Seite" because of its large number of lager beer shops and German immigrants. The prosperous German citizenry, mostly laborers, artisans, and small shopkeepers, formed the city's most numerous ethnic group. While Germans gave a particular flavor to the North Division, it was by no means a German ghetto. In fact the North Side was popular with middle-class families. Swedes, Scottish Americans, and Germans lived harmoniously in blocks of wood frame cottages. Harmony could not be said to have reigned over Kilgubbin, an Irish neighborhood that extended along the North Branch of the Chicago River and included a large island just above the forks. The island was called Goose Island, perhaps because of the flocks of fowl kept by some of the Irish families. Kilgubbin was notorious for its riotous street life, wretched shanties, and high crime rate. The slum contributed to the slightly gritty atmosphere of the North Side. Factories and shipyards along the river, and breweries and brickyards in the neighborhood, helped to reinforce this impression.[11]

The natural division of the Chicago River into a North Branch and a South Branch created a watery barrier between the central business districts and the western reaches of the city—the West Side. The east-west orientation of Lake Street rendered settlements across the river easily accessible to the main shopping district. Business and convenience made the West Side attractive to the bourgeoisie. Union Park, a lavishly landscaped refuge from the congestion of city traffic, became the focal point of an elite neighborhood. However, the large, well-built but unpretentious homes of the Union Park area were not the whole of the West Side. To the south, the Lower West Side was characterized by the ramshackled frame shanties of the "lumber shovers." Along the west bank of the river immigrant laborers, mostly German, Irish, and Bohemian, made their homes close to the lumberyards where they worked unloading schooners.[12]

———◇———

The convocation of the Republican party in Chicago swelled the population of the city by as many as fifty thousand.[13] In one day the Illinois Central Railroad, only one of a dozen railroads serving the city, brought twelve thousand people into Chicago. As the special trains poured into the city from all directions, the city's hotels filled up. Chicago had been given the nod for hosting the convention over rival Indianapolis because of its forty-two hotels, more than any northwestern city could boast. Yet, on the eve of the convention's opening, all hotels were filled. The elite "two dollar and a half a day" hotels had long since been booked by state delegations for politicking. Even the fleabag, dollar-a-day joints were filled to overflowing. "O, give me a cot" was the cry of many a visitor. Cots were jammed into every available space—underneath stairs, in hallways, and in storage rooms. Single rooms for ordinary delegates were unheard of; five and six people to a room was the rule. Billiard halls were also drafted into the hotel business. All day and into the evening their tables were used for sport. But as the night progressed the benches in the hall began to fill with homeless Republicans waiting for the games to cease. When the crowd was large enough the proprietor closed the tables, covered them with makeshift mattresses, and rented them as sleeping accommodations. "We looked in just after midnight, upon one *ranche* of this kind," a *Chicago Tribune* reporter noted, "where one hundred and thirty persons were making this use of billiard tables in a manner and zest, from the fatigues of the day, that would have excited the sympathy of the most unfeeling bosom."[14]

There were only 466 official, voting delegates to the convention, but thousands of other Republicans, part of a movement that had revolutionized the American political scene, flocked to the city. Born in 1854 in the midwestern corn belt, the Republican party had a meteoric rise to national prominence. Less than two years after its founding, the party held its first national convention in Philadelphia and nominated a politically inexperienced former explorer, John C. Fremont, for president. In spite of an incompetent candidate and only a fledgling party organization, the Republicans received 33 percent of the votes in a three-party race. The Republicans, although they were a sectional party and had little support in the South, clearly had a chance to challenge the Democrats for control of the federal government. To be successful, however, they had to find a way to synthesize a variety of dissident political elements. Among the most important of these was the American Know-Nothing party, which opposed the growing importance of Catholics and immigrants in American life. Abolitionists and former Liberty party supporters, although they were never numerous, were a highly articulate and well-organized group attracted to the Republicans. Former Whigs looked to the Republicans to lead a government that would actively aid industrial expansion. Old Free Soilers, who as early as 1848 organized a party to halt the expansion of slavery, looked to the Republicans to carry the banner of free labor. This latter group contained sizable numbers of German immigrants who were attracted to the idealism of antislavery but repulsed by the Know-Nothing's vulgar patriotism. It would be no small task for the young party to harmonize these diverse constituencies.

It was precisely because the Republican party was in flux that the Chicago convention attracted thousands of observers. They flocked to the city with their carpetbags to be part of a historic event and to argue for their vision of the party. Thanks in large part to the leadership of William H. Seward, the Republicans had begun to build a common philosophy. While delegates and party members might argue over the role of such issues as temperance or women's rights, and might even come to blows over abolitionism or nativism, there was agreement on many fronts. Republicans were opposed to slavery but advocated its restriction, not its abolition. The "peculiar institution," in their view, had robbed the South of the vitality and industry that comes from free men working hard to achieve their ambitions. Economic stagnation led to political oligarchies in the cotton states, which Republicans were loath to see expanded to the national government. The physical intimidation of northern representatives by southern legislators, proslavery gag rules, and the overthrow of the Compromise of 1850 by border ruffians in Kansas were cited by Republicans as evidence of slavery's pernicious influence on American democracy. The Republicans gathering in Chicago were animated by the common belief that their party alone could save the American experiment. This faith lent a "born-again" flavor to their public proceedings. But the very real differences which threatened Republican unity made behind-the-scenes politicking in Chicago intense and venal.

The unchallenged master of "hard ball" Republican politics was Thurlow Weed, party boss of New York State, a sixty-three-year-old newspaper editor from western New York. For almost thirty years he had been the leader of the Whigs and later the Republican party in the Empire State. Candidates he endorsed received superior press coverage across the state, lavish financial support, and shrewd political advice. His success at advancing his friends and influencing policy had earned Weed a series of unflattering epithets ranging from "the Dictator" and "the Wizard" to the "Lucifer of the Lobby." Yet, although Weed elevated and then broke many politicians and amassed millions in campaign funds, he was not personally ambitious for high office. He had devoted his considerable talents to furthering the political destiny of William H. Seward, serving for three decades as Seward's personal friend and political handler. The 1860 campaign found Seward at the peak of his political career and Weed at the apex of his New York machine. Chicago, they expected, would be the scene of a hard-fought battle, but inevitably it would be their greatest victory.[15]

Weed established his headquarters in a suite at the Richmond House, one of the most luxurious hotels in the city. From here the Wizard pulled the strings of literally thousands of assistants. The tall, gaunt man with thick white hair and bushy white eyebrows was generally pleased by what they reported. Straw polls taken on the trains arriving in Chicago showed that Seward was the clear favorite of both the delegates and the throng that accompanied them. A poll of Michigan Central Railroad passengers showed Seward leading all other candidates by a seven to one margin. Weed was also told of a poll on the Chicago and North Western which showed his man preferred over all other candidates by three to one. But the veteran politician's thin smile evaporated when a train from Indiana arrived and yielded a poll giving Abraham Lincoln 51 votes, Seward 43, with 131 delegates divided among a host of other candidates. Clearly Indiana's delegates were "at sea." Weed had not counted on their support, but he did not want them going over en masse to another candidate. Lincoln's strength would bear watching.[16]

Weed spent most of his first day in Chicago in strategy sessions with his supporters. The leaders of the New York delegation, which was solid for Seward, were his stalwarts. Edwin D. Morgan, governor of New York and national chairman of the Republican party, owed his office to Weed. But the Wizard did not want to dilute the potency of this highly respected ally by involving him in overtly partisan battles, so Morgan established his own headquarters at the Tremont House. Another member of Ward's brain trust was Henry J. Raymond, editor of the *New York Times*. Weed had provided the financial backing and political support that allowed the *Times* to thrive following its founding in 1851. As a newspaperman Raymond was a useful source of information on the progress of the numerous clandestine caucuses that would mark the convention. William M. Evarts, a distinguished lawyer renowned for his eloquence and irreproachable character, was chairman of the New York delegation. Unlike most of the delegation, he was not in Weed's pocket. But this, too, was part of Weed's calculation. Evarts' independence would lend substance to his pro-Seward speeches. All these men, while still confident of victory, were concerned by reports of Indiana's and Pennsylvania's opposition to Seward. The Pennsylvania delegation had been in town three days before the New Yorkers arrived. Immediate action would be needed to bring these states into line.[17]

Now that the New Yorkers were in town, Weed wanted to demonstrate Seward's strength. Parades, rallies, speeches, and socials were planned to plant the image of a Seward boom and sway the undecided delegates to the banner of "Old Irrepressible." To effect that plan Weed marshaled the loudmouths, the heavy drinkers, and the glad-handers who accompanied his delegation. Captioned by Tommy Hyer, a prize fighter of national renown, these men were prepared to take care of the unsavory details of the nomination.

Weed had an ample war chest to purchase champagne, cigars, and votes. For two years he had gathered funds by legal means and otherwise. One scheme alone netted the campaign perhaps as much as $1 million. Weed shepherded a lucrative street railway charter through the New York state legislature and saw to it that $250,000 in bribes were distributed. Even Governor Morgan was shocked by the audacious swindle, and he vetoed the bill, but Weed's forces easily overrode his opposition. The howls of the outraged public were still ringing in his ears when Weed left for Chicago. At the convention, money would be one of Weed's principle assets.[18]

It would be wrong, however, to view Weed as merely a corrupt political boss. He was a master politician. Illicit fund raising was among his lesser talents. Weed had a marvelous way of making small men feel important, an essential skill in coalition building. He also was a highly seasoned propagandist who knew how to adroitly plant a notion in citizens' minds and make them think it was their own idea. Most important for the battle in Chicago, Weed was a veteran of many nominating conventions. He knew the importance of emotion and momentum in an era when there were no primary elections and delegates were free to change their votes.

In the days before the convention Weed met with each arriving delegation. No sooner had the Kansas delegation arrived in the city on the morning train, for example, than one of Weed's assistants greeted them with an invitation to meet at Weed's suite. After refreshing themselves in their rooms, the Kansas Republicans, with a "touch of trepidation," mustered the courage to see the "political mogul." Weed knew his "Lucifer of the Lobby" reputation preceded him and intimidated strangers, so he personally greeted each Kansas man as he entered the parlor. His often impassive face was animated with gracious warmth as he shook each man's hand and immediately memorized his name. Soon the delegates were perfectly at ease and sat at a conference table with Weed. He spoke in complimenting tones about the important work they had done for the party during the "bloody Kansas" crisis of the past few years.

With personal pleasantries aside, Weed launched into the specific pitch he felt was necessary to win the Kansas men for Seward. As westerners he felt they might be intrigued by the prospects of Missouri's Edward Bates, a respected judge who had been active in the Whig party, or even by Abraham Lincoln. So Weed decided to stress that the crisis before the nation demanded an experienced statesman, qualities neither Bates nor Lincoln could claim. "Four years ago we went to Philadelphia to name our candidate, and we made one of the most inexcusable blunders any political party has ever made in the country," Weed began. "We nominated a man who had no qualifications for the position of Chief Magistrate of this Republic," said Weed, referring to John C. Fremont. "We were defeated as we probably deserved to be, and we have that lesson of defeat with us today." Weed now approached his main argument. "We are facing a crisis; there are troubled times ahead of us. We all recognize that. What this country will demand as a chief executive for the next four years is a man of the highest order of executive ability, a man of real statesmanlike qualities, well known to the country, and of a large experience in national affairs. No other class of man ought to be considered at this time."

Weed's soft speaking voice and gracious manner won over the bulk of the Kansas delegates. But Addison A. Procter, youngest of the delegates, could not help thinking, as he listened to the New Yorker, of Lord Byron's description of a pirate: "The mildest mannered man that ever scuttled a ship or cut a throat." Weed concluded his pitch:

> We think we have in Mr. Seward just the qualities the country needs. He is known by us all as a statesman. As Governor of New York he has shown splendid executive ability. As Senator he has shown himself to be a statesman, and a political philosopher. He is especially equipped in a knowledge of our foreign relations, and will make a candidate to whom our people can look with a feeling of security. We expect to nominate him on the first ballot, and to go before the country full of courage and confidence.[19]

The Kansas men voiced a hearty assent to Weed's remarks. He thanked them for calling on him. As he again shook hands with each delegate, he assessed the strength of his pro-Seward sentiment. He liked what he saw in their faces. The Weed magic was at work once again.

Not all the delegations visiting the Richmond House needed to be won over to Seward. The pro-Seward delegates also reported to Weed to get his assessment of the progress of the campaign and to receive his orders as to what they should do to further the cause. Some were veteran politicians from New England with whom Weed had worked before. But Seward also had great strength in the Upper Great Lakes states. Among those were men won to the senator's side by the idealistic and uncompromising tone of his rhetoric. Their battle cry was the "Irrepressible Conflict" with slavery. They had never had contact with Weed and his New York machine before. Typical of these idealists was Carl Schurz, chairman of the Wisconsin delegation, a short, black-bearded immigrant who had fled political oppression in the German states and found prosperity and political prominence in a frontier state.

Shortly after arriving in Chicago, Schurz marched his delegation, which was 100 percent for Seward, to the Richmond House. Full of enthusiasm, they wanted to report for orders. But the ardor of Schurz's idealism was immediately chilled as he made his way through Weed's headquarters. He was unable to find Raymond of the *New York Times* or William Evarts or Governor Morgan. What he did find were:

> New York politicians, apparently of the lower sort, whom Thurlow Weed had brought with him to aid him in doing his work. . . . They talked very freely about the great service they had rendered or were going to render. They had marched in street parades with brass bands and Seward banners to produce the impression that the whole country was ablaze with enthusiasm for Seward. They had treated members of other delegations with no end of champagne and cigars to win them for Seward. . . . They had hinted to this man and that supposed to wield some influence, that if he could throw that influence for Seward, he might, in case of success, count upon proper "recognition." They had spent money freely and let everybody understand that there was a great lot to spend.

Schurz observed that the only man of note in the crowd was Thurlow Weed. He "moved as the great captain, with ceaseless activity and noiseless step, receiving their reports and giving new instructions in his peculiar whisper, now and then taking one into a corner of the room for a secret talk, or disappearing with another through a side door for transactions still more secret."

Weed cordially greeted the diminutive German and asked for Schurz's opinion of the situation. He received an enthusiastic summary of the young Republican's devotion to Seward. Perhaps trying to cool down Schurz, Weed reminded him the problem at hand was how to impress those people who did not share their enthusiasm. Weed advised the Wisconsin men to "exhibit confidence in every possible way" so as to induce others to join the bandwagon. He asked Schurz to play the German card by visiting as many delegations as he could "and to let them know that no candidate could possibly receive as many 'German votes' as Mr. Seward." But Schurz had taken a dislike to Weed and already had begun to regard him as a "Mephistopheles" who would dishonor Seward. Instead of agreeing to Weed's request he equivocated, by replying, "I could not well say that, for I hoped it would not prove true in case Mr. Seward should unfortunately fail to be nominated."[20]

Weed did not have time to debate or to smooth Schurz's ruffled feathers. He had other delegates to meet, and there were plans to complete for a reception honoring prominent northeastern Republicans. Most important, there was a meeting to be arranged with Henry S. Lane, the key man in turning the Indiana delegation to Seward. Weed's political pragmatism might have alienated idealists like Schurz, but it would take more than platitudes to transform Seward from the leading contender to the nominated candidate. As Schurz went back to his hotel somewhat disheartened, Weed went back to spinning the web that would capture the necessary votes.[21]

While Weed worked to bind delegates to Seward, another politically powerful New Yorker labored just as hard against "Old Irrepressible." No sooner had the Kansas delegates returned to their rooms at the Briggs House when they were assailed by a pale, flaxen-haired man in a light, drab suit. He strode into the room, tossed his floppy felt hat on the table, and stood in the middle of the room looking over the delegates with his piercing blue eyes. A Democrat might have mistaken him for "a dairy farmer fresh from his cloven field," but, being good Republicans, the Kansas men immediately recognized Horace Greeley. As editor of the *New York Herald Tribune* Greeley headed the most influential Republican newspaper. His journalistic leadership in the fight against the expansion of slavery won him a great reputation in the Midwest, and his editorials were eagerly read and reprinted. To suddenly be face to face with the great man after being in the city only a few hours stunned the Kansas men.

After his dramatic entrance Greeley put his audience at ease with warm compliments for the news and correspondence that they had shared with him over the years. He immediately took on the attitude of an old friend and quickly won their confidence: as one delegate recalled, "He seemed to find a place in our hearts at a bound." After the exchange of pleasantries, Greeley asked if they had visited Weed at Seward headquarters. "I suppose they are telling you," Greeley said in a deliberate, drawn-out manner," that Seward is the be all and the end all of our existence as a party, our great statesman, our profound philosopher, our pillar of cloud by day, our pillar of fire by night, but I want to tell you boys that in spite of all this you couldn't elect Seward if you could nominate him."

Had the Kansas men not been so surprised by these words, they probably would have laughed at how perfectly Greeley had summarized, almost mimicked, Weed's pitch. Greeley had long been a highly visible supporter of Seward. They did not expect New York's leading Republican journalist to be against New York's leading Republican. Greeley went on:

> You must remember as things stand today we are a sectional party. We have no strength outside the North, practically we must have the entire North with us if we hope to win. Now there are states of the

North that cannot be induced to support Seward, and without these states we cannot secure electoral votes enough to elect. So, to name Seward, is to invite defeat.

After planting the seeds of doubt concerning Seward, Greeley left the Kansas delegation but not before promising to introduce them to "representative men" from New Jersey, Pennsylvania, and Indiana who were against Seward.[22]

Greeley was pleased with the effect of his first caucus with the Kansas delegates. The journalist was playing a deceitful game at the Chicago convention. Publicly he appeared to remain a loyal member of the informal Weed-Seward-Greeley partnership formed in 1838 that had helped each of them rise to great prominence, while privately he labored to boost another candidate into the nomination. It was Weed's influence and money that helped transform Greeley from a starving journalist to a would-be king maker. But the journalist wanted a more direct role in politics, and when in 1854 he was passed over as a gubernatorial candidate and then not even offered the lieutenant governorship, Greeley severed his ties with Weed and Seward. In a private letter to Seward he chided the senator for his lack of gratitude for Greeley's assistance over the years. But the letter remained private, and in the ensuing years Greeley continued to cooperate with Weed and Seward in their most important battles. Weed tried to formally heal the breech prior to the convention, but Greeley, an idealist, was offended by the Albany boss's recent swindles. The upshot was that Greeley was not offered a seat in the New York delegation. But the eminent journalist outflanked Weed and was credentialed by the State of Oregon when one of its delegates was unable to attend.[23]

Greeley was a loose cannon, rolling along the floor of the convention wreaking havoc in the Seward camp. The better informed delegates heard rumors of the rift, but many, particularly those from the Midwest, still thought of Greeley as a Seward man. This made his denunciations of Seward particularly damning. If even Greeley did not think Seward could win, perhaps the delegates needed to rethink their positions.

The candidate Greeley did support was Missouri judge Edward Bates, who was not even a Republican. He was an elderly Whig politician who had supported the Know-Nothing party four years before. Bates, however, was a favorite among conservative Republicans because of his ability to attract new elements into the party and because he came from a slave state. He was Seward's most important rival going into the convention. Another elderly jurist, John M. Read, a Pennsylvanian, also received considerable preconvention support. But Read's star, unlike Bates's, had already begun to set before the party convention in Chicago.

The Pennsylvania delegation came into the city largely committed to Senator Simon Cameron, whom historians have determined was "a crass businessman, a turncoat politician, and head of one of the most notoriously venal of state machines."[24] But his prospects could not be discounted because he represented a critical state and had a healthy war chest. Throughout the Midwest, "Cameron and Lincoln Clubs" had been established to champion the corrupt Keystone state politician and his choice for vice-president.

Ohio, another powerful Republican state, offered several strong candidates. Senator Salmon P. Chase was second only to Seward among the party's radical abolition wing. A brilliant, died-in-the-wool Republican, he was selfish, vain, and egotistical. Chase spent the year prior to the convention doing everything he could to snare support. But because of the conflicting ambitions of John McLean, an ancient who sat on the Supreme Court, and fiery Senator Benjamin Wade, the Ohio delegation was divided. Ohio's candidates needed a deadlocked convention to be able to make a stab at the nomination.

A deadlock was possible because of the usual number of "favorite son" candidates. Vermont advocated the cause of its senator, Jacob Collamer, while New Jersey championed former vice-presidential candidate Senator William L. Dayton. Illinois, only a week before the convention opened in Chicago, committed its entire delegation to a would-be senator, Abraham Lincoln.[25]

————◇————

Lincoln was a dark-horse candidate who could perhaps have secured the vice-presidential slot on the ticket. Had the convention been held in any other city but Chicago, he never would have won the presidential nod. This is not to say that there was nothing to recommend his candidacy. He was from one of a handful of critical states the Republicans needed to carry in the fall—Illinois, Indiana, Pennsylvania, and New Jersey. His magnificent showing against Stephen A. Douglas—leader of the Democratic party—in the 1858 senate campaign had won him admirers across the country. But that campaign and an undistinguished term in Congress twelve years before were the extent of his national political career, and in the end he did lose to Douglas. In the wake of the Great Debates, Lincoln had been careful to cultivate a national profile through well-publicized political speeches. In these appearances he backed away from the rhetoric of his famous "House Divided" speech and positioned himself with the conservative wing of the party. Yet in spite of these efforts, Lincoln, on the eve of the convention, was not well known among the party's rank and file.

That Lincoln persisted in his efforts as a presidential candidate is a tribute to his will to power and his political savvy. He brushed aside all attempts by Cameron and Seward supporters to depict him as a vice-president on their tickets, knowing that such talk would weaken his chances for the top spot. Although he was not optimistic about his prospects for success, he did want to make a strong showing as a foundation for another senatorial campaign. It was not until the Illinois Republican convention met in Decatur that the prairie lawyer's campaign caught fire. In a carefully managed exercise in political showmanship, Lincoln was carried to the podium on the shoulders of his supporters. Then, when enthusiasm was at a fever pitch two gnarled pioneers marched through the throng with a banner supported by two old wooden fence rails. The banner read:

> Abraham Lincoln. The Rail Candidate for President in 1860. Two Rails from a Lot of 3,000 made in 1830 by John Hanks and Abe Lincoln—whose Father was the First Pioneer of Macon County.

Never mind that the rails had been taken from a fence twelve miles away. Never mind that Lincoln's father was not Macon County's first settler. The vital fact was that the convention went wild. The rails symbolized Lincoln's rise from poverty and made a potent and picturesque political emblem. At that emotional moment, Illinois' many Seward supporters were effectively gagged, and the delegation named to Chicago was committed to Lincoln, not just on the customary first ballot, but enthusiastically to the end, whatever that might be.[26]

Three days later, Judge David Davis, Lincoln's campaign manager, arrived in Chicago. Thurlow Weed was already in town, and the Seward headquarters was established. Greeley had already raised the Bates banner. Although the convention was only four days away, Lincoln's people were unorganized. Davis was shocked to find that no one had even bothered to arrange for hotel rooms to serve as headquarters of the Lincoln forces. Davis quickly took two rooms at the Tremont Hotel, paid for them with his own funds, and began to marshal his supporters.[27]

Davis was a forty-five-year-old Illinois circuit judge who, like Lincoln, had made the political journey from Whig to Republican. He was a frank, industrious, and astute politician, who was bound to Lincoln by ties forged in the smoky taverns and drafty courtrooms of the rural Illinois legal circuit. At three hundred pounds, he was big in every respect: " 'He had a big head and a big body, a big brain and a big heart,' " recalled a contemporary. His bulk made him "the natural presiding officer of every company, social and otherwise, in which he happened to find himself." Lincoln chose him to lead his forces at the convention because of his superior organizational ability and because of a unique "way of making a man do a thing whether he wants to or not." Among his confederates at the convention was Norman B. Judd, a veteran of the state senate whom Lyman Trumbull called "the shrewdest politician . . . in the state" and whom Lincoln described as a "trimmer." Judd played a large role in securing the convention for Chicago. He was aided by a coterie of Lincoln's old legal and political associates: Leonard Swett, Ward Lamon, Jesse Dubois, and Samuel C. Parks.[28]

Davis needed all his political skill merely to harmonize the Republicans of Illinois, let alone lead them to victory. Only a few days earlier, Swett and Judd had been rival candidates for the gubernatorial nomination. When neither would yield to the other, a dark-horse candidate secured the nomination on the fourth ballot. The wounds from that battle were still open, and Davis had to handle the pair of them with care. "Long John" Wentworth, the Republican mayor of Chicago, was an even more serious problem. Although he was a personal friend of Lincoln's, he refused to support the rail splitter at the convention. He was in high dudgeon over the failure of the state party to name him as one of the prestigious four Illinois delegates-at-large to the national convention. Lincoln's decision to make Davis, not Long John, his manager further angered him. Wentworth noisily made his way through the preconvention caucuses denouncing Lincoln and praising William H. Seward. But even more noticeable was the division in the Chicago Republican press. Whenever Judge Davis looked out the window of his room at the Tremont, he saw a huge sign with one word emblazoned on it: "Seward." The sign and other bright Seward banners decorated the offices of the *Chicago Journal*, an influential Republican daily. At least Davis could console himself; he had the resources of the *Chicago Tribune* on his side.[29]

The first task for the Lincoln men was to try to slow the momentum of the Weed-Seward machine. This meant cooperating with all other possible delegates to expose the weaknesses of the senator from New York. An important ally was Henry S. Lane, Republican gubernatorial candidate in Indiana. He had an influential voice in the party, because he had served ably as chair of the 1856 national convention. Lane felt Seward could not win Indiana in November—his rhetoric against slavery was too strong for southern Indiana voters. Lane led the Indiana delegates to Chicago in search of a candidate who could win Indiana and thereby pull the rest of the state ticket into power. Another irreconcilable Seward opponent was Andrew Curtin, gubernatorial candidate in Pennsylvania, who opposed Seward on similarly self-interested grounds. Seward could not carry Pennsylvania, he maintained, because former Know-Nothings resented his early support for parochial (Roman Catholic) education in New York. Although many Indiana men leaned toward Bates and Pennsylvania was nearly solid for Cameron, the Lincoln supporters were cheered by their opposition to Seward. Every delegate knew Seward could win the nomination but not the election without Indiana, Pennsylvania, and Illinois; thus their enthusiasm for Seward was dampened on the eve of the convention.

The results of the initial round of caucuses heartened Davis enough to ignore vice-presidential offers and strive for the top spot on the ticket. First he needed to make Lincoln more than another "favorite son" candidate. He opened spirited negotiations with the Indiana delegation, which was open to offers from any candidate but Seward. From an impressive suite in the Tremont Hotel, Frank Blair managed the Bates campaign and was confident of securing their support. There were many more Bates delegates than Lincoln supporters among the Hoosiers. Fortunately, several Indiana leaders who had known Abe Lincoln during his circuit riding days were vigorous in their support of the "rail splitter." It is likely that Davis tipped the balance and secured the delegation's final support by promising Caleb Smith, one of their leaders, a spot in Lincoln's cabinet. However it was done, Indiana's secret promise to support Lincoln on the first ballot made him a genuine candidate. But because nothing bound Indiana to that pact, Davis could only hope that Bates or another candidate did not make them a better offer before the voting began.[30]

———◇———

On Wednesday, May 16, the convention formally opened. The 466 delegates filed into the convention hall, and thousands of spectators pressed eagerly toward the doors to be among those admitted to the gallery. The Republicans met in a large wood auditorium, dubbed "the Wigwam," near the Chicago River at the corner of Lake and Market streets. Politicians, particularly in New York, had long used the term "Wigwam" to describe their campaign headquarters, and local Republicans seized on the name for the convention hall. But there was nothing ordinary about the auditorium they built. The Wigwam was the "largest audience room in the United States." It was all the more remarkable because, as late as April 1, the lot where the structure was built was vacant. Once construction began, it went forward with marvelous speed. Using the wood framing techniques that were pioneered in Chicago, carpenters soon erected a hundred foot by hundred and eighty foot building. The cost was a mere $5,000, which was paid by local Republicans, and Republican builders were used.[31]

The Wigwam was capable of holding twelve thousand people—clearly more than needed for the 466 delegates and the members of the press to do their business. Chicago's other halls could have accommodated such a group easily but would not have held the thousands of enthusiastic supporters. When Thurlow Weed heard of the massive structure being built in Chicago, he became suspicious that perhaps the pro-Lincoln men intended to stampede the convention by sheer force of numbers. But the Lucifer of the Lobby was not so easily outflanked. The thousands of Seward supporters in town for the convention, including the hundreds of specially transported toughs from New York City, were Weed's insurance against local demonstrations. Simon Cameron also had a deep pocket and did his best to ensure that his name would be on many lips. His nearly six-hundred-man cheering section was given free rail transport to Chicago in exchange for political favors from the unscrupulous senator.[32]

These "professional" supporters mixed with thousands who were drawn to Chicago by the spectacle. Long before the convention was set to open, the vicinity of the Wigwam was a mob scene. The *Chicago Daily Journal's* reporter saw "thousands of people . . . crowded around the doors and windows, congregated upon the bridge. [They] sat on the curb stones, and in time, used every available inch of standing room. The doors were thrown open at half past eleven, and the vast throng poured in." The main floor was quickly packed with standing spectators. The gallery, which seated about three thousand, was reserved for ladies and their gentlemen escorts, making unattached women a valuable commodity. Enterprising Republican stalwarts offered startled school girls twenty-five cents to see them to the gallery. One girl made a tidy profit by taking six separate men into the Wigwam before she stopped, fearful that the doorkeepers were catching on to the game. An Irish laundress with a load of clothes under her arm seized the chance to make a little extra money and boldly walked up to the gallery with a Seward supporter in one arm and the clothes in the other. After this gambit worked, there was a mad scramble for any female. But when a spectator tried to draft a young Indian woman who had been selling moccasins to tourists, the doorkeepers barred their entry. A "Squaw," they rudely stated, could not be a "lady."

While the crowd patiently awaited the arrival of the remaining delegates, they could not help but admire the Wigwam's interior. The floors of the structure were pitched so that those in the rear could see over the crowd in front of them. The delegates sat beneath state banners on a huge stage that ran the length of the building. On the wall behind the stage were massive paintings of Liberty, Plenty, Justice, and other patriotic emblems. Wooden pillars rising from the stage and the main floor were artfully covered by boughs of evergreens and red, white, and blue bunting. Busts of George Washington and other heroes adorned the front of the stage, while at the west end of the platform hung a large banner which read "For President _____, For Vice President _____." Gaslights and skylights combined with the decorations to make the Wigwam a brightly lit firetrap.[33]

At 12:15 Governor Morgan of New York called the convention to order and in due course proceeded to a roll call of the states. Applause greeted the reading of each state's name (save for those of the Deep South which had sent no delegates and were received with derision and laughter). George Ashmun of Massachusetts assumed the responsibilities of chairman, several speeches were given, and various committees introduced. The convention then adjourned so that the delegates could go on a schooner excursion on Lake Michigan arranged by the Chicago Board of Trade.[34]

The delegates and their followers spent the evening alternately caucusing with the supporters of rival candidates and celebrating in the grog shops and ale houses of the town. The lobby of the Tremont House was packed with politicos. Murat Halstead of the *Cincinnati Commercial* was amazed at the spectacle:

> Men gathered in little groups, and with their arms about each other, and chatter and whisper as if the fate of the country depended upon their immediate delivery of the mighty political secrets with which their imaginations are big. There are a thousand rumors afloat, and things of incalculable moment are communicated to you confidently, at intervals of five minutes. There are now at least a thousand men packed together in the halls of the Tremont House, crushing each other's ribs, tramping each other's toes, and titillating each other with the gossip of the day; and the probability is, not one is possessed a single fact not known to the whole, which is the slightest consequence to any human being.

What was not so well known was that Thurlow Weed had gotten wind of the Indiana delegation's deal with Judge Davis. That evening Weed took out Henry S. Lane in an effort to bring the Hoosier state into the Seward camp. When cajoling comments and political arguments failed to move the gubernatorial candidate, Weed promised he "would send enough money from New York to ensure his election for Governor." Lane reacted indignantly, but it was probably more his knowledge of Indiana's conservatism than honor that led him to reject the offer.[35]

The Lincoln, Bates, Chase, and Cameron supporters were also active that night. The Maine delegation met with Illinois delegates; Ohio entertained Pennsylvania. At two o'clock in the morning, steins were still being raised with gusto, the Missouri headquarters was filled with song, and a brass band marched down Lake Street. Night gave way to day and bleary-eyed politicians swarmed to the Tremont House restaurant in search of breakfast. They could hear another marching band draw near, and the more alert recognized the song as "Oh Isn't He a Darling." Word spread through the hotel that a massive Seward demonstration was approaching. Heedless of the storm of dust they stirred up in the street, the Seward stalwarts marched four abreast. As they passed the Lincoln and Bates headquarters, "they gave throat-tearing cheers for Seward." As the sound reverberated through the throbbing heads of their hungover opponents, no one could deny that Seward's friends were irrepressible.[36]

That morning the convention wrestled with the credentialing of delegates. Anti-Seward forces were intent on disenfranchising the delegation from Texas on the grounds it was not properly constituted. Weed, however, was ready for the maneuver and produced evidence that the delegation had been chosen by a mass public meeting of legal voters. The Texas delegation was credentialed, and Seward won six more votes. The opposing factions also sparred over the question of whether a simple majority of delegates or a two-thirds majority would be necessary to nominate a candidate. The anti-Seward coalition had won this battle in committee the night before. A two-thirds rule would give them a virtual veto over Seward's nomination. But Weed demanded and received a vote of the full convention on this vital issue. In an impressive show of Seward strength ($358^1/_2$ to $94^1/_2$), it was determined that a simple majority would suffice. The Lincoln forces proved to be disorganized during these skirmishes, and they were disheartened by the results.[37]

The convention ratified its platform later that day. The document was drafted by John A. Kasson and Horace Greeley in the wee hours of the morning, and it successfully synthesized the diverse elements which came together to make the Republican party. The platform denounced the influence of slavery on American government and proclaimed the West as forever the bastion of free labor. Among the forward-looking features of the document was a strong plank advocating the rights of immigrants, a call for free homesteads for pioneers, and government support for economic improvements. The platform, neither conservative nor radical, was generally and enthusiastically received. It was not without amendment, however. Joshua Giddings, Ohio's grand old man of free soil politics, regretted that the rhetoric was less strident than the 1856 platform. In consolation, he demanded the reinsertion of the passage from the Declaration of Independence, "all men are created equal" which Republicans had long used to condemn slavery.[38]

A debate followed, which served only to slow the convention. When the amendment finally carried, with great enthusiasm and cheers, it was nearly six o'clock. A Minnesota delegate, no doubt hungry for his dinner, moved for adjournment. Cries of "No, no!" and "Ballot, ballot!" arose from the Seward supporters. The Minnesotan, a Seward man himself, hastily tried to correct his mistake. "I withdraw the motion, and move that we now proceed to ballot for a candidate for the Presidency." Benjamin Eggleston of Ohio jumped to his feet and renewed the motion to adjourn. The motion was denied. Old Irrepressible clearly had the support of most of the delegates, and a vote at that time might easily have produced a Seward victory. In desperation, the anti-Seward forces howled their opposition to a ballot. David K. Cartter of Ohio quickly jumped to his feet in an effort to salvage the chances of his candidate, Senator Benjamin Wade. A stuttering speech impediment made Cartter an unlikely spokesman, but he summoned up all the eloquence he could muster and said, "I call for a division of ayes and nays, to see if the gentlemen want to go without their supper." It was not Cicero, but it did remind the delegates of their empty stomachs. Momentum for a ballot was further broken when the chair announced that a few minutes' wait would be needed to prepare the tally sheets. The Seward forces wavered, and it was decided to wait until the morning.[39]

————◇————

Judge Davis and the pro-Lincoln forces had been given a reprieve of one evening, and they had to make the most of it. Seated behind the conference table in his room, Davis drew his men around him. Davis realized it was necessary to reverse the impression, unmistakable at the Wigwam that afternoon, that Seward had momentum. Even under the best possible circumstances Davis knew that Lincoln could not equal Seward's first- or second-ballot vote totals. It would be necessary, therefore, to give delegates a sense of Lincoln's rising fortunes by manipulating the atmosphere. Lincoln supporters had to overwhelm Weed's army of professional boosters. Ward Lamon and Jesse Fell were given the job of marshaling a thousand died-in-the-wool Lincoln supporters and insuring they were admitted to the Wigwam. (There was much talk later of counterfeit tickets and forged passes, but such dirty tricks were never proven.) The pro-Lincoln ranks were further swelled when a railroad attorney arranged free rail passes for downstate boosters. To lead the vocal chorus, Davis enlisted services of a Chicago doctor named Ames, who was reputed to be able, on a calm day, to shout all the way across Lake Michigan. He was to be echoed by an Ottawa Republican equally boastful about his bellowing ability. These two vocal bookends and the packed galleries assured Davis of a pro-Lincoln atmosphere for the balloting.[40]

Of course, such antics would be useless without delegate support. Davis told his aides that they would caucus through the entire night if necessary. Former New Englanders, such as Samuel C. Parks and Leonard Swett, were sent to those delegations. Weed counted on virtually a unified front among northeasterners for Seward. But Davis's earlier probes had revealed how weak those commitments were. The Lincoln representatives gradually made headway through the night by cannily pushing for second- and third-ballot pledges for Lincoln. Other Lincoln men followed a similar strategy in their dealings with Virginia and Maryland delegates. Bates and Cameron representatives crisscrossed paths with the Illinoisans all night long, but as Swett later recalled, "We let Greeley run his Bates machine, but got most of them for a second choice."

Although Weed was full of confidence, he left nothing to chance and kept his staff busy that evening. He clearly saw that Lincoln was the principal threat and sought to sidetrack him as a vice-presidential candidate. Davis fended off numerous offers from the Seward supporters to put Lincoln in a subordinate position on the ticket. When these failed, Weed tried with some success to convince New Jersey that the only road to Republican victory in that state was through a Seward-Lincoln ticket. He also tried to draw off some of Bates's considerable strength. Weed floated the balloon that Lincoln was much more of an anti-slavery radical than Seward, and that if Lincoln looked strong, the Bates men should rally around the banner of New York. In return, Weed promised that if Seward, with Bates's support, could not beat Lincoln, Weed would throw all of Seward's delegates to Bates. Weed did not expect the Bates team to agree to this prior to the balloting. But such overtures might prove the basis for an alliance later on.

While Weed maneuvered behind the scenes, his lieutenants hosted a lavish champagne supper. Three hundred bottles of bubbly were opened; as one observer recalled, "it flowed freely as water." After dinner a band was assembled and the "Irrepressibles" marched to the rooms of uncertain delegations and treated them to a serenade. Less organized groups abandoned caucusing and set to "raising h—l generally." Western Republicans were less than impressed with these demonstrations.

> They can drink as much whiskey, swear as loud and long, sing as bad songs, and "get up and howl" as ferociously as any crowd of Democrats you ever heard, or heard of. They are opposed, as they say, "to being too d—d virtuous."

These fellows made few converts when they walked up to other delegates, slapped them on the back, and blurted out with whiskey breath, "How are you, Hoss?" When a delegate expressed doubt about Seward's ability to sweep all northern states, they hooted loudly. If he persisted, the New Yorkers called him an "ingrate" for accepting their hospitality and "traitor" to the party. Such discussions often ended with the Seward supporters threatening, "If you don't nominate Seward, where will you get your money?"[41]

Such crude displays pushed more sober delegates toward the opposition. Bates and Lincoln agents followed in the wake of the revelers with reports of Weed's part in the street railway swindle and of political corruption in Albany. Seward's star could not help but be tarnished as the night wore on.

The center of anti-Seward intrigue was the Tremont Hotel. Representatives of the four states, New Jersey, Pennsylvania, Indiana, and Illinois, that doubted Seward could lead the party to victory, met in the rooms of Congressman David Wilmot. Judge Davis and Caleb Smith of Indiana doggedly argued Lincoln's cause. New Jersey delegates knew that their favorite son, William L. Dayton, could not win, and they were withholding their second ballot support for whoever looked likely to win so as to share in the spoils of victory. Although they were hardly united, Pennsylvania delegates held out vain hopes for Simon Cameron. They controlled a massive block of fifty-four convention votes, and since the anti-Seward forces had not united on Bates, Chase, or Lincoln, why not consider Cameron again? Discussion continued for four hours with little headway made. The meeting would have broken up, but there was no alternative. These states acting in concert with the right candidate could stop Seward; otherwise, his victory was assured.[42]

About ten o'clock, Horace Greeley, the loose cannon, rolled into the room. Anxiously he inquired as to their progress, but they had nothing to report. Discouraged, he headed downstairs to check on the other delegations. Wherever he went Greeley was stared at by the conventioneers. One observer said, "If he stops to talk a minute with someone who wishes to consult him as the oracle, the crowd becomes dense as possible, and there is the most eager desire to hear the words of wisdom that are supposed to fall on such occasions." But all of Greeley's eloquence and wisdom, however eagerly listened to, seemed to fall on deaf ears that night. He tried to turn the Kansas delegation to Bates by bringing before them Henry Lane of Indiana and Andrew G. Curtin of Pennsylvania. Although they both predicted Seward's defeat in November, Kansas remained staunch for Seward. Greeley saw that in the ad hoc street corner debates among delegates, Bates was losing because of adamant opposition from Chicago's numerous German Republicans. It seemed likely that not only had Greeley backed a looser but Seward would emerge the victor. And the "Irrepressibles" were taunting him. At one point they pinned a "Seward for President" button to his back, creating a stir of derisive laughter wherever he went. A Weed lieutenant in the Tremont told Greeley with mock solemnity that the conservatives had best decide who they wanted as vice-president, since the nomination was sown up for Seward. Bitterly, the editor replied, "Oh, never mind; fix up the whole ticket to suit yourselves."[43]

Greeley went to the telegraph office and wired home his dispatch for the *New York Herald Tribune*: "My conclusion, from all that I can gather tonight is, that the opposition to Gov. Seward cannot concentrate on any candidate, and that he will be nominated." Other journals had reached the same conclusion and the dispatches out of Chicago that night prepared Republicans for Old Irrepressible's nomination.[44]

Wearily, Greeley climbed the stairs to his room at the Tremont. He was not a night owl, yet he had spent most of the previous night caucusing. Now it was near midnight, he was defeated, and he wanted only to go to sleep. But as he passed the room of David Dudley Field, another anti-Seward New Yorker, he felt obliged to relay the bad news. He entered Field's room, threw himself on the couch, and said, "All is lost. We are beaten." The tired editor was roused, however, when Field excitedly responded: "No, all is not lost. Let us up and go to work." Rallying his strength, Greeley rose and they went downstairs. In the lobby they saw big-bellied David Davis in conference with Joseph Medill, another Lincoln man and copublisher of the *Chicago Tribune*. Medill eagerly pressed him for news of the meeting with the Pennsylvania delegation. Davis suddenly lost his poker face and triumphantly said, "Damned if we haven't got them." "How did you get them?" Medill asked. "By paying the price."[45]

The news electrified Greeley and Field. It did not bode well for their candidate. With Pennsylvania's support, Lincoln would be Seward's main rival. The deal, if it held up, would break the deadlock among the doubtful states. Greeley hustled off in search of Francis P. Blair, manager of the Bates forces. Their job now was to ensure a convention hung between Seward and Lincoln. Bates could then pose as a compromise candidate and still win in a late ballot rally. In any event, there was a chance to defeat Seward.

Meanwhile, Davis and Medill discussed the tense meeting that had just ended. The critical moment came at eleven o'clock. After five hours of fruitless discussion, the delegates from the four doubtful states decided to calculate as accurately as possible the delegate strength of each candidate. Davis shocked the other delegates when he revealed that he had secured votes from Maine, Massachusetts, Connecticut, Virginia, and Kentucky. The New England states were thought to be solid for Seward. New Jersey and Pennsylvania began to lean toward Lincoln. Two things tipped the balance—the Catholic issue and Davis's willingness to bargain. Seward was unacceptable to states with strong Know-Nothing contingents because of his support in New York of state aid for Catholic schools. Those states needed a candidate who could rally nativists to the Republican banner. Bates, a spokesman for the Know-Nothings in 1856, filled that bill nicely. But the Know-Nothings were bitterly opposed by German Republicans, many of whom were Catholic. Prior to the formal beginning of the

Republican Convention they had held their own meeting in Chicago's Deutches Haus. Although the meeting was less successful than its organizers hoped, it did send a clear signal that the Germans wanted nativism repudiated. Lincoln was untainted by either support for parochial education or by Know-Nothing connections. His lack of prominence on vital questions made him a logical compromise.

Compromise was possible because Judge Davis was willing to trade political favors for votes. This was directly contrary to Lincoln's instructions. When the rail splitter was informed that the nomination could be secured only by buying votes with promises, Lincoln wired back: "*Make no Contracts that will bind me.*" The telegraph demoralized his workers. "Damn Lincoln," said Jesse Dubois. Swett, more temperate, suggested, "I am sure if Lincoln was aware of the necessities . . .'"; others launched bitter attacks on Lincoln. But Davis silenced everyone. "Lincoln ain't here," he said decisively, "and don't know what we have to meet, so we will go ahead, as if he hadn't heard from him and he must ratify it." To the Pennsylvanians he offered a cabinet post for unscrupulous Cameron, and to New Jersey he promised prime diplomatic posts for favorite son William Dayton and his manager, Thomas Dudley. In return the negotiators promised to meet with their delegations and bring them into the fold.[46]

But Davis and Medill knew that promises were cheap on that hectic night. Virginia's support had been bought and sold several times to various candidates. They had no illusions that New Jersey and Pennsylvania would not try one final time for a better price. Indeed, it required the energies of every pro-Lincoln man to keep his strength intact, let alone expand it. All night long they kept after the delegates. At one o'clock in the morning a crisis occurred over the previously solid Indiana delegation. Henry Lane, "pale and haggard, with cane under his arm," walked "as if for a wager, from one caucus room to another" and put down the uprising. Davis then sent him to try to drive a wedge between Vermont and Seward. The tedious discussions and the endless cajoling of frazzled delegates in smoke clouded rooms went on until someone opened the shade on a window and saw the sunrise over Lake Michigan. Then it was time to wash their faces and secure several cups of black coffee. All that could be done had been tried. It remained to be seen who in the end would win.[47]

————◇————

William H. Seward met the dawn on the veranda of his country house near Auburn, New York. On the lawn was a cannon, primed and ready to salute news of his nomination. Judge Bates stalked about his farm outside St. Louis, disturbed by the news from his manager. In Columbus, Ohio, Salmon P. Chase prepared to go to his office where, in spite of reports to the contrary, he vainly expected to hear news of "a Chase boom."

In Springfield, Illinois, Abraham Lincoln was tense and uncertain. Davis had wired him to expect any outcome. The day before he had tried to release tension by playing a ball game known as "fives" and having a few beers with "the boys."

It would have been unseemly for any of the candidates to attend the convention or to politic openly on their own behalf. Candidates were not supposed to lust after public office or to personally proclaim their qualifications. They merely expressed their willingness to serve, pulled strings behind the scenes, and let their friends advocate their cause.

By eight o'clock in the morning Seward's advocates were shaking off the effects of the night's champagne bash and were forming ranks in the streets of Chicago. They oozed confidence. Rumors of the night caucus were dismissed. As one pro-Seward reporter noted: "The opposition of the doubtful states to Seward was an old story. . . . It was not imagined that their protests would suddenly become effective." At the head of their column was a "magnificent" marching band whose members were gaudily outfitted in bright uniforms with glittering epaulets and caps with white and scarlet feathers. Behind the band were a thousand Seward stalwarts ready to fill the convention hall with their enthusiasm. As the band struck up a patriotic air they set off in fine military style. The parade wound its way through the street of downtown Chicago, past the Tremont Hotel where Bates supporters, with pictures of the Judge proudly pasted to their hats, were finishing breakfast. The impressive demonstrations then turned down Wells Street to show off their strength to the Pennsylvania delegation at the Briggs House. The Cameron men, each wearing a resplendent white hat, had just come out of their final caucus. They had ratified, in the presence of Judge Davis, the bargain to back Lincoln on the second ballot, but secretly they had decided to vote for Seward if Lincoln did not look strong early in the fight. The Seward army was the sensation of the city that morning. All who saw it were impressed—except Thurlow Weed. By the time he saw the parade approach the Wigwam, the convention hall was surrounded by thousands of spectators. The parade pressed forward to the entrance but could not enter. The New Yorkers loudly demanded access. They had come all the way to Chicago to cheer Seward's nomination. But no amount of bullying or bribes could get them inside. Weed noted with frustration that while the New Yorkers were marching, the hall had been packed by Lincoln boosters. The Seward enthusiasts had to be content to wait outside with thousands of others.[48]

The Wigwam was filled beyond capacity, and the hall reverberated with the excited conversations of more than twelve thousand people. Ushers were forced to evict numerous Chicagoans who boldly occupied delegates' chairs on the stage. Joseph Medill looked over his handiwork. He and Norman Judd had acted as the local arrangements committee, and they used that power as much as possible to isolate the New York delegation. Thurlow Weed and the New York delegation were seated at the far end of the stage next to a wall. Next to them were staunchly pro-Seward delegations. There was no way for Weed and company to influence other delegations during the balloting. Pennsylvania, crucial to the Lincoln cause, was seated at the other end of the stage; its delegates could barely hear the pro-Seward orators. Illinois delegates sat between Indiana and New Jersey, the two other vital states.[49]

Sixty newspaper reporters were seated on the stage. They were given the best seats in the hall so that an accurate account of the proceedings would be made. The reporters, all men, were dressed in dark jackets. But on this day of the convention a young woman presented a press pass and took her seat with the journalists. Women reporters were practically unheard of at that time, and certainly they were not given assignments as important as the Republican Convention. The woman was Mary A. Livermore. An editor friend, unable to attend the climatic session, asked her to report the proceedings. She tried to make herself inconspicuous by dressing in black, "like my brethren of the press," she said. Just as the convention was about to come to order, one of the convention marshals spied a woman among the press. "In stentorian tones that rang through the building," she later recalled, "while his extended arm and forefinger pointed me out, and made me the target for thousands of eyes, he ordered me to withdraw my profane womanhood from the sacred enclosure provided for men." Stunned and embarrassed, Livermore automatically rose to leave. But the reporters would suffer no interference. "Sit still!" they ordered. Then they turned on the marshal. A chorus of jeers and cries of "Dry up!" forced him to back down. Mary Livermore was allowed to report the most dramatic convention in American political history.[50]

At ten o'clock the session opened with a prayer. Convention president Ashmun, perhaps acting on Weed's advice, ordered the vast audience to keep quiet during the proceedings. But such a blatant attempt to gag the throng fell on deaf ears. Montgomery Blair then tried, and failed, to pack the Maryland delegation with five "newly arrived" pro-Bates delegates. This effort also failed. The convention moved on to the business at hand.

William M. Evarts rose and said, "I take the liberty to name as a candidate to be nominated by this Convention for the office of President of the United States, William H. Seward." A prolonged applause filled the hall. But when Norman B. Judd rose to nominate Lincoln, his words were greeted by a thundering ovation. Burton C. Cook in the Illinois delegation then took out his handkerchief, which was the prearranged signal to launch the two great cheerleaders of the pro-Lincoln gallery. The result was an even mightier response "rising and ranging far beyond the Seward shriek." The crowd greeted the nomination of Bates, Chase, Cameron and other favorite sons with considerably less enthusiasm.

When the nominations were seconded, another vocal duel occurred between the Lincoln and Seward forces. Austin Blair of Michigan was followed by a storm of pro-Seward cheers.

> The shouting was absolutely frantic, shrilled, wild. No Comanches, no panthers ever struck by a higher note, or gave screams with more internal intensity. Looking from the stage over the vast amphitheater, nothing was to be seen below but thousands of hats—a black, mighty swarm of hats—flying with the velocity of hornets over a mass of human heads, most of the mouths of which were open. . . . The wonder of the thing was that the Seward outside pressure should, so far from New York, be so powerful.

Had the thousand professional rooters gained access, the Seward cheer might have caused permanent ear damage. As it was, Mary Livermore and other reporters covered their ears.

The roar finally subsided, and Columbus Delano of Ohio rose to second Lincoln. His motion let loose another uproar. A Cincinnati reporter said it was as if thousands of slaughtered hogs all gave "their death squeals together" and "a score of steam whistles going." When the swell began to ebb, Burton Cook again signaled with his handkerchief, and immediately there arose "a shriek that was positively awful." Henry Lane of Indiana leaped upon a table, and swinging hat and cane, performed like an acrobat. The presumption is he shrieked with the rest, as his mouth was desperately wide open," but "his individual voice was lost in the aggregate hurricane." The Seward delegation sat white-faced and still in the face of the dominating chorus. The crowd then began to stamp wildly, making "every plank and pillar in the building quiver." Editor Charles Ray of the *Chicago Tribune* feared the hastily erected hall might come down on their heads. Finally, the demonstration subsided, and the delegates heard John Andrew of Massachusetts call for a vote.[51]

The roll was called, and state after state announced its vote. Weed must have blanched when Virginia, whose support he had bought several days before, gave Lincoln the majority of its votes. Lincoln also showed strength in New England that worried Weed. The first-ballot totals showed Seward far ahead with 173$\frac{1}{2}$ votes, Lincoln with a formidable 102, Cameron with 50$\frac{1}{2}$, Chase with 49, Bates with a disappointing 48, McLean 12, Dayton 14, and Collamer of Vermont 10.

The convention moved on to the second ballot. Now was the time for Davis's bargains to be tested. It was essential to make Lincoln's vote total rise or else convention support might build for a dark horse. Joseph Medill, a former resident of the Buckeye state, moved to the Ohio delegation, thus violating the convention's rules. Without ceremony, white-haired Joshua Giddings ordered him out. But Medill's friends came to his rescue, and after a prolonged argument, he was allowed to stay. Medill smoothly prodded Chase supporters to switch to Lincoln and did his best to restrain a boom for native son Benjamin Wade.[52]

The second roll call brought Weed more grief. Lincoln snared 9 votes from New Hampshire and Vermont's entire total of 10. The later vote startled the New Yorkers "as if an Orsini bomb had exploded." Judge Davis was pleased, but he was too anxious about New Jersey and Pennsylvania to celebrate. New Jersey, Thomas Dudley announced, would give 4 votes to Seward and 10 for Dayton. Now it was Davis's turn to look stunned. New Jersey had reneged on its agreement.

Would Pennsylvania hold true? Yes! Within an instant 48 Cameron votes were added to the Lincoln column. The concluding tally showed Seward with 184½, Lincoln 181, Chase 42½, Bates 35, Dayton 10, McLean 8, Cameron 2, Cassius Clay of Kentucky 2. Seward had gotten only 4 votes closer to the 233 necessary to win: Lincoln was gaining on him.[53]

Weed saw the prize he had labored for for almost ten years slipping from his grasp. He desperately needed to slow Lincoln's momentum. The greatest political manager of the day was faced with his supreme challenge. He needed to secure a large block of votes, and the Bates people were the most logical source. Weed had laid the groundwork for cooperation the night before. He sent for Charles Gibson of the Missouri delegation and tried to strike a deal, but there was too little time. While Weed and Gibson met in an anteroom, the Lincoln forces were crying for a third ballot. The Bates forces, like Weed, had miscalculated. They did not expect Lincoln's strength to rise after the first ballot. Things were moving too fast. The Bates forces, in spite of their weak showing, would not join Seward, even after Weed offered Francis Blair the vice-presidency. So Weed was forced to promise Seward votes for Bates; such a bold move might break Lincoln's momentum and allow Seward's forces to regroup. But while the two men dickered, the third ballot already began. Weed told Gibson that Bates would have all his votes if they could survive the next ballot.[54]

Weed listened tensely to the roll call, calculating the totals as the votes were called out. Seward was dead in the water, and the sharks were closing in for the kill. Massachusetts switched 4 votes from Seward to Lincoln, New Jersey gave the Illinoisan 8, Pennsylvania gave Lincoln 4 more. Each Lincoln gain struck Weed like a personal blow. Worst of all was

Maryland abandoning Bates and giving Lincoln 9 votes, in spite of Weed's promise of votes on the next ballot. Didn't they trust him? Or did they sell out for a spot in a Lincoln cabinet?

There was still hope; Lincoln's total reached $231^1/2$ at the end of the roll call. He was $1^1/2$ votes shy of the nomination. It appeared that Seward had survived the ballot and Weed could try his last ditch maneuver. But in the Ohio delegation Joe Medill counted the Lincoln votes as quickly as Weed, and he tried to push Lincoln over the top. He whispered to Ohio spokesman David K. Cartter, "If you can throw the Ohio delegation for Lincoln, Chase can have anything he wants." "H-how d'dye know?" Cartter stuttered. "I know and you know or I wouldn't promise if I didn't know," Medill replied. Cartter quickly thought over what Medill had said. Up to this time no one had paid much attention to him—here was a chance to play kingmaker. The would-be Warwick rose to his feet. "I rise, eh, Mr. Chairman, eh," he said, "to announce the change of 4 votes for Ohio from Mr. Chase to Mr. Lincoln."[55]

There followed a brief moment of silence. For an instant, the Republicans held their breath. No one spoke. The massive Wigwam was still. The fate of the nation was suspended. Thurlow Weed's face went ashen. Then the crowd reacted.

> The nerves of the thousands, which through the hours of suspense had been subjected to terrible tension, relaxed, and as deep breaths of relief were taken, there was a noise in the Wigwam like the rush of great wind in the vane of a storm—and in another breath, the storm was there. There were thousands cheering with the energy of insanity.

The convention secretary held up the tally sheet and shouted to a man in the rafters, "Fire the salute! Abe Lincoln is nominated!" As the crowd outside the Wigwam received the momentous news, a great cheer arose. It was so loud that, for a moment, those inside were stilled. Then came the great crescendo of the artillery salute. The thundering discharges carried across the city, and the acrid scent of gunpowder filled the convention hall.[56]

Norman Judd walked to center stage with a huge charcoal portrait of "Honest Old Abe" and jubilant David Davis followed with a moss-covered rail bearing a sign, "Split by Lincoln." These emblems drove the audience into a frenzy. According to one Chicagoan, "Handkerchiefs, hats and umbrellas went so high that their owners never saw nor heard of them again. Men were beside themselves. Old grizzly-bearded fellows acted like boys, and appeared reckless of consequences to themselves or their belongings." The drama and enthusiasm of the moment was too much for many men. After forty-eight hours without sleep, marked by almost ceaseless negotiation of the most delicate type, and the tortuous balloting, many Lincoln supporters completely broke down. Judge Davis sat down and wept. Henry Lane and Andrew Curtin collapsed into their chairs and "sank down in an excess of joy."[57]

Thurlow Weed was broken. He cried bitter tears of regret, his head bowed and his face buried in his hands. Horace Greeley was triumphant and joined unreservedly in the celebration. But the New York delegation was sullen. When the revelers tried to wave the New York State banner with the other state ensigns, they were warded off. Silently, they watched the proceedings, loath even to smile.[58]

When order was finally restored, William H. Evarts mounted the secretary's table and presented a melancholy and moving concession speech on behalf of Senator Seward. Then, one by one, the pro-Seward delegations rose and changed their votes so that Lincoln's nomination might be unanimous. With the healing process begun, the convention adjourned for lunch.

The delegates filed out into streets filled with jubilant, jostling crowds of people. The insatiable politicians among them went to the Tremont House for dinner and discussion of who the vice-presidential candidate should be. But many others were too moved for such sober considerations. An overwrought pro-Lincoln man sat down at a table in that hotel and immediately began to harangue the diners. "Talk of your money and bring on your bullies with you!—the immortal principles of the everlasting people are with Abraham Lincoln." Although he did not know anyone at the table, he continued, "Abe Lincoln has no money and no bullies, but he has the people."

When a waiter asked him what he wanted to eat, he shot back, "Go to the devil—what do I want to eat for? Abe Lincoln is nominated . . . and I'm going to live on air—the air of Liberty. . . ." But his long-winded response and the hearty chops before the other diners soon awakened his appetite. He ordered "a great deal of everything" because if he was going to eat that day then why not "the whole bill." On a day like today he felt he could "devour and digest an Illinois prairie."[59]

Most of the Lincoln and Seward men had no thought of eating. They had been through an emotional wringer that morning and many "were hardly able to walk to their hotels." A reporter remarked:

> There were men who had not tasted liquor who staggered about like drunkards, unable to manage themselves. The Seward men were terribly stricken down. They were mortified beyond all expression, and walked thoughtfully and silently away from the slaughterhouse, more ashamed than embittered.[60]

2
◇

A HOUSE
DIVIDED

———

I t was a night like no other in Chicago. That morning Abraham Lincoln had been nominated for the presidency. In the afternoon, Hannibal Hamlin of Maine was selected for vice-president, and the Republican National Convention ended. Chicagoans had begun to celebrate as soon as the cannon on the roof had boomed. Ad hoc parades snaked through the downtown streets. Bands played and people danced in the street. As night fell, laborers and countinghouse clerks joined the revelers. The delegations of Pennsylvania, Indiana, and Ohio were nearly as enthusiastic as the Chicagoans. The Cameron delegates tipped back their white hats and swallowed huge drams of corn liquor to further fuel the celebration. They had given Lincoln the support he needed to win, and they rejoiced in anticipation of the spoils a Lincoln victory would bring them. Others hooted and hollered, overcome by exuberance—a coarse westerner (like themselves) was to be president. The sound of gunshots fired triumphantly in the air rose above the din. Though there was much liquor drinking, so joyous was the throng that no one seemed drunk.[1]

A great rally held in the Wigwam was packed with enthusiastic Republicans. Party luminaries delivered fiery speeches and the cheering audience did their best to "raise the roof"! Skillfully working their way through the densely packed gallery were seven or eight pickpockets, thankful for a last opportunity at an easy harvest. When the speeches were done, several processions formed and made their way through the central business district, which was brilliantly illuminated by hundreds of lights. The well-lit *Chicago Tribune* office was a natural stopping place for the revelers. From its third-story windows hung a giant transparency on which was inscribed:

For President,
"Honest Old Abe."

For Vice President,
Hannibal Hamlin.

The demonstrators' cheers were answered in chorus by the more than one hundred printers inside who were laboring to produce the next day's newspaper.[2]

The German Republicans of Chicago organized their own procession. Several thousand citizens made up a contingent led by hundreds of "Wide-Awakes," a Republican marching club started in Connecticut and now established throughout the North. They were resplendent in black enameled capes and glazed military fatigue caps, each sporting a brass eagle. Trained in precision drill and bearing lanterns, the Wide-Awakes were guaranteed to thrill any Republican crowd. Behind them were men bearing rails—some liberated from lumberyards, others from citizens' fences, and a few "authentic" rails from downstate Decatur. The Pennsylvania contingent was so taken by these rails that they wired to Decatur, offering to buy every one Abe ever made. Others had the same idea, and Republicans across the country spent considerable sums on weathered fence rails.

The processions met outside the Tremont House at a great bonfire, thirty feet in circumference. The crowds were led in cheers for Lincoln, a genuine "bottom dog." Others took up the cheer, "Hurrah for Lincoln and Hamlin—Illinois and Maine!" or "Hurray for Honest Abe." Then, from the top of the hotel, boomed thirty-three small-bore cannons. One hundred shots rang out in honor of the first Illinoisan nominated for the White House.[3]

Large, spontaneous, and enthusiastic though the crowds churning through the streets of Chicago were, they did not represent a universal sentiment in the city. Chicago was not a Republican city. It was, in 1860, rather evenly balanced between the young Republican party and the old Democrats. The latter were loath to join the pro-Lincoln rallies. Their shades were drawn and lights extinguished at an early hour. As one Republican organ noted the next day, "Everybody was happy, every heart filled with joy—except the Douglasites. They refused to be comforted."[4]

Chicago Democrats, almost to a man, were proud of the appellation "Douglasites," referring as it did to their unswerving devotion to the man the nation knew as the "Little Giant of Illinois," Stephen A. Douglas. Born forty-seven years before in Brandon, Vermont, he headed west at the age of twenty, armed with a smattering of classical and legal knowledge, to make his fortune as a frontier lawyer. He settled first in Jacksonville, Illinois, and in spite of his youth and limited education, became a successful attorney and a prominent figure in local politics. During these years Douglas came to know David Davis, Lyman Trumbull, John A. McClernand, and Mary Todd. He held his first debates with another young and ambitious politician, Abraham Lincoln. By the time he moved to Chicago in 1847, both he and the lakefront city were poised for greatness. Chicago was a town of seventeen thousand people, and its prospects were bright. After eleven years of disputes, the Illinois and Michigan Canal was near completion, and work had begun on the town's first rail connections. By age thirty-four, Douglas had already served as a state's attorney, judge, and congressman, and in 1847, he was the newly elected junior senator from Illinois.[5]

As Chicago emerged as the great city of the Northwest, Douglas became the region's most prominent spokesman. He called for free homesteads on the prairie and supported westward expansion at the expense of Mexico and Great Britain. He accelerated the city's rise to greatness by making it the terminus for both the Illinois Central Railroad and the projected Pacific railroad, thereby putting the federal stamp of approval on Chicago's evolution as the nation's rail center. Through the early 1850s Douglas was the prophet of the Democratic party's "Young America" faction, a group of men like himself, mostly from the West, who hoped to revive American politics through vigorous nationalism and direct democracy. In contrast to the "old fogies" and political jobbers who played such a large role in government, Young America was idealistic and energetic.

But Douglas and Young America were laden in their march to political power by the heavy baggage of slavery. The South's insistence on maintaining and even expanding its "peculiar institution" meant that slavery was a facet of almost every political question. No politician could avoid it. Stephen Douglas was particularly vulnerable to the slavery issue because he insisted on addressing a national constituency. He wanted a unified Democratic party as the anvil on which to forge an American Republic that stretched from sea to sea and whose trade, industries, agriculture, and power would dwarf the monarchies of Europe. For that to be achieved, the slavery question could not be allowed to divide either the Democratic party or the nation.

Douglas had been a leading figure in the agonizing nine months of negotiation that produced the Compromise of 1850. He stood with Senate leaders Daniel Webster and Henry Clay in the debate over the measures that determined the fate of the territories won in the Mexican War. It was Douglas's pragmatic principle of "popular sovereignty" that finally settled the issue of whether the territories of California, Utah, New Mexico, and Oregon would be slave or free. Let the people decide for themselves was his expedient and successful formula. The Compromise quelled southern cries for secession but at the cost of creating new enemies for Douglas in the North.

Douglas's faith in popular sovereignty led him into even more dangerous waters in 1854. In an effort to secure southern support for a Chicago based transcontinental railroad, he proposed an act that would open the Kansas territory to settlement. Slave owners from the adjacent state of Missouri were then free to move west. If they could command the votes, they would be able to make Kansas a slave state. Northerners howled that the bill was tantamount to a repeal of the venerable Missouri Compromise of 1820, which promised there would be no slave state farther north than Missouri's southern border. Douglas quickly went from being the most popular statesman in the North to being despised as a traitor to his region. The Little Giant joked that he could travel from Chicago to New York by the light of his burning effigies. He was less good humored when two years later his stand on the Kansas-Nebraska Act cost him the Democratic presidential nomination.[6]

Douglas found himself increasingly isolated during the late 1850s. As a nationalist he tried to represent neither North nor South. Slavery, he believed, should not be a political question. If the people of a given state wanted slavery, that was their business. He did not view slavery as either a moral question or a constitutional right. But his Jacksonian moderation was out of temper with the times. Attacks on Douglas by fire eaters on both sides of the Mason-Dixon Line and the Buchanan administration made him politically vulnerable. Abraham Lincoln tested the strength of the wounded Little Giant in 1858. Their seven debates during the campaign for the Senate were closely watched across the country. Although Lincoln impressed many with his eloquence and the debates began his national career, it was Douglas who won the race. The campaign saw Douglas re-emerge as the leader of northern Democrats and southern conservatives. His pragmatic, nationalist message still held broad appeal.

Lincoln went on to be a dark horse candidate for the Republican nomination, while Douglas, in the spring of 1860, was the front-running Democrat. But while Lincoln's chances were buoyed because the Republicans met in Chicago, Douglas's supporters had to journey to the camp of the enemy in quest of the nomination. The Democrats met in Charleston, South Carolina, the seed bed of southern extremism. Although the pro-Douglas forces were in the majority, the galleries were packed with aggressive proslavery sympathizers. When Douglas's delegates rejected a platform guaranteeing the expansion of slavery into all territories, most southern delegates walked out of the convention. At the very time Chicago Republicans were dancing in the street to celebrate Lincoln's nomination,

Democrats in the city were dejected over Douglas's failure and the prospect of a divided party.

A month after the Republicans concluded their work in Chicago, the Democrats held a second national convention, this time in Baltimore, in an attempt to reunify the party. By this time the country was a caldron of conflicting politics and passions. The Republicans, for all their talk of choosing a moderate candidate, did not expect to campaign for any southern state. Moderates, disgusted with the squabbles of the Democratic party and the sectionalism of the Republicans, formed their own group, the Constitutional Union party. They nominated John Bell, a Tennessee senator, and Edward Everett of Massachusetts. Their platform was admirably simple: They would uphold the union by strictly adhering to the Constitution. Although this rather naive, if patriotic, message was popular in the states that bordered the North and South, it did not command enthusiasm across the country. The Constitutional Union party was a group of political has-beens, tainted by nativism, whose only real hope was to deny other candidates enough electoral votes and throw the election into the House of Representatives. The Democrats, for all their trouble in Charleston, were the only national political party and the only realistic hope against the rising tide of sectionalism.

Stephen Douglas was keenly aware of this as the party reassembled in Baltimore. He still nursed the ambition to be president, and his support by Illinois, Wisconsin, Michigan, and other western Democrats was almost religious. They saw Douglas as the party's only chance of success in the North and demanded his candidacy. Only the technicality of a two-thirds majority kept them from nominating Douglas in Charleston after the southern extremists walked out. They would not be denied in Baltimore. Yet, Douglas knew that the sacrifice of his candidacy might be the price demanded by southerners to hold the party together. In a letter to his campaign managers, he wrote:

> If therefore you and any other friends who have stood by me with such heroic firmness at Charleston and Baltimore shall be of the opinion that the principle can be preserved and the unity and ascendancy of the Democratic Party maintained, and the country saved from the perils of Northern abolitionism and southern disunion by withdrawing my name and uniting upon some other non-Intervention and Union loving Democrats I beseech you to pursue that course.

It was one of the hardest letters Douglas ever had to write. To make sure there was no doubt of his sincerity, he sent a similar letter to Dean Richmond, head of the New York delegation.[7]

Douglas's offer to withdraw his candidacy was never revealed at the convention. From the beginning the proceedings were marred by uncomprising rhetoric and bitter denunciations. Douglas's supporters tried to prevent the readmission of those southern delegations that had bolted from the Charleston meeting. For their part southern Democrats haughtily demanded Douglas's withdrawal while at the same time rejecting the names of other moderates. The spirit of compromise, essential to party unity, was submerged by a flood of partisan prejudices. In the end, the southern extremists again bolted. They reconvened in another hall and drafted Vice-President John C. Breckinridge as their candidate. The regular convention nominated Stephen Douglas. The Democratic party was hopelessly split. Douglas accepted his nomination, but the prize he had sought for so long was tarnished by the prospect of the dissolution of the United States.

In Chicago it was, at last, the Democrats' turn to celebrate a nomination. The initial news bulletins mentioned only Douglas's success. Unreserved in their delight, Democratic clubs formed ranks in the streets of each neighborhood and marched by torchlight to the city center. Bonfires were lit at various street corners, and from the flickering shadows rose the strains of patriotic airs on the South Side. War whoops cut through the evening air. Older residents of Chicago might have thought the Potawattomi were returning to reclaim their lands, except that the cries came from the direction of Bridgeport. Irish laborers with whiskey breath and Douglas's name on their lips were drawn from the suburb to the partisan celebrations like flies to a molasses barrel. They were the "Dimmycrats"—born in the Emerald Isle, faithful to the Mother Church, and the "People's Party." Their exuberance was testimony to their loyalty to the Little Giant and to their willingness to line the streets with his broadsides and stuff the ballot boxes with votes. The crowds convened outside the offices of the *Chicago Times,* a Douglasite journal. The newspaper building was brightly lit and decked out with Douglas banners. After a round of cheers, the celebrants marched to the Tremont House. Blazing tar barrels bathed the street in an orange glow, and a salvo of three hundred cannon shots thundered from the roof of the hotel. Through the smoke from these discharges, speakers ascended to the second floor balcony and harangued the crowd. Douglas and his lieutenants were in Washington, but lesser politicos were able to rally the troops on such a festive night.[8]

About nine o'clock, the crowd's enthusiasm began to wane. Amid the raucous cheers and ratification speeches a rumor circulated. At first it was discounted, yet it persisted. Then came confirmation that the party had split in Baltimore, and Breckinridge was also in the already crowded field of candidates. There was "a general dropping of jaws" at this an-

———◇———

nouncement, and like a railroad engine suddenly relieved of its steam pressure, the meeting went flat and stopped cold. The sobered celebrants filed home through the streets still hazy from the cannon salute and the smell of gunpowder in the air.[9]

———◇———

The division of the Democratic party along sectional lines crippled Douglas's campaign before it began. It was July before he was in the field as an official candidate, giving the Republicans and the Constitutional Union party more than a month's head start. He was further hurt by his running mate, Benjamin Fitzpatrick, who changed his mind about working with Douglas and declined the nominiation after the convention. Douglas was then forced to choose a second running mate mostly on his own. Herschel V. Johnson of Georgia accepted the position, but the damage was done. Independent voters who otherwise would have been inclined toward Douglas began to doubt his chances and look to other candidates such as Lincoln. In the North, Republican strategy was successful. Lincoln appeared to be a moderate who might keep the Union together. In the South, however, the prospect of the Rail Splitter's election was regarded by the fire-eaters as grounds for secession. Moderate men in the region looked for and wanted an alternative but were split between Douglas and John Bell.

In all sections of the country Douglas was haunted by President James Buchanan's vendetta against him. Buchanan, the sitting Democratic president, would not forgive Douglas for breaking with administration policy on the Kansas Territory. In many areas of the country the patronage troops, so important to a Democratic candidate, refused to rally to the Little Giant or were downright hostile to his candidacy. Such troubles made it difficult to raise campaign funds, and Douglas was hampered by lack of money throughout most of the race. The Illinois senator's health was poor that summer of 1860. He suffered from a throat condition and nearly submitted to surgery—no small matter considering the state of mid-nineteenth century medical science.

Even his friends in Chicago had to admit that Douglas was politically wounded and surrounded by partisan sharks. Yet, the bantam-sized candidate had earned the title Little Giant because of his tremendous stamina and political power. In mid-July he summoned all his strength and launched one of the most remarkable campaigns in American history. Douglas decided to fight for his political future, fight to reunite his party, and fight to save the Union.

Douglas strongly doubted that he could win the election, but he felt that it was possible to elicit principles that could serve to reunite the party after the election. A party united, North and South, might inspire enough confidence in the political system to prevent secession after a Republican victory. To achieve that end, Douglas embarked on a nationwide campaign to take the issues to the American people. Never before had a candidate personally stumped for votes. Tradition dating back to George Washington and nineteenth-century standards of political propriety frowned on presidential candidates acting as ordinary office seekers. Yet Douglas flaunted convention and hit the campaign trail.

He began in New England, where he tried to disguise his speaking tour under the cloak of visiting friends and family. But soon he cast aside this pretense and openly sought the voters' ears. His actions were denounced in the press as "vulgar." When he moved his campaign to the South, Jefferson Davis criticized Douglas as "an itinerant advocate of his own claims." Yet, wherever Douglas went, crowds gathered to listen. He spoke several times each day, often from the back of a train. His hectic travel schedule and the demanding pace of his speeches taxed his already weak health. Sometimes his voice was so strained that it was reduced to a "spasmodic bark" barely audible to the crowds before him. He took to having a plate of lemons at hand and used the juice to sooth his throat during long speeches.[10]

Douglas did not pull punches. In the South he proclaimed that southerners who spoke of secession after a Lincoln victory were traitors and that he would support force to prevent such an action. "There is no evil, and can be none, for which disunion is a legitimate remedy," he said in Virginia. Dressed in a backwoodsman's slouch hat, his clothes wrinkled and dusty from constant traveling, Douglas spoke throughout the Southeast. Southern hotheads denounced him as Lincoln's ally; others, Jefferson Davis included, spoke intemperately of lynching enemies of their region. Yet, wherever Douglas went, he strengthened moderate sentiment. Douglas was not disheartened if many of the moderates were actually John Bell supporters; his goal, win or lose, was to break Breckinridge and the bolters who threatened national and party unity. American unity was the central theme of his campaign. "But for my apprehensions on this subject, I would not have taken the stump this year," he told a group of Marylanders. "I am not seeking the Presidency. I am too ambitious a man to desire to have my death-warrant signed now. . . . My object is to preserve this Union by pointing out what, in my opinion, is the only way it can be saved."[11]

Early in October Douglas took his message to the Midwest, his base of support. Yet even here his campaign was in trouble. Democrats in his hometown of Chicago were beset by divisions. Chicagoans of Virginia or Kentucky origin were sympathetic to Breckinridge; a minority of others were inclined, because of the patronage still wielded by the Buchanan administration, toward the vice-president. Republican journalists took great delight in Democrats' confusion, as an anecdote from the *Daily Journal* indicates.

> "Whooraw for Douglas and Johnson!" shouts the man who reads and swears by the Chicago *Times*. Whooraw for Breckinridge and Lane!" responds the Kentuckian Democrat on the other side of the street. "You are no longer a Democrat," indignantly exclaims the *Times* reader. "You are a miserable sectionalist, just as is your leader," replies the Kentuckian.
>
> A Republican, who comes along just in time to prevent a collision, holding in one hand an old copy of the Chicago *Times* and in the other an old copy of an Administration organ, says to them, "Why look here, friends—these organs of yours say, *We are all Democrats.* If that is so, what's the use of quarrelling? Brethren should dwell together in unity."
>
> "Whooraw for Breck and Lane!" ejaculated the chivalrous Kentuckian, with redoubled emphasis. "Whooraw for Douglas and Johnson! responds the other 'Democrat,' and each goes his way rejoicing in his own " 'Democracy.' "[12]

Douglas's presence was clearly necessary to clarify the issues among midwestern Democrats.

———◇———

"A set of crazier men than the Republicans of Chicago . . . have seldom been seen," complained a Douglas supporter. "Great numbers of them seem to be wholly unable to tell whether they walk the streets on their heels or their heads."[13] Since Lincoln's nomination, Illinois Republicans had done so much celebrating the Democrats may have been right. Rallies were held in the Wigwam as touring Republican luminaries made their campaign swings through the city. Lincoln himself neither campaigned openly nor did he comment on public issues, save in meaningless generalities. He left it up to other party leaders to wage the partisan fight. The most effective of those surrogate warriors was the man rejected by the Chicago convention, William H. Seward.

For Republicans, the climax of the 1860 campaign in Chicago was Seward's appearance in the city. Although he was bitterly disappointed that his presidential prospects were torpedoed by the convention, Old Irrepressible shook off his depression to take the stump for Lincoln. Wherever he went, particularly in the Great Lakes region, he drew enthusiastic crowds. Chicago, drunk with politics, gave him a greeting so ecstatic as to give the impression that Seward had actually won the nomination. A delegation of prominent citizens and several uniformed militia units met his train and led him to an elegant open carriage, where he was seated with Mayor John Wentworth. Four perfectly groomed bays pulled Seward's carriage through the streets of downtown Chicago. Men waving top hats and women raising their parasols in salute crowded the sidewalks. While fireworks lit the night sky, a mounted band serenaded him. "Deafening huzzas" greeted Seward's party when they reached the Tremont House. Ironically it had been in this very hotel that Illinois Judge Davis, through adroit maneuvers and extravagant promises, labored to deny Seward his fondest wish. Now the shifting dictates of politics demanded that he mount the stairs to the hotel's second-floor portico and speak on Lincoln's behalf.

On the balcony were more dignitaries, among them the British Consul, who was that evening escorting Lady Jane Franklin, a world-wide celebrity and a Victorian icon. Fifteen years earlier her husband, a Royal Navy explorer, had sailed in search of the Northwest Passage never to be seen again. Her refusal to accept his death and her appeals for search expeditions had launched a flurry of Arctic voyages. More significantly she became a symbol of the faithful wife. Her presence was greeted by "a round of honest cheers" and Senator Seward dutifully offered her a cordial handshake. As he approached the speakers dais, he saw before him a sea of faces. In the street below Republicans were packed shoulder to shoulder. In front of him people spilled out of windows, jammed onto the balconies, and lined the rooftops of the buildings along the street. Anxiously they awaited Seward's remarks.[14]

But it was Mayor Wentworth who first addressed the throng. Long John, as the six-and-a-half-foot-tall mayor was known, was a favorite with Chicago voters. He arrived in the city in 1836, barefoot and ambitious. His fortunes rose as fast as Chicago grew. Wentworth was soon a newspaper editor, a congressman, and a man of property, but he never lost the common touch. Whether he was debating with neighbors over a pint of lager or brawling in the streets with an enemy, he remained a raw westerner. When the Prince of Wales visited Chicago a month earlier, Wentworth introduced him to a gawking crowd in frontier fashion: "Boys, this is the Prince of Wales! He's come to see the city, and I'm going to show him around. Prince, these are the boys." Some elite Chicagoans cringed for fear that Wentworth would offer a repeat performance. Considering Chicago's prominent role in Seward's defeat, tact was required. Wentworth was tactful that evening, but as always he was also controversial. He praised Seward's recent speeches attacking those who would expand slavery: "They have placed the devotees of human liberty under additional obligations to you, and given them new proof that you had 'rather be right than be President.' " But he went on to paint both Seward and Lincoln in colors more abolitionist than either would have preferred.[15]

It was, of course, Republican strategy to appear moderate on the slavery issue. When Seward finally got his chance to speak, he thanked Wentworth for his introduction and immediately set about defining the true campaign gospel. Slavery, he argued, was not an issue for which northerners need concern themselves: "Neither you nor I have any power to disturb those of our fellow citizens in the southern states who maintain a different system; and having no power we have no responsibility." He concluded, "Nonintervention in the states by free men is but half, however, of the motto of the Republican party—nonintervention by slave holders in the territories of the United States is the residue." The New Yorker's remarks drew "long, continued, deafening cheers."[16]

Chicagoans were reassured by Seward's moderate rhetoric. Although southerners often denounced the city as a "nigger loving town" and a den of "Black Republicanism," Chicago was not strongly abolitionist. Like most northern cities, it had cells of dedicated antislavery crusaders and a nascent, free black community. During the stormy years of the 1850s, the city was home to *Free West,* the leading abolition journal in the West. Although it is doubtful that there was a well-organized network of aid stations, as is implied by the term "underground railway," the antislavery minority gave active assistance to fugitives and offered open resistance to slave catchers. It was not unusual for an abolition crowd to forcibly retake a fugitive from a slave-catcher armed with a legal warrant. A proslavery editor in Cairo, Illinois, complained that Chicagoans were "the most riotous people in the state. Mention nigger and slave-catcher in the same breath and they are up in arms." Most Chicago Republicans, however, ranged in sentiment from sympathy with the abolitionists to outright resentment of their extremism. One contemporary recalled Chicago's abolitionists as men and women "possessed of devils" who were "ready to see the country torn to pieces to get rid of the evil spirit of slavery."[17] This militancy threatened to stampede voters to Douglas's unity banner and was resented by most Republican politicians, except, of course, John Wentworth.

The next day, October 2, 1860, Seward again addressed the faithful. He was escorted to the Wigwam by the Lincoln Rangers, an honor guard of five hundred young, uniformed Republicans. The convention hall was packed, as was the area surrounding the structure. One Republican newspaper, the *Daily Journal,* claimed that the rally had drawn one hundred thousand visitors to the city from neighboring states. That, of course, was campaign rhetoric, but there were thousands of excited Republicans in the city. Seward and the other speakers stuck to the official moderate tone of the campaign, although they did not hold back jibes at the Democrats. General J. W. Nye of New York drew cheers when he claimed that although Breckinridge and Douglas bitterly criticized each other, there was no real difference between them; they "eat milk from the same dish, sweeten their pancakes in the same syrup." Full of humor and optimism, Nye concluded by asking Republicans in the audience to be kind to their Democratic neighbors because "they feel bad":

> If my Democratic friends are here—and I know there is one by that groan. . . . I have a simple cure for them; join the Republican party. Wash seven times in the water of Republican purity and be healed.

Amid good feeling and confidence, the Republicans concluded their formal rallies. The real show, however, had just begun.[18]

Chicago Republicans planned one of the largest torchlight parades ever attempted. It took two hours to organize Wide-Awake units from New York, Iowa, Wisconsin, Indiana, Michigan, and twenty-two Illinois towns. At seven o'clock in the evening, the 850-man Chicago Wide-Awake unit, their black rubber capes shining beneath the torchlight, led the massive procession through the streets. Behind them came Seward, his colleagues in their horse-drawn carriages, hundreds of Turners (a German workers club), the Swedish Republican Club, the Plough Boys (a marching company from Downers Grove, Illinois), Seward Clubs, and, of course, marching bands. The parade passed the Tremont House, which was decked out for the occasion with hundreds of Chinese lanterns. The massive demonstration climaxed at the courthouse square with a few harangues and prizes for the best banners. The impressive show of strength was too much for one Irish Democrat, who threw a stone at the tightly packed ranks of the Lincoln Rangers. Fortunately, he immediately fled the scene or there might have been a lynching. But this incident could not ruffle the Republicans. They returned to their houses and hotels that night confident of victory in November.[19]

Two days later Stephen Douglas returned home, and it was the Democrats' turn for celebration. He arrived on a brisk, clear autumn evening. Cook County Democrats had done their work well, and he was met by a large crowd of supporters. They escorted his carriage from the railroad station through the streets of cheering Democrats. The parade included hundreds of mounted riders and several thousand torch-bearing attendants. It was much like the Seward parade a few days earlier; cannon salutes echoed over the city, fireworks lit the night sky, in place of the Wide-Awakes were the Little Giants and Ever-Readies, uniformed Democratic marching clubs. Yet, no one would have mistaken Douglas's torchlight reception for a Republican rally. In place of the long columns of middle-class tradesmen and clerks in black suits, the Democratic procession featured a much less formally attired retinue. Some wore the blood-splattered leather aprons of the hog butcher, others the sweat-stained red union suits and durable canvas pants of the lumber shovers. Even a charwoman walked among the ranks of the marchers waving her kitchen broom above her head, crying, "Hooray for Doog."

"Little Doog" was how the Irish laborers, who made up the bulk of the parade, affectionately referred to the Illinois senator. Republicans noted disapprovingly that most of the saloons along the way were illuminated in honor of Douglas, and the stars and stripes flew above each door. The more enthusiastic barmen even threw a few planks over empty beer barrels and sold whiskey right in the street. Detours at these refreshment counters tended to disrupt the procession from time to time, prompting one reporter to remark, "Falstaff's army had met its match." Occasionally, a brawl would break out where a band of Republican youths heckled the "Dimmycrats." Yet, all in all, the parade proved to be an impressive demonstration of the Little Giant's enduring political strength in Chicago. To the uncertain voter it showed that Douglas still had the magic to bring people together. For his staunch supporters it was a magical night, a grand party for people who had few entertainment outlets.[20]

The next day was reserved for speeches. At noon Douglas was led from his rooms at the Tremont House and escorted through the streets by an army of two thousand supporters. The parade headed west to the cricket fields beyond the city center. Lacking a Wigwam of their own for giant political rallies, the Democrats improvised an outdoor arena. Temporary bleachers were erected around a speaker's platform. Fortunately, the weather cooperated, and on a clear, brisk afternoon a crowd of eight to ten thousand people made the journey to hear Douglas speak.

The senator was with old friends that afternoon. Unlike his audiences in the South, these were not men he had to win over to his side. He was the "sun" of Cook County Democrats' political universe. Yet the Republicans' surprising nomination of Lincoln and the hopeless split in the Democratic party had shaken their confidence. As he looked out over "five acres of densely packed Democrats," Douglas wanted to bolster their confidence for the last days of the campaign, so he served them a healthy slice of partisan pie. He attacked the Republican party as a band of extremists determined to destroy slavery even at the cost of destroying the country. "Their propositions mean revolution—undisguised revolution." Aware of the large number of Irish-Catholics in the audience, Douglas made sure he raised the specter of two of their most feared bogey men. First he accused the Republicans of seeking to put the black man on the same political and economic footing as the white laborer. As Douglas heatedly denounced Negro equality, Irish brogues rose in assent from the crowd, "God for yees, Steevin!" "Down with um!" "No, be jabers!" Douglas then played on the Catholic's fear of the Protestant majority. He described the dominant role of Protestant clergy in the abolition movement and darkly hinted at the political influence anti-Catholic clergy would have in a Republican administration. This, too, brought howls from the crowd of thousands.[21]

After expertly warming the crowd with a mixture of canards and caricature, Douglas moved on to his main point. The future of the Union was "much in danger"; only a Democratic president could hold it together. He drew shouts of delight when he said that after having campaigned in Kentucky, he was sure that he, not Breckinridge, was the only Democrat with a chance of victory. In fact, the Little Giant was now certain he would defeat Lincoln. Again a chorus of cheers rose from the crowd, excited by the prospect of victory and the Little Giant's pugnacious style.

Douglas's address was followed by other political harangues designed to keep the partisan fire burning. At day's end the crowd made its way back to the center city in yet another torchlight parade. While a barrage of twelve hundred Roman candles lit up the sky above the city, Stephen Douglas retired for the night. His arm was numb from handshakes, his throat raw from yet another oration. Yet he slept content that, in Chicago, the party was united in his favor. He rested the next day in his home town before resuming the campaign in Iowa and Wisconsin.[22]

As Douglas left Chicago he was encouraged by the solidification of support among Democrats and by unmistakable signs of discord among his Republican opponents. He had plenty of time on the train to Iowa to read the Chicago newspapers. They all carried articles about the city's latest political embroilment, at the center of which, Douglas was not surprised to see, was "Long John" Wentworth.

During the 1850s, Douglas and the mayor had been close political allies. Wentworth's *Chicago Democrat* was the official Douglas newspaper in northern Illinois. But during the controversy over the Kansas-Nebraska Act, the Little Giant felt that Wentworth had betrayed him, and Long John was driven out of the Democratic party. Douglas must have been amused that, six years later, Wentworth, Republican mayor of Chicago, might turn out to be the key to winning Illinois for the Democrats.

The seeds of discord among the Republicans first bore fruit during Seward's highly successful campaign appearances in Chicago. Wentworth had tried unsuccessfully to set a radical, abolitionist tone to the rallies. His remarks were not merely rhetorical excesses; rather, they were part of a conscious political maneuver. While almost every Republican leader knew the key to electoral victory lay in moderation on the slavery issue, Wentworth, ever the wildcat, became an outspoken abolitionist. He hoped to set in motion a wave of antislavery sentiment that would sweep him into Lyman Trumbull's senate seat. As mayor of the city and editor of the *Democrat*, Wentworth was difficult to ignore, but as luck would have it, in the fall of 1860 the federal district court in Chicago tried a case that aroused abolitionists across the country. Long John's radicalism became an important issue in the waning days of the 1860 campaign.

The trial that gave Wentworth such attention was the Ottawa Rescue case. The incident began in September 1859 when a slave, James Grey, escaped from his master in New Madrid, Missouri. Grey made his way to Illinois and crossed more than half the state before he was suspected of being a runaway and apprehended. The Fugitive Slave Law of 1851 required that federal officials cooperate in the arrest and return of escaped blacks. So in short order, a federal judge in Ottawa, Illinois, turned Grey over to a U.S. marshal, who intended to return the runaway. The proceedings were interrupted, however, when John Hossack, one of Ottawa's leading citizens, burst into the court. He reached out to Grey and said, "If you want liberty, come!" Grey dashed toward him, and the two fled the court. When the marshal tried to pursue them, seven fellow abolitionists barred his exit from the courthouse. Hossack and Grey sped away in a waiting carriage. Grey was helped to safety in Canada, while Hossack returned home to face prosecution. A grand jury indicted Hossack and six others who aided the escape.[23]

The trial, held a year later in Chicago, came during the heat of the presidential campaign. Hossack, who had political ambitions, did his best to appear a martyr. The case against him was cut and dried; the crime, after all, had been committed in a federal court. But in order for Hossack to be convicted, the state had to convince a jury. Republicans universally regarded the Fugitive Slave Law as obnoxious, but they were divided on whether to push for Hossack's conviction as a signal of goodwill to southerners and their sympathizers. Some of the party's leading attorneys agreed to serve as Hossack's counsel.

The climax of the closely watched trial came when Hossack, a strong and hardy man in his thirties, rose in his own defense to address the court. In his bearded face and intense eyes, some abolitionists saw an Illinois equivalent of John Brown. Certainly in rhetoric and self-righteous confidence the two men were similar. "I am an abolitionist. I have no apologies to make for being an abolitionist," he proudly proclaimed to the jury of eight Republicans and four Democrats. Nor did Hossack argue his guilt under the Fugitive Slave Law. He justified his actions under the Declaration of Independence and the higher law of God: "The law so plainly tramples upon the divine law that it cannot be binding upon any human being under any circumstances to obey it." These remarks thrilled the abolitionists in the gallery. Yet, after only two hours' deliberation, a conviction was returned.[24]

The law had been upheld over local Free Soil sentiment. That was all Lincoln supporters wanted. The court itself saw no reason to be vindicative. Hossack and the other defendants were given ten-day jail sentences and confined until a modest fine was paid—lenient treatment indeed for men who attacked a federal court. But it did not satisfy Hossack, who sought martyrdom. His speech to the court had been printed in almost every newspaper in the region. He was determined to keep the political spotlight focused on abolitionism. With a flourish Hossack went to jail in Chicago's Bridewell lock-up, proclaiming that he would rather stay in that hellish prison than acknowledge his guilt by paying the fine.

The idealistic Mr. Hossack gave the opportunistic Mayor Wentworth a chance to avenge himself on those Illinois Republicans who had elbowed him out of Lincoln's circle and at the same time to make political hay with the state's abolitionists. Wentworth visited Hossack in prison and ingratiated himself to the abolitionists. As mayor he had complete control over the conditions of Hossack's confinement. In short order, city workers refurbished the abolitionist's cell. The wife of the city jailor became Hossack's personal maid and cook. Banquets were arranged at municipal expense. Wentworth himself took Hossack out of jail on daily paroles. Proudly Long John drove around town in his carriage, exhibiting Hossack like a boy with a new pet.

In his newspaper, the *Daily Democrat,* Wentworth printed huzzas to the abolitionist cause. He even gave a column to Hossack so that the crusader could address the public from prison. Lincoln supporters wanted the Hossack case out of the press as quickly as possible, but rather than risk an open breach in party ranks, they bore Wentworth's antics in silence. Wentworth went too far on October 8 when he called for the Republican State Central Committee to pay Hossack's fine. The rival Douglas newspapers immediately seized on the call as proof of Lincoln's abolitionist leanings. The *Illinois State Register* referred to Wentworth's *Daily Democrat* as "Mr. Lincoln's organ in Chicago" and assured downstate readers that the Republicans intended to use Hossack as "a martyr exhibiting wounds sustained in the cause of Abraham Lincoln."[25]

In city taverns and around the pot-bellied stoves of country general stores, Douglas men worked to paint Lincoln with the same extremist brush they applied to Wentworth. "Look here," they would say to their neighbors, "here is the Chicago *Democrat.* Is it not Republican? Did not John Wentworth nominate Lincoln? Is he not his right-hand man? Will you doubt evidence like this?" Usually such political pitches ended with the warning that a vote for Lincoln was a vote for "Nigger Equality" in Illinois and an invitation to slave insurrection in the South.[26]

Lincoln supporters could no longer remain silent. They turned to Joseph Medill and Charles H. Ray at the *Chicago Tribune* to help disassociate Lincoln and the Republican party from Wentworth. Speakers were dispatched into the countryside to counteract the charge that Lincoln was an abolitionist. Meanwhile, the *Tribune* took on Wentworth directly. For a week the newspaper ran stories that either overtly attacked the mayor's character or mocked his political savvy. At first these attacks were veiled as letters to the editor signed by such appropriate *noms-de-plume* as "An Old Line Abolitionist," but by week's end the assaults became more open and bitter. Wentworth was described as "a secret but fortunately harmless enemy of the Republican party." According to Medill and Ray, "His object is to so identify Mr. Lincoln and the Republican movement with the Abolition party proper that they will fail in all doubtful districts."[27]

This Republican family quarrel gradually fizzled out during the second week of October. Long John had planned for a stirring climax, but he could not get the supporting cast to follow his script. After leading a public subscription campaign to pay Hossack's fines and court costs, Wentworth held a rally to honor the freed abolitionist. Loyal Republicans stayed away, and the half-empty auditorium at Metropolitan Hall embarrassed both Hossack and the mayor. The two quarreled, and the abolitionist used the occasion to hurl barbs at Wentworth as well as at slave owners. Medill saw that Long John was losing steam, and he began to dismiss him as having been "struck with idiocy or insanity." The *Daily Democrat,* according to its rival, might have done "irreparable mischief if its reputation were decent and its circulation wider." With the sound of laughter ringing in his ears, Wentworth gave up the fight.[28]

Fortunately for Lincoln, right in the midst of the controversy over the Ottawa Rescue case, Illinois received word of statewide elections in Pennsylvania, Ohio, and Indiana. Politicians looked to these campaigns, which came only a month before the presidential vote, as tests of strength. The canvas in those states vindicated the Republican party's moderate strategy as their gubernatorial candidates were swept into office. These auspicious triumphs reinvigorated Chicago Republicans, while their Democratic rivals, who were just beginning to gather momentum, were thrown into despair.

Despair brought desperation. Less than a week before the elections the always manipulative city council made a bid to affect the outcome. Two Democratic aldermen proposed to increase the number of polling places in each precinct. Perhaps they merely sought to increase the turnout for Douglas among the ethnic working class by making voting more convenient. In any event, Republicans were deeply suspicious of the proposal. More polling places would compound the problem of policing against vote fraud. An even greater danger in the proposal was discovered by the party's lawyers. State statute specified the number of polling places in each precinct. To create more without approval of the state legislature would be illegal and would call into question ballots cast at those locations. The anticipated Republican majority in Chicago could conceivably be thrown out. Republican aldermen were unwilling to step into the trap. Confident of victory, they wanted no change in the political ground rules.[29]

They were not so confident, however, that they would forgo the political low road—no holds barred campaigning. As the election neared Republican newspapers trotted out the old canard, "Was Douglas Catholic?" The Little Giant had a Catholic wife and legions of Catholic supporters. For those with Know-Nothing leanings, this was proof enough that he was a papist. Republicans also raised the anti-Irish banner. In the sheriff's race they boosted their German-born candidate by saying that he was more American than Francis Sherman, the native-born Democratic candidate: "The German . . . will fill his office with Americans, and employ its patronage for the benefit of Americans." In contrast, the Republicans charged, "if Sherman is elected, his deputies will be Irishmen and soreheads." In its final pre-election editorial, the *Tribune* prodded undecided voters out of their homes with the warning the Irish would vote in large numbers.[30]

On the other side of town, William J. Onahan, one of the Irish voters so feared by the Republicans, sat down with his diary. In the quiet of his cottage home, he reflected about the coming elections. Full of regret and yet clutching faithfully to his belief in the Little Giant, he wrote: "Tomorrow decides the character of our government for the next four years, at least. Republicans are confident, Douglas men have only the courage of despair to animate them. Yet they will not give up."[31]

———◇———

For Stephen Douglas, the doomed campaign came to an inglorious conclusion on November 4 in Montgomery, Alabama. After a day of campaigning, the senator from Chicago boarded a steamboat bound for Selma. In the middle of a farewell address to his Montgomery supporters, the crowded upper deck from which he was speaking gave way. Douglas, his wife, Adele, and a hundred others crashed to the deck below, a jumble of broken decking, baggage, and struggling bodies. Douglas and his wife were rescued from the wreckage and carried to shore. Adele Douglas was badly bruised and remained in Montgomery. Her husband, however, with only one day remaining in the campaign, borrowed a crutch and gamely continued his swing through the South. He was in Mobile on election day. The initial returns were discouraging, and as he entered his hotel that evening, a friend noted that the limping Little Giant looked "more hopeless than I had ever before seen him."[32]

Election day in Chicago was a ward committeeman's dream: the weather was beautiful, the voter turnout high, and fraudulent voting rampant. Elections in Chicago were often marred by rain, sometimes even snow, but in 1860 the city enjoyed a cloudless blue sky. Republicans crowed that it was "just the kind of day for the Democrats to lose." Long lines formed early outside the polling places and continued throughout the day. The old maxim of Chicago politics, "Vote early and often," was in full force. Voter registration laws were lax, and there was little but dread of long lines at the polling places or personal scruples about lying under oath to prevent a citizen from casting several ballots for his candidate. One of the most important uses of money in the campaign was securing multiple voters. Republicans accused their rivals of "importing" men from "their strongholds to doubtful districts, where by the defect in the statutes, they will be sure to vote." Both parties were aware of opportunities to steal votes, and neither blanched at doing what was necessary to win. Party stalwarts spent the day securing very possible vote, by fair or foul means. The sick were taken from their beds, the lame were carried to the polls, the blind were provided with escorts, the old rode to the polls in carriages.[33]

In spite of the intense competition for votes, there were few disturbances at the polls. Crowds swarmed around the polling places, but there was no violence and little verbal banter. Perhaps because the chief rivals were natives of the Prairie State and one was a Chicagoan, few voters had not made up their minds long before. By election day voters were weary of arguing with their neighbors and anxiously awaited the results. Those of a sporting disposition bet on who would win the White House and placed side bets on local contests. A *Tribune* reporter noted, "Large sums of money, oceans of hats, stacks of boots, miles of pants, acres of coats, cords of cigars, and legions of oyster suppers" were wagered.[34]

After the polls closed, the drama shifted to the streets outside the newspaper offices and other telegraph locations. For the Douglasites it was a short evening. The midwestern returns came in first, and they presaged a Lincoln landslide in the North. Lincoln carried Chicago. The city that was so influential in nominating the Rail Splitter gave him 10,697 votes. Douglas did well in his hometown, securing 8,094 votes. His rival for control of the Democratic party, Vice-President Breckinridge, netted a mere 87 votes in the city. Democrats consoled themselves with the thought that at least Douglas would control the party in the North. By ten o'clock the Republicans were beginning to celebrate. Standards proclaiming the death of "squatter sovereignty" appeared in the crowds. The choruses for every Lincoln campaign song swelled as the evening progressed. At about midnight the news came across the wire that New York, Lincoln's last remaining obstacle, had fallen to the Republicans. Jubilant Republicans toasted victory with jugs of free liquor and surged through the streets proclaiming their victory to the sleeping city. At the head of their column a band cheerfully played "Dixie."[35]

Republicans celebrated their party's first presidential victory for two days. Rallies, parades, and speeches dominated the city until not a single Roman candle remained unfired and all Republican voices were rendered hoarse by songs and shouts. A Douglasite, weary of the noise, described one rally as a "grand blow out." "Cannons were fired on the lakeshore," he complained, "cannons were fired on the prairie; cannons were fired toward the university; cannons were fired toward the cemetery as if to wake the dead." Finally, even the Wide Awakes began to find the smell of their torches disagreeable and constant marching trying. Slowly order returned to the streets and quiet to the nights. Both Republicans and Democrats gratefully came together in the sentiment "all over at last."[36]

The object of the Republican's long celebration, the former rail splitter and future president, visited Chicago two weeks later. He arrived without fanfare and escorted by only a few friends. For the staff of the Tremont House the sight of the tall, thin president-elect waiting patiently at the registration desk was a shock. No sooner were Mr. and Mrs. Lincoln ensconced in the best available suite than every reporter, job seeker, and politico in town descended on the hotel. A troop of Wide-Awakes marched to the Tremont and serenaded the Prairie State's most distinguished couple. The next morning the hotel clerks were startled once more when equally as unceremoniously, Vice-President-elect Hannibal Hamlin arrived. Reporters lounging in the lobby dashed to the telegraph office. A major political story was clearly in the offing. Lincoln and Hamlin were meeting for the first time since their names had been linked in the Wigwam six months before.

Because neither Lincoln nor Hamlin campaigned for election, and because the office of vice-president then had few responsibilities other than presiding over the Senate, there had been no reason for the two men to meet. Victory in the general election put two urgent items on Lincoln's agenda: dividing the political spoils of the executive branch and determining a political posture toward those southern states that threatened to secede from the Union. Hamlin had been an early Lincoln supporter in New England. The senator from Maine, however, was placed on the ticket not out of expectation that he would work with Lincoln but because he was a friend of Seward's who could bring regional balance to the ticket. Although Lincoln and Hamlin would never become what the *Chicago Daily Journal* proclaimed them to be, "friends, personally and politically," the president-elect wished to have a cordial relationship with his running mate.[37]

When Hamlin was shown into Lincoln's suite, the Rail Splitter greeted him pleasantly: "Have we ever been introduced to each other, Mr. Hamlin?" As they shook hands Lincoln mentioned that as a young congressman he had been impressed by a speech Hamlin made to the Senate: "It was filled 'chock up' with the very best kind of anti-slavery doctrine." The man from Maine was a born politician, and without missing a beat Hamlin mentioned the first time he heard Lincoln address Congress, "a speech that was so full of good humor and sharp points that I . . . was convulsed with laughter."[38]

The two men were discussing cabinet appointments when throngs of Lincoln's Chicago friends burst into their conference. Social activity took center stage as introductions were made and acquaintanceships renewed. Some of his closer friends may have chided Lincoln about the beard he had begun to grow. Perhaps one of them noted that there had never been a bearded president. The group then went on a sight-seeing tour. This allowed the Chicago Republicans to show off their president, and it gave Lincoln and Hamlin a chance to inspect the Wigwam and other sites that figured in the convention fight. Hamlin was greatly impressed by all that he saw. "This place," he wrote to his wife, "is a marvel indeed." Also on the itinerary were the post office, the customs house, and the federal court building. These stops were convenient opportunities for Chicagoans to lobby for patronage jobs.

The post office was a particularly tricky decision for Lincoln. The *Chicago Tribune* was exerting powerful pressure to secure the postmastership for John L. Scripps. Control of this post would give Medill and Ray an unrivaled opportunity to expand their paper's circulation. Lincoln, however, parried any attempt to secure a commitment and, with the vice-president in tow, beat a retreat to the Headquarters Restaurant and an oyster supper.[39]

The next morning Lincoln and Hamlin held an official reception. Although the day was cold and blustery, thousands turned out to shake hands with the Rail Splitter. From nine until noon, citizens queued up from the Tremont House's Ladies Parlor, down the stairs, out the Lake Street entrance, and along the block. Some were job seekers; others wanted to meet the man in whom all Illinois took pride. For most, meeting Lincoln was a memorable experience. The angular president stood six feet, four inches tall, and in order to shake hands with the majority of his well-wishers, he stooped slightly, and offered a warm two-handed greeting, a friendly smile, and a word of salutation. The guests moved along the receiving line to Charles Wilson, Mrs. Lincoln, and the vice-president elect.

Charles Wilson was the influential editor of the *Chicago Daily Jour-*

nal, an old-line Free Soiler and an ardent Republican. He loved the give and take of a political fight. When Thomas Hoyne, U.S. district attorney, crossed him in 1856, Wilson assaulted the Democrat on Clark Street and forcefully punctuated his arguments with well-placed punches until he knocked Hoyne through "the show window of the State Bank, and safely deposited him among the other 'smallcoin.' " Such a man was not shy about promoting himself for the job of postmaster for Chicago. Lincoln got some relief from Wilson and other job seekers when a young boy, about five years old, appeared before him. "The child," a reporter noted, "was boiling over with enthusiasm, his cheeks glowed with pride, and he could not contain his feelings, so he cried out, 'Hurray for Uncle Abe!' " Lincoln smiled broadly and took the lad in his arms. He treated the boy to a gentle "tossing up," which delighted him and brought applause from the crowd. By the time the reception ended, about three thousand hands had been shaken, and Hannibal Hamlin complained that he was "squeezed out."[40]

Lincoln tried to spend the rest of the day in conference with politicians from Ohio, Wisconsin, and northern Illinois. But by this time, the lobby of the Tremont was a sea of patronage hopefuls. Even the New York reporters, no strangers to patronage, were surprised by the particularly obnoxious genus of "homo politico" found in Chicago. "The vultures are on the alert," a reporter from the *Herald* remarked as he looked out on the milling mob of job seekers. Each one kept one eye on the hotel entrance, so as to ambush any newly arriving dignitary, and the other on the main stairway, in case Lincoln or Hamlin ventured forth. The Tremont's staff were kept busy bringing dozens of gentlemen's calling cards up to the Lincoln and Hamlin suites. Only a few people, "known not to be bores or office seekers" were let in. Most had to cool their heels with the hoi polloi below. Chicago's political elite, knowing that such treatment was not meant for them, continually broke in on Lincoln and "worried him nearly to death [with invitations to] dinners, parties, Sunday school meetings, church visits, levees, etc. etc." So little business was conducted that day that Lincoln was obliged to extend his visit to Chicago. But to make best use of this time, he needed to find a more tranquil setting than the chaotic Tremont House.[41]

Lincoln's old friend Judge Ebenezer Peck volunteered the use of his house in Lakeview, then a rural district north of the city limit. The next morning, Lincoln, Hamlin, and Lyman Trumbull, Illinois' Republican senator, eluded the job seekers in the lobby and escaped by carriage to the suburbs. Even there the president-elect was not entirely free from patronage concerns. Judge Peck was a gracious host, but he made it clear that he wanted to be named postmaster of Chicago. Lincoln was discovering that a president could have too many "friends."

No record was kept of the Lakeview meeting, although it is not difficult to discern the principal topics of the conversations. The selection of a cabinet would be the first and one of the most important tests of Lincoln's administrative ability. He wanted Hamlin's advice, because Hamlin was an easterner and a Washington insider. Many American vice-presidents before 1860 were outright hostile to the policies of the chief executive. Lincoln wanted above all to avoid intraparty conflict in the first Republican administration. He told Hamlin that his chief rivals for the nomination— Bates, Chase Cameron, and, of course, Seward—all represented rival factions of the Republican party. His goal was to co-opt these factions by bringing their leaders into the cabinet, where they would be responsible to him, yet still be in a position to reward their followers. The cabinet, therefore, was to be the glue of party unity. To make that work, however, appointments had to be made in such a way as to balance the egos of the men involved with their political clout and personal talent. Lincoln presented his initial thought on each position and solicited Hamlin's response.[42]

Trumbull and Hamlin agreed to become Lincoln's go-betweens in negotiating with prospective cabinet members. In return for this valuable service, Lincoln told Hamlin to pick a New Englander for the cabinet. This was a rare opportunity for Hamlin to exert influence, although Lincoln qualified the commission by giving him a list of four men to choose from. The vice-president used his choice well and invited Gideon Wells of Connecticut to serve as secretary of the navy.[43]

The acid test that Lincoln applied to all cabinet appointees was their willingness to enforce the fugitive slave laws. These laws loomed large in Lincoln's thinking about the second great issue he faced, the threat of southern secession. South Carolina voted on November 9, 1860, to hold a secession convention. Four days later, the governor of Mississippi called for his state to consider secession. Alabama's legislature had voted for a secession convention months before, just in case Lincoln won the general election. Georgia and Florida teetered on the verge of secession. Lincoln was urged by many to offer the South some reassurance and thereby stem the rising tide of secessionist sentiment. Historians have been critical of Lincoln because he remained silent during this period. Yet, the president-elect was caught in a dilemma, and he knew there was no way out of it. The South demanded concessions, notably some guarantee on the extension of slavery in the West. Yet, Lincoln was the representative of a party whose central doctrine was to stop the expansion of slavery. Some Republicans wanted Lincoln to make clear to the South that slavery would be contained. Moderates urged him to hold out the hope of concessions. If Lincoln did the former, he might stampede more states into secession; but if he appeared ready to make concessions, he would divide the young Republican party before he took office. What made his position particularly difficult was his status as president-elect. Everyone agreed he was the critical figure, but he had no real powers. Lincoln tried to deal with the dilemma by making as few comments on the political situation as possible. He was regularly invited to speak to groups and he refused. He knew how much would be read into each word he said.[44]

Even when Hannibal Hamlin tried to raise the issue of South Carolina's action in the privacy of Judge Peck's drawing room, Lincoln "dismissed the incident in a general way" and changed the topic of conversation. Some people interpreted Lincoln's reticence on this subject and his amiability as naivete and ignorance of the gravity of the crisis. Over dinner one night, Don Piatt, an old acquaintance of Lincoln's and a Republican leader from Cincinnati, insisted on drawing out the president-elect on the issue. "The Southern people," he contended "were dead earnest." Piatt "doubted whether [Lincoln] would be inaugurated." Lincoln tried to laugh off Piatt's remark and change the subject. But the Cincinnatian only grew more insistent. "In ninety days," he predicted, "the land would be whitened with tents." Lincoln managed to keep his good humor over this badgering, but would not comment on the issue. He merely smiled and said, "Well, we won't jump that ditch until we come to it. I must run the machine as I find it."[45]

Lincoln was particularly determined to remain reticent on the issue of secession while he was in Chicago, because only two days before he had reluctantly issued a "semi-official" statement through Lyman Trumbull. This message was conciliatory to the South, although it offered no change in Republican principles. He gave the South the assurance that "all of the states will be left in complete control of their own affairs," and they could choose "their own means of protecting property and preserving peace and order." This underscored his earlier commitment to uphold the law of the land "firmly and even obdurately to the end." More than this Lincoln could not promise without undermining his own base of support.[46]

What he could do was encourage southerners to believe what he said about respecting the slave codes. Therefore, potential cabinet appointees had to be willing to back enforcement of the fugitive slave laws. It is very likely that those laws also were the subject of considerable discussion between Lincoln and Chicago Republicans. The celebrated Ottawa Rescue Case did nothing to enhance goodwill between North and South or create the image of northern respect for slavery's legality.

Only a week before Lincoln's visit, another attempt to enforce the fugitive slave laws was foiled in Chicago. Eliza Grayson eluded her master and fled to Chicago in 1858. For two years she worked as a domestic servant in a Clark Street bordello. Then she made the mistake of confiding her secret to one of the prostitutes, who together with a "friend" turned Eliza over to a slave catcher for a $200 reward. The scheme failed when the girl was "liberated" from the rather loose temporary custody of a Chicago deputy by a mob of angry blacks. Eliza was immediately sent north to Canada via the underground railroad. Her liberators were arrested, but spent only a night in the lock-up. The *Chicago Times* decried the incident as a threat to sectional harmony, while the Republican *Tribune* spoofed such notions by headlining the story "The Union Again Threatened! Colored Person Loose!"[47] Lincoln may well have been angry that while he was carefully trying to cultivate sectional trust based on the law, Chicagoans were flaunting its violation. What happened in Illinois and what was printed in the *Tribune* reflected on the president elect. Because of this the fugitive slave laws would be more strictly enforced in Chicago in the months before the Civil War than at any other time.

The worst incident occurred in April 1861 after Lincoln was inaugurated. Abolitionists were warned that as a gesture to appease the South, federal marshals would make a sweep of Chicago's free black community. The *Daily Journal* warned runaway slaves to "make tracks for Canada as soon as possible. . . . You are not safe here and you cannot be safe until you stand on English soil. . . . Strike for the north star." More than one hundred of the city's small black community were runaway slaves and answered the warning. Although about one thousand escaped slaves passed through Chicago in 1860, 104 people was too large a group to be smuggled north at one time via the underground railroad. Therefore, abolitionists and black leaders pooled their resources to secure four freight cars from the Michigan Southern Railroad to carry the refugees to safety. On the day of their departure the runaways came together for an emotional religious service at the Zoar Baptist Church. They were then packed into freight cars. The refugees were given plenty of food and water, but their trip north would be crowded and cold in the dark cargo cars. Most were young men, several had their families with them, and they were in good spirits. The elder runaways, according to one reporter, "evinced no levity but acted like those who had been hardened by troubles, and were now suffering a lot foreseen and prepared for." Many of those who came to see them off had tears in their eyes. Someone called out, "Never mind, the good Lord will save us all in the coming day." Then the engine bell rang out and the train pulled out of the freight yard bound for "the other side of Jordan."[48]

Many blacks who lacked certificates of freedom yet chose to remain behind lived to regret it. On April 4, 1861, the city's new federal marshal raided the black community and arrested five people as fugitive slaves. A family living on South Clark Street was also arrested and sent below the

Mason-Dixon Line. These actions caused a panic, and many fled the city in haste. Dr. C. V. Dyer, a prominent abolitionist, fought back. A black man in his employ was seized by a southern slave catcher. Dyer caught up with the man in a small tavern on Lake Street. A quarrel ensued over the legality of the warrant, but the question was settled when Dyer broke his walking stick over the southerner's head and made off with the runaway. Only the firing on Fort Sumter a short time later saved the black community from further arrests.[49]

These events were in the future when Lincoln visited Chicago in November 1860. But they underscored the importance he placed on the enforcement of the fugitive slave laws as part of a conciliatory, if conservative, response to the threat of secession. Another conciliatory gesture to the South that Lincoln discussed in Chicago was to name a southerner to his cabinet. Lincoln liked the idea in principle but wanted someone he could trust. Unknown to the press, Lincoln secretly met with his first choice during the Chicago conference.

One evening, Lincoln secretly left his suite and visited the rooms of Joshua Speed, a merchant from Kentucky and an old friend. They had spent time together in Springfield when Lincoln was a rising attorney and Speed a leading merchant in that town. The slavery question eventually split their friendship. Speed felt so strongly about the issue that he sold his extensive investments in Springfield and moved to a slave state. For years no correspondence passed between them. But as Lincoln prepared for his Chicago trip he reopened communication with Speed. At their clandestine meeting the conviviality between the two men returned. Speed had known Lincoln well, and it did not take him long to see what the Illinois politician was leading up to. Before Lincoln could formally invite Speed to join the cabinet, the Kentuckian declined any office with the new government. He did agree, however, to try to help Lincoln secure another southerner for the cabinet. Lincoln did not want to write to people he did not know well for fear that his negotiations might be leaked to the press. Speed agreed to act as a confidential agent. Eventually he approached James Guthrie of Kentucky for a post, but Guthrie declined because of advanced age. In the end, no southerner was included in the cabinet.[50]

Lincoln hoped to conclude his visit to Chicago by spending Sunday with friends and acquaintances. But he was too much in demand and was pulled in several directions. In the morning he attended services at St. James Episcopal church, the congregation of the Chicago elite. He was escorted by Congressman Isaac N. Arnold, and in the pews around him were William B. Ogden, the city's first mayor, Gurdon Hubbard, a former fur trader who helped pioneer the meat-packing industry, and descendants of John Kinzie, one of the city's founders. After the service the president-elect returned to his hotel and joined friends for one of the Tremont House's unrivaled Sunday dinners. In the middle of the meal John V. Farwell, a Chicago merchant, arrived and said his carriage was waiting. Lincoln was confused, until Mrs. Lincoln mentioned that the day before, while Lincoln was in Lakeview, Farwell had called and invited him to visit a Sunday school. Without complaint, Lincoln left his meal and joined Farwell in his carriage. He made one request to the Republican merchant—that he not be asked to make a speech.[51]

The Sunday school to which Lincoln so obligingly allowed himself to be taken to was no ordinary one. Farwell took Lincoln to the infamous district north of the Chicago River. Here, among the sailors' dives, gambling houses, and brothels, they found Dwight L. Moody preaching to several hundred ill-clad street urchins.

Moody was the most aggressive of Chicago's evangelical ministers. He roamed the streets of the city like a modern-day Socrates. Children and young people were drawn to him by his forthright nature, his penetrating concern for them as individuals, and the seemingly endless supply of candy that he doled out from his pockets. To many adults, however, he was a self-promoting, self-righteous, humorless fanatic. His practice of buttonholing strangers on the street and challenging them with, "What is the status of your soul?" created consternation among some and inclined the press to dub him "Crazy Moody." Farwell was among a handful of prominent Chicagoans who believed Moody was a genuine man of God. The determined manner in which Farwell separated Lincoln from his dinner was an indication of how firm a disciple he was.

Lincoln heard Moody give one of his brief, down-to-earth sermons, but these remarks were only prelude to an address by Lincoln himself. When Moody introduced him to the children, they gave him an enthusiastic reception. "Speech, Speech!" they shouted over and over again. Perhaps Moody's enthusiasm infected Lincoln, or it may have been the pleas of the dirty children in the dingy hall, but Lincoln agreed to speak, the only time he did so during his trip to Chicago. In a few words he underscored the importance of Biblical study and the challenge of trying to live up to the Bible's message. "With close attention to your teachers," he concluded, "and hard work to put in practice what you learn from them, some of you may become president of the United States." This drew more cheers from the children, and Lincoln made his exit. The presidential visit was a boost to Moody's nascent organization and a spur to reporters, who addressed him more kindly thereafter as "Brother Moody."[52]

No sooner did Lincoln return to his hotel than he was visited by Henry C. Whitney, an Urbana attorney who had ridden the Eighth Judicial Circuit with Lincoln in days gone by. After recalling old times,

Whitney—like everyone else—had a request: he wanted Lincoln to sit for a picture by Urbana photographer Samuel G. Alschuler. Lincoln knew Alschuler; he had been photographed by him three years earlier. But the president-elect could not have been enthusiastic about being photographed at this time. His beard had not fully grown in and was restricted to a fuzzy patch along his chin. Whitney, however, was insistent; besides, Alschuler had brought all of his equipment. Lincoln finally acquiesced. The result was a portrait showing the confident prairie politician on the eve of crisis, his features smooth and youthful, save perhaps for his eyes, which seemed wary and a bit weary.[53]

One thing Lincoln was not troubled by on Sunday was job seekers. Word had been spread that the president left town Saturday night. The last night Lincoln spent in Chicago was peaceful. He would never again see Chicago, the home of many friends and the scene of several political triumphs. At 9:00 A.M. Monday, he and Mary Todd quietly left the city. It was a cold, gray day, and by the time the Lincolns reached Springfield it had started to rain. But this did not deter the mob of reporters and office seekers "who had been lying in wait for him since Saturday." They leapt from the twilight shadows pressing their cases and questions. The president, as always, preserved "the even tenor of his temper" and went immediately to his reception room and the task of creating an administration.[54]

The enthusiasm generated by Lincoln's election blinded many Republicans in Chicago to the approaching dangers of civil war. Mayor Wentworth, for one, was unworried by the thought of secession, because he knew that southerners liked to "bully, and brag and bluster," but if put to the test they would "eat dirt." In the *Chicago Democrat* he bragged, "Seventeen men can conquer a state full of chivalry, and they know it." The *Tribune* satirized the southern states by reporting the fanciful secession of the largely democratic Bridgeport area. The election, the *Tribune* mockingly declared, revealed such a "flagrant disregard . . . for our feelings . . . as well as our most sacred rights" that the working-class community had no choice but to secede. In more sober moments Joseph Medill and others at the *Tribune* realized there might be something more than bombast in the South's declarations. But the newspaper wanted no concessions to be made. Rank-and-file Chicago Republicans, according to one reporter, "think of apologizing to nobody for voting for Honest Old Abe. They do not dream of conceding one plank in the Republican platform nor one beam in the grand old constitution of these states." Only after December 20, when South Carolina formally seceded from the Union, did brave words give way to the grim realization that a war was imminent.[55]

Wars demand heroes, and even before the conflict began Chicago found one in Major Robert Anderson, commander of U.S. troops in

Charleston, South Carolina. President James Buchanan, fearful of irritating southern secessionists, not only refused Anderson's request for reinforcements but negotiated with South Carolina to transfer federal military installations to the rebel states. While his irresolute policy made Buchanan anathema in Chicago, Major Anderson boldly acted to strengthen the position of his troops. On the night of December 26, 1860, Anderson skillfully extracted his meager force from Charleston and occupied Fort Sumter. Carolinians were chagrined and outraged by Anderson's strategic coup, while in the North, citizens were relieved to see some sign of resistance to the growing rebellion. One Chicagoan enthusiastically wrote the major, "You are today the most popular man in the nation." A meeting of Chicago Germans voted to send an inscribed sword to Anderson.[56]

Mayor Wentworth, always ready to share the luster of another's glory, declared January 8 the anniversary of the Battle of New Orleans, as a day for honoring the actions of Major Anderson and the memory of Andrew Jackson. Public buildings were closed, flags were flown, and bells were tolled. But there were no parades. Chicago's militia had no desire to muster on a cold January day, or to muddy their fancy uniforms in the sloppy streets. "The citizens were not very jubilant," the *Tribune* noted. "The day is past for rhapsodies over our 'gar-r-r-eat country' and wrapping of figures of speech in star spangled banners and setting off word pyrotechnics. We have come upon a new era. We know the country is large; but *will it hold together?*"[57]

Stephen A. Douglas worked desperately to answer that question affirmatively. From December 1860 through the spring of 1861 he lobbied and caucused with colleagues in the Senate to draft a compromise plan that might halt the drift toward dissolution of the Union. He proposed new amendments to the Constitution that would offer guarantees to southerners and impose limitations on the growth of slavery. As recipient of nearly 1.5 million votes in the presidential election he had considerable clout in Washington. But moderates such as himself had little ground on which to maneuver. Republican senators were cool to any compromise that might limit the power of their new administration. Southern fire eaters talked compromise in Congress, yet wrote to their constituents in the manner of Robert Toombs of Georgia: "All further hope of looking to the North for security for your constitutional rights in the Union ought to be instantly abandoned."[58]

Extremist sentiment ran so high that even Republicans began to doubt whether Lincoln could be safely inaugurated. Senator Seward hired several New York detectives to investigate security risks in the capital. A Chicago detective, Allan Pinkerton, investigated security along Lincoln's route to the city and claimed that a plot was afoot to assassinate the president-elect when he transferred trains in Baltimore.

Pinkerton was a forty-two-year-old Scot who had immigrated to America in 1842. After failing as a barrel maker, he founded a detective agency in Chicago. His reputation as an innovative crime fighter grew apace with his reputation as a racial abolitionist. Lincoln knew Pinkerton and did not doubt his word. He allowed the detective to secretly escort him through Baltimore, disguised as an old woman. The *Chicago Tribune* credited Pinkerton's action with saving the Rail Splitter's life. Mayor Wentworth, however, near the end of his term, branded the whole incident a shameful hoax designed to enhance Pinkerton's business. "There was no conspiracy at all," he wrote, "save in the brain of the Chicago detective." Several weeks later, Pinkerton let Long John know he did not appreciate such comments. He saw Wentworth crossing one of the city's muddy streets and accosted him. Before onlookers could separate them, the detective thoroughly "thrashed" the former mayor.[59]

At the inauguration, Stephen Douglas stood with his long-time opponent from Illinois. As Lincoln made the inaugural address, Douglas held Lincoln's distinctive stove-pipe hat. Throughout Lincoln's conciliatory but firm speech, Douglas nodded his head and muttered "Good" and "That's so." A Chicago merchant in the audience wrote, "I felt glad and rejoiced" at the sight. "Mr. Douglas was the first to shake hands with the president after the inaugural speech. I thought I saw conversion in the man."

Although Douglas made a public display of determination to support the president, he had not been "converted." Significant differences continued to separate the two men. During the weeks following the inauguration Douglas tried to draw Lincoln away from the uncompromising posture of the radical Republicans and forge an agreement with southern moderates. But it was too late for such manuevers. While Douglas worked in Washington, Alabama secessionists in Montgomery were preparing a constitution for the Confederate States of America.[60]

By this time many of Douglas's Chicago supporters regarded secession as a reality. What they wanted to avoid was civil war. "Let them go in peace," was the advice of *Chicago Times* editor James Sheahan and publisher Cyrus Hall McCormick, two of Douglas's most important constituents. Republican William B. Ogden, the city's first mayor, was also fearful of conflict and urged compromise to bring peace and unity. For a time Douglas hoped to unite Democrats and peace Republicans into a popular movement for sectional negotiation. But the secessionists put an end to these hopes on April 12, 1861, when rebel batteries opened fire on Fort Sumter.[61]

Like a sudden and violent midwestern coldburst, the attack on Fort Sumter cleared the political atmosphere. The worst had happened. There would be civil war. On April 14, 1861, Major Anderson surrendered his garrison, and the next day Abraham Lincoln requested seventy-five thousand troops to put down the rebellion. The *Chicago Tribune,* speaking for "a patient and reluctant, but at last an outraged and maddened people,' proclaimed, "The gates of Janus are open, the storm is on us. Let the cry be, THE SWORD OF THE LORD AND OF GIDEON!"[62]

Thousands of Chicagoans, perhaps as many as twenty thousand, packed the streets surrounding the courthouse square on the evening of April 18. Bathed in torchlight, the city's political elite appealed to the assembled citizenry's patriotism. But such appeals were unnecessary at so emotional a moment. Young men flocked to join militia units. The climax of the rally was a song performed by the Republican party's favorite troubadours, the Lumbard Brothers. The song "The First Gun Is Fired" had been written only the day before by George Frederick Root, a Chicago music teacher. The lyrics captured the city's rising war fever:

> The first gun is fired,
> May God protect the right,
> Let the free born sons of the North arise,
> In power's avenging might,
> Shall the glorious Union our fathers made,
> By ruthless hands be sundered?
> And we of freedom's sacred rights,
> By traitorous foes be plundered?[63]

Stephen Douglas met with Lincoln on the day of Fort Sumter's fall. He pledged his support to fight secession and advised the president that at least two hundred thousand troops would be needed to combat the Confederacy. The Little Giant then returned to Illinois, where the war had thrown his party into chaos. Many leading Democrats in Chicago and downstate immediately rallied to the administration. Others found it difficult to embrace their partisan foes. The *Chicago Times* responded to the Fort Sumter attack with salvos of their own against Lincoln: "He cannot have our commendations for smothering the last hope of the American Union in the blood of American citizens."

Nationally, the party needed leadership, and the state needed unity; Douglas left Washington to provide both.[64] He went first to Springfield where he addressed the state legislature. There he gave one of the greatest speeches of his career. When Douglas described his "sadness and grief" over the sorry condition of the Republic, even the bearded cynics in the state house wept openly. He cast aside partisan causes and called for Illinoisans to resist secession: "It is a duty, we owe ourselves, and our children, and our God, to protect this government and that flag from every assailant, be he who he may." Men of both parties loudly cheered the Little Giant. By the time Douglas reached Chicago even his arch enemies at the *Tribune* hailed him as a modern Demosthenes or Patrick Henry.[65]

On May 1, 1861, about nine in the evening, Douglas came to Chicago for the last time. His train was met by a delegation of long-time supporters and recent enthusiasts. Uniformed militia companies complete with marching bands escorted the senator through the illuminated streets of the city. Thousands lined the sidewalk to cheer while hundreds more preceded his entourage on horseback, leading the parade toward the Wigwam. The main floor and galleries of the convention hall were packed when Douglas made his way to the vast wooden stage. Although he was not feeling well, to the audience below he looked his old confident, combative self. A "hearty cheer" rent the heavy air of the hall as he approached the speaker's rostrum.

"I can say before God, my conscience is clear," proclaimed the Little Giant, as he recounted his numerous attempts at compromise with the South. Indeed, he faulted himself for going "to the extreme of magnanimity." Angrily he noted, "The return we receive is War, armies marching upon our Capital, obstructions and dangers to our navigation, letters of marque to invite pirates to prey upon our commerce, a concerted movement to blot out the United States of America from the map of the globe." The reason for the conflict was neither slavery nor Lincoln's election, according to Douglas. These were "mere Pretext." "The present secession movement is the result of an enormous conspiracy formed more than a year since . . . by leaders of the Southern Confederacy."

He then moved to the central theme of his address, a rallying cry that united the North: "There can be no neutrals in this war: *only patriots—or traitors.*" Democrats and Republicans needed to work together. The southern conspirators counted on throwing a united South upon a politically divided North.

> There is but one way to defeat this. In Illinois it is to be defeated by *closing up the ranks.* War will thus be prevented on our own soil. While there was hope of peace I was ready for any reasonable sacrifice or compromise to maintain it. But when the question comes of war in the cottonfields of the South or the cornfields of Illinois, I say the farther off the better.

He closed his address by highlighting once more the twin themes of duty and unity: "The greater our unanimity, the speedier the day of peace."

> It is a sad task to discuss questions so fearful as civil war, but sad as it
> is, bloody and disastrous as I expect it will be, I express it as my con-
> viction before God, that it is the duty of every American citizen to rally
> round the flag of his country.

Douglas concluded his speech to loud applause and cries of "More." As the
reception committee escorted him off the stage, nine cheers in his honor
thundered from the packed galleries of the Wigwam.[66]

Douglas's impassioned speech to his fellow Chicagoans was the climax of his long and tumultuous public career. His challenge, "Only
patriots—or traitors," brought the bulk of the Democratic party behind
Lincoln's call to arms and was the cornerstone of the "War Democrats," a
branch of the party that proved vital in bringing a northern victory. The
ovations of the Wigwam still rang in his ears when the Little Giant finally
returned to his suite at the Tremont. He embraced his wife Adele as groups
of citizens serenaded them from the street below. He had reason for
guarded optimism. Although the America he had worked to expand and
strengthen for so many years was in turmoil, a path through the crisis,
however violent, had begun to emerge. Since he returned to Illinois, his
new role as a war leader had begun to take shape. But Douglas was a weary
man. For one year, from the breakup of the Democratic party at Charleston through the presidential campaign and the secession crisis, he had been
at the center of American politics, under more pressure than any politician
before or since.

Douglas planned to return to Washington soon after his speech. But
the next day he felt weak and feverish. So his wife decided they should remain in Chicago for a much needed rest. Each day his condition grew
worse. The fever rose, and rheumatism inflamed the muscles of his arms
and shoulders. Soon he was forced to remain in bed, unable even to write.
He rallied briefly on May 19 and was able to leave his bed and take some
fresh air. Thereafter, his condition deteriorated rapidly. Liver and throat
ailments sapped his strength. The succession of physicians, family, and
clergy visiting the stricken senator convinced the press of the seriousness of
the illness. Straw was placed in the street in front of the Tremont House so
that passing carriages did not disturb the patient. On June 3 the weakened
and feverish Douglas suddenly called out, "Death! Death! Death!" His
wife rushed to his side. Holding his head in her arms, she saw he was
dying. Gently she asked if he had a message for his two sons. "Tell them,"
he said, "to obey the laws and support the Constitution of the United
States." He died several hours later.[67]

The body of the forty-eight-year-old senator lay in state at Bryan
Hall for two days. Across the country, from the Chicago courthouse to the

White House in Washington, public buildings were draped in black. On June 7, 1861, Roman Catholic Bishop James Duggan led a funeral procession made up of five thousand mourners, many of them Irish laborers who were deeply affected by the loss of their champion. The procession ended south of the city limits on a meadow near Lake Michigan. On land where he once had hoped to build his permanent home, Douglas was buried. For many Chicagoans the brief graveside service that June morning marked an appropriate end to the drama of a divided nation and the beginning of a tragic civil war.

3

◇

THE FIRST BLOOD

L incoln stared out the window and across the lawn of the White House toward the river. The eddying current swirled in dark brown circles. For a moment, it looked rather like the Illinois River back home, but it was the Potomac, still heavy with spring runoff, carrying the loamy soil of northern Virginia to the sea. Across the room the door opened. Who was it this time?

Senator Henry Wilson of Massachusetts quickly crossed the library floor and stood at the president's side. Lincoln turned and shook hands, then quickly broke away. "Excuse me," said, "but I cannot talk," and he began to cry. The president buried his face in his handkerchief, and for some moments sobbed softly. Wilson himself was on the verge of tears and did not press the president. Finally, after he composed himself, Lincoln took a seat. "I will make no apology . . . for my weakness," he said sadly, "but I knew poor Elmer Ellsworth well and held him in great regard."[1]

The man for whom Lincoln grieved was a militia officer from Chicago whom chance had chosen to be the first Union officer killed in the Civil War. Only moments before, Lincoln had learned of the details of his heroic death. Within days his name would be on the lips of every northern patriot, his image printed in scores of periodicals. Today the name of Elmer Ellsworth is all but forgotten, yet to Chicagoans of 1861, Ellsworth was the epitome of manly honor and patriotic glory. His life and death go far to explain why Chicagoans in particular, and Northerners in general, rushed so enthusiastically to the slaughterhouse of civil war.

Ellsworth arrived in Chicago in 1854, a seventeen year old with little to his credit but a proud demeanor and a modest education. Both qualities appealed to Arthur F. Devereux, a young New Englander who had a pat-

66

ent business. Devereux offered Ellsworth a position as clerk and junior partner. The two young men shared an interest in all things military. Ellsworth would have gone to West Point if his education had been better. Devereux belonged to a private military company, the Cadets of the National Guard, which Ellsworth soon joined. As a boy in the Hudson River Valley, Ellsworth had played the role of drill sergeant with his playmates; as a young man in Chicago, he read William J. Hardee's manual of arms for amusement. He was perfectly suited for the Cadets and became one of the most popular and active members of the company and a successful man of business.[2]

In 1857, Ellsworth's rapid social and economic progress came to an end. Devereux and Ellsworth entrusted all of their funds to a man who turned out to be an embezzler. Not only was their firm ruined, but each man was saddled with a heavy burden of debt. For a time, Ellsworth may even have had to sever his connection with the Cadets. His pride made his poverty worse than it needed to have been. He refused his many friends' offers of assistance and struggled to pay his debts by whatever means he could manage. He chafed under the "insults and infernal stare" of his creditors and lamented that he had become "the sport and foot-ball of fortune." He went for days without food. On one occasion a fellow member of the Cadets bought him an oyster stew. Although Ellsworth had not eaten for three days, he refused the supper until his friend threatened to have it thrown out. As soon as he had money, Ellsworth sought out the friend and paid him back. He would endure no blot on his rigidly defined personal honor.[3]

It took more than a year, but Ellsworth eventually got back on his feet again. To better support his parents in New York, he began to study for a legal career. But he could not resist the allure of military life. His reputation as a drill master was well established in Chicago, and other companies in the region invited him to help them improve their military bearing. In December 1857 he was invited to Rockford, Illinois, to spruce up a volunteer company known as the Rockford Greys. By summer they were a trim, precision drill team, and Ellsworth was in love with Carrie Spafford, sixteen-year-old daughter of a Rockford banker. In less than a year they became engaged. But the engagement, her father insisted, was conditional upon Ellsworth starting a legal career. For months he studied law, sleeping in a Chicago lawyer's office and subsisting largely on crackers and water.

In April 1859 Ellsworth faced an agonizing choice. The members of his old company, the Cadets, asked him to assume the captaincy of the unit. They had fallen on hard times, and their membership lagged; only eight to ten men would report to meetings. They were in debt and without leadership. They believed that only Ellsworth's discipline and personal popularity could save the unit. Like most of the military companies in Chicago, the Cadets functioned more as a men's social club than a real militia unit. Elegant uniforms, dress balls, and parades were the reward for the tedium of drill. The members of such clubs shared with Ellsworth a longing for military glory. They saw military life as a connection with the Minute Men of three generations before and such nineteenth-century romantic heroes as Napoleon and Garibaldi. In their trim uniforms they could imagine themselves as the knights errant depicted in Alfred Tennyson's popular *Idylls of the King*. The difference between Ellsworth and the remaining Cadets, however, was that for Ellsworth, being a soldier was less a weekend fantasy than a long-term goal. In spite of the demands of his law studies and the conditions of his engagement, Ellsworth seized the chance to head the Cadets.[4]

The manner in which Ellsworth overhauled the Cadets set in motion a wave of interest in volunteer companies across the North. Like many young men Ellsworth had closely followed the recently ended Crimean War. He was particularly struck by the illustrated newspapers' depictions of the French light infantry units known as the Zouaves. This was reinforced by his friendship with Charles A. DeVillers, an Algerian Frenchman who came to Chicago as a fencing instructor and physician. DeVillers had served as a surgeon with the Zouaves and told his eager young friend much about the unit. The strange name came from the Zouave warriors of North Africa, whose courage and lightening assaults helped the French in their invasion of Algeria in 1830. Eventually, the French army modeled several "Zouave" units after them. With DeViller's encouragement Ellsworth sent to Paris for the Zouave manual. He was thrilled by the absolute precision and gymnastic demands of Zouave tactics and by the baggy red pants, the collarless dark blue jackets, and the yards of gold trim that made the uniform visually striking. He assumed the captaincy of the Cadets and immediately changed their name to the United States Zouave Cadets. His bold goal was to make them a company second to none in the America.[5]

It took the young captain only a few months to revive the company and make it the most popular and colorful military unit in Chicago. At the National Agricultural Society fair in September 1859, the Zouaves competed for the title of champion company of the United States and Canada. Only one unit competed against them, and the Zouaves easily claimed the "champion colors." The Zouaves were further honored with the title "Governor's Guard of Illinois." Ellsworth's growing reputation drew him to Springfield. At the state capital, he formed important new friendships with young law clerks John Hay and John Nicolay as well as with Governor William H. Bissell. Ellsworth was given the honorary title of Assistant Adjutant General of Illinois. But more significantly, he became a friend of Abraham Lincoln. After Ellsworth returned to Chicago he continued to correspond with his new supporters in Springfield. Lincoln was particularly eager to have Ellsworth join his law office. A mutual friend wrote that Lincoln "assures me no pains on his part shall be lacking to perfect [you] in the study of the Law—he has taken in you an interest I have never known him to take in any." In the spring of 1860 Lincoln was a prominent Republican politician, and Ellsworth wanted to accept his patronage. But he had one more goal to accomplish with the Zouave Cadets.[6]

The unit's claim to "champion colors" had been criticized by militia companies throughout the country because the Zouave Cadets had competed against only one other unit. Ellsworth decided to silence doubters by challenging rival companies on their home ground. He proposed that the Zouaves undertake a twenty-city tour. Financing for the tour was scraped together, and in a carnival-like mood, thousands of Chicagoans turned out to wish the departing Zouaves good luck. The unit in top condition after months of intensive physical training, was also disciplined in moral conduct. Each man swore not to enter a saloon, brothel, gambling den, or billiard parlor. They agreed to commit their free time to drill, reading, or chess, and swore an oath to help any member struck by illness or unemployment. Of the more than two hundred men who first signed the Zouave muster roll, only forty-seven survived the physical and moral selection process for the tour.[7]

On the forty-three day tour the Zouaves performed in twenty cities to universal acclamation. The *New York Tribune*'s report of their performance before a crowd of ten thousand was typical. The reporter was impressed by the "superb" rendition of the oblique march, firing, bayonet drills, stacking arms, and double and rapid-time drills. The climax of the review was a wonderful piece of showmanship. The soldiers charged with fixed bayonets, stopping just short of the audience to give a cheer in chorus: "One, two, three, four." At each number they doffed their caps. "Five, six, seven! Tig-a-r! Zouaves!" This brought "shouts of delight, waving of umbrellas, handkerchiefs, parasols, sticks, and hats." The reporter claimed that the Zouaves justly deserved their champion status, and "their fame . . . had not been trumpeted too loudly." What made the Zouaves national heroes, however, was their moral example:

> Here are forth young men, who had voluntarily given up what are considered enjoyments by too many of our American youth, abstaining from dissipation in all its forms, restraining their appetites, sub-

mitting almost to the training of the professional athlete . . . not with
the design of ultimately pounding an antagonist, but simply to gain
excellence in a certain direction, for its own sake.

The Chicago Zouaves became nationwide heroes of middle-class morality.[8] They were cheered by President Buchanan on the White House lawn
and by thousands of Philadelphians in front of Independence Hall. At
West Point they drilled not only for the cadets but also for the nation's
leading military experts, Major William J. Hardee and Lieutenant General
Winfield Scott. Grudgingly the West Pointers joined in the chorus of praise
for the Zouaves. By August, Ellsworth's picture was hawked by street corner vendors. A contemporary recalled that "school-girls dreamed over the
graceful wave of his curls." Several songs were written in the unit's honor,
and numerous imitation Zouave companies were formed in their wake.
Young Elmer Ellsworth was the "most talked of man in the country."[9]

On August 14, 1860, the Zouaves returned home to Chicago on the
night train. In spite of the late hour a torchlight parade and thousands of
friends and relatives met the conquering heroes. Roman candles were fired
and bands played. A rally in the Wigwam was followed by midnight supper at the Briggs House. "We claim you as our own," Mayor Wentworth
announced, "and as our own, we have rallied tonight as Chicago people
have never rallied before." It was near dawn before the celebrations and
congratulations ended and the Zouaves broke up to return to their separate homes.[10]

The triumphant Zouave tour proved to be a powerful stimulus to volunteer companies in Chicago and throughout the North. From Chicago to
Boston thousands of young men, caught up in the Zouave craze and the
growing secession crisis, crowded into militia armories. Ellsworth's almost
knightly image appealed to romantic and idealistic young men. The temperate reputation of the Zouaves helped to counter the middle class's disdain
for the military, which was more often associated with idleness, drinking,
and gambling. The tour proved that military units could preserve and protect the country's honor *and* a Christian's personal honor. The tour was also
a clear indication of the glory and fame that could be won via the military.
What twenty-three year old man of business, letters, or the clergy could
claim half the fame Ellsworth had gained in his year with the Zouaves? The
Zouaves contributed to the naive impression in the North that self-
discipline, hard work, and character were the requirements of military
victory—not death, dismemberment, and destruction.[11]

After the tour Ellsworth left Chicago, joined Lincoln's law office,
and campaigned for the Republican ticket. In March 1861, he was part of
Lincoln's bodyguard during the risky journey to Washington. In the capi-

tal he worked to create a federal militia bureau, but abandoned this task when Fort Sumter fell. With a cadre of his old Chicago comrades he formed a regiment of Zouaves made up of volunteers from the New York Fire Department. This unit participated in the first Union advance into Virginia where Ellsworth was killed. His death was a sobering reminder of the terrible cost of war. Yet this lesson was not widely accepted because of the romantic way Ellsworth fell.

On the evening before his troops entered the rebel state, Ellsworth wrote his parents: "Whatever may happen, cherish the consolation that I was engaged in the performance of a sacred duty." The next morning his troops occupied Alexandria, Virginia. While passing the Marshall House, an inn in that city, Ellsworth noted a Confederate flag flying from the roof. For weeks the flag had taunted Unionists in Washington; it could even be seen from the White House. Impulsively Ellsworth and a squad of riflemen rushed into the building to tear it down. While the troops below cheered Ellsworth ripped the flag from its pole. But as he descended to the street, he was shot in the chest by a rebel sympathizer. He died moments later, still draped in the captured battle flag. Death came quickly in a moment of glory for Ellsworth, and it immortalized him in the eyes of his fellow northerners. The romantic saga was complete when his wake was held in the White House. The nation mourned, and Ellsworth's bride-to-be, Carrie Spafford, was presented with her fallen hero's sword. Chicago provided the North with its first martyr.[12]

As the secession crisis accelerated and political marching units such as the Wide-Awakes disbanded, more young men looked to the militia companies. Besides the Zouaves, the militia of Chicago in 1860 consisted of eleven companies that together would have been fortunate to muster 150 fully equipped soldiers. This situation gradually changed during the first months of 1861. The Zouaves had disbanded after their tour, but regrouped. A Hungarian immigrant, Geza Mihalotzy, formed the Lincoln Rifles with volunteers from the city's Eastern European community. In February the Highland Guards, composed of Scots, Irish, and Welsh, began an active campaign to arm themselves. Other old companies dusted off their equipment and began to drill regularly. The attack on Fort Sumter found Chicago, by the standards of the day, the Illinois town best prepared for war.[13]

Governor Richard Yates responded to Lincoln's appeal for troops by calling on the armories and drill halls of the city. Germans swarmed to the North Side Turner Hall, a social and athletic center, and within two days enlisted two companies. A crowd of volunteers for the Zouaves packed the street in front of the armory. Mexican War veteran Frederick Harding hoisted the guidon of the Chicago Light Infantry in front of a vacant Dearborn Street store and quickly got the one hundred enlistments necessary to form a company. Joseph Kellogg and James Hugunin each succeeded in raising companies within two days. With the assistance of the Swedish consul, Swedish army veteran C. J. Stoltrand began to organize a company of his countrymen. Those who were too old to enlist for service formed "Home Guard" units. Within a year the Home Guard swelled to ten companies.[14]

On Saturday, April 20, only five days after Lincoln's request for troops, recruits were ordered to report to their company armories. New regiments with no facilities were billeted in public halls. Friends and relatives swarmed outside these buildings, eager to watch every bit of military drama. Young men tried to join units by sneaking through back doors of armories, and guards were posted to control access. Inside, recruits learned to form lines and march. At night they got their first real taste of the army as, after a dinner of coffee and bread, they slept on the hard armory floor.

Presiding over this nascent army was Brigadier General Richard K. Swift, a cigar-smoking banker who had no military experience. He surrounded himself with a staff that was nearly as large as the staff Grant had when he defeated Lee. Governor Yates had so little faith in Swift that he ordered Swift's aide, Captain Joseph D. Webster, to countermand any outrageous order he might give. On the other hand, the governor was not able to provide Swift with what his troops needed most—guns. The state arsenal contained only a handful of weapons, most of which were better suited for the museum than the battlefield. Rather than look to Springfield, the city decided to take care of its own. At a mass public meeting, a war fund was established to arm and equip Chicago troops as well as to care for soldiers' families. Private citizens administered the $30,000 fund. Within two days they purchased practically every rifle, shotgun, and revolver in the city, and additional muskets were borrowed from Milwaukee. Thousands of tin cups, plates, and cooking sets were bought, fourteen hundred uniforms were ordered, and blankets disappeared from the shelves of every dry goods store. Hardware stores made canisters for the city's artillery. This timely, resourceful job of supply was done none too quickly. On the evening of April 2, Governor Yates ordered Swift to occupy the key river port of Cairo in southern Illinois.[15]

Located at the junction of the Ohio and Mississippi rivers, Cairo controlled two of the nation's most strategic waterways. A state official visiting the town a few days after Fort Sumter witnessed "ostentatious and overbearing" demonstrations in favor of the Confederacy. Recruits for Southern forces were treated like heroes. The War Department in Washington wanted Cairo to be a Union base of operations against the South. The governor feared that unless action was taken quickly, rebel forces or their sympathizers might seize control of the town.[16]

At ten o'clock in the evening of April 2, the troops marched from their amories to the Illinois Central Railroad's lakefront depot. Swift's command was composed of 595 men, 46 horses, and 4 pieces of artillery. It included the Chicago Light Artillery, the Chicago Light Infantry, two companies of Zouaves, and two ethnic companies: the German Turner Union Cadets and the Slavic Lincoln Rifles. The depot sheds were jammed with people by the time the troops arrived. Wives and sweethearts rushed to embrace the departing soldiers, and mothers and fathers, their eyes wet with tears and faces gravely pale, gave their sons "last injunctions." As the long line of cars pulled out of the station and moved along the lakefront pier, artillery boomed a salute, church bells rang, and steam engines blew their shrill whistles.[17]

The expedition's first action occurred at Centralia, where the train made a water stop. The soldiers, in spite of food thrust into their hands when they left Chicago, were hungry and thirsty. They stormed the railroad lunch stand, overwhelmed the opposition, and devoured "anything edible, to say nothing of drinkables." At this stop General Swift heard that Southern sympathizers threatened to destroy the log trestle bridge over the Big Muddy River. If this occurred, rail communication between Chicago and Cairo would be disrupted for months. Swift detached a company of Zouaves to guard the bridge while the rest of the train, with an artillery flatcar at its head, proceeded to Cairo. The troop train entered the city on the evening of April 22 to the surprise of the residents. All train traffic and telegraph communication between Chicago and Cairo had been cut off so as to prevent word of the expedition reaching rebel supporters. The town's defenses were occupied with no incident.[18]

The troops mounted their handful of artillery pieces on the levee and began to inspect southbound steamboats for war supplies. They had secured an important base for the Union but were ill prepared to defend it from attack. The governor could find plenty of volunteers to help them, but he needed weapons if his patriots were to become an army. (The Chicago Citizens Committee had realized that there were barely enough weapons in Illinois for one regiment, let alone the six called for by the governor. They sent an agent east to secure rifles by any means he could, and for a time the agent opened negotiations with the government of Canada.) The troops in Cairo knew where there were plenty of weapons—at the U.S. Army arsenal at Jefferson Barracks in St. Louis, but in April 1861, St. Louis was a city deeply divided between Unionists and rebels. Any overt shipment of weapons to Cairo was likely to be hijacked by the rebel forces camped outside St. Louis, waiting for a formal ordinance of secession to seize the arsenal for themselves. In a desperate effort to secure eight thousand of the arsenal's weapons (the amount authorized by Washington), Governor Yates dispatched a secret agent to St. Louis.[19]

The agent was James H. Stokes, a Chicagoan who would soon rise to the rank of general. He traveled incognito to St. Louis where he found the arsenal surrounded by a large crowd of people, most of them secessionists. The arsenal commander at first refused to comply with Stokes's requisition for rifles, complaining that the rebel forces in the city would prevent any such shipment. Stokes countered by pointing out that if rebel forces were feared, it was better to try to save some of the weapons than let them all fall into rebel hands. Besides, Stokes had a plan to secretly remove the rifles.

At two the next morning the steamer *City of Alton* crossed the Mississippi River and slid alongside the arsenal's wharf. Stokes had dispersed the crowd of rebel sympathizers who frequented the area outside the arsenal gates by sending several boxes of old flintlock muskets by wagon to the railroad depot. The mob followed this shipment and later hijacked it amid great exultation! The few Confederates outside the arsenal that morning were easily rounded up and confined by a corporal guard from the arsenal. For several hours Stokes and army volunteers transferred boxed weapons to the steamer. They took much more than the 8,000 rifles ordered by Washington. By the time their work was finished, they had loaded 23,000 arms and more than 110,000 cartridges. For good measure Stokes also took a complete artillery battery.

Stokes's luck began to turn, however, when the steamer tried to leave for Illinois. It was so heavily loaded that it was grounded on a rock. At the same time one of the officers at the arsenal, Captain Nathaniel Lyon, accused Stokes of being a rebel agent. Stokes was Southern born and educated and did not speak like a Yankee. It was only with great difficulty that Stokes convinced the captain that he was a Unionist from Chicago. Refloating the steamer was more difficult. For more than an hour the already weary men struggled to move the boxes of rifles from the bow to the stern. Finally the boat floated free, and Stokes cast off.[20]

"Which way?" the steamer skipper asked apprehensively. He knew there was a rebel battery on the St. Louis levee. "Straight to Alton, in the regular channel," Stokes replied. This was not the answer the captain wanted to hear. "What if we are attacked?" he asked. "Then we will fight," Stokes said. "What if we are overpowered?" the boatman again complained. "Run the boat to the deepest part of the river and sink her," said Stokes. At this point the steamer captain gave up and said, "I'll do it," as he guided the vessel into the regular channel. Stokes could not relax. While the arms were afloat, they could easily be retaken by a rebel sortie across the Mississippi. But the *City of Alton* was not challenged by the Southern battery, and by 5:00 A.M. the steamer arrived at her namesake town.

As soon as the boat touched the wharf, Stokes ran to town and rang the fire bell. The streets filled with men and women in nightshirts and gowns, and Stokes appealed to them for help. For the next few hours they transferred the cargo over the levee and onto a waiting freight train. It was well after dawn before the last crates were in the boxcars. Stokes clambered aboard the train, which moved down the track toward Springfield, while the tired citizens of Alton, standing along the tracks in ruined night clothes, cheered the Union coup.[21]

Stokes's capture of weapons from the Jefferson Barracks arsenal not only provided Illinois with arms for six regiments but also allowed the state to lend assistance to Wisconsin and Indiana. These weapons, together with thousands of additional rounds of ammunition purchased in the east by the Chicago Citizens Committee, put the state on secure military footing. The aggressive response of Chicagoans to the start of the war ensured that Illinois would be the staging ground for victory in the West.

The first weeks of the Civil War were marked in Chicago by waves of enthusiasm. The phrase "War Spirit" was emblazoned on the front of every newspaper; the streets were filled with volunteers and bustling quartermaster and commissary aides. The city's foundries worked overtime as units ordered supplies of round shot. In lead works "the tap, tap of the molds [kept] pace to the increase of ounce bullets and wicked looking Minié balls." A *Tribune* reporter found the saloons and hotels filled with the "excited and ravenous quest of news sought from all sources. . . . Scraps of street talk falling upon the ear in the kaleidoscope conversation overheard, mingling war and volunteering, and rumor and fact, stiff canard, and doubtful report, in one ever changing tissue." Particularly sought after was news concerning enlistments. Many more volunteers came forward than were needed for the six regiments that the government asked for from Illinois. Rumors that the government would accept more men were picked up like gold coins by street urchins who would loudly proclaim such reports as fact and cause a tidal wave of eager men from the shops and counting houses of the business district to sweep into the recruiting stations.[22]

The federal government slowly began to realize that to preserve the Union it would require more than seventy-five thousand ninety-day volunteers. The call for more troops to serve for up to three years was tempered, however, by the sad reality that Simon Cameron's War Department was incapable of supplying, equipping, and organizing a national army. While Chicagoans rallied to the Union, Cameron steadfastly refused to accept more troops from Illinois and other enthusiastic states. Lincoln and other federal officials were barraged by requests for various volunteer companies and regiments to be accepted into government service. By July 1861 Richard Yates, governor of Illinois, wanted thirteen additional regiments from Illinois accepted. "Illinois demands her right to do her full share of the work of preserving our glorious Union from the assaults of high handed rebellion," he wrote, "and I insist you respond favorably to the call which I have made."[23]

In spite of the fact that only a handful of Chicago units were accepted into the state's first six regiments, newly formed units continued to spring into existence. By May 1, 1861, the city had produced thirty-eight separate companies, twenty-four of which were not accepted into service. One such unit was the Sturgis Rifles, made up of "some of the best shots in the city," many of whom were members of the Audubon Club. Solomon Sturgis, a wealthy man of business, personally bore the cost of arming the unit with the new Sharps rifle, sword bayonets, and two eight-inch revolvers. He also paid the entire unit's expenses for nearly two months while they waited for acceptance into government service. At one point the War Department announced it would accept the unit if it would join with another group of Chicago recruits known as the Yates Phalanx, but the Phalanx was made up of ordinary citizens and boasted none of the fine equipment or uniforms of the Sturgis Rifles. So Sturgis's group rejected the proposed union, and soon they were sent to General George B. McClellan's command. He took one look at their natty outfits and made them his personal guard. The Yates Phalanx waited more than half a year to be called into service. Its officers were forced to disband the unit at one point because the men, "sick and tired" of waiting, went home. Twice the unit sent emissaries to the secretary of war in Washington. Only the tenacity of the officers, who paid many expenses out of their own pockets, kept the unit together.[24]

One reason officers were willing to go to great lengths to hold prospective units together was to preserve their prospects of a commission. Officers were elected by the men of a company. Generally, a wealthy man who took it upon himself to organize a company and provide for the needs of the recruits could count on being elected captain or at least first lieutenant of the unit. Men had the option, in a place like Chicago, of choosing to join many different companies. If they did not like the look of the people organizing a unit, they were free to move down the street to the recruiting table of another company. However, money and social position did not necessarily translate into a higher rank. In 1862, Uranus H. Crosby, a wealthy distiller, started to raise a company, but the press of business forced him to allow two other young men to oversee the enrollment. When the time came to go before the army mustering officer and enlist for three years, Crosby balked. He did not know the men who had enrolled in his company and who would vote for officers. If he signed the muster roll, he would have to "risk the possibility of having to carry a musket for three years as a private soldier."[25]

Because soldiers chose the unit they served in, they had a stake in having their company accepted into the service. The system also made it possible for men to choose with whom they would spend their military career. The experience of Alexander C. McClurg is an example of how men sought out others of a similar background. McClurg, a junior clerk in a wholesale business, had recently come to Chicago to make a career for himself in business. He and several other clerks he knew were college educated and hoped "to secure commissions as lieutenants and subaltern officers." When this was not possible, McClurg wrote, "We finally determined to form a company among ourselves, in which all the men might be of somewhat the same condition in life, and more or less congenial, that so we might tone down some of the asperities of the private soldier's life." In this way Chicago sent to war a variety of units that reflected diverse economic, social, and ethnic communities. Units of Germans, Swedes, Slavs, and Scots fought next to units of sailors, clerks, railroad men, and farmers.[26]

One of the most celebrated ethnic units organized during the frantic spring of 1861 was the Irish Brigade. On April 20, a newspaper advertisement called on the Irish of Chicago: "For honor of the Old Land, rally. Rally for the defense of the new." That evening a meeting was held to organize an Irish unit. The force behind the newspaper notice and the principal speaker of the evening was James A. Mulligan, a new-style Irish leader. Born in America, college educated, and trained in law, he seemed destined to take a prominent place in Chicago politics. Drawing on his colorful and spellbinding speaking abilities, he appealed for volunteers from the crowd gathered at the North Market Hall. By evening's end he had secured 325 recruits, and within four days the number climbed to nearly 600.

In the days that followed, the unit continued to grow rapidly. Irish from such neighboring towns as Joliet, LaSalle, and Waukegan flocked to the city to enlist. Prewar Irish militia companies such as the Emmet Guards, Shield's Guards, and Montgomery Guards were folded into what the Sons of Erin grandly called the Irish Brigade. Within a week the Brigade's ranks swelled to twelve hundred men. The entire Irish community in Chicago, from parish priests to politicians to packinghouse workers, took pride in the Brigade. A women's committee was formed to raise funds for a flag, and everything was proceeding famously when the Brigade received word that the government would not accept their offer of service.[27]

Mulligan called the men together. There were angry cries of discrimination. Some said that because they were mostly Democrats, the government was denying them a chance to defend the Union. Mulligan, however, mastered the situation. He claimed that the government needed them, whether it realized it or not and promised the men he would appeal the rejection to the president himself, if necessary. The Brigade was then called upon to vote whether to disband, and only four of the twelve hundred raised their hands, although several hundred would reconsider during the next week. Mulligan hurried to Washington and secured the War Department's acceptance of the Brigade.

Mulligan returned to Chicago and assembled his men in a large brick building, formerly the Kane Brewery, on West Polk Street. Mulligan tried to create a military image for the place by naming it "Fontenoy Barracks," after the eighteenth-century victory of the exiled Irish "Wild Geese" over English regulars. Most people, however, referred to the building as "Hotel d'Shamrock" or simply "the Brewery." Chicagoans joked that it was a particularly appropriate place to billet the hard-drinking Irish recruits, yet it proved an excellent training site. It was large enough that each company could be quartered separately, for kitchens and mess rooms to be established, and for the troops to drill rain or shine.[28]

Most units awaiting orders created camps on the outskirts of the city. One such staging area was Camp Webb, located in a parklike setting near Wright's Grove (about Clark Street and Wrightwood Avenue today). Camp Slemmer, a "camp of instruction" for several companies, was located at Maine Station on the Chicago and Northwestern Railroad near the Desplaines River. The most popular campground was near Cottage Grove, south of the city limits. There, in a forested setting at the end of the line of the street railway system, were several music pavilions and a beer garden. These were popular with the German-American community and virtually every summer Sunday were the scene of picnics and parties. By May 1861 military units were establishing encampments near the beer garden. Camp Sturges, Camp Long, Camp Blum, and Camp Hecker, formed by units waiting to be called into service, started as tenting grounds and gradually became more elaborate as permanent barracks were built.[29]

On weekends a carnival atmosphere permeated the camps. Families and friends joined the soldiers, bringing cold chicken dinners, pastries, and buckets of beer. Music, played by either a military or a polka band, filled the air. Among the favorite songs were the "Star Spangled Banner," "Hail to Columbia," and "Dixie." Often there would be ceremonies honoring newly elected officers, who with much flourish were presented with swords. Some married men had their families stay in camp over Saturday night. For single men this was a time to show off in front of "mere" civilians. The proudest peacocks were those who had just received their uniforms. No regulations defined uniforms of the various volunteer units, although the most popular colors were "cadet grey" and the scarlet and blue of the Zouaves. While these colors were not prudent on the battlefield, the young men were handsome figures at Sunday picnics. After such a Sunday, a recruit wrote his parents that he was having "a first rate time."[30]

The atmosphere of the camps near the beer garden was not conducive to the one thing the new soldiers needed most, discipline. During the first few weeks of the war, the military of Chicago were a greater threat to each other and to the citizens of the city than they were to Jefferson Davis. During target practice, troops repeatedly sent civilians scurrying for cover and bullets crashing through drawing room windows. City officials were pleased to have the troops in camps outside the town limits because they wanted to end such incidents. But the flat topography of the region made any rifle range a threat. On May 13, Solomon Sturgis's unit decided to show off their new Sharps rifles and fired at targets across the open prairie. A mile away, a farmer had to duck for cover. Another frequent problem was drunkenness. In July members of the Highland Guard were deterred from mutiny only by the fixed bayonets of the Zouaves after the lads had a wee too many drams of whiskey.

The close proximity of the city made it a source of temptation some men could not resist. Absence without leave was a common problem, compounded when the troopers in question returned drunk and belligerent. Newly elected officers were sorely tested by such incidents. Captain Alexander McClurg was awakened one night by reports that a drunken private had stabbed the sergeant with a bayonet. The men of the company hung back, some out of fear, others out of interest to see what the boyish officer would do. With much bravado, McClurg walked up to the man and disarmed him. The private had threatened to "make mincemeat" out of the "d____d little militia captain," and several times he raised his arm to strike. But the officer's insignia inspired enough sense of discipline to make him give up peacefully.[31]

The citizen soldiers had two principal complaints about the army: poor food and the long delay between enrollment and service. The longer the delay, the worse the men felt about the food. Chicagoans lavished special attention on the men of certain upper-middle-class companies. One unit stationed in Cairo was sent Sunday dinners by friends in the city. In contrast, the Irish brigade, made up of the town's working class, languished in their brewery for two months with poor rations indifferently prepared. Some men left the barracks at meal time and ate at local restaurants at their own expense. Finally, on June 22, a riot broke out at dinner. Fortunately, Major Mulligan was present and rushed into the fray to quiet the soldiers. But they

———————◇———————

were insistent that the quality of the food and its service be improved. The major promised to do what he could on both counts, and to show he was in earnest he unbuckled his sword and assumed the duties of waiter. For five hours he served dinner to each company of the brigade. By the time he was finished the quality of the food had not changed, but the men's dispositions had. With three hearty cheers, they saluted the major.[32]

Funds for the Brigade's food initially were raised among the Irish of Chicago as were funds for equipment. Eventually the U.S. Army Quartermaster Corps would provide all recruits with uniforms, camp equipment, shoes, and supplies, but in the hectic early days of the war, these were community responsibilities. Many Irish were willing to make sacrifices for the unit because it was a source of pride. Within days of the unit's organization, the saloons of the South Side were echoing with a song honoring the Irish Brigade.

> Ye sons of green Erin assemble,
> And join in the battle's array;
> The usurpers and traitors shall tremble,
> When they see the Brigade in the fray.
> Go! march to the battle field proudly,
> Let the foe at your might be dismayed;
> And the trumpet of fame shall sound loudly,
> The praise of the Irish Brigade.

Yet the size of the Brigade and the long delay in their formally entering government service strained the Chicago Irish community. The Cook County government provided each soldier with a uniform consisting of a blue jacket with green facing, gray pants with green stripes, a blue cap, and a gray shirt. The Brigade was provided no medical or camp equipment.[33]

On July 15, 1861, the Irish Brigade was ordered to entrain for the front in Missouri. The Irish tried to make the sendoff impressive, and hundreds showed up to cheer the boys as they left. A high mass was held at St. Mary's Church, presided over by the bishop. An observer, however, could not help note that the Brigade looked rather like "Falstaff's tatterdemalions." Their blue jackets and gray pants were torn and ragged. According to the *Tribune*, the men were "a credit to any section" but their poor equipment and clothing were "a disgrace to Chicago as a city, Cook as a county, and Illinois as a state." It was not until the men reached St. Louis and were placed under the command of General John C. Freemont that they were fully armed and equipped. Yet, shabby though the Irish Brigade looked when it departed Chicago, it was destined to quickly become a source of great pride and a powerful stimulus to the city's "war fever."[34]

The Irish Brigade (or the 23d Illinois Infantry Regiment, as it was officially known) played an important part in the seesaw battle for control of Missouri. The state never formally seceded, although it fielded a rebel army. On August 31, 1861, General Freemont ordered the brigade to reinforce Lexington, an important crossroads on the banks of the Missouri River. Several Missouri and Illinois units were already there, making a combined force of 2,640 men. Five hundred of those, however, were Missouri Home Guards, whose lack of discipline and resolve made them, in Mulligan's opinion, "in peace invincible; in war invisible." Mulligan, now a colonel, was the senior officer, even though he had little more than a month's service. He assumed command of the town and set up headquarters at Masonic College, on a hill overlooking Lexington.

Three days later, Sterling Price, rebel commander in Missouri, appeared before the town with a force of seventeen thousand soldiers. Union officers held a council of war, and all of the colonels advised withdrawal save for Mulligan, who had faith that Freemont would send reinforcements. "We'll fight 'em!" he said. For four days the entrenched brigade was besieged by Price's army. Brief periods of intense, sometimes hand-to-hand fighting were followed by protracted bombardment. The stench of dead horses rotting in the Missouri sun and a lack of water plagued the defenders. On the third day of the siege, Price was able to close in on Mulligan's position by adopting a brilliant strategy. Bales of hemp were soaked in the river and used as movable breastworks. Rebel soldiers crouched behind the bales and rolled them toward the Irish Brigade's position. Bullets could not penetrate the barrier, and even Mulligan's small cannon had little effect on the advancing bales. The Missouri Home Guard panicked and abandoned their positions, refusing to fight any longer. The Brigade hospital was captured and with it all medical supplies. Only an unofficial truce prevented the Union position from being overrun. The Union officers held another council and decided to surrender.[35]

While the Brigade was fighting in Lexington, its members were enshrined as heroes across the North. For a week newspapers in Chicago headlined the Brigade's battle. A Chicago Irishman wrote in his diary, "Mulligan and Lexington are on every tongue and according to all accounts he holds out gallantly." Rumors concerning the "unequalled bravery of the Brigade" and the "prodigious fighting at Lexington" were eagerly accepted and passed on. General Freemont was accused of acting "sluggishly" and was roundly castigated for not sending reinforcements. Suspense built to a fever pitch. When news of the surrender finally reached the city, people were "greatly cast down." But defeat did not tarnish the unit's image; instead, the detailed report of the battle glorified their gallant stand. "Mulligan is the hero of the war now," one Chicagoan wrote.

The combative Irish Brigade seemed to embody the city's pugnacious self-image. Rather than surrender their green regimental banner, the Brigade tore it into little pieces and each soldier took a shred. The troops were marched to Hannibal, Missouri, to await parole. One soldier was asked to take an oath not to bear arms against the Confederate States of America. The press, with relish, reported his reply: "If there were any Confederate States he didn't believe the United States knew of any such government and he was sure he didn't."

The story of the battle reinforced Chicago's image of war as a heroic drama. Mulligan offered his sword to General Price, but that officer chivalrously refused to accept it from so gallant a foe. Although twenty-four Chicagoans were buried in Missouri, most of the men were back in Illinois two days after the battle ended. Mulligan was not paroled until October 30, 1861, and his return to Chicago was greeted by a parade, bonfires, and skyrockets. From the balcony of the Tremont House, surrounded by the elites of the city and with thousands cheering in the street below, he said, "I am deeply impressed . . . the great city of the Northwest, has risen in all her wealth and dignity and power, to honor me, one of the humblest of her children."[36]

Members of the Brigade celebrated their return to the city in various ways. Henry Bradburn, for example, treated all his "friends," several of whom were prostitutes, thieves, and gamblers, to free drinks. He took them on a spending spree and they all got new clothes, and then the party attended a series of footraces. In "a state of gross intoxication" Bradburn bet and lost heavily. By day's end he had spent $1,900. The police became curious about where he got this much money, and they discovered that during the siege of Lexington, Bradburn and others took $15,000 from the Farmer's Bank of that town. Government detectives were called in and more soldiers were investigated. John Brown was arrested in Grand Haven, Michigan, with $155 from the bank, while Patrick Kelley fled as far as Detroit before he was caught. This tawdry postscript to the saga of the Brigade, however, did little to tarnish the brigade's luster. The boys from Bridgeport were heroes, and by the end of 1861, Chicago was in desperate need of heroes.[37]

————◇————

The thousands of Chicagoans who packed the streets to cheer Mulligan's return were eager to make heroes of the defeated soldiers, because Union victories had been few and far between. The disastrous defeat at Bull Run in July 1861 jarred the city, as it did the entire North. But it did not have a lingering effect on morale, because Chicago troops did not play a significant role in the battle. Indeed, the reaction was one of greater determination to close with the enemy. Spirits rose in August when the War

(*Above*) A bird's-eye view of Chicago in the 1860s. (Frederick F. Cook, *Bygone Days in Chicago*, 1910)

(*Left*) The courthouse was the center of city life in 1860. (Frederick F. Cook, *Bygone Days in Chicago*, 1910)

(*Right*) Chicago's lakefront railroad depot as it looked when delegates arrived for the Republican National Convention. (A.T. Andreas, *History of Chicago*, 1885)

Delegates to the Republican National Convention arrive in Chicago. This sketch by W.B. Baird appeared in *Harper's Weekly.*

The famed Wigwam, Chicago's first convention center. The size of the Wigwam, which could hold 10,000 people, played a significant role in securing the nomination for Abraham Lincoln. Prairie State politicians packed the galleries with Lincoln supporters. (A.T. Andreas, *History of Chicago,* vol. 2, 1885)

Inside the Wigwam as the convention was about to begin. The view is from the ladies' gallery. (*Harper's Weekly*)

(*Below*) Joseph Medill, editor of the *Chicago Tribune* and an important early supporter of Lincoln. (F.F. Cook, *Bygone Days in Chicago*, 1910)

(*Above*) Abraham Lincoln as he appeared in 1865. When the prairie politician ran for the White House in 1860, he had neither a beard nor a grave demeanor. (T.M. Eddy, *The Patriotism of Illinois*, 1865)

Courthouse square in the 1860s was bounded by Randolph, Clark, Washington, and La Salle streets. (A.T. Andreas, *History of Chicago,* vol. 2, 1885)

(*Left*) Stephen A. Douglas, Chicago's Little Giant. (A.T. Andreas, *History of Chicago,* vol. 2, 1885)

(*Middle*) The Reverend Dwight Moody. When Lincoln met him in 1860, Moody was still regarded by many Chicagoans as "Crazy Moody," but maturity and the experience of the Civil War made Moody one of America's leading religious figures. (Frederick F. Cook, *Bygone Days in Chicago,* 1910)

(*Right*) Mayor "Long John" Wentworth, the first of a series of colorful Chicago chief executives, arrived in the frontier town a barefoot boy and became one of its leading real estate investors. (Frederick F. Cook, *Bygone Days in Chicago,* 1910)

(*Left*) Elmer E. Ellsworth, a young Chicago law clerk, came to symbolize the romantic image of war. (A.T. Andreas, *History of Chicago,* vol. 2, 1885)

(*Right*) Colonel James A. Mulligan, commander of the Irish Brigade. (A.T. Andreas, *History of Chicago,* vol. 2, 1885)

The Chicago Zouaves at drill. (Frederick F. Cook, *Bygone Days in Chicago,* 1910)

(*Left*) General John B. Turchin, an uncompromising soldier, symbolized Chicago's drift toward "total war" mentality. (A.T. Andreas, *History of Chicago*, 1885) (*Right*) George Frederick Root, the North's leading writer of war songs. His "Battle-Cry of Freedom," written for a Chicago recruitment rally, became an anthem for the Union cause. (Frederick F. Cook, *Bygone Days in Chicago*, 1910)

McVicker's Theater housed the offices of the Northwest Sanitary Commission during the Civil War. (A.T. Andreas, *History of Chicago*, vol. 2, 1885)

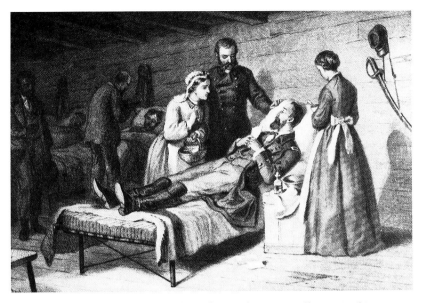

Mary Livermore visiting a Union Army hospital in Cairo, Illinois. In this
J.J. Cade engraving, a Union officer wounded at Island No. 10 dies while
clutching a letter from home. Incidents such as this during Livermore's 1862
tour of western military hospitals convinced her to commit herself entirely to
war work. (Mary A. Livermore, *My Story of the War*, 1887)

(*Above*) Mary Livermore twenty
years after the war. (G. Schlecht engraving, from Mary A. Livermore,
My Story of the War, 1887)

(*Left*) The Reverend Robert Collyer
was one of the clergymen who led
the effort to improve the lot of
wounded soldiers. (Frederick F.
Cook, *Bygone Days in Chicago*,
1910)

The Soldiers Home, built in 1865–66 to care for men disabled during the war, still stands near the corner of 35th Street and Lake Avenue, across from the Douglas Memorial. (A.T. Andreas, *History of Chicago*, vol. 2, 1885)

The Northwest Sanitary Fair. This illustration of the 1865 fair gives an indication of the scores of booths and shops that made the fair such an attraction to shoppers in 1863 and again in 1865. (Frederick F. Cook, *Bygone Days in Chicago*, 1910)

Department was finally ready "to accept all troops willing to enter the service." One Chicagoan later commented, "Thank God for that much!" and noted that the open enlistments "gave new heart to the people."[38]

The defeat at Bull Run demonstrated the danger of rushing into battle unprepared. Troops need discipline and some degree of training before they can be committed to combat. To provide this for troops raised in the northern district of Illinois, the governor ordered the creation of a mobilization center and camp of instruction. Because numerous companies were already gathered south of Chicago near Cottage Grove, that area was selected. In September the mobilization center was established on land donated by the estate of Stephen A. Douglas. Colonel Joseph H. Tucker was appointed by the governor to build what became known as Camp Douglas and to be its first commandant.[39]

When Tucker first visited the site, he saw a broad, flat prairie. Several structures stood nearby, the most prominent being the campus of the University of Chicago (not to be confused with the contemporary institution in Hyde Park). This school had been founded in 1857 under the joint sponsorship of Stephen A. Douglas and the Baptists. The school was housed in an impressive Gothic-style limestone building with numerous turrets and towers. It had been built away from the city in part because of a desire for a quiet setting conducive to study. But once Tucker began his work, Cottage Grove was anything but peaceful. He purchased lumber from the massive yards along the Chicago River and directed the building of barracks, mess hall, and officer quarters. By winter, the camp could accommodate eight thousand soldiers and stable two thousand horses. In time, a hospital and warehouse were also built. The camp covered about sixty acres between what is now 31st Street on the north, 33d Street on the south, Cottage Grove Avenue on the east, and Giles Avenue on the west. The construction program was completed by winter but due to cost restrictions, Tucker did not install a proper drainage system, which eventually led to much sickness and death.[40]

Rapid construction of the camp was accomplished by the Mechanic Fusiliers, a unit made up entirely of carpenters and other skilled tradesmen. The unit was raised from Chicago and several other Great Lakes towns by Colonel J. W. Wilson, who promised the men extra pay, fifty cents a day more than other soldiers. This proved a boon to enlistment, and by October there were six hundred men in the unit and at work on Camp Douglas. The Mechanics Fusiliers did excellent work but trouble erupted when they discovered that they had been mustered into service as an Illinois infantry regiment rather than as a special force under direct federal control. Nor was the extra pay Wilson had promised forthcoming. Unable to get a satisfactory response to these grievances from either

Tucker or their own Colonel Wilson, the men went on strike. The army, however, had no patience with a job action. When a hundred men refused to stand inspection, Tucker called on the camp guard and charged the Fusiliers with disobedience and put them under arrest. The ringleaders were sent in irons to St. Louis for court martial, but the rest were back at Camp Douglas within a week or two, by no means humbled by the army's action. Instead, they changed tactics. One of their number, E. C. Jones, applied to the U.S. Circuit Court in Chicago for a writ of habeas corpus, contending that he should be discharged from the service because he had been deceived into enlisting by fraudulent promises. By this time most of the men in the unit demanded to be discharged. The army tried to "stonewall" both the men and the court. When a writ was issued for Jones's release, it was ignored. Eventually the court decided against the Fusiliers, ruling that they volunteered freely and were bound by that contract of service.[41]

By the end of January 1862 the army had enough of the contentious Mechanics Fusiliers and decided to discharge the regiment rather than trust its members with loaded weapons. The unit left with a flourish. The men formed ranks and marched with their regimental colors flying from Camp Douglas to a saloon on Randolph Street, where steins of lager were ordered all around. They were still angry, especially the out-of-state men, who were disgusted with Illinois in general and Chicago in particular. "We should like to be clear of you, both city and state," they complained, "but we want our pay. . . . We are cheated and humbugged by everybody. . . . Let us go home wiser men, but not altogether beggars." They drafted an official claim for their extra pay and left for home.[42]

By the time Camp Douglas was built, the city had lost patience with rebellious citizen-soldiers like the Mechanic Fusiliers. With the establishment of Camp Douglas, troops were, for the first time, given uniform instruction in bayonet and close-order drill. The state appointed two former Ellsworth Zouaves as the official instructors at Camp Douglas. Tucker established a schedule that gave the recruits at least four hours of drill each day. Saluting officers was enforced, and officers were held responsible for men missing from roll call as well as the quality of their company's drill. These reforms helped to improve the quality of troops sent by Illinois to the battlefield, but they barely muffled the growing chorus of civilian complaints against drunken and undisciplined soldiers.[43]

The establishment of Camp Douglas on the outskirts of Chicago intensified the city's contact with young recruits. Between April 18, 1861, and January 25, 1862, 44,811 Union soldiers passed through Chicago. Many trained at Camp Douglas or its predecessors. The city could not avoid some negative contact with large numbers of high-spirited young men away from home for the first time. Residents of the small farms and homes that stood between the city limits and Camp Douglas bore the brunt of abuse. Soldiers weary of army beans and bacon would often pry a gap in the wall that surrounded the camp and raid local farms for chickens and eggs. Troops returning from leave in the city were boisterous, and citizens accused them of "taking over" street railway cars. A large number of those who lived in the Cottage Grove area were Irish Democrats and were opposed to the "Black Republican War." In June 1861 an Irish farmer quarreled with a German recruit on a street car. The Irishman produced a gun and shot the soldier dead.[44]

Most incidents were related to the use of liquor. Soldiers "in their cups" occasionally took over a saloon. Even the army had trouble controlling such men. A squad of drunken soldiers returning to camp one February night attacked and captured the post guardhouse. Enlisted men were not the only ones guilty of improprieties. The adjutant of the Irish Brigade was arrested and charged with seducing a "respectable girl." Worse still was the example of Captain Robert Crofton, who fatally stabbed a railroad employee after being barred from entering a train car.

Officers and enlisted men alike had little fear of the city's undermanned police force. In June 1862, Captain J. Rourke of the Irish Brigade was returning to camp by street railway with several enlisted men. Rourke, who was probably inebriated, insulted several women in the car, challenged one woman's husband to a duel, and flourished his loaded revolver in a menacing way. An off-duty policeman stepped in and prevented any further trouble, but when he tried to leave the streetcar, Rourke had his men arrest him. He was detained at the Camp Douglas guard room for several hours and told to either sign an apology or face isolated confinement. The *Tribune* complained that many volunteer officers needed to be reminded "that their commissions do not place them out of the pale of the law."[45]

The heroic image of Chicago's soldiers and the war itself received a much needed boost in February 1862. Ulysses S. Grant emerged from the shadow of dismissal from the army for drunkenness in 1854 by driving rebel forces from Kentucky and most of Tennessee. He did this by seizing control of the vital river and rail routes in the region. On February 6, 1862, his troops and gunboats attacked the Confederate stronghold at Fort Henry, which guarded the Tennessee River. After brief resistance the post surrendered. Grant's gunboats steamed 150 miles up the Tennessee River battering rebel watercraft all the way into Alabama. The general then sent his fifteen thousand troops twelve miles east to attack Fort Donelson, the rebel post controlling the Cumberland River. This citadel proved a more difficult target, for the garrison housed seventeen thousand soldiers defending three miles of trenches. On February 15 the rebel garrison launched a bruising attack on Grant's forces in a desperate effort to break out. General John A. McClernand's Illinois troops bore the brunt of the attack. The rebels were on the brink of succeeding when Grant rallied the federal forces and restored his siege lines. That night, Confederate commanders abandoned their troops and escaped downriver. The next morning General Simon Bolivar Buckner, an old comrade of Grant's, asked what surrender terms would be offered. "No terms except an unconditional and immediate surrender can be accepted." Grant replied. "I propose to move immediately on your works." The Confederates had no choice but to capitulate.[46]

Chicago exploded with celebrations on February 17 when the news arrived. Crowds rushed from store to store, shouting, "Fort Donelson is taken!" Men stopped each other in the streets to shake hands, embrace, and literally dance with delight. The celebrating was so spontaneous because everyone had been braced for bad news. The announcement of complete victory "was like the bursting of some mountain stream, long fettered, carrying everything before it and sweeping on with resistless might." From the windows of the city's hotels people waved handkerchiefs or red, white, and blue banners. The delirium infected every corner of the city. Amid the cheering, schoolboys ascended the roofs of their schools and raised flags. For the day the entire curriculum focused on the Union triumph:

> National songs were sung, patriotic scraps of speeches found in the reading-books were recited, and the location and importance of Fort Donelson were explained to the young people. When the hour of dismissal came, they added to the joyful confusion of the streets by shooting out of the schoolhouses like bombs from mortars, with shrill and prolonged hurrahs leaping from their lips as they rushed through every part of the city.

Hats flew in the air, flags flew from almost every home, and church bells rang in a chorus of celebration.[47]

The public party continued into the night. People flocked downtown to sing the "Star Spangled Banner" and celebrate around bonfires, for the victory was the most important of the war up to that point. Not only did it drive the rebels away from the middle Mississippi Valley and open up the deep South to invasion, but it also forced them to abandon the industrial center of Nashville, the first Confederate state capital to fall to Union troops. Celebrations rocked the North, and U. S. Grant was a national hero. His initials now stood for "Unconditional Surrender." Chicagoans were particularly pleased because their boys "had compelled the rebels to surrender and had planted the stars and stripes upon the rebel fortress."

More than a few people ended the happy day at evening church services, where they thanked God for the victory.[48]

Concrete proof of Grant's victory soon appeared in Chicago. Union forces took twelve to thirteen thousand rebel prisoners at Fort Donelson, and Camp Butler in Springfield and Camp Douglas in Chicago were selected to house the rebels until their parole was negotiated. At midnight on March 1, 1862, the first of 7,850 prisoners arrived in Chicago by train. In spite of the late hour a considerable number of people assembled to get a view of the enemy. Some ministers were particularly shocked by the large number of "young ladies" who were out late "to get a glance at the prisoners." Chicagoans had heard much of southern chivalry and their boasts that one of them could "whip five times their own individuality!" They were curious to see the real thing. For several weeks arriving trains of rebels (or "secesh," as they were called) were greeted by crowds of people anxious to get the measure of the enemy.[49]

What they saw was unimpressive. A minister's wife noted:

> A more motley-looking crowd was never seen in Chicago. They were mostly un-uniformed and shivering with cold, wrapped in tattered bedquilts, pieces of old carpets; hearth rugs, horse blankets, ragged shawls—anything that would serve to keep out the cold and hide their tatterdemalion condition. They had evidently suffered severely in the terrible three days' fight at Donelson, not only from the arctic weather but from insufficient food and clothing.

Instead of haughty planters in plumed hats, Chicagoans were faced with a pathetic mob of suffering men. "We were filled with pity," another woman wrote, "for those poor fellows when we saw their feet peeping out through their poor shoes on the day in February with a slight fall of snow on the ground." Some men noted that the rebels looked "wolfish" and "seedy," and even the *Tribune* had to admit that on the whole they were a "woebegone . . . set of men . . . sallow faced, sunken eyed, and apparently famished."[50]

Even more disillusioning than the sorry appearance of the dreaded enemy was the dawning realization in the month following the Fort Donelson victory that the Confederacy was not teetering on the brink of defeat. Like the North after Bull Run, the South, in the wake of Donelson, stiffened its resolve. Defeat was sobering, but it did not deter them from continuing on their course. This was underscored by the Battle of Pea Ridge, May 7–8, 1862. Rebel forces were routed and the Union secured control of Missouri, but the Confederacy remained a determined and formidable foe.

Perhaps the event that more than any other single action eroded the illusion of the war as a brief romantic conflict was Shiloh. In the forests and meadows around the log meeting house in southern Tennessee, Chicago's image of war as a patriotic sporting contest was washed away by the blood of its sons and the tears of their mothers.

The great Battle of Shiloh surprised the people of Chicago as much as it did General Grant. In the weeks following Fort Donelson, newspapers expected the armies of Grant and General Don Carlos Buell to unite and drive into Mississippi. But Union forces were timidly directed by General Henry "Old Brains" Halleck, and the link-up and advance moved at a snail's pace. By early April the principal focus of Chicagoans had shifted to the Mississippi River, where Union forces besieged a critical Confederate stronghold on Island No. 10. Each day, Chicagoans eagerly sought newspapers to get the latest news on the progress of the siege. Hopes were high for another Union victory. On the morning of April 9, 1861, word was received of a great triumph. General John Pope and Flag Officer Andrew Foote secured Island No. 10. In the process their men suffered very few casualties and took seven thousand rebel prisoners. Once again the city began to celebrate, but the joy was subdued when, later that afternoon, news came that General Grant's forces were under attack by a rebel army headed by General Pierre G. T. Beauregard, the victor of Bull Run.[51]

On April 6, 1862, a Confederate army of forty thousand men launched a surprise attack on Grant's base camp on the Tennessee River. The initial assault overwhelmed the bulk of the Union encampment, and scattered regiments fought a desperate and disorganized battle. Some union units firmly held their ground, others fled pell-mell after the first attack, and still others rallied to make periodic stands against the advancing waves of rebels. For much of the day it looked like the rebel plan to drive Grant's forces into the river and recover control of Tennessee would succeed. Fortunately for Grant, several battered but not completely broken divisions, mostly Illinois troops, held back the Confederate advance until the general could organize a last line of defense. This line held. Although the day ended with Shiloh looking to all the world like a rebel victory, Grant was not finished fighting. He spent the night bringing up his reserve forces as well as the advance units of Buell's army. At dawn he counterattacked and, after another day of vicious slaughter, drove Beauregard's army from the field and back to Corinth, Mississippi, in defeat.

Shiloh was a great strategic victory for the North. In concert with Island No. 10, it opened the way for the Union conquest of the Mississippi Valley. But it was won at a terrible cost. Grant's soldiers inflicted 10,699 casualties on the enemy; of Grant's own troops, 13,047 were killed, wounded, or missing. No victory celebrations were held in Chicago for Shiloh. People greeted one another with condolences, not congratulations. Newspapers were eagerly scanned not for the details of victory but for names of friends and relatives in the appallingly long columns of casualties. Chicago grieved because Shiloh was up to that point the most costly battle ever fought in America and because so many of the troops involved were from Illinois. Out of the sixty-five Union regiments in the battle, twenty-eight came from Illinois.

Chicagoans were in the thick of the fighting at the Hornet's Nest, where a group of federal units stalled the rebel advance for most of the day. The 57th Illinois, largely made up of Chicagoans, helped hold this position until it was surrounded by Confederate infantry. The men then attacked and cut their way clear to the Pittsburg landing, suffering 187 casualties.

Action near the Hornets nest severely wounded Chicago attorney David Stuart. A year earlier, in an attempt to clear his reputation after being mentioned in a celebrated society divorce case, Stuart had raised a regiment of northern Illinois men. At Shiloh the regiment was caught in a crossfire where Minié balls were thick as hail. Half of Stuart's troops fell that day. General John McArthur, who in 1861 organized the Highland Guard, was wounded trying to relieve Stuart's men. One of the regiments under his command counted 366 casualties.[52]

Shiloh not only gave Chicago its first long list of casualties but also provided a glimpse of the reality of combat in the industrial age. James Milner, a member of Battery A of the Chicago Light Artillery, sent a detailed description of the battle to his father so that he might know what he "saw, heard and felt during those terrible two days." The *Tribune* later published the letter in full on its front page. Unlike most correspondents, Milner had seen many friends die, and he could not help but dwell on that aspect of the battle.

> Ed Russell, a young man whom you have often seen behind the counter of Smith's bank, as gentlemanly a young man as we had in the battery, had his bowels torn out by a solid shot. He lived but half an hour. His last words were as he lay on his face, "I die like a man." And good man Farnham, a Christian man, my tentmate for six months . . . was shot through above the heart. . . . Flanigan a merry hearted Irishman and the intimate friend of Ed Russell, was shot through the mouth.

At one point in the chaotic fighting, panic-stricken Union infantry fled directly in front of Milner's battery. "We yelled at them to keep away from our fire, but they mostly didn't hear us," he recalled, "I ran and waved my hat, but to no purpose, and I went back to my post and fired through them."[53]

Milner's battery eventually retreated to Pittsburg Landing, where Grant's nearly defeated army made their "last stand."

> I felt then that I had never witnessed so painful a sight as a disorganized army. Here I found Billy Williams . . . riding on a baggage wagon. He said to me in a pitiable tone, "Jimmy, won't you come and take care of me? I am shot through." I had to refuse. This to me was truly painful. I helped him down and put him into an ambulance, and helped Paddock in too. I got up into the ambulance, and examined Paddock's wound, found that he was shot through the liver. . . . He was very frail and I thought he must die. I put his handkerchief over the wound and went back to my gun.

Later, he heard that his friends had died.

> [M]y heart was filled with hatred and revenge against the enemy. . . . As I talked about the death of the boys, I could not restrain the tears and felt that I could then hazard my life in any position to mow down their ranks with canister.

After this, Milner fought with the "utmost indifference as to my fate," determined to resist the enemy and not surrender or be made prisoner. Such desperate spirit helped Grant's line hold on the evening of April 6 and provided the opportunity for victory the next day.[54]

Shiloh changed the soldiers who survived the slaughter. "The men look serious," a Chicago minister remarked, "as if they had grown older." Before the battle they had longed for a major engagement:

> Never again do I expect to hear the same wish from the lips of our men. We are just as ready now to do our duty as we were, but to desire another hard battle, with the same chances of loss to our company, is quite a different thing.

This realistic view of combat and its risks was tempered by an increasingly bitter attitude toward the South. As the army advanced from Shiloh toward Corinth, Mississippi, John Wilcox, an officer from Elgin, Illinois, advocated punishing the farms and families of rebel soldiers. In a letter to his wife he complained of army restrictions on foraging:

> I begin to think the better way would be to utterly desolate wherever we went. . . . If I had control when this army had marched through

the Gulf states no landmarks would be left to show the boundaries of towns, counties, or states.[55]

Shiloh also tempered, but did not destroy, the soldiers' view of war as an honorable, gallant activity. James Milner told his father that the battery requested that none of their letters home be published. "We wish our conduct to speak for itself," he said. "I am proud of the battery, and without boasting, I know it isn't surpassed anywhere." Yet to maintain such an image Milner had to withhold some of what he saw. Although he told his father about the battle, so that he might know "exactly what war is," Milner omitted a description of the battlefield. He felt it necessary to spare his father "the horrid and disgusting details of the thousands of suffering wounded and the mangled corpses."[56]

In Chicago, a committee was organized to care for the dead and wounded from the city; $1,225 was raised to bury the men of the Chicago Light Artillery in a special plot at Rosehill cemetery. On April 14, 1862, the body of Captain R. D. Adams arrived in Chicago. The Church of the Redeemer's bell tolled when his heavy, metal coffin was carried into the house of Adam's father-in-law. He had been wounded in the thigh by two Minié balls during the retreat from the Hornet's Nest. Army surgeons had amputated the leg, but Adams died from shock. The family opened the casket and gazed in "mute grief" at the blood-stained corpse. After a brief prayer the casket was closed and the remains turned over to the undertaker. Four days later, another body, that of Captain Irving W. Carson, U. S. Grant's chief scout, was received in the city with full military honors. Fortunately, the morbid procedure of opening the coffin was dispensed with. Carson's head had been torn off by a cannonball while he was reporting to Grant near the end of the second day's fighting.[57]

The long casualty lists in the newspapers and the parade of wounded soldiers and coffins passing through the city robbed the citizens of any joy of victory and left them eager to punish those who were to blame for the heavy losses. Initially, much of the blame fell on Grant, who was faulted for not having his troops entrenched. The *Tribune* urged Chicagoans to "withhold all censure from Gen. Grant . . . until the facts are known." Shiloh cast a shadow over Grant's great victory at Donelson and the string of Union successes in the West. The grim details of the battle continued to arrive in Chicago on April 16, 1862, when the city's municipal elections were held. The Republicans had dominated all recent campaigning, but the election found them divided and dispirited. The Democrats were resurgent due to working-class anxiety over abolitionist influence in the federal government and complaints against Republican conduct of the war. Turnout was slight on the cold, rainy election day. Democrat Francis C. Sherman, a brick manufacturer who owned and operated the Sherman House, was elected mayor.[58]

After Shiloh, many Chicagoans assumed a much harsher posture toward the South. The editors of the *Tribune* were intent upon keeping war fever at full pitch. But the attitude of the troops also influenced public opinion. Rumors of rebel atrocities were relayed by soldiers to their families and friends; Confederate guerrillas were reported to have cut the nose and ears off one captured Illinois soldier. Southern soldiers at Shiloh were said to have bayonetted sleeping Union troops during their first surprise attack. Other stories recounted poisoned wells, refusal to bury slain Union soldiers, even the "making of tools and utensils of their bones." According to the *Tribune*, the institution of slavery had forced Southerners to subdue their better natures and become vicious and cruel. Instead of Southern Christianity being used to convert the slaves from barbarism, the *Tribune* maintained, slavery succeeded in "barbarizing the American." Southerners had themselves become slaves "of the malignant fury and foul lust of the savage."[59]

For one year, from Fort Sumter in April 1861 to Shiloh in April 1862, the elan inspired by Lincoln's call to arms and Douglas's call for unity had sustained Chicago's war effort. Defeats and the high price of victory eroded that spirit. Douglas's proclamation that there were "only patriots—or traitors" began to give way to partisan politics and a profoundly different view of the war. The image of war as heroic action, embodied in the life and death of Elmer Ellsworth, endured among both soldiers and civilians, yet increasingly it was modified by the frightening reality of mass slaughter and closed casket funerals. The innocent times of Sunday picnics and patriotic songs with the troops, like the vision of a quick, easy victory, were over.[60]

4

◇

"GOD BLESS THE SANITARY COMMISSION!"

During the week after the battle, rain fell steadily at Shiloh. As he walked over the muddy battlefield, Robert Collyer, a Unitarian minister from Chicago, commented, "It seems as if the cannon had broken the windows of heaven." Because of the heavy rain, army burial squads made little progress. Five days after the fighting ceased, most of the dead still lay where they had fallen. Collyer was appalled by what he saw:

> Dead bodies stark and stiff lie in every conceivable position, distorted in the death agony, or stretched out with faces staring upward, washed by the pitiless rain. Here and there are limbs torn away by shot and shell, or cast aside in the hasty field offices of the surgeon. Dead horses lie scattered over the ground. The air is heavy and tainted with the odors of decomposition.

Sickened and sad, he turned away from the dead and reminded himself that he was there for the living. He returned to Pittsburg Landing where steamboats were being loaded with Shiloh's wounded.[1]

The Reverend Collyer was one of several hundred people, mostly relatives of soldiers in Grant's army, who rushed from Illinois when word of the great battle was received. In the weeks following the fight, they crowded the river landings of Cairo and Mound City, anxious to secure passage for the 225 mile trip up the Tennessee River to Shiloh. Those unable to get tickets or passes appealed for special consideration. As steamers prepared to leave the wharf, the unfortunate cried out, "I have a son in ____ regiment and that regiment is cut all to pieces." "I had a son in the fight and he is wounded, I must go!" "I had a brother killed in the battle, and I am after his body." Among those who managed to get up river were the inevitable curiosity seekers for whom the war was a spectacle. They slogged through the soggy battlefield, stepping over corpses, gathering "canes marked with shot, gunflints, Bowie-knives, balls, cartridges, pelican buttons," and other souvenirs. Collyer, however, was not in search of relatives or mementos. He was at Shiloh to nurse the wounded.[2]

Collyer was part of a team of forty-eight nurses and eighteen surgeons dispatched from Chicago as soon as the scale of the battle was known. When their train reached Cairo, they immediately transferred their 154 boxes of hospital supplies to the steamers *City of Louisiana* and *Hiawatha*, hospital boats with operating rooms and wards of clean beds. When they arrived at Shiloh, the landing was so congested with other steamboats that they were forced to make fast in a line three vessels deep. Planks were laid across the boats, and the nurses were at last able to reach shore. With some difficulty they tried to scramble up the steep river bank, which rain and the army had reduced to a wall of mud. Only by stepping over large sacks of corn, stacked and awaiting transport, could they reach the top of the bank. There they were immediately struck by the sight of thousands of dead and wounded men. "The first sight of these brave men made the heart sink," a nurse reported, as he walked past "a continuous line of prostrate heroes, gashed and torn and scarred by every conceivable form of ghastly wounds, with firm compressed lip, and an expression of triumph and defiance, modified by pain upon their every countenance; yet uttering not a murmur." The regimental surgeons had long been at work, and hundreds of amputees awaited transport. Most of the men were in surprisingly good spirits, considering the ordeal they had been through. As they ate their ration of brick-hard biscuits, someone joked that if the doctors needed any splints, the biscuits could be put to better use. This brought a hearty laugh even from those who were bleeding. As one of the Chicago surgeons dressed a neck wound, he tried to make conversation with the patient victim. "Have you ever been wounded before?" he asked. The veteran jerked open his tunic and revealed a score of battle scars from fighting in Europe.[3]

Collyer's medical team was only one of several relief expeditions dispatched to the battlefield. The Sisters of Mercy, also from Chicago, arrived on Palm Sunday with the hospital boat *Empress*. Richard Yates, governor of Illinois, led a combined fact-finding commission and relief mission aboard the steamer *Black Hawk*. Hospital steamers from St. Louis and Cincinnati also had arrived. With more than two thousand wounded in the vicinity of the landing, there was more than enough suffering for each hospital. Occasionally the half-loaded hospital boats left the landing and went up river because the stench of the battlefield became overpowering. So great was the number of casualties that the army converted numerous cargo transports to hospital vessels, and the volunteer medical teams were divided to staff them. As soon as possible, the boats were loaded with several hundred wounded each and sent to waiting hospitals in Mound City, St. Louis, and Cairo. Some vessels made more than five trips between Shiloh and the hospitals.[4]

In the immediate aftermath of Shiloh, Chicago's City Council went into special session and voted $10,000 for relief of the wounded. The Board of Trade collected an additional $3,000. Individual donations of bandages, towels, sheets, brandy, and porter were sent to the front. Like the governor's relief mission, these were not gestures of public charity but the only effective way to aid wounded soldiers. The Army Medical Department had demonstrated in previous battles that it was wholly incapable of providing for its wounded. Its surgeons were either incompetent or lethargic, and its supplies were inadequate or spoiled. At Shiloh the problems were magnified by the fact that many hospital tents had been overrun by the enemy on the first day of battle. If General Buell's nearby army had been properly equipped, it should have been able to redress this loss. As it was, there were soldiers wounded on Sunday, April 6, whose wounds were not dressed until Thursday, April 10. The state of Illinois and communities like Chicago had learned from previous battles that they had to step into the breach if the wounded were to be saved.[5]

The organization that coordinated the efforts of the relief missions from Illinois, Ohio, and other states and that transported individual donations to the front and established hospital boats and permanent medical centers was the Sanitary Commission, a volunteer civilian group dominated by philanthropic women and religious leaders. Shiloh was the largest relief project the commission had as yet undertaken, and through their intervention thousands of lives were saved. The experience of Shiloh taught the commission that in the future even more would have to be done. Yet, for the soldiers carried off Pittsburg Landing and onto a hospital boat, the men and women of the commission were some of the battle's true heroes. "God bless the Sanitary Commission," the wounded soldiers told Reverend Collyer as the steamers headed north.[6]

The Sanitary Commission grew in part out of the experience of the British Army in the Crimean War. Camp diseases harmed the British forces in southern Russia far more than had the tsar's troops. Near the end of the conflict, the shocked English public demanded the organization of a British Sanitary Commission to investigate the high death rates. When the Civil War broke out, Henry Bellows, a Unitarian minister in New York, called for a similar investigatory and advisory commission. Despite the initial hostility of the Army Medical Bureau, the United States Sanitary Commission played a major role in the Union effort. In addition to dispatching sanitary inspectors to military camps to advise the troops on the disposition of latrines, drains, and fresh water supplies, the organization acted as a combination Red Cross and USO. By the war's end the commission was engaged in all aspects of the soldiers' lives except combat.[7]

The Sanitary Commission was able to play such a dominant role in the war effort because of the strong desire of civilians, especially women, to aid the volunteer soldier. Prior to the emergence of the commission as an organizing force, this desire was carried out through a plethora of organizations. In Chicago, the wives, sisters, sweethearts, and mothers of men of a newly formed company would band together to aid their heroes, raising money for flags and making uniforms. At first this was thought to be enough. But no sooner were troops sent south to Cairo than complaints about camp conditions were received in Chicago. In June 1861 a soldier at Cairo wrote about the troops:

> Many are sick from exposure and lack of proper protection. For these we need very badly, beds, blankets, pillows, socks, and something in the way of food besides "hardtack and salt junk."

Only families and friends were in a position to respond immediately, so they came together again and formed "relief societies" for specific regiments.[8]

The regimental relief societies and similar organizations attached to various churches had mixed success. When motivated by an emergency appeal they would quickly respond with clothing, mosquito nets, and blankets, but such aid was sporadic and sometimes frivolous. When the men of a Chicago regiment stationed in Springfield (the 19th Illinois Volunteer Infantry) appealed for aid, the women of the city mobilized to outfit them. Thirty sewing machines were installed in the upper floor of J. H. McVicker's theater, and volunteers made the unit its needed clothing. Often, however, efforts to aid the troops went astray or were misdirected to begin with. Friends of the first companies sent to secure Cairo took up a collection for "the boys" after they were gone a few days. Three hundred dollars was spent to buy them a lavish Sunday dinner, which was sent by messenger service from Chicago to Cairo. When the messenger reached the town, he wired back that the soldiers did not have enough blankets.

The soldiers, of course, enjoyed receiving delicacies from home, but the regimental relief societies proved inefficient in getting such donations to them. Homemade pastries and jelly and fresh fruits and vegetables were often packed in boxes with clothing, stationery, books, and blankets.

Some such "care packages" were lost en route, others arrived in the camps weeks later, the food rotted and the clothing ruined.[9]

Concern for sick and wounded soldiers was also demonstrated early in the war. Even before the Cairo expedition left the city, the women of Chicago volunteered for nursing duty. At the first great war rally on April 18, 1861, two women shocked many of those present by offering to accompany the troops. One of these bold ladies, Jane A. Babcock, made good her desire and, by the end of the month, she helped establish a military hospital at Cairo. Most of the early women volunteers were easily discouraged by the military surgeons, who were unenthusiastic about having women at the front.[10] But such prejudice did not extend to Roman Catholic nuns; the nursing experience and discipline of those women, particularly the Sisters of Mercy, allowed them to play a vital role in army relief work.

The Sisters of Mercy had come to Chicago in September 1846. Within months they had established St. Francis Xavier Academy for Women. Although the emphasis of the community was on teaching, the Sisters of Mercy were experienced nurses. In 1851 they established their first hospital in "a small ramshackle frame building on the lake shore." The small hospital won the respect of the city when cholera ravaged Chicago in 1854. The sisters first went to the battlefield when the largely Catholic Irish Brigade was in combat at Lexington. Aided by the Union Defense Committee of Chicago, Mother Mary Francis Monhalland dispatched twenty nuns to the scene of the fight. The women, all born in Ireland, were especially eager to reach the besieged brigade. Renaming themselves "the Soldiers of Mercy," they embarked on a steamer and tried to break through the Confederate positions along the Missouri River. Only after the vessel was badly shot up and the hull damaged did they turn back. Instead, a field hospital was established in Jefferson City, where for several months they tended to the casualties of the Missouri campaign. The Sisters of the Holy Cross, based in South Bend, Indiana, also took a lead as nurses. At both Cairo and Mound City, Illinois, they transformed abandoned warehouses into hospitals capable of handling thousands of patients.[11]

Although there were a few notable exceptions, Protestant women were largely excluded from nursing for the first year of the war. Surgeons "entreated" with relief organizations to send "Catholic sisters." "Protestant nurses," one surgeon complained, "are always finding some mare's-nest or other that they can't let alone." So, while convents were being emptied, hundreds of women in Chicago were forced to find other means of aiding troops. Their first efforts were "misdirected" and "blundering," as one of their number later recalled.[12]

The first blunder was the Havelock craze. At the beginning of the war a newspaper article recounted the invention by British General Sir Henry Havelock of a successful sunscreen device, a white linen headdress with a cloth flap that hung over the soldier's neck. Since troops were going to be sent south during the summer, Havelocks seemed to be a useful piece of clothing. (In the twentieth century, Havelocks would become well known to American movie goers when Hollywood costume designers made them standard issue for actors portraying French Foreign Legionnaires.) Civil War soldiers, however, called them "white night caps" and despised having to wear them. Nonetheless, thousands of northern women went to work making the unappreciated head gear. "Women who could not attend the 'sewing-meeting' where the 'Havelocks' were being manufactured," one Chicagoan recalled, "ordered the work sent to their homes, and ran the sewing-machines day and night till the nondescript headgear was completed." The Havelock craze in Chicago came to an end one July afternoon, when a large group of women went to Cottage Grove in part to treat the men of the 19th Illinois to a picnic lunch, but also to get a look at the soldiers in their new headdress. When the unit was assembled "a shout went up from the officers, soldiers and lady visitors." The men had taken the Havelocks and fashioned them into turbans, scarves, sunbonnets, sweat bands, and bandages—any purpose but that intended by Sir Henry Havelock. The ludicrousness of the Havelock was apparent even to the women, and one of their number recalled, "No more time nor money was wasted in their useless manufacture."[13]

No sooner was the Havelock craze dispensed with than the "lint and bandage mania . . . set in with great fury." Women came together to cut cloth into strips and roll them into bandages. More time consuming was the making of lint. Early in the war surgeons used cloth fibers to help stop bleeding. The fibers were known as lint, which was made by scraping old linen with broken glass or a knife. On April 23, 1861, a thousand Chicago women met in Bryan Hall to organize the production of bandages and lint. With great enthusiasm they established committees for the job when several male physicians in attendance stepped forward with "a bucket of cold water and a wet blanket." The doctors said it would be a waste of time for women to make lint by hand because "any corner drug store" had machines to make it easily and cheaply. This was dispiriting news for the eager women, but they pressed ahead with the meeting, intent upon focusing their efforts on bandage production. Again, a medical man stopped the effort, advising the women to send the whole cloth to the field surgeons as most preferred to have it cut to their own specifications, and they had access to machines for that purpose. The second announcement took the steam out of the meeting's organizers, and the assembly broke up bitterly disappointed.[14]

The "lint and bandage mania" did not end there. The next day many of the women were angry. Their gathering was supposed to have been "a meeting of women," yet it "was spoiled by . . . the interference . . . of some individuals of the other sex." The doctors may have been well meaning, one of the women argued, but they "sent a chill of disappointment to those who had been glad in the thought of doing their little something with their own hands for the poor soldier." The *Tribune* picked up on this theme and, in a patronizing fashion, argued that lint and bandages made by a lady's "gentle hands" would have more healing power. It also recommended that women not form a citywide organization but merely cooperate with their neighbors. This advice was taken, and for several months many Chicago women, anxious to be able to help, labored in isolation.[15]

Among the most important home-front activities Chicagoans initiated during the spring of 1861 was a fund for the care of soldiers' families. The official War Finance Committee disbursed donations from the business community to care for families and equip the new troops. Initially, most of the funds went to equipment, but by the time the fighting started in the fall of 1861, claims forms began to come in from destitute women and children. Rich and working class alike contributed to this fund. The iron molders at the Eagle Works Foundry established their own subscription for soldiers' families. Men pledged twenty-five cents to a dollar per week to the fund and challenged clerks and mechanics in the city to do the same. Churches and regimental relief societies also helped raise funds for needy families. In spite of this, by December the official war fund was nearly exhausted, as were the funds of many regimental organizations, such as the Ladies' Association of the Irish Brigade. The county then stepped in and authorized tax funds to be committed to the purpose.[16]

Throughout 1861 a steady stream of regiments from Wisconsin, Michigan, and Minnesota were funneled into the city by the railroad. As they awaited connecting transportation, church groups offered them coffee and sandwiches. Units marching from one station to another initially attracted attention and were an occasion for cheers and patriotic songs. But by August 1861, the *Tribune* noted, they had become an "everyday occurrence," and most Chicagoans only "bestowed upon them a casual glance." The burden of providing gallons of coffee and mountains of sandwiches exhausted the funds and energies of community groups after the first two months of the war. It became clear that if the city was going to continue to extend hospitality to troops in transit, an organized effort was required.[17]

————◇————

The United States Sanitary Commission gradually emerged as the principal coordinating force of almost all war relief activities. It took almost six months, however, for the commission to begin to be organized into an administrative, action-oriented agency instead of the purely advisory body Lincoln thought he created. A critical phase in effecting this metamorphosis was the dissemination of the findings of the commission's agents in the course of their inspection of army sanitary conditions. In the summer of 1861 the Commission appointed Robert Collyer agent for the Missouri front.

The selection was propitious. Collyer was a Yorkshire-born Unitarian minister who a reporter once described as a "brainy muscular Christian." The big-shouldered preacher had been a blacksmith before taking the cloth and later won a national reputation as a religious writer and speaker. In 1860 he headed Chicago's relief mission to rural Iowa after a devastating tornado. So vigorous was his response to Fort Sumter that for years afterward members of his congregation loved to relate how he draped his pulpit with the American flag and said there would be no more preaching until the war was over. What he saw as sanitary agent in Missouri shocked him. Battle casualties suffered in understaffed, poorly equipped hospitals with only their comrades to keep the ever-present flies off their wounds. Camp hospitals were jammed with young men suffering from diseases such as measles and mumps. Diarrhea was also a problem, because many officers did not know the first rule of camp sanitation—get water for coffee upstream from the place the horses are watered.[18] With his pen and voice, Collyer dramatized the suffering of Illinois troops. In his distinctive Yorkshire burr he called on Chicagoans to rally behind the Sanitary Commission.

On October 17, 1861, at a meeting at the Tremont House, Judge Mark Skinner was elected president of a Chicago branch of the U.S. Sanitary Commission. Skinner, the son of a former governor of New Hampshire, amassed a fortune in pursuit of a legal career. As a leading War Democrat and one of the city's most active philanthropists, he was the perfect choice to oversee the Chicago Branch's activities. Eliphalet W. Blatchford, a founder of the Chicago Academy of the Sciences, was treasurer, and Ezra B. McCagg, another well-heeled patron of the arts and sciences, was elected secretary. All of these men were considered by the community to be Christian gentlemen who, because of their wealth, religious convictions, and belief in civic duty, donated money and leadership to worthy undertakings. The wealthy of Civil War era Chicago were still motivated by a sense of noblesse oblige. They took on the task of directing the Sanitary Commission in Chicago because it was, like their other philanthropic activities, a worthy cause. The demands of war made the Chicago Branch an urgent and demanding priority, but overall the officers of the organization treated the Sanitary Commission like their other charitable responsibilities. Their job was to inspire public confidence in the management of the Commission, to help raise funds, and to oversee long-term strategy.[19]

The Chicago branch of the Sanitary Commission was typical of other charities in the city, such as the Orphan Asylum and the Home for the Friendless, in that its officers were mostly men. The work was done by the "benevolent ladies" of the city. Men were seen as essential to make tough administrative decisions, and women were necessary to provide the loving care that was seen as part of the female nature. This was the structure of the national U.S. Sanitary Commission. Even though women and Protestant ministers created the organization, only men were appointed commissioners. There was no challenge to male domination of the leadership because this was the way most previous philanthropic efforts had been organized and because women were intent on helping the soldiers. Throughout the war the women of the commission's rank and file worked well with the male directors. Nonetheless, the Sanitary Commission became a training ground for the leaders of the postwar women's suffrage movement.[20]

The first order of business for the Chicago Branch was to establish headquarters where it could gather donations for relief of the soldiers. Initially this was a small room on Wabash Street, but soon the operation was moved to a large set of rooms under McVicker's Theater on Madison. Operations there were directed by Eliza C. Porter, wife of a Presbyterian clergyman. She was a quiet, gentle woman of forty-five, whose outward manner concealed a passionate hatred of slavery. She was at breakfast with her husband, son, and two nephews when word was received that Fort Sumter had fallen. "If I had a hundred sons," she said in a fervent tone that surprised the young men, "I would gladly send them all forth to this work of putting down the rebellion." All three young men joined the army, and her husband became chaplain of the 1st Illinois Light Artillery. During her first few months on the job, Eliza Porter had a difficult task explaining to donors that the commission could not and was not intended to act as a forwarding agent for gifts to specific companies. Its goal was to do the most possible good. Therefore, supplies of medicine or food were sent to those hospitals or units that were most in need. This larger, nonparochial view of its mission quickly set the commission apart from the regimental relief societies that had previously dominated war work in Chicago.

Porter was also involved with Robert Collyer in establishing the Chicago Protestant Female Nurse Association. This group worked with the commission to screen suitable candidates for needy military hospitals. Porter was more concerned with nursing than managing the relief efforts of the Chicago Branch. After five months she left her post as superintendent of the headquarters and led a team of nurses to Cairo. Eventually, she followed the western army on its victorious march from Vicksburg to Chattanooga to Atlanta. Her post with the commission in Chicago was assumed by two remarkable women, Jane C. Hoge and Mary Livermore.[21]

Hoge and Livermore first became involved with the commission in December 1861 when they attempted to raise funds for the relief of the soldiers by hosting a festival. Independent of any male direction, they planned a gathering rather like a church bazaar, at which items donated by cooperating merchants were auctioned and food and beverages donated by local restaurants were sold. Music and a few patriotic speeches made the entire gathering an enjoyable way to spend a winter day. After all, the expenses were paid; they had collected $675.17 for the soldiers. A draft for that amount was sent to the commission with the following note:

> To the Chicago Sanitary Commissioners:
>   Accept this as our Christmas gift. We regret that it is not larger.
> We shall condense into a permanent organization for active hospital
> service, and hope to aid you, in a small way, through the war.

The confident efficiency and independence of Hoge and Livermore impressed the male commissioners, and the two women were invited to become agents of the commission.[22]

Their first assignment was to inspect conditions at the military hospitals in St. Louis, Mound City, and Cairo, paying particular attention to the personnel and logistical needs of the hospitals. The trip was an important step in the women's evolution into two of the home front's most effective leaders. The experience also helped to draw the two women, who had cooperated on several prewar charitable programs, closer together as friends.

Jane Hoge was an unlikely war heroine. The mother of thirteen children, she had had the advantage of some advanced education. She was a devout Presbyterian, which led her into several charitable projects before the war. When two of her sons joined the army, she threw herself into war work. Latent skills as a public speaker and executive thrust her into a leadership role. "The inspiration of the war developed in her capabilities of whose possession she was not aware," a friend wrote, "and she surprised herself, as she did others, by the exercise of hitherto unsuspected gifts."[23]

Mary Livermore had demonstrated that she was an exceptional woman long before the war. As a child she reveled in books and lectures. In the woodshed behind her parent's house she rigged up a small pulpit and delivered sermons to the stacks of cord wood. By age thirteen she attracted

forty neighborhood children to a summer school, over which she presided
for a fee of ten cents per week. Even her strongly conservative father was
led to remark, "If that girl were only a boy I would educate her for the
ministry, for she has it in her." However, her father gave in to her desire for
"higher" education and sent her to the Baptist Female Seminary in Charles-
town, Massachusetts. She later said her years of study were the happiest of
her life. Education reinforced her independent nature. Upon graduation
she overrode her father's objections and accepted a teaching position on a
Virginia plantation. "Do you know that you are running away from home
like a boy?" were her father's parting words.

In Virginia she learned something of the psychology of the planter
class and saw firsthand the abuses endured by slaves. The flogging of a
slave for a minor infraction left her nauseated and "paralyzed with hor-
ror." On quitting the plantation she again demonstrated her independence
by becoming engaged to the Reverend Daniel P. Livermore, a young Unitarian minister. She was immediately shunned by all her Baptist friends,
and her father was outraged. Yet she stayed her course, married the minister, and a short time later moved to Chicago. Reverend Livermore was
owner-editor of a struggling Universalist newspaper, *The New Covenant*.
Mary wrote many articles for the paper, some of which were later published as a book, and as its associate editor she was the only woman reporter at the Republican Convention in 1860. She also became involved in
charitable works in Chicago, particularly the Home for the Friendless
(which seems to have been a training ground for Sanitary Commission
workers) where she met Jane C. Hoge.[24]

Nothing Hoge and Livermore had ever experienced prepared them
for what they saw on their hospital tour. They began at the St. Louis Military Hospital, which was choked with casualties from Grant's victory at
Fort Donelson. "The sickening odor of blood and healing wounds almost
overpowered me," Livermore later recalled. But because she and Hoge
wished to learn nursing techniques, they began to work with the surgeons.
The army still had a strong prejudice against female nurses, and perhaps
because of this, they were first led into a ward of eighty beds which contained the worst cases. Mary was assigned to assist a surgeon who was
changing a wounded man's bandage. He had been hideously wounded in
the face. His lower jaw was gone, and his tongue had been cut off. As the
bandages were removed and the raw flesh of his mutilated face was exposed, a "deathly faintness" overcame Mary, and she rushed from the
ward. Three times she returned, only to be led away nauseated and faint.
Finally, the surgeons told her to stay out of the ward, explaining that some
people cannot adjust to such sights and smells. "But was I to shrink from
the sight of misery which these brave men were so nobly enduring?" she

later wrote. "The thought was a tonic, and despising my weakness, I forced myself to remain in the ward without nausea or faintness." Through an exercise of "iron control," she went from bed to bed with the surgeon.[25]

Jane Hoge, the more retiring of the two women, had an easier time adjusting to nursing. By the time they finished inspecting the hospitals of St. Louis and southern Illinois, both women were virtually immune to the horrors of war. What they saw and experienced did not change their romantic concept of courage and patriotism. The soldiers were in their eyes heroes, not victims of war. This was how most of the men wanted to be seen by the folks back home, and they did their best to project that image to visitors from Chicago. Jane Hoge nursed a young man referred to by the surgeons in Mound City as the "miracle" case. He had been wounded in one of the preliminary assaults on Fort Donelson and had lain helpless on the battlefield for about thirty-six hours in temperatures hovering just above zero. His clothes froze to the ground, and he could not move. Yet, when he saw the American flag raised over Donelson, he and the other wounded cheered. A wounded man near him raised the stump of his shattered arm in triumph. By the time he reached the hospital, both arms and legs were shattered and unmovable. Amputation seemed the only course, yet after five weeks care he surprised the staff by regaining the use of his limbs. He even hoped to return to his company. "I fear you've got more than you bargained for," Jane said when he finished his story. "Not a bit of it," he replied. "We went in for better or worse, and if we got worse, we must not complain." Jane heard another soldier, dying of his wound, say, "Thy will, O God, be done! 'Tis a privilege, even thus, to die for one's country."[26]

Hoge and Livermore's inspection tour lasted just short of three weeks. As they left St. Louis, they saw thousands of newly inducted troops march off to the front in southern Tennessee. The hospitals were nearly clear of the wounded from Fort Donelson, but many people predicted another large battle. The two women hurried back to Chicago, where they took charge of the Sanitary Commission headquarters. Familiar with the needs of the wounded and the limitations of the military hospitals, they were in an excellent position to distribute the most desired supplies to the appropriate locations. Hundreds of boxes of hospital goods were assembled and shipped south. Agents from Chicago established supply depots at Cairo and Paducah, Kentucky. Nearly one thousand packages of supplies were shipped to Shiloh when the fight began. After Shiloh, the rooms of the Chicago Branch were astir with activity.

When the stream of donations began to slow, the women placed notices in the newspaper. Old underwear, sheets, shirts, and pillowcases were particularly sought after. Hoge and Livermore also worked to prepare hospital beds in Chicago for those needing long-term care and for wounded men in transit. Half of the large Marine Hospital, on Michigan Avenue near the river, was turned over to the swelling ranks of wounded. Hoge, in particular, worked to supplying the needs of these patients.[27]

The activity of commissioners Skinner and McCagg in raising funds and the executive abilities of Livermore and Hoge allowed the Chicago Branch to operate five hospital steamers for three months following Shiloh. The commission also fitted out three steamers to return wounded soldiers to their native state, two for Illinois and one for Wisconsin. The ability of the Chicago Branch to anticipate the needs of the army before Shiloh and keep aid teams in the field for months afterward saved hundreds, perhaps thousands, of lives. By spring of 1862, the Chicago branch of the Sanitary Commission emerged as the leading army relief organization in the West and was one of the most successful in the Union.[28]

————◇————

"Our people all have the 'blues,' " Joseph Medill wrote in the winter of 1862. "The feeling of utter hopelessness is stronger than at any time since the war began." Chicagoans had actually begun to give way to disappointment during the summer of that year, after the rush to aid the wounded of Shiloh subsided. The great Union victories of the spring—Fort Donelson, Island No. 10, and the capture of New Orleans—were eclipsed by the news of McClellan's failed attempt to take Richmond. High hopes were dashed by this defeat. On July 2, 1862, church bells in Chicago rang, flags were raised, and celebrations began because of a rumor that the Union army had captured the Confederate capital. When it became apparent that McClellan was in retreat, the people felt worse than before. Grant's forces spent the rest of the year in fruitless maneuvering to besiege Vicksburg, while rebel cavalry launched raids as far north as Cincinnati in spite of the government's claim of control over most of Tennessee and Kentucky. In September there came more bad news from the East, where the Second Battle of Bull Run (fought on August 29–30) destroyed the reputation of General John Pope, victor at Island No. 10. The Battle of Antietam halted Lee's invasion of the North, but no one felt like celebrating when the casualty lists were posted. Sentiment hit rock bottom after December 13, when thirteen thousand Union soldiers fell at Fredericksburg. The defeat, Joseph Medill wrote to a friend, "leaves us almost without hope."[29]

Discouragement eroded the fervent unity of the patriotic response to Fort Sumter, "the spirit of 1861." All through the summer of 1862 abolitionists pushed the administration to act against slavery, while conservative Democrats decried the influence of radical Republicans on war policy and demanded Lincoln stand firm on the Constitution and leave military matters to the generals (i.e., McClellan). On September 4, 1862, radicals in Chicago held a mass meeting in Bryan Hall, claiming to represent the "Religious Community of Chicago." They contended that Union defeats were a sign of God's displeasure with America, and until the nation purged itself of the sin of oppression, the war could not be won. Two ministers were sent to Washington and relayed this demand for an emancipation decree to the president. Actions such as these led James Sheahan, editor of the Democratic *Chicago Post*, to remark that the abolitionists were "rebels of the North" who were intent on driving Lincoln "to acts of folly and madness." Meanwhile, the *Tribune*, not noted for its restraint, had begun to refer to its Democratic rivals as "secessionist" newspapers.[30]

Illinois was further divided during the summer of 1862 by a referendum on a new state constitution. Downstate Democrats dominated the convention that drafted the document and produced a constitution that was highly favorable to their party and their section of the state. To Republicans it was a "Secession Constitution"; to the Democrats it was a working man's document. The vote on June 17 defeated the constitution, although the people of Chicago, perhaps as a sign of disenchantment with the Republicans, approved the document by 995 votes. Chicagoans also voted in favor of special referendum issues directed at blacks. Two articles were put before the voters: one prohibited the immigration of blacks and mulattoes to the state; the other prohibited those who were already in Illinois from voting. Both articles passed by overwhelming majorities.[31]

Considerable anger was directed at blacks in Chicago during the summer of 1862. Federal victories along the Mississippi had induced thousands of slaves to flee bondage and seek refuge with the Union army. Technically, these runaway slaves were still property. They were labeled "contraband" (enemy property) and herded into camps near army bases. One such camp was in Cairo. Democrats contended that these refugees were the first of a wave of blacks who would overwhelm the working men of the state. Many Republicans, on the other hand, thought it would be wise to use their labor if it was available. When a few farmers employed the blacks, it seemed as if the Democratic prophecy was coming true. Working men throughout the state were alert for any sign of increased economic competition from blacks.[32]

It was in this atmosphere that racial violence broke out in Chicago. On July 14, 1862, a black man, W. E. Walker, boarded the Clark Street omnibus. He paid his dime, took his usual seat in the far corner of the bus, and waited with the patience of a veteran commuter for the bus to leave. After a few minutes, Richard Kelly, the driver, mounted his seat. He had been in the saloon across the street, passing his break time with other bus drivers, who envied Kelly because he was regularly scheduled to make the 12:15 run down Clark Street. This was one of the busiest routes of the day, and because drivers were paid a percentage of the fares, it was a much coveted assignment. Few of the drivers felt good about blacks riding the omnibus. It did not take too many drinks on Kelly's part for his colleagues to convince him that letting blacks ride on the bus during his busy route hurt the other drivers, because it made whites less likely to want to ride buses. Kelly had this in mind when he noticed Walker sitting in the omnibus.

"Come out of here, you God damned nigger!" he screamed. Walker was surprised and quietly asked why he must leave. "I won't carry any damned niggers in my bus," Kelly replied. "Why," Walker again said, "I have ridden in these buses for years and always pay my fare. I was never ordered out before." But Kelly wanted no arguments and once more rudely ordered Walker out. The black man refused to move from his seat.

> At this, in a boiling rage, the driver entered the bus, seized Walker by the collar and roughly dragged him out and after getting him to the bottom of the steps dealt him a savage blow in the face. Walker had hitherto made little or no resistance, but upon receiving the blow seized the driver, threw him down, and with remarkable forbearance, did not return the blow, but contented himself with holding down his assailant.

By this time a crowd had gathered, and the two men were pulled apart. Walker probably would have been injured if Edward Salomon and a police officer had not arrived on the scene. Salomon was a former alderman of German-Jewish background who at the time was training a German regiment for active service. With the help of the police officer and one of the men of his regiment, Salomon escorted Walker away from the crowd.[33]

The confrontation, however, was not over. Walker still wanted to take the bus north on Clark Street, and Kelly still intended to stop him. The Irishman had gathered a mob of supporters a short distance away at the southern terminus of the line. Rather than risk open provocation, the police officer told Walker to slip off the bus before it entered the turnaround and catch it at the next stop on Clark Street. At the terminus Kelly angrily mounted the bus several times in search of Walker. Another driver then took the bus north. But he refused to stop for Walker at the next stop, citing Kelly's instructions not to admit "niggers." The black man persisted, however, and he ran down the line to another stop. Another crowd was gathering to watch what the bus driver would do. The drama ended when the driver admitted a black woman and, at the next stop, allowed Walker to enter. The violence was not over, however; during the afternoon black people were randomly attacked by small gangs of irate whites.[34]

To the *Tribune*, these actions were the work of secessionists who were emboldened by McClellan's defeat. A mob assault on blacks was depicted by *Tribune* editors as a treasonous attempt to undermine Chicago's war effort. Blame for the violence was also laid at the door of the rival *Chicago Times*, "and kindred treasonable prints, which love slavery better than the Union . . . [they] have pandered to, and egged on this mob spirit." That whites' fear of blacks was widespread was left unstated. Kelly was fired from his job, arrested, and indicted for assault.

The omnibus riot was not an isolated incident. A month later another riot directed against blacks occurred. A gang of white stevedores were underbid by a crew of blacks for the job of unloading a schooner. Before the blacks could begin the job, they were violently attacked by the white stevedores. Police broke up the fray, but it erupted again as soon as they left. Only after the arrival of another squad of officers armed with firearms was the riot brought under control.[35]

It was in the midst of this atmosphere of hostility, rancor, and discouragement that Chicago received another federal request for troops. On July 2, 1862, Lincoln asked for 300,000 new three-year volunteers that he hoped would bring the war "to a speedy and satisfactory conclusion." A month later Congress made an additional manpower request. A new federal militia law gave Washington the power to call the state militia into national service for nine months. When states did not have adequate militia forces to be called forward, the administration was empowered to draft individuals into service. Under this legislation the War Department requested an additional 300,000 troops for the prescribed nine-month term. Illinois' quota under these new calls was 52,296.[36]

This second great call to arms did not elicit the same enthusiasm as Lincoln's initial appeal a year earlier. Shiloh's bitter lesson of the reality of war had been widely appreciated. Many men who wanted to enlist in 1861 but had been turned away were now accustomed to being in the sidelines. The local economy was booming, and there was money to be made at home. More sophisticated recruiting techniques were required to revive enthusiasm for volunteering. Whereas in 1861 it was simply a matter of pitching an enlistment tent and opening a muster roll, in 1862 grand rallies, financial inducements, and propaganda were needed to prime the pump of patriotism.

The first of these giant recruiting rallies was held on July 21. The well-planned affair produced a great turnout, perhaps as many as fifteen thousand people. Republican clubs, War Democrats, the Board of Trade, and church groups all did a good job of creating interest in the rally and turning out their people. More than ninety honorary vice presidents, including almost every mayor Chicago had ever had, presided over the gathering. The core of the rally was the courthouse square. Two halls adjacent to the square, Bryan Hall and Metropolitan Hall, were patriotically decorated for the principal addresses. For several hours the crowds in these halls were harangued by the city's notable businessmen and clergy. From a third speaker's platform, erected outside in the square, lesser dignitaries addressed those who could not be seated inside. Highlighting the evening were bands playing their stirring renditions of patriotic songs. The entire gathering sang "Marseillaise" with great gusto. Also popular was a new song by Stephen Foster, "We Are Coming, Father Abraham, Three Hundred Thousand More." Resolutions adopted at the rally supported the call for troops and urged a more vigorous prosecution of the war.[37]

Giant war rallies were held again on July 26 and August 1, 1862, each affair attracting about ten thousand people. The August 1 rally was notable because of the abolitionist tone of the program. Owen Lovejoy shared the speaker's platform with Governor Yates and Senator John Sherman of Ohio. Not only did they propose the use of free blacks as soldiers, but they advocated full emancipation as well. Such sentiments had been suppressed during the first year of the war, lest they create rifts between War Democrats and radical Republicans. The fact that such ideas were openly cheered by thousands indicated the growing desire of Northerners to pursue any course necessary to destroy the Confederacy. The July 26 rally also premiered one of the war's great songs: "The Battle Cry of Freedom."[38]

George Frederick Root began work on the song soon after Lincoln's call for more troops. Root was a music educator, whose teaching experience gave him a background extemporizing melodies. He came to Chicago in 1860 and joined the music publishing firm of Root and Cady, which his brother had founded. He enjoyed a modest reputation as a writer of sentimental ballads and hymns. His song "The First Gun Is Fired" was a hit at Chicago's first war rally in April 1861, but that song never became as popular as "The Battle Cry of Freedom." Several days before the July 26 rally, Jules and Frank Lumbard, the city's most popular patriotic singers, visited Root at his store. They had been asked to sing at the rally and wanted to present something new to stir the crowd. The ink was hardly dry on "The Battle Cry of Freedom" when Root put it into their hands. They went through the song there in the shop and were immensely pleased with it.

Saturday, July 26, was hot and muggy. By two in the afternoon the courthouse square was jammed with thousands of people. The Board of Trade, which sponsored the rally, placed three speaker's platforms at different places in the square. Without an electronic outdoor public address system it was impossible to speak to fifteen thousand people at once, so a different program was arranged for each platform. After a long speech by

Congressman Isaac Arnold, Jules Lumbard mounted the north platform
and began to sing "The Battle Cry of Freedom." His deep, rich bass was
backed by a small choir and a band.

> Yes, we'll rally 'round the flag, boys,
> We'll rally once again,
> Shouting the battle cry of Freedom.
> We will rally from the hill-side,
> We'll gather from the plain,
> Shouting the battle cry of Freedom.
> *Chorus:* The Union forever, Hurrah! boys, Hurray!
> Down with the traitor, Up with the star;
> While we rally 'round the flag, boys,
> Rally once again,
> Shouting the battle cry of Freedom.

The song went on for three more verses. Each time the chorus was repeated, more and more of the audience joined in. By the time the final re-
frain rang out, thousands were turned toward the north platform "shouting the battle cry of freedom."[39]

The song had an electrifying effect, and it spread in the weeks that
followed across the nation. Scarcely any Union rally would ever again be
considered complete without at least one verse of the song. One reporter
referred to it as the "Northern Marseillaise" because of the immediate popularity it enjoyed among the fighting men. It was introduced to the Army
of the Cumberland just after the vicious battle of Stone's River. Many officers from border states had recently resigned their commissions in protest
of the Emancipation Proclamation. A glee club from Chicago introduced
the song to the men of an Illinois regiment. "The effect was little short of
miraculous. It put as much spirit and cheer into the army as a victory. Day
and night one could hear it by every camp fire and in every tent. I shall
never forget how the men rolled out the line, "and although he may be
poor, he shall never be a slave.' "

A *Tribune* reporter heard it one evening near Vicksburg sung by a
clear tenor voice from the Union gunboats. Just as the last notes died
away, an equally clear tenor from the rebel batteries responded with
"Dixie." After the war a Confederate general recalled that the first time he
heard the song it sounded like "the knell of doom" for the South. It was on
a rainy night after several days of fighting, and Lee's forces had thoroughly
beaten the Yankee opponents. Someone inside the Union lines began to
sing the song "and others joined in the chorus until it seemed to me the
whole Yankee army was singing." A rebel picket turned to the general and

said, "Good heavens . . . what are those fellows made of, anyway? Here we've licked 'em six days running, and now on the eve of the seventh they're singing Rally 'Round the Flag."[40]

The song proved to be lucrative for Root and Cady. Several years after the war they claimed to have sold "between five and seven hundred thousand" copies of the sheet music. At one point during the war, fourteen printing presses were at work making copies of the song. Music stores bought thousands of copies at a time; one store bought the "Battle Cry" in increments of twenty thousand copies. Such success encouraged Root to continue to write songs about the war. Some, such as "Lay Me Down and Save the Flag" and "Who'll Save the Left" glorified the heroics of Chicago soldiers and enjoyed only limited national appeal. However, his sentimental ballads "Just Before the Battle, Mother" and "The Vacant Chair" enjoyed popularity in the drawing rooms of the North as well as around military campfires. "Tramp, Tramp, Tramp, the Boys Are Marching," a stirring march about rescuing Union prisoners of war, sold thousands of copies and, for a time, seemed destined to become as popular as "Battle Cry." After the war the tune was adopted by Irish revolutionaries as the anthem "God Save Ireland."

Root's assistant, Henry C. Work, was his only rival as a wartime song writer. Work was an impoverished printer when Root signed him to a five year contract to write exclusively for Root and Cady. An abolitionist, he viewed the war as a holy crusade; he had served time in a Missouri prison for aiding escaped slaves. His exuberance over the fall of the "peculiar institution" was best illustrated by "Marching Thro' Georgia," which also became one of the best known Civil War songs and the favorite of postwar veterans' reunions.[41]

More rallies were held in August and September. At the September rally, General Samuel E. Curtis, victor of Pea Ridge, and General John A. McClernand, an Illinois Democratic politico turned soldier, exhorted the crowd to stand by the government. To further inspire the audience in Bryan Hall, the tattered battle flag of the 8th Illinois Infantry was displayed with all the solemnity of a holy relic. A parade and rally on August 19 featured one of the city's most colorful soldiers and controversial heroes, Russian immigrant John B. Turchin, born Ivan Turchinenoff. Trained from his youth to be a soldier, he quickly rose to a position on the general staff. During the Crimean War he planned and constructed Russia's Baltic coastal defenses. There he met George B. McClellan, who was sent by the U.S. Army to observe the war, and it is likely that McClellan induced him to emigrate to America. Turchin arrived in the United States in 1856 and became a construction engineer for the Illinois Central Railroad. In July 1861 he was made Colonel of the 19th Illinois Infantry, which included the Chicago Zouaves, and made it one of the best drilled volunteer units in the army.

Turchin was probably more surprised than anyone that Chicago would choose him to preside over a great war rally, when only a month before he faced a court martial and the likely prospect of a disgraceful discharge. The controversy over Turchin began during an aggressive probe he led up the Tennessee River Valley into northern Alabama. At one point an Ohio regiment attached to his brigade occupied the town of Athens. The people of the town claimed to be Unionists, and the troops carelessly failed to post pickets. Rebel cavalry seized the advantage and drove the Ohio unit out of town. As they fled, the townspeople jeered and threw garbage at them, and several shots were fired from the houses. The 19th Illinois was quickly brought up and recaptured the town. Once more the townspeople professed their loyalty to Washington, but the Chicagoans were not fooled. They broke ranks and sacked the town. Turchin described the action as a measured reprisal against a deceitful foe. Confederate accounts also accused the soldiers of raping the students at a female seminary. Later, when the 19th retreated northward to rejoin the main army, they were periodically fired on by guerrillas. As casualties mounted Turchin adopted a strategy of burning the house nearest to an ambush site. "It was pitiful, but it was war," a veteran later wrote. But Don Carlos Buell, the commander of the army, saw things differently and arranged a court martial to investigate the Athens atrocity. Turchin was charged with "neglect of duty, to the prejudice of good order and military discipline." Probably he would have been found guilty and dismissed from the service had it not been for the determined action of his wife.[42]

Madame Turchin was as resourceful and determined as any soldier. She was a soldier's daughter and had lived with her father and then with her husband during all of their Russian Army commands. When her husband joined the Union army, she followed him to camp. She became a familiar sight at Camp Douglas, riding side saddle through drill fields— serene and imposing. When the unit went to the front, she readied herself by carrying a dirk and revolver. She nursed soldiers when they were wounded and is reputed to have, on one occasion, directed the regiment in battle when her husband was ill. "Dear Madame Turchin!" a veteran recalled, "how we all respected, believed in, and came to love her for her bravery, gentleness, and constant care of the sick and wounded in the Regiment." When she saw the direction of the court martial's proceedings, she hurried to Washington and appealed to the secretary of war. Her appeal was answered, and she made a dramatic return to the regiment just as the court martial was set to discharge Colonel Turchin from the service. She delivered to her husband new orders assigning him to command a brigade, with the rank of brigadier general.[43]

Turchin's promotion to general made him the first Chicago volunteer to attain that rank and a fitting figure around which to build a rally. He was escorted into Bryan Hall to the tune of "Lo! the Conquering Hero Comes" and the "din of clapping hands, stamping of feet, vivas and huzzas." A special introduction was afforded to Madame Turchin, who also received a loud ovation. Introductory speakers praised Turchin as a man "who handled our enemies roughly." His promotion, they proclaimed, was a sign that "this kid glove business is played out." When it was the general's turn to speak, he did not disappoint the rally's organizers. In a stirring speech he accused the rebels of waging "a war of extermination" and concluded "we must do the same, and until we use all men, slaves included, we cannot put them down." For General Buell, who was unpopular in Chicago because of his unaggressive direction of the army in Tennessee, Turchin expressed disdain. He closed his speech by observing, "What I have done is not much; but what I could do, were I allowed might amount to something. . . . We have been talking about the Union and hurrahing the Union a great while. Let us now talk and hurrah for conquest."[44]

Turchin's aggressive call for total war, like the display of tattered battle flags and the playing of such patriotic tunes as "The Battle Cry of Freedom," helped to create the proper emotional atmosphere for recruiting activities. The giant rallies organized throughout the summer of 1862 proved to be a tonic for morale and a boost for enlistments. While Lincoln's second call for troops drew only a small response in some sections of the North, Illinois quickly filled its quota.

As in 1861, Chicagoans went to war not so much as individuals but as members of distinct ethnic, religious, and occupational groups. "Clear the track!" was the battle cry of the 89th Illinois Infantry, organized in August by employees of ten railroads that served Chicago. Father Dennis Dunne, pastor of St. Patrick's parish, organized a second Irish-Catholic regiment, which he grandly dubbed the "Irish Legion." The Irish community in Chicago was already beginning to cool toward the war. They viewed talk of emancipation as a threat of more competition for unskilled labor jobs. Dunne worked so hard at raising the "Irish Legion" that he was elected its temporary colonel.

The Germans had no intention of letting the Irish outdo them in the war effort. Frederick Hecker, who had organized a regiment in 1861, returned to the city to raise a second German unit. One company of this second Hecker regiment was composed of Scandinavians, while another, the Concordia Guards, was made up entirely of Jews. By mid-August, war fever struck the small Jewish community in Chicago. In thirty-six hours they held a series of rallies, raised more than $11,000, and enlisted a full company of recruits. Even the *Chicago Tribune* got caught up in the excitement and organized a company of its employees and friends.[45]

The Chicago Board of Trade led the city's most effective effort to fulfill Lincoln's call for troops. Their initial response was to raise and equip a company of light artillery. In a matter of days they filled the enrollment book and collected the necessary money to organize the unit. On July 23, at a mass meeting on the trading floor, the board resolved to raise a regiment of infantry. The members cheered, save for one fellow who shouted, "Humbug extraordinary!" The man was seized and lifted over the crowd, hand over hand, then hustled downstairs and hurled into the street. Later, the board joined with the Young Men's Christian Athletic Association to raise a total of three infantry regiments. A war fund of $55,000, raised in less than a month, was used to pay each volunteer $60 over the federal bounty of $100. Every employee of the board who enlisted was guaranteed his job back when the war was over.[46]

Bounties and threat of the draft no doubt helped to spur enlistments. Republican newspapers like the *Tribune* and the *Journal* carried warnings that a draft was inevitable, and men were well advised to enlist while they could. By enlisting, a man received a bounty and could pick the men and officers with whom he would serve. As August 21, the date for fulfilling Chicago's quota, approached, enlistments accelerated. The *Tribune* described the recruiting tents in front of the courthouse as "beehives." This was not the case in many Indiana, Wisconsin, and Ohio towns. Those states failed to meet their quotas and were forced to endure a draft.[47]

The draft inevitably produced draft dodgers, or "skedaddlers." By late August, Chicago began to receive hundreds of such reluctant travelers, most seeking rail or boat passage to Canada. An observer of the exodus noted that the Michigan Central Railroad, the main line from Chicago to the north, reaped "a rich harvest in the way of fares . . . while every steamboat that leaves our wharves is loaded down with passengers for the North who are not very particular as to upper deck cabin accommodations." The "skedaddlers" were widely scorned. Even the *Chicago Times*, no friend of the administration, declared, "Citizens, whether natural or adopted, who leave their country in such a crisis, cannot expect . . . good will should they ever return." The paper went on to say the "skedaddlers" were "cowardly" and deserved to be punished as deserters.[48]

For a time, "skedaddlers" threatened to undermine the draft. Secretary of War Edwin M. Stanton was forced to order that no citizen of draft age be allowed to leave their county or state, let alone the country, without a pass from the local militia committee or police authorities. The pass system was an almost unprecedented violation of an American citizen's freedom to move about the country without restraint. The War Department promised the Chicago police a $5 reward for every draft dodger they caught, so Superintendent C. P. Bradley and his men enforced the pass system with enthusiasm. On the day the order went into effect, Bradley cast his net broadly to catch as many "skedaddlers" as possible. His officers inspected every train. At the mouth of the Chicago River he stationed a police tug, with a cannon mounted on its bow to stop and search every outward bound vessel. That night his men made thirty arrests, fourteen of whom turned out to be draft dodgers. The "unfortunate cowards" spent several hours in the city lock-up before they were unceremoniously marched to Camp Douglas and inducted into the army.[49]

Superintendent Bradley instructed all ticket agents to restrict bookings even to those who held valid passes. This sent a deluge of stranded salesmen and other travelers into police headquarters, all clamoring to be allowed to leave town. One by one they were let into the superintendent's office and their eligibility was hastily assessed. A reporter for the *Chicago Times* described one such interview. A man stood, hat in hand, in front of the policeman's desk:

> Superintendent—"What is your name?"
> Traveler—"Robert H. Brooks. I am going to Chennango County, New York."
> Superintendent—"Where is your home?"
> Traveler—"I've been living for the last two months in Davenport, Iowa, but my home and family are in New York."
> Superintendent—"Well, sir, you must give a bond, with some citizen as security, in the sum of one thousand dollars, conditional for the performance of military duty, if you should be drafted."
> Traveler—"I don't know any one in Chicago, and I must go to New York; my family are sick, and my presence is necessary."
> Superintendent:"Can't help it; you can't go. Who's next?"

Incidents such as this frustrated legitimate travelers and led even many Republicans to ask that the pass system be revised. The *Times* was much less restrained. It complained, "Chicago is virtually *under martial law*."[50]

The pass system remained in effect for less than a month, and it succeeded in stopping what one Chicagoan called "the great stampede." It was followed, however, by a more serious breach of civil rights. On September 24, 1862, Lincoln suspended the writ of habeas corpus for all people discouraging compliance with the draft or giving "comfort to the rebels." The decree gave federal officials the means not only to deal with draft riots in Wisconsin and Indiana but also to arrest antiwar activists and hold them without trial. Administration opponents inevitably linked this decree with Lincoln's preliminary Emancipation Proclamation, which threatened the South with the loss of their slaves if they did not return to the Union by January 1, 1863. Wilbur F. Storey, editor of the *Chicago Times*, caustically observed:

> Mr. Lincoln once declared that it was impossible for the Union to exist half slave and half free. He is, of course, anxious to prove the truth of his prophecy. After the emancipation proclamation had failed to verify his assertion by rendering the people all free, is it possible that his proclamation suspending the habeas corpus was another attempt at demonstration by making them all slave?

In a more serious vein, Storey reflected the fears of many Chicagoans when he wrote on the very day habeas corpus was suspended that traditional and constitutional freedoms were being "trampled under foot." Such actions were proof: "Our chart is gone, our course is lost, and amid the din of the tempest around us, can be heard the maddened voice of mutineers."[51]

In spite of the heroic relief efforts in the spring of 1862, the Chicago Branch of the U.S. Sanitary Commission nearly became a casualty of the discouragement and political division that infected the homefront during the summer and fall of that year. The organization's coffers had been emptied by relief efforts for Shiloh's casualties, and new funds were slow to come in. Certainly Lincoln's call for more troops focused the city's attention on fulfilling its quota and avoiding a draft. Moneys previously available for wounded soldiers went to inflate enlistment bounties. The commission also faced direct criticism of its motives and competency. "Systematic assaults began . . . to be made upon the commission by opponents of the administration," a Sanitary worker remembered, "who, now, unreserved in their condemnation of everything helping to sustain the army, pronounced its labors unnecessary, and its management inefficient."

Even more dangerous than the sniping of disgruntled peace Democrats, and certainly less predictable, were the complaints of returning veterans. Soldiers on sick leave or furlough often made "loud complaints" that they saw little of the thousands of dollars worth of goods sent to the front. Stories circulated that nurses and doctors gorged themselves on food meant for the troops, or worse still, that the hospital staff sold them for a profit to the soldiers. Nor was there any real accountability of branch societies in towns like Chicago to the U.S. Sanitary Commission. The Cincinnati branch actually tried to assert its autonomy after several large donations gave it financial independence. All of these issues forced the commission, in November 1862, to reorganize.[52]

The restructuring was effected through the Women's Council, a conference of the leading female relief organizers in the North. Jane Hoge and Mary Livermore journeyed to Washington to represent Chicago at the meeting, which determined that the branches of the commission would coordinate the collection and distribution of supplies to the troops. The Chicago branch, for example, would receive boxes of supplies from Wisconsin and northern Indiana and assume the responsibility of shipping them to Cairo to a warehouse and a forwarding agent. The agent would ensure distribution to the neediest front. The new cooperative system put tremendous pressure on Chicago's Sanitary Commission workers as they became the coordinators for the entire northwest.[53]

Organizational improvements and the recognition that, flawed though it might be, the commission did a better job of helping the soldiers than any other body, succeeded in restoring the flow of money and supplies to the Madison Street depot. Drays and carriages arrived continuously, laden with crates, boxes, and packages. The shouts of draymen were barely heard over the "incessant hammering and pounding within [the depot] caused by opening and nailing up boxes." The din was further increased by the sounds from the second floor, where thirty to forty sewing machines operated throughout the day. "Upstairs and downstairs, and over our heads, the women of the soldiers' families maintained a ceaseless tramp from morning till night, coming to sew, to receive or return work, or to get their greatly needed pay." Mary Livermore wrote of those busy days: "Add to this a steady stream of callers, on every imaginable errand, in every known mental mood—grieved, angry, stupid, astonished, incredulous, delighted, agonized—all talking in the tones of voice in which these various moods betray themselves."

Few visitors to the Chicago Sanitary Commission left without remarking on the depot's smell. "The odors of the place were villainous and a perpetual torment," wrote Livermore. "Codfish and sauer-kraut, pickles and ale, onions and potatoes, smoked salmon and halibut, ginger and whiskey, salt mackerel and tobacco, kerosene for lamps, benzine for cleaning purposes, black paint to mark boxes, flannel and unbleached cotton for clothing—these all concentrated their exhalations in one pungent aroma that . . . clung tenaciously to the folds of one's garments when one departed."[54]

Jane Hoge and Mary Livermore, together with John Freeman, the shipping clerk, and William Goldsmith purchasing agent, presided over the organized pandemonium of the depot. When they were not visiting the front, they arrived at the depot about nine o'clock each morning. Both women had already bundled their husbands and children off to work and school before they themselves hastened to the omnibus. Often work began before they could even take their coats off. In a newspaper article, Mary Livermore described one such "Day at the Rooms of the Sanitary Commission":

> We enter the office. Ladies are in waiting, who desire information. The aid society in another State, of which they are officers, had raised at a Fourth of July festival some six hundred dollars, and they wish to know how it shall be disposed of, so as to afford the greatest amount of relief to the sick and wounded of our army. They are also instructed to investigate the means and method of the Commission, so as to carry conviction to a few obstinate skeptics, who persist in doubting if the Sanitary Commission, after all, be the best means of communication with the hospitals. Patiently and courteously, the history, method, means, views and successes of the Commission are lucidly explained for the hundredth time in a month, and all needed advice and instruction imparted—and the enlightened women leave.
>
> An express messenger enters. He brings a package, obtains his fee, gets receipted for the package, and without a word departs. Next comes a budget of letters—the morning's mail. One announces the shipment of a box of hospital stores, which will arrive today; another scolds roundly because a letter sent a week ago has not been answered—which has been answered, as the copy-book indisputably asserts, but has been miscarried; the third has a bugaboo, mythical story to relate to the surgeons and nurses in distant hospital, with large development of alimentiveness, who save little for their patients, being mainly occupied in "seeking what they can devour" of the hospital delicacies; a fourth pleads earnestly and eloquently that the writer may be sent as a nurse to the sad, cheerless, far-away hospitals; a fifth is the agonized letter of a mother and widow, blistered with tears, begging piteously that the Commission will search out, and send to her, tidings of her only son . . . not . . . heard from since the battle of Grand Gulf; a sixth seeks information concerning the organization of an aid society in a remote town, which has just awakened to its duty; a seventh is a letter from nine-year-old little girls, who have earned five dollars, and wish to spend it for the "poor sick soldiers." God bless the dear children! An eighth begs that one of the ladies of the Commission will visit the society in her town, and rekindle flagging zeal of the tired workers, who forget that our brave men do not stop in marches, and postpone not their battles and their victories because of the heat, or of weariness; a ninth announces the death of one of our heroic nurses, who was sent by the Commission a few months ago to Tennessee, a blue-eyed, broad-browed, serious-faced, comely girl, with heart loyal as steel, and soul on fire with patriotic yearnings to do something for

her country, and who has now given her life; and so through a package of twenty, thirty and sometimes forty letters.

Now commences the task of replying to these multitudinous epistles; a work which is interrupted every five minutes by some new comer.

Most of the callers were relatives of wounded soldiers anxious for word of their condition. Perhaps the most dreaded duty was to convey the news of a soldier's death to his family. Gently they dealt with the grief-stricken and made arrangements to secure the soldier's remains. Finally, at six or seven in the evening, or whenever the complaints, donations, and sorrows stopped for the day, Jane Hoge and Mary Livermore rode a streetcar to their home and the "cheerful companionship" and "thoughtless gaiety" of their children.[55]

By spring of 1863 the commission was so well organized that it was able not only to continue its work for the wounded but also to launch an ambitious new program. In February, Jane Hoge visited General Grant's army in Mississippi. Camped in low, swampy terrain, the Union battalions had been reduced by disease to one-third their original number, and the twelve thousand men on the sick list lacked nutritious food and good water. Sanitary Commission agents began a campaign to improve camp hygiene, while Jane Hoge launched a drive to secure fresh fruits and vegetables for the soldiers. Scurvy, a disease caused by a lack of vitamin C, further threatened Grant's men. From Chicago, the Sanitary Commission sent out the following dispatch: "Rush forward anti-scorbutics for General Grant's Army." Affiliates throughout the region scurried to meet the emergency.[56]

The army had tried and failed to secure vegetables for its men. March was a difficult month in which to get products from the countryside. Spring rains rendered roads all but impassable, and little produce was available in Illinois and Michigan due to a severe drought the summer before. Crops had been better in Wisconsin and Iowa, and it was there the commission turned. Cabbage, potatoes, onions, horseradish, and pickles were gathered for Grant's men. "The aid societies gave themselves up to the occasion," a Sanitary Commission worker wrote, "Regular meetings, extra meetings, and canvassing expeditions filled up the time. . . . These gatherings were, with ready tact, seized and made useful for the packing and forwarding of the onions and potatoes, and for the preparation of the sauerkraut and horse radish." So thorough was the commission's collection of vegetables that almost the entire supply of such products was acquired. By July 1863 the Chicago depot had shipped 18,468 bushels of vegetables and 61,056 pounds of dried fruit. Some of these went to Grant's troops and the rest to the Army of the Cumberland.[57]

—————◇—————

The success of the Sanitary Commission was not limited to aid for troops at the front. By the summer of 1863 the commission had an impressive system of services in place in Chicago: it helped care for wounded soldiers recuperating in the city's hospitals, and it also established a shelter for men in transit. The Soldiers' Rest provided every soldier in need with a temporary bed and a meal. For men who were too ill to travel and who had nowhere to go, a more permanent Soldiers' Home was founded in July 1863. For a time, both functions were technically housed in the same facility, but the demands on the Soldiers' Rest were so great that most meals were served in the basement of Bryan Hall. There whole regiments could be served dinner at one time.[58]

—————◇—————

In the corner of Dwight Moody's office in the YMCA was a bushel filled with playing cards. He kept those symbols of dissipation as a graphic reminder of the success of his mission to the soldiers of the Civil War. Moody was an important member of the United States Christian Commission, a rival of the Sanitary Commission. The Christian Commission was born in November 1861 through the leadership of the YMCA. While it was concerned about the physical condition of the soldiers, its principal focus was their spiritual welfare. Eventually the Christian Commission directed hundreds of local committees and over five thousand field agents stationed with Union forces.[59]

The Christian Commission shared with the Sanitary Commission a belief that a good soldier was a virtuous and temperate man. As historian Gerald F. Linderman has recently pointed out, Americans of the Civil War era linked nearly all aspects of character: "One could not be virtuous in courage and unvirtuous in other aspects of life." Christianity, which stood at the heart of middle-class morality, was seen as an indispensable element in the character of a good soldier. A soldier who was undisciplined, cowardly, and quick to complain was also believed to be un-Christian. Mary Livermore found one such man during a tour of a St. Louis military hospital. She and Jane Hoge had seen many men quietly enduring horrible wounds. Yet here was a young man suffering from a stomach wound and an amputation who cried and complained loudly. "I ain't fit to die. I have lived an awful life, and am afraid to die. I shall go to hell." Mary sat down by him and in a scolding tone said, "Stop screaming. Be quiet. If you must die, die like a man, and not like a coward." She then reminded the boy of God's saving love. Later a Methodist minister arrived and sang the boy a hymn. Mary saw the "burden" roll "from the poor boy's heart." He turned to the minister and said, "It's all right, chaplain! I will trust in Christ! God will forgive me! I can die now!"[60]

Although Sanitary Commission workers like Mary Livermore believed in the link between Christianity and courage, there were deep differences of method and philosophy between the two relief organizations. While the Sanitary Commission was dominated by mainline, liberal Protestant churches, the Christian Commission was essentially an evangelical crusade, and put more importance on the soldiers' spiritual welfare. At Shiloh, Chicagoans of both groups tried to cooperate, but the differences caused a certain amount of tension. On the railroad journey from the city, Dwight Moody led the evangelicals in a prayer meeting, while at the rear of the car some of the Sanitary Commission workers played cards. Later, as the hospital boats neared the battlefield, a joint service was held for the entire relief team. Moody "exhorted his hearers" to attend to spiritual as well as medical wounds. "Many of them have doubtless been wicked men," he said, "but you can, at least, remind them of divine mercy, and tell them the story of the thief on the cross." These words angered Robert Collyer, a Unitarian minister, and he quickly came forward. "I cannot agree with the last, brother," he said. "I believe we shall best serve the souls of our wounded soldiers by ministering, for the present, simply to their bodies. For my own part, I feel that he who had fallen fighting for our country—for your cause and mine—is more of a man than I am. He may have been wicked; but I think room will be found for him among the many mansions above." These words were greeted with "a hearty, spontaneous clapping of hands" by the Sanitary Commission workers.[61]

Dwight Moody and Benjamin F. Jacobs began the work of the Christian Commission in Chicago. Jacobs was a lay Baptist who worked with Moody in the Sunday School movement before the war. In May 1861 they began to organize prayer meetings for recruits at Cottage Grove. The successful services soon became a regular feature of camp life, prompting Moody and Jacobs to enlist the aid of the YMCA. In time they were able to offer eight to ten prayer meetings a day during the week, while on Sundays the services were "almost continual." In October, when outdoor meetings became difficult, the YMCA built a camp chapel. Later, when the Christian Commission was founded, Moody and Jacobs affiliated with that group, and John V. Farwell, Moody's patron, became Chicago's representative on the executive committee of the national organization. Moody and other evangelicals received a warm reception from some soldiers. The Chicago Dragoons, eventually part of the 12th Illinois cavalry, went to war determined to remain strict Christian soldiers. When the unit was invited to a theater benefit to raise funds for their equipment, the men unanimously voted to reject the offer and held a prayer meeting instead. Moody and the YMCA stepped in and helped provide equipment for the Dragoons.[62]

For Dwight Moody, war work with the Christian Commission was a critical phase of his life. He would go on to become one of the giants of evangelical revivalism and a major figure in American religious history. But in 1861 he was scoffed at by most Chicagoans as a religious crackpot. While he would boldly accost strangers with, "Are you a Christian?" and he was the master missionary to the city's street urchins, he was shy about formal preaching to adults. He lacked the scriptural training of the ordained minister. His early attempts to speak on religious topics in Congregational circles were discouraging failures. Even friends in the YMCA admitted that, in 1861, Moody was "a young man with more zeal than knowledge." The war thrust him into the role of a minister; he felt a fearful urgency in his work with wounded soldiers and his prayer meetings with men on the eve of battle. The troops were receptive to his unvarnished sermons and fortified Moody's natural inclination to focus on the immediate individual acceptance of Christ.[63]

After the hotly contested battle of Stone's River in December 1862, Moody worked as a Christian Commission nurse. The medical teams were hard pressed to deal with room after room of suffering soldiers. "For two nights I had been unable to get rest, and after being really worn out, on the third night I had lain down to sleep," Moody later recalled. "About midnight I was called to see a wounded soldier who was very low." The tired evangelist tried to put off the request, but the messenger said the man would be dead by morning. So Moody lit a candle and made his way to the proper ward. The wounded man asked Moody to "help him die." He had never been religious, but he knew he was near death. Moody tried preaching the Gospel, but after each passage the man only shook his head and said, "He can't save me; I have sinned all my life." Finally, Moody read the passage, "Whosoever believes in Him should not perish, but shall have eternal life." Immediately the wounded man became animated. "Is that there? . . . I never knew that was in the Bible." Three times he asked Moody to repeat the passage, which he then memorized. Later that night the soldier died, quietly, calmly, repeating the Gospel passage. To Moody, the incident was a powerful example of practical Christianity at work.[64]

When the war broke out Moody agonized over whether he ought to enlist. Seventy-five members of his Sunday School joined the army, most in that first flush of enthusiasm in 1861. "I felt that I could not take a gun," Moody explained, "and shoot down a fellow being." He did, however, become a constant and popular visitor to the troops in the field. He campaigned against drinking and convinced men to exchange their playing cards, which were linked by the evangelicals with gambling and drinking, for hymnals. After a visit by Moody to the 19th Illinois, one soldier wrote, "Many of the boys have signed the temperance pledge and commenced to lead a different life." The men of the 19th liked Moody so much that they asked him to become their chaplain; but he neither wanted his work restricted to one regiment nor did he want to abandon his Sunday Schools in Chicago.[65]

There were soldiers who regarded the roving ministries of Christian Commission agents such as Moody with suspicion. Clergy who appeared pompous and self-righteous did not fare well at the front. In 1863, Mary Livermore unwittingly interrupted a young Chicago soldier's mimicry of a preacher.

> The men were standing or sitting in a body, and a chaplain was delivering an address, or preaching a sermon. As I listened he seemed to be setting the sins of his audience before them in a manner that savored more of frankness than tact, and he was exhorting the men to repentance. The boys, however, seemed to enjoy the recital of their shortcomings and sins . . . and frequently assisted the preacher's memory to facts which he had forgotten, or did not know, suggesting peculiar punishments for them, all of which was immediately adopted into the discourse. I thought the interruptions of the soldiers needless and profane. Little as I sympathized with the queer exhortations of the chaplain, I tried to infuse into my manner an expression of reverence, that would rebuke the wild fellows. The service was brought to an abrupt close by one of the men shouting out, "I say, Harry, you'd better wind up your gospel yarn, and see who's behind you!"

Only then did Livermore realize the speaker was "an irrepressible wag." Although she herself was a minister's wife, she had to admit the mimicry was "perfect," and she joined the soldiers' hearty laughter.[66]

Moody was not mocked by the troops, because he seemed to practice what he preached. "The secret of Mr. Moody, both here among the soldiers and at home," a Chicago soldier wrote, "is that he makes a personal application of the Gospel truths to those whom he meets, and living a life devoted to his master, his advice and example convinces and converts." Through the activities of Moody and others of the Christian Commission, revivalism became an important part of army camp life, particularly among the Army of the Cumberland.[67] In September 1863, those men were defeated in the bloody battle of Chickamauga and besieged in the city of Chattanooga. The beaten and hungry troops barely hung on to the city. By fall, U. S. Grant arrived as their new commander. Among his orders was the directive that Christian Commission agents be given free and unobstructed access to the troops. A revival swept through the ranks, and the enthusiasm of the army was resuscitated by religious zeal as well as by supplies and reinforcements. The rebirth of the army was climaxed by the spectacular storming of Missionary Ridge. Twenty-three thousand soldiers were ordered to attack the formidable center of the Confederate Army. When they reached the base of the ridge, however, their enthusiasm overran both Grant's orders and common sense, and they charged ahead. Among the troops was the 19th Illinois, the Chicago Zouaves, which Moody had earlier visited. The unexpected assault completely routed the rebels and opened the road to Atlanta. A War Department observer wired Lincoln that the victory was one of the "greatest miracles in military history," made possible only by the "visible interposition of God." A reporter for the *Chicago Evening Journal* claimed that after the battle, Missionary Ridge seemed to ring with the anthem "Give Thanks to the Lord."[68]

Military historians tend to credit the victory more to the poorly positioned defenses of the demoralized rebel army than to the effect of a revival among the Union forces. Yet, for the Christian Commission, it was an example of the power of Christ mobilized for the Union. They were proud to proclaim, as did a veteran of the Battle of Chattanooga, "I have been an instrument of Almighty God."[69]

The Fourth of July 1863 was one of the quietest in memory. Children, of course, could not be restrained from lighting firecrackers, but there were no official fireworks displays, no parades, and little celebration. Chicago was filled with apprehension. Robert E. Lee had invaded Pennsylvania; Grant continued his protracted siege of Vicksburg. In lieu of a formal celebration many families packed picnic lunches and enjoyed a railroad excursion to Evanston or other suburban environs. The only important gathering in the city was the opening of the Soldiers' Home. The Sanitary Commission managed to raise enough money to buy the ramshackled Mansion Hotel, a relic of Chicago's log-cabin past. After much cleaning and repair, the shelter was ready for a gala opening.

The ladies of the commission invited three hundred soldiers from Camp Douglas and wounded men from the city's hospitals to be their guest at the opening. All morning long, omnibuses discharged their cargoes of wounded veterans, and the men were helped into the dining room, gaily decorated with red, white, and blue bunting. Just as a dinner of "home victuals, such as they did not often get" was laid before the men, news was received from Gettysburg. Cheers and songs greeted the news that the rebels had been checked. Two years of war had taught Chicagoans to be leery of preliminary reports of victory, but this report sounded authentic. To the women of the Sanitary Commission, news from Gettysburg was seen as a good omen for the new Soldiers' Home.[70]

The opening of the Chicago Soldiers' Home severely taxed the already depleted financial resources of the Chicago Sanitary Commission.

The spring antiscurvy campaign had cost the commission more than $42,000. As the number of wounded from Vicksburg mounted, the commission's agents called for more supplies from Chicago—supplies the commission was not in a position to send. Even the Soldiers' Home would not have been possible that summer had it not been for the women of the commission. Their volunteer labor helped to transform the dreary old hotel into a pleasant shelter, while their strawberry festivals helped to attract the financing for the building's expenses. When the Chicago Sanitary Commissioners met in mid-July to discuss the financial crisis, it was these women who proposed the solution.

"Languidly," the male officers of the commission approved of Mary Livermore's and Jane Hoge's plan to hold a fair to raise funds. Most towns in the North had sponsored fairs and festivals to raise funds for hospital work. Livermore and Hoge had arranged one in December 1861, and fairs had proved useful in raising money for the Soldiers' Home. The men of the commission responded unenthusiastically to the suggestion because they wanted to raise thousands of dollars; fairs garnered hundreds of dollars at best. They "laughed incredulously" when Livermore declared that a fair could raise $25,000.[71]

With the sound of that laughter ringing in their ears, the women set about planning their fair. Livermore and Hoge envisioned something more than a local social event; they wanted a giant fair, held in Chicago, and supported by all of the branch commissions in the northwestern states. To build support for the idea they held a mass meeting of Chicago women in Bryan Hall, and an executive committee was appointed, which included women from every major religion in Chicago—Protestants, Jews, and Catholics. This committee issued circulars calling on the women of the Midwest to join in a convention in Chicago on September 1 and 2. The three hundred best educated and most energetic women in the region gathered at this second meeting. The first evening took place in the parlors of the Tremont House, allowing the delegates a chance to meet informally and form acquaintanceships. The next day, in formal session, the women's convention focused on what would be required of each participating community. The fair, it was determined, would raise money largely by selling donated products. Therefore, numerous donations of highly desired items must be obtained. So that "all classes" might be represented, the fair would have items to sell for as little as a dime and as much as a thousand dollars. After a round of patriotic speeches that, according to one eye witness, "kindled a flame in the hearts of the women," delegates returned to their communities determined to make the fair a success.[72]

Immediately after the convention Hoge and Livermore disseminated twenty thousand circulars listing the items most desired for the fair. Out of the Chicago offices of the Sanitary Commission flowed a steady stream of correspondence pleading for the support of governors, generals, legislators, teachers, ministers, and, in particular, women. This alone was a mammoth task in the days before computerized mailing labels. In just one day seventeen bushels of mail were sent from the Sanitary Commission headquarters.

Jane Hoge journeyed to Philadelphia, her birthplace, and Pittsburgh, where she had many friends, to organize women in support of the fair. Former new Englander Mary Livermore took Boston under her wing. Soon the Chicago headquarters was swamped with express deliveries of such incongruous items as Oriental fabrics and art sent by international merchants and breech-loading steel canon, sheets of iron, and kegs of carbon oil from Pittsburgh's manufacturers. The rush of such costly and exotic wares into the headquarters awoke the men of the commission, in particular, and Chicago, in general. In became clear that the women had started something great, and "fair mania" soon overcame men as well as women of the city. Potter Palmer, six years away from building the first Palmer House hotel, but prospering as owner of one of the forerunners of Marshall Field's, used his connections with New York merchants to obtain nearly $6,000 worth of merchandise for the fair.[73]

The massive donations sent to the Chicago fair were a reflection of the resilient war spirit and the remarkable prosperity of the North. "What a marvel is here!" a Pennsylvania soldier wrote, "something new under the sun! A nation, from internal resources alone, carrying on the most gigantic war of modern times, ever increasing in its magnitude, yet all this while growing richer and more prosperous!" The northwestern states shared in this prosperity, and in every town of any size there was a Sanitary Commission fair committee organized to collect donations. "One after another," Mary Livermore recalled, manufacturers came forward with their "mowing machines, reapers, threshing machines, corn planters, pumps, drills for sawing wheat, cultivators, fanning mills—until a new building, a great storehouse, was erected to receive them."[74]

The week before the fair found the Sanitary Commission absolutely deluged with donations. Hoge and Livermore had to contend with stables full of beef cattle, oxen, and horses. Fortunately, they received wagons loaded with hay, oats, and grain. While they were uncertain about what to do with several boats loaded with rubblestone, they knew exactly how to arrange the donations of pianos, china, and perfume. The gift they prized the most came from Washington, D.C. Abraham Lincoln sent the original manuscript of the Emancipation Proclamation. "I had some desire to retain the paper," he wrote, "but if it shall contribute to the relief or comfort of the soldiers, that is better."[75]

The most vexing problem concerned the massive amount of manufacturing equipment that had been received, from steam engines to threshing machines. Such large, bulky equipment would have crowded all other items out of the available space in Bryan Hall, the main fair building. Livermore and Hoge decided to have a temporary exhibition center for the machinery, so workmen were ordered to build a Manufacturers Hall behind Bryan Hall. The tradesmen, at first, refused to work, because the building contract had been signed by two women. They contended, correctly, that Illinois statute stipulated that a married woman needed her husband's signature on a contracted agreement. Livermore, in particular, was outraged, but she obtained his signature and vowed to change the demeaning legislation.[76]

The fair was set to open on October 27, 1863, and a grand inaugural parade was initiated to rally every ethnic and religious group. Hours before the parade the streets were packed by people dismissed from work by their patriotic employers. Near the head of the procession was a carriage filled with Confederate battle flags, "the flaunting rags which the rebels had borne on many a battlefield, and which our braves soldiers had torn from the hands of their standard bearers." The crowds cheered each division of the parade, particularly the marching bands. Popular, too, were several omnibuses filled with children waving small American flags and singing "John Brown's body lies a-molding in the grave!" The loudest cheer was given the carriages containing the crippled and maimed convalescents from nearby military hospitals.

Wheeling into line with the rest of the parade were more than a hundred wagons driven by Lake County farmers. The first of the wagons bore a banner that read: "The Gift of Lake County to Our Brave Boys in the Hospitals, through the Great Northwestern Fair." Behind that wagon rolled a succession of other wagons loaded with barrels of cider, potatoes, and other produce. The cheerful, motley procession snaked its way through the streets to the courthouse square, where the inevitable patriotic addresses were delivered. Finally, at noon, thirty-four cannons were fired, and the crowd, "like a tidal wave" surged into the fair buildings.

The first day of the fair was a tremendous success. "Such a sight was never before seen in the West upon any occasion, and we doubt whether a more impressive spectacle was ever presented in the streets of the Imperial City itself," the *Tribune* reported. "The vast procession of yesterday, with its chariots and horsemen, its country wagons and vehicles, its civic orders and military companies, on horse and on foot, with their various designs, and mottos, and brilliancy of color, converted Chicago, for the time being, into a vast spectacular drama."[77]

The fair was arranged around the courthouse square. Bryan Hall was transformed into an Oriental bazaar with scores of booths arranged in a semicircle. In the middle of the hall was a two story octagonal pagoda, the lower level of which was a sales booth, while the upper story featured a bandstand from which music emanated every afternoon and evening. Everywhere in the hall were seen the colors red, white, and blue. Flags hung from the ceiling, from arches, from doorways, and even the columns were entwined in patriotic bunting. The booths were stocked with needlework, silverware, and china. One booth boasted a pair of pianos from Root and Cady, another displayed the latest fashions in women's hats. All items were priced and marked with a card indicating the donor. Bargaining by visitors was discouraged by the words, "Buy for the sake of the soldiers!" These words Mary Livermore said "provided 'open sesame' " to purses and pockets. The lower level of the hall was converted into a giant dining room where as many as three hundred guests could be served at one time.

The Manufacturers Hall displayed and sold industrial wares. In the courthouse itself was the "curiosity shop" where trophies of war and tattered battle flags attracted much interest. Chicagoans were drawn in particular to the banner of the 19th Illinois, which was inscribed "Who'll save the left?" referring to the unit's brilliant defense at the battle of Stone's River. More poignant were the tattered flags of Wisconsin's famed Iron Brigade, which had absorbed the full fury of Lee's army during the first day of the battle of Gettysburg.

A gallery set up at McVicker's Theater, under the direction of Chicago sculptor L. W. Volk, displayed an impressive array of art work. Of particular note were an original Rembrandt and two paintings by Frederick Church of the romantic Hudson River school.

Metropolitan Hall, at the corner of Randolph and La Salle, was the scene of the fair's entertainments. Every night musicians, singers, and players performed for large audiences. The Detroit Sanitary Commission thrilled Chicagoans by staging a dramatic series of tableaus. The colorfully staged scenes depicted biblical and mythological incidents. Cries of "encore!" and enthusiastic cheers were lavished on several of the scenes, particularly the finale, "Liberty," in which the goddess of liberty, flanked by Union soldiers and sailors, sang the "Star-Spangled Banner."[78]

The most popular performer at the fair was neither musical nor dramatic, but a "young girl of not more than twenty summers," Anna Dickinson. She was the unlikely star of the eastern lecture circuit, where she appeared in lecture series with Ralph Waldo Emerson and Wendell Phillips. Before the war Anna Dickinson had been a Quaker school teacher with strong abolitionist leanings. Her outspoken abolitionism and eloquent pleas for a more vigorous prosecution of the war cost her a job in the

United States mint but won her an ever-increasing audience. Her impassioned lectures moved fans and critics alike. Prior to her arrival in Chicago, one critic armed with a pistol sought out the "Girl Orator." Fortunately his aim was as bad as his temper, and he only hit "one of [her] dainty black corkscrew curls." Such incidents made her more of a sensation; by the time she was booked for the Sanitary Fair her ticket sales far outstripped her $300 lecture fee. Metropolitan Hall was completely filled, even standing room, on the nights of her lectures. Her topic, the crisis of the Union, was not original, nor were the arguments she offered; yet, in the words of Mary Livermore, "she held an immense audience spellbound by her eloquence, now melting them to tears by the pathos of her voice and of her speech, and now rousing them to indignation as she denounced the enemies of the country, fighting against our armies at the South, or plotting treason at home."[79] The "Second Joan of Arc," as Chicagoans proclaimed Anna Dickinson, was able to earn $1,300, after all expenses were paid, for the Sanitary Commission.

Like many women who were active in war work, Anna Dickinson became a staunch advocate of women's rights after the war. She continued to be much in demand as a lecturer until 1866, when she became a popular actress and later a playwright and novelist. But the success Anna enjoyed in her youth abandoned her later in life. Because of eccentric behavior off stage, she was committed to an asylum. A sensational trial followed which, although it failed to find her mentally deranged, left her reputation forever ruined. During the many years before her death in 1932, she must have often thought of her celebrated appearances in Chicago when thousands were moved by her every word.[80]

The northwestern Sanitary Commission fair was a huge success. The halls were crowded from eight in the morning until ten at night. When the press of humanity became too great, the gates were closed, and prospective patrons were forced to wait for hours to get into the fair. Thousands came from all over, lured to the city by half-price rail fares and curiosity about what newspapers were calling the "Great Fair." Sales were brisk on virtually all items, from patriotic pin cushions to lottery tickets for a grand piano. Heavy equipment and breeding stock were auctioned off to the highest bidder, who was happy to pay more than the item's real value. The dining hall served meals to fifteen hundred people each day, the food prepared by volunteers who cooked roasts, pies, and stews at home and sent them via special express wagons to the fair, where they were reheated and served. Hundreds of ducks, turkey, and chickens were consumed each day. Hundreds of gallons of milk came each day from the dairies of Elgin, Illinois. The dining room was the most vexing logistical problem faced by "lady managers," but like the rest of the fair ran without a hitch. The Sanitary Commission fair gave nineteenth-century midwesterners a blend of the modern shopping mall and the traditional county fair, and they loved it.[81]

The scope of the fair and its smooth management drew tremendous praise for Hoge, Livermore, and the other women of the commission. They earned "the gratitude of thousands," the *Tribune* wrote. But the *Tribune*'s rival, the Democratic *Chicago Times* saw things differently, and accused the fair of being "scandalously partisan" in its conception and management. Such claims were supported by the suspicious scheduling of the patriotic festival at the climax of the county election, which was seen to ensure a Republican victory. Evidence of partisanship could be found in the fair itself. A steam engine, for example, was displayed with a sign identifying it as a donation from P. W. Gates & Company. Gratuitously added to the identification was the phrase "Not one copperhead in the whole institution." Anna Dickinson went out of her way to attack the Democratic party during her lectures. Of course, such carping observations were evidence of the *Time*'s own partisanship. While the Sanitary Commission fair was exhibiting the Emancipation Proclamation as an historic document, Wilbur Storey of the *Times* was demanding that the Supreme Court declare it unconstitutional. During the fair, the *Times* attacked the commission; the paper printed letters from soldiers saying they never received Sanitary Commission supplies or, if they did, they had to pay for them. In reply, the Chicago Sanitary Commission explained that the bulk of its aid was for wounded soldiers, and healthy troops may indeed have paid for some supplies labeled "Sanitary Commission," but only after they had been officially traded with army sutlers for goods needed by the wounded.[82]

The *Times* also questioned the integrity of the fair's managers. Calling the gala benefit a "magnificent abolitionist swindle," the Democratic press attacked the competence and honesty of the female managers. The *Times* dropped broad hints that Mary Livermore was misusing relief funds. Livermore was cast as a power-hungry woman whose motto was "Rule or ruin." The paper claimed that she and Hoge would use their "mighty power" to "crush all who dare assume the responsibility of saying anything derogatory to their respectability or Sanitary Commission transactions." Such attacks were potentially dangerous because, as the war progressed, raffles, benefits, and gift concerts for the aid of the soldiers became popular schemes for swindlers. Chicagoans grew leery of benefits that served only to line the pockets of their organizers. It was because of the Sanitary Commission's good reputation that the *Time*'s charges did little damage to the immensely successful fair.[83]

For two weeks the northwestern Sanitary Commission fair bustled with excitement. Donations continued to flow in, even after the fair opened, so when one stock of goods sold out, it could be replaced by another. It soon became clear that the fair would net more than the $25,000 that had been its goal. The Emancipation Proclamation alone sold for $3,000, purchased by Thomas B. Bryan, a failed mayoral candidate, who gave the document to the Solders' Home. Copies were lithographed and sold to raise more funds for the home. Later, the original document was given to the Chicago Historical Society. (Unfortunately, it was destroyed in the Chicago Fire.) When the final proceeds of the fair were counted, Hoge and Livermore reported to the chastened men of the Sanitary Commission that the fair had raised a staggering $86,000!

The fair cemented the working relationship between the Chicago Branch of the Sanitary Commission and the other midwestern relief organizations. In recognition of this, Chicagoans voted to change the name of their organization to the Northwestern Sanitary Branch. The fair also inaugurated a valuable new tool to raise funds for the troops. For the next year and a half fairs were held in rapid succession across the North. In Cincinnati, Boston, Brooklyn, New York, Philadelphia, Baltimore, St. Louis, and other cities, giant fund-raising fairs were held in imitation of Chicago's fair. Eventually, nearly $4.4 million was raised for relief of soldiers by means of these fairs. Sanitary fairs helped keep the Union Army strong and served to rally patriotic sentiment in the North. The *Chicago Tribune* described the opening parade of the Chicago fair as "a grand, sublime protest, on behalf of the people, against the poltroons, and traitors who were . . . opposed to the war." "I always knew that the heart of the people was right," said one old fellow who watched that parade. "They did not know their danger for a long while; now they have found it out, and this is what they say about it."[84]

The first sanitary fair had a long-term effect on the women who organized it. War work in general fostered a degree of independence and political engagement that was rare among antebellum women. Sanitary fairs proved to be training grounds for the postwar women's suffrage movement in Illinois. Myra C. Bradwell, who organized the war relics display, became a lawyer, editor of *Legal News*, and an advocate of women's rights in the legal profession. Anna Dickinson returned to Chicago in 1869 to decry the feminization of poverty and to demand equal rights for women. "What is wanted, is that women shall have a chance to do well-paid, as well as ill-paid work," she said on that occasion. "Women were never accused of abandoning their sphere, so long as they did servile and poorly paid work." Mary Livermore was buoyed by the success of the fair, but stung by the restrictions of the "laws made by men for women." She kept her vow to change the legal status of women and after the war became one of the country's leading suffragettes. The sanitary fairs helped to initiate a movement that would eventually transform American society.[85]

The fair closed on November 7, 1863, with a dinner for the wounded soldiers in Chicago. Six hundred men limped into the dining hall to the tune of "Brave Boys Are They." The women greeted them with a loud cheer, which soon broke down into a series of "audible sobs" as they saw the veterans make their way to their seats, some armless or legless, others blind, deaf, or emaciated. "I have not come here today to make a speech," said young Anna Dickinson in her greeting to the men, "but simply as an American woman out of full heart and with trembling lips to thank you." Looking upon their broken bodies she promised, "The future will do you more justice and better honor than the present, and history will emblazon your names upon its records forever as the grandest heroes of this most grand and memorable time." Meanwhile, the waitresses filled the tables with a wide variety of items: fish, turkey, game, soup, vegetables, followed by pies, puddings, ices, coffee, and tea. Even an after-dinner cigar was offered to each man.[86]

The officers responded to the fine dinner with speeches, while the enlisted soldiers gave "three cheers for Abraham Lincoln! A Diamond in the Rough!" and "three cheers for the ladies of the Northwestern Fair!" When the party broke up, the fair was finished. Hoge, Livermore, and the other women could finally relax their efforts. They had successfully concluded an enterprise few men had thought likely of prospering. But no sooner had the soldiers left the hall than two hundred young gentlemen from the business circles of the city "descended on the dining hall determined to treat the ladies, who had labored so hard for two weeks, to a dinner. Brooking no opposition, the young men bade the women rest for two hours, and then return for their treat."

The experiment in role reversal did not go well. When the women returned, the men were dressed in waitresses' white caps and aprons. The tables, one woman recalled, had been set in a "motley" manner, and the women braced themselves for "a frolic." Soon the waiters were running "hither and thither like demented men, colliding with each other, to the great damage of tureens and coffee urns, and the immense bespattering of the fair ones waited upon." The women shouted with delight at the clumsiness of their hosts. "Faster and faster ran round the awkward waiters," wrote Mary Livermore, "until at last the masculine attendants, whose caps had fallen on their necks, and whose aprons had got twisted hind-side-before, gave up in utter despair." Throwing themselves into chairs and benches, the men declared they were "completely tuckered out." If the ladies wanted anything else, they said, they would have to "help themselves."[87] The men of nineteenty-century Chicago were clearly not as ready for sexual liberation as the women.

5

$\diamond$

CAMP
DOUGLAS

W hile Chicagoans celebrated the success of the Sanitary Commission fair, the tide of war continued to ebb and flow. The heady successes of summer at Gettysburg in the east and Vicksburg in the west were followed by the escape of Lee's army back to Virginia and a bloody rebel victory at Chickamauga in September 1863. As fall gave way to winter, the conflict showed no signs of abating. The jetsam of civil war—sealed coffins, wounded men, and prisoners—continued to arrive at the Lake Michigan city with depressing regularity. Funeral notices in newspapers and uniformed men on the streets, many with empty sleeves or hobbling on crutches, were regular reminders of the war. However, the most persistent reminder, if Chicagoans needed one, was Camp Douglas.

The camp had been founded in 1861 as a training center for Union recruits. Following Grant's victory at Fort Donelson, it became a major prison camp for captured rebel soldiers. As a prison camp location, Chicago developed something of a notorious reputation among Southerners. Inevitably it was compared by some of its tenants with Andersonville or Libby prison, where thousands of Union prisoners suffered in ghastly squalor. Such comparisons were overdrawn. Neither in terms of overall mortality nor the brutality of its management was Camp Douglas as bad as Andersonville. Nonetheless, more than forty-four hundred Southern soldiers lie in Chicago cemeteries because of the poor conditions at Camp Douglas. More rebels died in Chicago than at the battles of Shiloh and Vicksburg combined.[1]

The city was less than an eager host to the defeated rebels. When rumors first surfaced that prisoners would be sent to Camp Douglas, many Chicagoans scoffed. The *Tribune* led the chorus of skeptics:

An Absurd Rumor—The rumor was prevalent upon the streets yesterday that orders had been received to put Camp Douglas in readiness
for the accommodation of five thousand rebel prisoners. This is decid-
edly *the* joke of the season. The idea of keeping five thousand prisoners in a camp, where the strongest guard couldn't keep in a drunken
corporal, is rich. The whole population would have to mount guard
and Chicago would find herself in possession of an elephant of the
largest description. If the authorities will give Chicago permission to
hang the whole batch as soon as they arrive, let them come.[2]

Editors Ray and Medill were more than a little red faced when a week later
the first trainload of Southerners arrived in the city.

Chicago was ill prepared for prisoners of war. There were few troops
to guard the rebels, so the Chicago police were pressed into service as
guards. The sixty-man police force was no model of efficiency, and many
Chicagoans feared for the safety of the city if that force was all that stood
between them and the rebels. Mayor Rumsey frantically wired General
Halleck that the city did not have the men to guard prisoners. "I have taken
these Confederates in arms from behind their entrenchments; it is a great
pity if Chicago cannot guard them unarmed for a few days," was his caustic reply. Rumsey ordered the police force doubled through the use of special volunteer constables.[3]

Fortunately for Chicago the wretched rebel prisoners were even less
prepared for escape than the city was for guarding them. Even before their
surrender, many were suffering from exposure to the near-zero-degree
cold at Fort Donelson. Chicago in February was no warmer, and the hungry, dispirited rebels were obliged to wrap themselves in old carpets, horse
blankets, ragged shawls, and scraps of cloth to fend off the cold. Escape
into the snow covered countryside offered few allurements to the original
prisoners of the camp. After several weeks of guard duty, the police turned
over Camp Douglas to Colonel James Mulligan and the paroled Irish Brigade.[4]

Chicagoans flocked to the camp to see Johnny Reb in the flesh. On
weekends in particular the streetcars were crowded with curious Yankees.
Initially, Colonel Mulligan was liberal with passes to the camp, and Chicagoans mixed freely with the prisoners, eager to engage the rebels in political discussions. Few people had an opportunity to hear what the average
Southerner felt about the issues behind the war. Most of the news they had
read in the years leading up to the conflict had been filtered through highly
partisan newspapers. Now the circumstances of war created "the rather
extraordinary spectacle at almost every hour of the day, of coteries of Illinoisans and Texans, loyal men of the North and rebel soldiers of the South

debating politics and abolition and aspects of the Negro question, without rancor."[5]

Among the prisoners were several former Chicagoans. An elderly woman frantically searched the milling crowds of Confederates for her son. The lad left the city five years before to "make his fortune" in the South. When she spotted him they rushed into each others arms. Tearfully she led the boy to the camp gate where her husband waited. As father and son embraced, the mother sobbed, "Oh, my dear boy, you have been the subject of many prayers, and you are not past praying for yet." The touching reunion induced camp authorities to immediately initiate steps to release the prodigal son. Much less sentimental was the reunion of John B. Miller with his former neighbors. Miller operated a soda fountain and later a saloon on Lake Street. When his whiskey sales faltered, he assumed numerous debts, then skipping town. Miller's sudden return to Chicago as the captain of a captured regiment was as unexpected as his departure. One by one his creditors descended on the camp. Although he was in no position to pay his debts, they could at least gloat over his confinement.[6]

Conditions at the camp degenerated as more and more prisoners arrived. At that time, Camp Douglas could accommodate about eight thousand prisoners. Local authorities had been told to prepare for seven thousand, but more than nine thousand men entered the prison in the wake of Fort Donelson. To make matters worse, many arrived in Chicago weakened by cold and fever. Within a week of their arrival, more than two hundred men flooded the hospital, while an additional three to four hundred sick prisoners languished in their barracks. Twenty-nine men had already died. A public meeting was held at Bryan Hall to raise funds to aid the stricken rebels. A city relief committee brought wagon loads of supplies to the camp. Colonel Mulligan hastily converted a horse barn to a second hospital, and Chicago doctors, including former Mayor Levi Boone, worked side by side with Confederate surgeons. The women of the city, led by those who had been born in Kentucky and Tennessee, prepared special delicacies for the stricken soldiers, and clothing drives brought in old coats, blankets, and bedding. Camp chaplain, the Reverend E. B. Tuttle, estimated that nearly $100,000 worth of clothing was given to the prisoners that first year.[7]

In spite of these efforts, the mortality rate at Camp Douglas climbed steadily. By April, more than two hundred rebels had died, and by June the number had climbed to nearly five hundred. Initially the principal problems were pneumonia and bronchitis, but as the weather moderated the sick list continued to grow. Increasingly the doctors found themselves treating patients with severe diarrhea. Some felt the cause of this might, in part, lie in the food rations of beef and bread, which were new to Southern boys raised on corn meal and bacon. But a more serious concern was apparent to those who had experience treating dysentery.[8]

Camp Douglas in the spring and summer of 1862 was covered with human excrement and garbage. Henry Bellows, one of the founders of the Sanitary Commission, was shocked by what he found; the very soil was reeking "with miasmic accretions, of rotten bones." The pools of standing water and urine were "enough to drive a sanitarian to despair." The number, the size, to say nothing of the drainage of the latrines were totally inadequate. As the dysentery spread, each latrine became a revolting scene of human misery. One rebel looked at the latrine behind his barracks and

> saw crowds of sick men, who had fallen, prostrate from weakness, and given themselves wholly to despair; and, while they crawled or wallowed in their filth, they cursed and blasphemed as often as they groaned. At the edge of the gaping ditches . . . there were many of the sick people, who, unable to leave, rested there for hours, and made their condition hopeless by breathing the stenchful atmosphere. Exhumed corpses could not have presented anything more hideous than dozens of these dead-and-alive men, who, oblivious to the weather, hung over the latrines, or lay extended along the open sewer, with only a few gasps intervening between them and death. Such as were not too far gone prayed for death, saying, 'Good God, let me die! Let me go, O Lord!' and one insanely damned his vitals and his constitution, because his agonies were so protracted. No self-respecting being could return from their vicinity without feeling bewildered by the infinite suffering, his existence degraded, and religion and sentiment blasted.[9]

On warm days the overflowing latrines filled the entire camp with a loathsome smell.

The camp's deteriorating conditions strained the good will that existed between captives and captors. The *Tribune* noted that where visitors to the camp once found the rebels open and friendly, "now they are upright, curt and belligerent." It was not uncommon for the prisoners to pelt an isolated sentry with stones or bottles. By the end of March a group of Tennessee soldiers were desperate enough to plan a sudden rush on the guard in an effort to achieve a mass breakout. A stool pigeon in their midst, however, notified Colonel Mulligan, and their plan was easily foiled.

Singly or in pairs rebels often tried to get out of the camp. On March 16, 1862, a Tennessee volunteer was detected as he tried to slip past the sentries. He was challenged and began to run. After a second warning, he was shot dead. Such incidents did little to dampen the interest in escape. James G. Blanchard, a Confederate corporal captured at Island No. 10, was among the irrepressible. In April he scrambled over the camp fence and made it into the city before being arrested. A month later he bribed his way out and just about made it to Canada before being retaken. Undeterred by these failures and confinement in the camp dungeon, Blanchard began to tunnel his way out. Unfortunately, his efforts were detected, and he was punished. Federal authorities were relieved when he was exchanged for Union prisoners and returned to the Confederacy.[10]

By July 1862, forty-five men had successfully broken out of Camp Douglas and managed to evade recapture. Like Blanchard, most escapees were easily retaken. Many headed for the saloons of Chicago and, by the time they were apprehended, were in no position to offer resistance. Others, particularly during the spring and summer, fled south to the marshes of the Calumet. Game was abundant in the vast wetland, and along its margins were small farms where eggs or a hen might be taken. Such an existence was only marginally better than camp life. Genuine escape, back to the South or to Canada, required luck and help, for dressed in butternut and rags, escaped prisoners were easily spotted. On April 4, 1862, several city aldermen were out hunting ducks in the Calumet marshes when their dogs flushed two escapees. The aldermen immediately identified them because of their "Dixified Appearance." But if a prisoner had money and a change of clothes his chances of avoiding detection were much improved.[11]

The press blamed Southern sympathizers for the frequent escapes from Camp Douglas. The *Tribune* was particularly shrill on this point. Those who tried to relieve the misery of the camp, particularly if they were known Democrats, were branded "rebel sympathizers." Only a day after the first prisoners arrived in Chicago the *Tribune* reported,

> a hack load of crazy and half-witted females astonished the camp by a harangue borrowed from Bedlam's, in which the astounded prisoners found themselves vigorously abused for not cutting their way out upon Cottage Grove avenue with their case-knives.

Even those whose sole motive was humanitarian did sometimes unwittingly help rebels to escape. One of these was Levi Boone, who had been given free run of the camp by Colonel Mulligan. The grand nephew of the hero of the Kentucky frontier, Boone felt a Christian duty to help the pitiful prisoners. He established a committee of Chicagoans who received money from Southerners and distributed it to the appropriate prisoners. Boone naively thought the funds would be used only to purchase supplies from the camp sutler, but in reality, many rebels bribed the guards into abetting their escape. Eventually, Boone was arrested, and he would have faced a stiff penalty had he not been a former mayor of Chicago and the father of a Union volunteer.[12]

Bribery proved to be significant in many of the early escapes from Chicago's prisoner-of-war camp. The men of the Irish Brigade were from the poorest sections of the city, and they were particularly vulnerable to offers of cold cash. Private William Temple escorted two rebels right through the front gate in exchange for a bribe. Other men merely looked the other way when on guard duty. Subtler forms of connivance were more difficult to detect. Suspicions fell even on Lieutenant Patrick Higgins, one of the Irish Brigade's officers. Eventually Colonel Mulligan ordered money to be kept from the prisoners. Even so, they were still able to pool financial resources for an occasional breakout. On July 23, 1862, rebels engineered a successful mass escape. Twenty-one men charged the camp wall and scaled their way to freedom on makeshift ladders, and several guards were suspected of looking the other way. Certainly Private Charles White (of the 67th Illinois) was involved in the plan. He left his uniform on the parapet and fled with the rebels.[13]

Discipline among the guard units was poor, and the Irish Brigade was particularly rambunctious. Off-duty soliders, unable to secure passes, eluded the camp guard to enjoy a spree in town. On one occasion a group of lads from the Irish Brigade returned to camp too well liquored to scale the fence. When the guard at the main gate tried to bar their entrance, a genuine donnybrook broke out. Only the timely arrival of sober reinforcements prevented the inebriates from dismantling the entire guardhouse.

On at least one occasion, alcohol led to tragedy at the camp. A drunken sentry from the Irish Brigade loudly proclaimed that he would "shoot a 'secesh' before leaving camp," but his fellow soldiers did not take him seriously until they heard a shot ring out. The drunk had pointed his musket into a crowd of Confederates and fired—wounding three men, one of whom later died. Colonel Mulligan and other camp officials tried to maintain discipline by publicly punishing men found drunk. Four or five drinking companions would be tied to a twenty-foot, two-hundred pound log and forced to drill all day on the parade ground. Although such punishment drills would go on for as long as ten days, they did not check the restlessness of the troops.[14]

It was Colonel James A. Mulligan who was held responsible for the camp's ghastly sanitary condition, the frequent escapes, and the discipline of his bored men. This was a heavy weight for the thirty-two-year-old lawyer whose leadership was more effective in active service than in administration. He was a caring individual who, because of his job, presided over the deaths of hundreds of helpless men. Mulligan organized the prisoners into work details to dig drains for the camp, but the project brought only a slight improvement. He took a personal interest in the hundreds of rebels languishing in the post hospital and helped to recruit Chicago doctors to assist Confederate surgeons. Father Thaddeus Butler, Irish Brigade chaplain who worked in the Camp Douglas sick ward, told a friend that Mulligan visited the hospital every day. Nevertheless, as one rebel later recalled,

> every morning the wagons came to the hospital and deadhouse, to take away the bodies; and I saw the corpses rolled in their blankets, taken to the vehicles, and piled one upon another, as the New Zealand frozen-mutton carcasses are carted from the docks!

Mulligan should have done more to improve sanitary conditions at the camp.[15]

The commander of the Irish Brigade did move to check disturbances and escape attempts among the prisoners. Acting on orders from William H. Hoffman, the Union's commissary general of prisoners, Mulligan attempted to collect the prisoners' money. Each man was to be credited for what was taken from him, and the camp sutler was instructed to honor drafts up to that amount. The system worked well for a time. But after Mulligan left the camp for the front, his successor found the prisoner's fund $1,450 short. What happened to the money was never explained. Mulligan was briefly arrested over this matter; indeed, the kindest thing that can be said about his handling of the fund was that he mismanaged it.[16]

Escape from Camp Douglas was retarded, if not stopped outright, by the control of money in the prison. For those who persisted in their attempts Mulligan designed a special dungeon, or cooler. According to a *Tribune* reporter:

> It consists of a building in the shape of a cross, of about 25 superficial feet in each direction. The first story walls are blank. . . . there is not a window, door or hole to be seen. The second story is fitted with a guard room, and from this hatches open to the room below. By a ladder . . . prisoners are lowered through the hatchway, and are left in that dark hole to amuse themselves. . . . The place is not an attractive one, especially when occupied by over one hundred, with but barely standing room.

Malcontents of every stripe were sent to the cooler, or "white oak," as it was officially known because of the type of wood used in its construction. Bread and water were the usual rations in white oak. When Governor Yates's tour of the camp was marred by several rebels yelling, "Hurrah for Jeff Davis; and d__n the men who oppose him," the perpetrators were sent to white oak. Prisoners who threw rocks or snowballs also were sent to the dungeon. "Nothing so readily takes the starch out of these 'rampageous secesh,' " the *Tribune* noted, "as a dose of 'white oak.' "[17]

Although Mulligan was not especially competent at Camp Douglas, he was by no means a tyrant. Early in his tenure at the Camp he had good rapport with the prisoners. In April 1862 the government transferred 821 prisoners from Camp Douglas to a prison camp in Madison, Wisconsin. As the train left the depot, the rebels, according to the *Chicago Times*, "arose and gave three cheers for Col. Mulligan so well satisfied were they with the kind of treatment they received at his hands." Mulligan was a natural leader and had the ability to relate well with men of all ranks. He was no professional soldier but a lawyer and politician familiar with the nod-and-a-wink Irish-American approach to rules and regulations.

During the spring of 1862 Mulligan participated in the courts martial of several Mississippi soldiers. The men were prisoners at the camp when a group of wealthy Chicago women arrived with a wagon of gifts for the inmates. The soldiers admitted that they stormed the wagon and plundered it as quickly as possible. When the women appealed to their "Southern honor" and asked them to stop, they replied, "Hang your honor" and continued to grab packages. Finally, the women tried to ward off the swarm of rebels with curses and blows. But the raiders did not desist until the entire wagon had been emptied. As Mulligan listened to the testimony of how the women were then driven from the camp under a hail of snowballs, he doubled up with laughter. The presiding adjutant tried to restore the dignity of the court, but Mulligan continued to laugh so hard, in fact, he fell from his chair. For Mulligan, the incident, while certainly a breach of discipline, was too ludicrous to take seriously.[18]

Mulligan and the Irish Brigade were relieved of their task as jailers in June 1862, and sent to West Virginia, where they spent two years in intermittent combat with rebel guerrillas. In July 1864, Mulligan attempted to block a rebel army marching up the Shenandoah Valley toward Washington. In a hard-fought delaying action, Mulligan was mortally wounded. His men tried to carry him safely behind Union lines, but he was reported to have ordered them, "Lay me down, and save the flag."

The colonel was captured by Jubal Early's forces and tended to by rebel surgeons. His wife frantically tried to reach him, but by the time she reached the Confederate camp her husband's life had ended. She tearfully brought his body back to Chicago, a city draped in black for its Irish hero. Poems were issued in his memory, and resolutions were passed by the city council and the bar association. George Root, moved by Mulligan's last words, wrote a new song in his honor, "Lay Me Down and Save the Flag," which enjoyed enormous popularity in Chicago. Such adulation was little consolation for the colonel's wife. Not only had she lost her husband in the battle, but her nineteen-year-old brother, an officer in the Irish Brigade, was also killed trying to rescue Mulligan. At the memorial mass at St. Mary's, she collapsed in her pew. That afternoon she composed herself and with her three young daughters dressed in black at her side, she trailed her husband's casket, stone-faced and stoic, as the procession escorted Mulligan to Calvary Cemetery.[19]

Camp Douglas continued to fascinate Chicagoans during the summer of 1862. Young people flocked to the camp on Sunday afternoons, not that there was a lot to see at the prison camp: the army had reversed its liberal pass policy, and access to the camp was no longer easily obtained. But it was possible to stroll around the camp and look at the wooden walls that contained the horde of butternut-clad fiends. For most visitors to Camp Douglas, a reporter later recalled, "it was enough that the place brought them in imagination in contact with something resembling the seat of the war." For those who wanted a closer look, there was the option of digging into their pockets and paying for the privilege of climbing to the top of a fifty-foot wooden observation tower, built by a shrewd Yankee. Few parents could resist the incessant entreaties of their children or their own curiosity about the enemy. From atop the platform the gaping, sometimes gloating, spectators could see the entire camp.[20]

From the tower the excursionists could see that the camp was divided into discrete sections. Immediately before them was the sand-covered parade ground; a large flag pole in the middle was flanked by one-story barracks that housed the camp garrison. Adjacent to the barracks was the hospital, a large two-story white-washed wood building. Most visitors looked past the hospital to the prison yard behind it, where a board fence about fourteen feet high separated the prisoners from the rest of the camp. Guards walked outside the wall, atop a raised platform, and sentries were posted every 120 feet. Several large lamps dotted the top of the wall to ensure visibility at night. Visitors looked for the "deadline," a low railing, thirty feet from the fence. Any prisoner crossing that line was assumed to be trying to escape and was shot by the sentries. Well behind the deadline milled hundreds of rebels. In summer they loafed about the dusty camp in homespun butternut shirts or tattered gray tunics. During the colder seasons they covered themselves with rags and blankets. The Confederates lived in one-story frame barracks about ninety feet long and twenty-four feet wide. Approximately forty-eight barracks were arranged along narrow streets.[21]

The actual number of rebel prisoners varied from month to month. The great battles of the spring of 1862—Fort Donelson, Island No. 10, and Shiloh—sent a flood of defeated Confederates into the camp. When

Colonel Mulligan and the Irish Brigade left for the front, there were 7,850 prisoners in Chicago. The problem of caring for them devolved to Colonel Joseph H. Tucker. A year earlier he had been responsible for the establishment of the camp as a Union training center, and he briefly had charge of the camp when the first prisoners arrived. Tucker disapproved of Mulligan's haphazard management of affairs at the prison and immediately set about reforming day-to-day operations. It was Tucker who instituted the policy of recording the exact number of sick and dead prisoners. He also repaired the stockade fences and barracks roofs. However, his plans to improve the drainage of the camp were vetoed by U.S. Quartermaster General Montgomery Meigs as too expensive. Tucker's plans to increase the number of barracks were initially approved, but before the work had progressed far the order was countermanded.[22]

The army wanted improvements at the camp halted because of the signing of an exchange agreement with Confederate representatives. Neither side was prepared to care for large numbers of prisoners of war. When the summer campaigns of 1862 demonstrated that the war would not soon be over, interest grew in an agreement, or cartel, as it was called, to exchange prisoners. Privates were exchanged on a one-to-one basis, while officers were valued according to their rank. A lieutenant counted for only four prisoners, yet an enemy general would fetch sixty privates in return. During the later part of August the surviving rebel prisoners at Camp Douglas were gradually loaded on rail cars and sent back south. By September, only 150 sick men remained in the camp.[23]

While the niceties of nineteenth century warfare removed from Camp Douglas its burden of rebel prisoners, Colonel Tucker was confronted with the almost as difficult task of managing paroled Union soldiers. Parole was a curiously archaic custom of releasing captured soldiers so long as they promised not to participate in the war, at least until they were formally notified that they had been exchanged for paroled or captured opponents. The parole system was based on the honor principle. Once a man gave his word, regardless of the circumstances, he was bound to uphold it.

Parolees were in limbo. Early in the war, when paroles were granted by local commanders, troops such as Chicago's Irish Brigade could return home and assume light duties until their parole ended. But the army soon found that return to hearth and home made capture too attractive to dispirited soldiers. To discourage men from purposely falling into rebel hands, the government began to send paroled forces to camps of instruction for drill. The prisoner exchange agreement worked out with the rebel army further complicated parole. According to the cartel, paroled troops were forbidden to undertake field duties, including guard, police, or constabulary operations. Many soldiers interpreted this to mean they were not bound to obey any orders, and indeed, some officers felt it forbade them to give commands. By early October 1862, Camp Douglas was filled with almost nine thousand dispirited, insubordinate, paroled Union soldiers.[24]

Most of the parolees had been captured at Harper's Ferry by Thomas "Stonewall" Jackson during the Antietam campaign. Due to inept commanders, the entire garrison capitulated after only token resistance. In haste to rejoin Lee at Antietam, Jackson paroled the entire Union force. After a brief time in Annapolis, Maryland, most were shipped north to Camp Douglas, even though most of the men were from New York and Ohio, and one division included a regiment from Vermont. Their arrival in Chicago was as ignominious as their surrender. After enduring several days packed into cattle cars with no water, let alone toilet facilities, they were billeted in barracks still filled with the filth left by the wretched rebel prisoners. Indeed, the barracks were worse than they had been when the rebels occupied them. The cold October rain leaked through the roofs of some, while others were filled with rubbish. The grounds of the camp were mud interrupted only by pools of stagnant water. The luckiest troops arrived after the barracks were filled. They were bunked in barns and stables, where the reasonably fresh hay made a comfortable bed.[25]

Colonel Tucker was not prepared to handle the sudden influx of men. Food supplies were inadequate, and even those who were issued rations were unable to cook in the rain and mud. Many officers, after taking one look at the camp, found housing in the city. Without their restraining influence, there was little Tucker could do to prevent the enlisted men from making their own authorized forays into town. Soldiers with money were welcomed in saloons of the city. While orders for beer and whiskey were paid for, the men were free to help themselves to trays of food at the end of the bar. When their funds expired, they were out on the street, intoxicated and resentful, outraging shopkeepers and insulting women. Hundreds begged for bread in the streets. Some Chicagoans opened their doors to the pitiful parolees. Those denied food simply took what they needed. A group of soldiers entered a State Street produce market and brazenly made off with all the peaches they could carry. Another group forced their way into a home on 12th Street and smashed dishes and glasses in their quest for food.[26]

Only after several days of repeated disorders did Illinois troops and the Chicago police restrict the bulk of the men to the camp. This, however, only concentrated the disorder. The men wanted to be discharged and allowed to go home. When the *Chicago Tribune* published the terms of their parole, many ceased to perform all soldiery duties. The 9th Vermont, for example, was ordered to do guard duty, but the men refused. Only a detachment of the 93d Illinois with fixed bayonets coaxed them to obey. Fires began to break out at the camp, and one night an entire row of barracks were burned. Five days later three more went up in smoke and more than a hundred yards of the camp fence was torn down. When part of the fence was replaced, the troops ripped it down the next night. The camp was in a state just short of guerrilla war. During the day the men sullenly obeyed orders; at night they were difficult to control. One night riotous troops demolished the post sutler's store; another night, they destroyed the guardhouse. Night guards were pelted with stones, and windows were repeatedly broken. The nadir was reached when the 60th Ohio threatened to mutiny. Camp authorities had no choice but to arm the other paroled units and use them to restore order. There was considerable doubt about whose side the men would take, but at the moment of crisis, they obeyed their officers, and the Ohio volunteers were put under guard.[27]

Fortunately, most of the parolees did not stay long at the camp. The New York troops, which were among the most incorrigible, began to leave on November 20. Their parting gesture to Camp Douglas was to burn their barracks. By the beginning of December most of the paroled troops had been formally exchanged and reassigned to active duty. Two regiments of Vermont infantry, however, lacked political clout in Washington and remained unexchanged. They spent a dreary winter in Chicago fighting boredom, dysentery, and smallpox; fifty soldiers succumbed to the disease. When the 9th Vermont finally received notice that it was exchanged and therefore off parole, the happy news was accompanied by orders to remain at Camp Douglas as prison guards. In spite of this, the morale of the Vermonters improved as they were reissued weapons, and the men, once more, began to respond to their officers. General Jacob Ammen, the camp's new commander, was a strict disciplinarian, and this further improved the atmosphere at the prison.[28]

The Vermonters were needed for guard duty because of a new consignment of prisoners in January 1863. Rebels captured at the Battle of Murfreesboro and at Arkansas Post began to fill the prison. By the end of the month more than thirty-eight hundred were assigned to the dilapidated barracks. Mostly from Texas and Tennessee, the prisoners included a number of Cherokees and Mexican-Americans. Chicago evidenced little of the curiosity that swept the city when the Fort Donelson prisoners arrived a year earlier. When the prisoners detrained at Archer Avenue, only a small crowd gathered. Most were silent, although three Bridgeport toughs, filled with liquor and patriotism, began to harangue the wretched P.O.W.'s. "Every devil of them should be hung to the first tree," one of them shouted. Unfortunately for the home-front hero, he strayed too close to the Texans when he spoke, and the prisoners grabbed him and, before the guards could intervene, gave him a sound thrashing. The rebels had a more friendly greeting for the men of the 9th Vermont. Many of the Texans had been with Stonewall Jackson when the Vermonters had been taken prisoner. "Hello! old fellow—turn about fair play," joked the Texans, "we had you at Harper's Ferry, and now you got us here. Let's have some beer for old acquaintance sake."[29]

Certainly the arriving prisoners needed something to cheer them. The long journey from a winter battlefield, much of the way exposed to the elements, left many of them sick and weak. Short of overcoats, they used pins improvised from telegraphic wire to hold blankets or rugs about their shoulders. It was no wonder that eight hundred prisoners were under medical care when they arrived. A reporter watching their entrance into Camp Douglas noted, "There seemed a continued cough from one end of the procession to the other." Smallpox, which had been slowly taking its toll on the Union parolees, found the shivering Confederates easy prey. Within three weeks 260 men perished. The hospital was choked with nearly 400 patients, and many sick rebels languished in their barracks. "At this rate," a Union officer confided in a letter, "we shall have our responsibilities all under ground before the last of spring. . . . Early every morning the melancholy procession of four Butternuts, bearing a stiffen Butternut corpse on their shoulders, begin to go past my window, and it is kept up all day."[30]

So weakened were most of the rebels that there were few escape attempts. Those who left the prison did so in the undertaker's wagon. Each day a federal contractor arrived at the camp and picked up his load of pine coffins. He was paid $1.50 per burial. In a large account book he dutifully gave each coffin a number. He then drove his team to the government cemetery located in what is now Lincoln Park, where his men dug shallow graves, sometimes just barely covering the coffins. The undertaker, however, made sure the number of the grave was entered into the account book. Within a month of their arrival, 10 percent of the prisoners had made the journey to the cemetery. The mortality rate alarmed the Chicago Board of Health, which sent a team of physicians to the camp. The doctors were disturbed by the army surgeon's methods of treating smallpox. Victims were kept in the same wards as men stricken with other illnesses, thereby exposing them to the deadly virus. They recommended that a separate hospital be built for the smallpox victims, that the clothes of the dead be burned, and that the healthy prisoners be vaccinated as soon as possible. Even so the disease leapt the stockade walls and spread to the city. By mid-March there were five hundred cases in Chicago. Greater mortality was prevented only by the exchange of the rebels at the end of March.[31]

Federal officials were slow to learn from the high mortality rates of the first two contingents of prisoners at Camp Douglas. Hospital facilities remained inadequate and sanitation was wretched. Instead of making the needed improvements to the prison, army officials pondered whether to move the camp to a less exposed, better drained location. In the end nothing was done, which for several months appeared to have been the right decision. The prisoners were gone, and the number of Union troops being trained at the camp declined. Occasionally, wounded men from the front were sent to Camp Douglas, but for most of the summer of 1863, there was little activity at the camp. Then, on August 19, 1863, a new group of Confederate prisoners began to arrive in Chicago.

The new men were not the pathetic survivors of a winter campaign, but hardy veterans of one of the South's most infamous units, Morgan's Raiders. In July 1863 General John Hunt Morgan led twenty-five hundred Kentucky horsemen across the Ohio River and into the northern heartland. The raiders galloped through southern Indiana and across the state of Ohio, robbing banks, seizing horses, and skirmishing with Union troops. Gradually, the Yankee generals hemmed in the Kentuckians, forcing many to surrender and others to flee in groups of two and three across the Ohio River. Morgan himself was cornered near the Pennsylvania border. With 364 men he surrendered and was imprisoned in the Ohio State Penitentiary. Yet, by Christmas he was back in the Confederacy, having led a daring escape from the prison. Most of his men, however, were not so fortunate. After a brief stay at Camp Morton near Indianapolis, the raiders were sent to Chicago for internment. The press dubbed them "Morgan's desperadoes" and described them as "mostly . . . horse thieves and highway robbers." But they also had to admit that the Kentuckians were "picked men . . . far better looking . . . than any of the secesh prisoners we have had here before." They also would prove to be a far greater source of trouble than any of the previous inmates.[32]

From the moment they arrived, Morgan's men began to plot their escape. Their initial efforts were ineffective. Four or five prisoners would band together, charge the wall, and try to boost one another over. A rifle shot in their general direction was enough to cause the men to raise their hands and call for "quarter." More imaginative prisoners searched the stockade for blind spots, where sentries could not detect them; others tried to take advantage of drainage ditches to shield them from the sentries' view. In October two of the most daring Kentuckians crawled into a sewer eighteen inches wide and only two feet high. Even though it was nearly filled with water, they squirmed their way under the camp walls toward Lake Michigan. It took sixteen hours to make the journey in ice cold water up to their necks. Finally, they reached the mouth of the sewer and emerged free men. They must have been suffering from exposure to the water and the autumn air, for they made their way to the city, where they found it impossible to resist the lure of a warming drink of whiskey. One drink led to another and soon they both were drunk. Suspicious patrons of the saloon summoned the police, who managed to retake one of the two escapees. Other escapees were even less fortunate. Several were wounded by the guards' Enfield rifles. To curb further attempts the camp commandant ordered his men to shoot to kill, but this had little effect as a deterrent. White oak, the camp detention dungeon, remained packed with incorrigible Confederates.[33]

Sending the most persistent escape artists to white oak did not work to the Yankees' advantage. At any one time white oak was filled with the most desperate and imaginative rebels, what the *Tribune* called "the worst of the whole pack of rascals in the Camp!" Confinement to the dark dungeon on a ration of bread and water kept their desire to escape keen and allowed them plenty of time to discuss new schemes with their most talented compatriots. It is no wonder that the first major escape from Camp Douglas by the Morgan Raiders was engineered by the white oak men. They cut a hole in the wood floor, gained access to a drain, and dug a tunnel under the feet of the guard and past the camp stockade. They skillfully disguised their activities from the guards and timed their escape perfectly between one and three o'clock in the morning during a violent thunderstorm. Not until daybreak did the guards discover that twenty-five men had made their escape.[34]

The white oak break made tunneling the rage among the prisoners. In short order tunnels were initiated from several barracks toward the stockade wall. Such tunnels required excavations well over one hundred feet and required careful planning. The Kentuckians responded imaginatively. The tunnel from the barracks of the 8th Kentucky Cavalry was a thing of beauty. It was four feet high, two feet wide, and carefully timbered to prevent cave-ins. The main tunnel included several underground chambers, one which functioned as a subterranean carpenter shop, where timbering was cut from wood scrounged from about the camp, while another was a rest station, complete with a straw tick mattress where weary tunnelers could relax between shifts. By early November the main tunnel was within a few feet of the fence, and the men of the 8th Kentucky were full of anticipation.

Unfortunately for the prisoners, the camp commandant, Colonel C. V. DeLand, anticipated their escape. He may have been warned by an informant or his suspicions may have been aroused by their actions. DeLand knew someone was trying to tunnel out of Camp Douglas. What he did not know was who and where. His means of detection were as imaginative as the rebel tunneling tactics. He ordered the drainage ditch that ran along the edge of the stockade to be flooded. DeLand reasoned that if a tunnel passed close to the flooded drain, the water would inevitably leak down into the escape route. For several days he monitored the water levels in the drain. Then one day he knew his plan had worked. The drain was completely dry—a tunnel had been found. The prisoners were assembled but no one would reveal its location, so DeLand's men deepened the ditch until they struck a tunnel. At first the rebels were confused by the Yankee actions. But as the excavation neared the tunnel location, the rebels became increasingly uneasy. When the tunnel was discovered, the disappointed Confederates angrily tried to stop the guards. A volley of shots rang out, severely wounding three men and scattering the rest. Later that day Deland's diggers discovered a second tunnel. A Kentucky private remembered, "How detestable seemed our prison life after this. It was ten times as hard to endure it after having liberty so near within our grasp." That night the Camp Douglas prison barracks were filled with quiet, dispirited men.[35]

Yet the idle rebels had little to do with their time, so within days another tunnel was begun. For four weeks a group of conspirators alternated going below ground. They dug with floor planks and carried the dirt from the tunnel in bags made from shirts. The excess dirt was dumped under the joists of the barracks floor. They did not worry about Colonel DeLand's flooded ditch because cold weather froze the water. Finally the prisoners estimated that the tunnel extended past the camp wall. Carefully they began to make an exit hole, but the closer they got to the surface the harder the digging became. The December chill had frozen the ground. When they at last breached the surface, the prisoners discovered they were only a few feet past the wall. Extreme care would be needed to ensure that the sentries did not spot men exiting the tunnel. They established a relay system; prisoners waited until the guard on the parapet turned his back and walked the other way. Then several men scrambled out of the tunnel and dashed away into the night. As the sentry's round brought him back near the hole, the prisoners hid in the tunnel. The Kentuckians timed their escape perfectly. Seventy-eight men successfully fled the camp before the morning light revealed the tunnel.[36]

Within two weeks more than fifty of the escapees were recaptured and brought back to Camp Douglas. The red-faced federal jailers resolved to foil future "gopher" tactics by removing the floor boards from every barracks. That way the guards could spot tunnels during their daily inspections. Morgan's Raiders responding by abandoning tunneling and adopting what they called "opossum" tactics. Prisoners removed wooden slats from their bunks and hammered them into makeshift ladders. They would wait for a stormy night and scale the stockade wall. With a certain amount of luck four or five men could be out of the camp within minutes. Unlike tunneling, however, "oppossum" tactics involved greater risk of being shot and offered fewer men the chance of escape.[37]

Some prisoners had help from outside the camp to make their escape. Relatives of captured rebels frequently visited the camp to plead for their release or simply to deliver comforts. A new pair of boots, a woolen overcoat, or a home-baked pie were all valued presents from loved ones. Some packages, however, offered more than comforts and furnished the means to escape. Camp guards screened hundreds of letters and packages each day. Initially this job was not taken seriously. Prisoners were free to receive turkeys stuffed with greenbacks or cakes with knives baked in them. Occasionally even a pistol would make it through.[38]

Regular security sweeps netted many of the weapons, but the prisoners were ingenious at hiding money and putting it to use. Corruption among guards remained a problem. Several made a business of it—they discovered which prisoners had money by watching the sutler's store. Men making large purchases would be offered a way out of camp for $20. The prisoners would purchase civilian clothes from the sutler and be escorted out of the camp by one of the guards. Several Kentucky families visiting the prison got wind of this and collected $1,200 to get a group of young men out over a period of several weeks. At first the project went well. The guards escorted the first two prisoners right out the front gate. The boys were supposed to take the first train out of Chicago and hired a hack to take them to the depot. But they arrived late, so they went back to the Tremont House to spend the night. When the hackman charged them $4 for the fare they quite rightly thought they were being gouged, and they went to the police to file a complaint against the driver. The next morning, after receiving a refund in court, they cooly made their escape for Kentucky. Another prisoner let out on the same bribe was equally bold but less fortunate. He went straight to a saloon, got drunk, and shouted for all the world to hear who he was. Within hours of his escape he was locked behind the stockade. This particular bribery conspiracy came to an end when one of the men who made good his escape sent a letter written in invisible ink back to his comrades. The camp authorities suspected the letter and held it over a candle. In moments they knew the details of the escape. To prevent future episodes of this sort, Colonel DeLand prevented gifts to the prisoners from anyone but their families, and all money was deposited with the camp command.[39]

Conditions within the camp were no inducement for the rebels to remain. Some of the older barracks were unheated, their doors and windows broken and left unrepaired. After the floor boards were removed, the cheerless shelters became even colder and damper. Puddles formed in some units, and all were filthy. The new drainage system failed to keep the latrines from filling with human waste and impregnating the atmosphere with foul odors. This problem became more acute as more prisoners arrived from battles near the Cumberland Gap and Chickamauga. Fortunately, the camp did not become as overcrowded as it had during 1862, and the men who arrived in Chicago were much healthier than the earlier prisoners. Still, the death toll from typhoid, pneumonia, and measles climbed during the autumn.

In November a number of Southern newspapers ran stories describing the bad treatment Confederate soldiers received in the Northern prisons. Camp Douglas was mentioned specifically as a place where Southern soldiers were starving. At the same time Northerners were learning of the wretched state of their men in Richmond's Libby Prison and other Southern detention centers. Initially, the complaints of the Southern press were rejected out of hand. Union officials maintained that prisoners at Camp Douglas received the same food as their guards. After further complaints from Confederate authorities, Brigadier General William W. Orme, who was given charge of the prison in December, personally investigated the commissary situation in the camp.[40] Not surprisingly he discovered that the Chicago contractor who was paid to supply beef to the prisoners had been cheating. While most of the rations assigned to the rebels were delivered as ordered, the contractor shortchanged the rebels by as much as 40 percent of their beef. The camp command, it was discovered, never bothered to monitor the contractor. Colonel DeLand was brought before a court martial for that neglect. Lincoln himself became concerned with the scandal. The Camp Douglas contracts had been let by his old friend Ninian W. Edwards, who got his job as commissary of subsistence through Lincoln's influence. Lincoln wanted the affair dealt with quietly and quickly. The contractor was fined and forced to make up the shortfall with a cash donation to the prison fund. A new contractor was hired, and his deliveries were monitored by the army. The story provided a bit of ammunition for the war of words between the pro-Lincoln *Tribune* and the anti-administration *Times*, but within a few weeks it was forgotten.[41]

Five months later the government consciously chose to cut rations at Camp Douglas and other prisons in retaliation for the abuse of Union prisoners. The change of policy was the inevitable result of what one historian called the growing "war psychosis in the North." The Republican press grew increasingly hostile toward the South and Southerners. Illustrations of cadaverous Yankee prisoners draped in rags convinced many ordinary people that Secretary of War Stanton was right when he accused Southern prison camps of "a deliberate system of savage and barbarous treatment."

George Root, Chicago's great composer of war songs, drew even more attention to the plight of Union prisoners of war with his mournful ballad "Starved in Prison" and the even more popular "Tramp, Tramp, Tramp, the Boys Are Marching." The thought of rebels getting fat while the boys in blue languished, however erroneous, drove the North to reduce prison rations from equal to that of Union soldiers to equal that of the Confederate army.[42]

The reduction in rations was bitterly resented by the rebel prisoners because it came as part of a general program to tighten the security at Camp Douglas. The stockade walls were made stronger and higher, and barracks were raised and placed on posts four feet off the ground, ending any chance of tunneling. Access to the sutler was restricted, and men were forbidden to gather in large groups. "Our good times were fast drawing to a close," one of Morgan's Raiders later recalled. At the same time, hope of exchange had all but vanished. The South's refusal to treat captured black Union soldiers as prisoners of war forced Lincoln's government to end the prisoner exchange program. During the spring of 1864 officials at Camp Douglas were getting ready to hold their prisoners for a long time.[43]

Much of the new rigor at Camp Douglas was due to Colonel Benjamin J. Sweet, who became camp commandant in May 1864. His brief active service had ended in October 1862, when he led the 21st Wisconsin infantry in crossfire during the Battle of Perryville. In a matter of moments 179 men were killed or wounded. Sweet himself, hit in the elbow and chest, was disabled and stayed behind the lines thereafter.[44]

His wounds did not cool his ambition or reduce his penchant for discipline. Eager to make a name for himself, Sweet set about making Camp Douglas tight as a drum. Sentries were ordered to shoot at any prisoner out of barracks after taps. During the day, if more than three prisoners gathered together outside, the guards were ordered to shoot to kill. "We had to be very cautious in every act," a Tennessee volunteer recalled, "for the simplest and most innocent mistake would cost a man his life, or a severe wound." After dark, even within the barracks, the prisoners were ordered to be perfectly quiet and to stay in their bunks. If a guard heard talking from a barracks or saw a flicker of light or a man by a window, he fired his rifle in that direction. "Many a Minié ball went crashing through our barracks at night at some real or imaginary noise," one of Morgan's men later maintained. "It was dangerous, even to indulge in a snore." If it was necessary to answer the call of nature during the night the prisoner had to go half naked, regardless of the season, and not deviate from the outhouse or likewise be shot. While the tactics seem extreme, they were not unique among Civil War prison camps.[45]

There were, of course, a host of punishments short of being shot that

Colonel Sweet used to maintain discipline. As the months went by without an exchange, and the camp became more crowded with new arrivals, the new prisoners' patience with their situation began to erode. Minor breeches of camp regulations were strictly enforced in an effort to head off more serious trouble. The most common form of camp punishment was a ride on "Morgan's mule," a four-foot-long piece of lumber with four legs nailed to it, rather like a carpenter's sawhorse, except that it was ten or fifteen feet off the ground. A prisoner due for punishment would mount the "mule" with a ladder. After he straddled the narrow beam, the guards would tie a brick to each leg. After four or five hours on the four-inch board or "saddle" as the guards called it, a prisoner felt as though he were being cut in half. The punishment was painful but did no real harm, save in winter, when a sadistic guard might leave a man on the "mule" long enough to suffer from exposure or even frostbite.[46]

Another punishment drill was called "reaching for grub." Prisoners were ordered to bend over, keeping their knees straight, and touch the ground with their fingers. A prisoner recalled that after a half-hour or more of remaining in that position many "would fall over in the snow in almost insensible condition." Others would remain in punishment position until "the blood would run from the nose and mouth." On other occasions men would simply be marched into a foot of snow and ordered to remain at attention for an hour, or worse, be ordered to sit in the snow. More conventional and less injurious were the ball and chain, which cut down on the mobility of an escape-minded prisoner. A variation was to make a man slip a half barrel over his head and parade back and forth all day.[47]

Enforcing the strict new regimen at Camp Douglas were several companies of the 8th and 15th regiments of the Veterans Corp, made up of men who had been wounded in combat, weakened by disease, or otherwise judged permanently unfit and discharged from active duty. Like thousands of other Union soldiers, however, they still wanted to serve. The Veterans Reserve was a mechanism that allowed them to contribute to the war effort and free healthy men for combat. Because they were "true believers" in the Union cause as well as veteran troops, they tended to be better disciplined and less open to bribery than previous guards at the camp. Initially they were referred to officially as the Invalid Corp and given baby-blue uniforms. Field troops and stay-at-home street toughs made light of them as "half-soldiers." Most were kind and sympathetic to the camp's wretched inmates, but there were a handful who used their authority to humiliate and bully the defenseless men.[48]

The most infamous of the guards was William O'Hara, known to the prisoners as "Red Bill" or "Old Red" because of his red hair and fiery temper. O'Hara was a burly Irish bully who delighted in patroling the camp and personally disciplining the prisoners. O'Hara carried two large army pistols tucked in his belt, and there was little the prisoners could do but submit. His favorite punishment was to hang a man by his thumbs. The memoirs of former prisoners make note of his quick, violent temper. Kentuckian R. T. Bean claimed to have witnessed a brutal demonstration of this one winter afternoon. "One cold day he slipped and fell a real good, jolly fall," recalled Bean, "and a member of the 64th North Carolina standing near laughed. Old Red shot and killed him on the spot." Many of the other guards were out of sympathy with O'Hara's strong-arm tactics and occasionally refused to back him up. On his own, Old Red could be less than brave. On one occasion he physically assailed a prisoner who was rooting in a garbage can for something extra to eat. Unexpectedly, the prisoner counterattacked with a stout piece of board. Old Red immediately turned and ran for the guardhouse with the prisoner in hot pursuit. The rebels watched in stunned silence, expecting at any moment that the angry prisoner would "be riddled with bullets," but the other guards "were not disposed to interfere." O'Hara made it to the guardhouse safely and demanded that the officers there provide a guard so that Old Red could go back and arrest and flog the prisoner. The officers refused, although they did give him "permission to go alone and flog him to his heart's content, provided he would leave his arms at the quarters." This checked the bully for a time, because he dared not venture into a rebel barracks without guns and a guard.[49]

Eventually, Old Red's temper got the best of him. While on leave in Chicago he became drunk and abusive, and the saloon owner had him arrested. Reportedly, he swaggered into jail boasting of his physical prowess and the "tortures he had inflicted upon the Rebel prisoners." A fight soon broke out with another Irishman, and by the time the police separated the two men, O'Hara was mortally wounded by a knife. No tears were shed behind the stockade at Camp Douglas.[50]

Most of the guards were ordinary men, serving their country and hoping for the war to end. Prisoner John Copley recalled, "There were many guards and noncommissioned officers who were disposed to treat us strictly as prisoners of war, and as humane as their instructions and orders from their superiors would permit." R. T. Bean formed friendships with several of the guards. For this reason barracks inspectors were rotated every few months. Many prisoners worked with the guards as part of the camp staff and did much of the cleaning and clerking. Work was a welcome way to gain money and make the time pass.[51]

Baseball was popular during clement weather. Inevitably someone would hit the ball past the deadline, a line even the most determined outfielder would not cross. The game would have to be suspended until one of the guards would fetch the ball. Less active men played marbles on the sandy ground or quoits, a game similar to horseshoes. Card playing was particularly popular during the winter and in the evening. It was not unusual for several hundred dollars of Confederate money to be wagered on a single hand. Real gamblers played for rations; a big pot might include several hunks of bread or plugs of tobacco stacked in the middle of the table.[52]

The camp guard was careful to confiscate all obvious weapons, but they allowed the prisoners to keep pocket knives. Bored rebels put these to good use whittling. Some made models for their own amusement; others produced items that were sold via the guards in exchange for credit with the camp sutler. One man transformed a pine shingle into a fiddle, another made an ox bone into a clarinet. Eventually, a Camp Douglas band was formed, which entertained many Chicagoans. Pipes were among the most popular products of the whittlers. One soldier was so proficient at making meerschaums from corncobs that his barracks became known as "Lappins Factory."[53]

A handful of books circulated in the camp and were greatly appreciated by those who could read. Tennessean John Copley secured several books on mathematics, a subject of which he was woefully ignorant. With the help of a messmate who acted as his tutor, he learned algebra during his stay in camp. A couple of literary prisoners organized *Prisoner Vidette*, Camp Douglas's unofficial newspaper. Editor T. B. Ball founded the paper because of the "need of literary sheet of some description in our midst." It was not printed; copies were written out in longhand on sheets of paper. Brief articles were written by prisoners for prisoners (the camp authorities did not sponsor its production). The first issue announced a concert by "Morgan's Nightingales," a glee club made up of musically inclined prisoners. It also struck a defiantly unrepentant pose toward the war. "A casual observer, knowing us not as we 'are' but as we seem would unhesitantly pronounce us as contented and resigned to our fate," the editor wrote, "but we knowing best our own desires feel the loss of liberty, and each day brings with it a stronger desire to be free and in the field."[54]

———◇———

During July and August 1864 the success of Northern troops continued to net large numbers of rebel prisoners. Camp Douglas received another twenty-five hundred men that summer, raising the total to seventy-five hundred. During November and December an additional forty-eight hundred Confederates were sent to Chicago. With more than twelve thousand men in the camp, sanitary regulations had to be strictly enforced in order to prevent the awful sicknesses that had struck the camp in 1862.[55]

The camp grounds were kept perfectly clear of all trash; no human waste or animal bones were tolerated. Under Colonel Sweet prisoners were even prohibited from emptying dirty water in the street. The barracks were also kept clean. Prisoners swept the floors daily and scrubbed them each week. A few Southerners had a hard time adjusting to the rules against spitting tobacco on the barracks floor, but a two-hour ride on "Morgan's mule" served to enforce the regulation. The rebels were allowed to wash themselves and their clothes on any day, although Friday was the "official" day all men were required to see to their laundry and toilet. The wealthier prisoners hired someone else to do their laundry, which gave some men a chance to earn a little tobacco money. The prisoners themselves, anxious to ensure that their barracks passed the weekly inspection, forced all men to wash once a week. A prisoner suspected of being dirty was hauled before a mock court and tried for slovenliness before a jury of his peers. A convicted prisoner would be roughly scrubbed until his skin was raw and fined one or two plugs of tobacco.[56]

In spite of these improvements, a new hospital, and a new drainage system that kept the camp fairly dry, the death rate at Camp Douglas began to swell during the summer and fall of 1864. In August, 94 rebels died in camp; the next month the toll climbed to 123. "Life in prison was going from bad to worse," wrote R. T. Bean in his prison memoir. "Half-fed, cursed, kicked and abused for imaginary more than real misdemeanors, hope was dead and life an existence only that gave no promise of relief or escape." Low morale combined with scurvy to make things worse. "The scurvy broke out in a most virulent and aggravated form. Lips were eaten away, jaws became diseased, and teeth fell out." Camp rations were the problem. Salt pork had been substituted for fresh beef and vegetables. Colonel Sweet personally intervened to eliminate the hominy rations, which he claimed had been wasted. The prisoners were still given more food than many rebel troops in the field, but it was by no means a balanced diet.[57]

The post surgeon as well as Colonel Sweet were slow in reacting to the growing threat of scurvy to the camp. A delegation from the prisoners, led by a Confederate surgeon, tried three times to see Sweet before he finally heard their demand for anti-scorbutics. Within two days onions, potatoes, and vinegar were distributed. The scurvy, however, proved to be a mere stalking-horse for smallpox, which raged through the camp in its wake. Not a virulent strain of the disease, it had little effect on healthy men, but it took a heavy toll among the men who had been weakened by scurvy.[58]

The susceptibility of the prisoners to scurvy and their suffering from hunger varied greatly. Those men whose families were behind Union lines could maintain regular correspondence with their loved ones. They regularly received money which could be put on credit for them with the post sutler. R. T. Bean, for example, did not like the loaves of bread given to the prisoners, so he paid the sutler $5 to smuggle him a fifty-pound barrel of flour, which he used to bake biscuits for himself and his friends. When the barracks guard let it be known that he did not like camp bread either, Bean promised to provide him with biscuits if the guard would provide butter for the barracks. "Many a good meal we had together after that," recalled Bean, although "I could never convince him [the guard] that I would be a much better boy 'out' of prison than 'in.' "[59]

Hunger had its biggest effect on men who had gambled away a portion of their ration or traded it for tobacco. After the war some former inmates claimed the camp rations were "intolerable" and that they were "half starved." Certainly they were hungry much of the time, because they were fed only twice a day. The meat ration was given out each morning and cooked in large boilers by the barracks kitchen crew. After it was cooked it was handed out with one-third a loaf of bread. John Copley claimed his meat ration never weighed more than "four to four and a half ounces," and after cooking it had the consistency of "an old dish rag." The second meal came at one o'clock in the afternoon and consisted of another one-third loaf and a thin "soup" made from the boiling of the morning's beef ration with beans or potatoes added to it. The rebels would crumble a portion of their bread into the soup to thicken it and then reheat it on the barracks heater. This resulted in "a first rate meal of thickened hot water." With nothing more to eat the rest of the day, the prisoners naturally dwelled on the gnawing feeling in their empty stomachs. By evening the afternoon gruel had long since been digested and there was nothing to do but talk about prewar Sunday dinners at home, favorite pies, and fried bacon with cornmeal.[60]

Hungry rebels made canine life at Camp Douglas dangerous and short. Confederate veteran J. J. Moore claimed that several prisoners avenged themselves against Old Red by seizing his puppy and cooking it. Lieutenant Fife, for whom the prisoners had no particular grudge, also lost his pet. The "beautiful black terrier" was actually a favorite among the rebels who petted and often played with it. But one afternoon the men of one barracks were able to entice the dog into their kitchen, where they quickly killed and butchered the beast. Boiled dog meat was savored by the assailants and their friends and a soup was made of the terrier's bones. After the pet was missed, Lieutenant Fife posted a notice offering a $10 reward for the dog's return. One of the prisoners could not help adding an addendum:

> For lack of bread the dog is dead,
> For want of meat the dog was eat.

Unfortunately, this piece of doggerel led to the identification of the dog eaters, who had their rations suspended for three days. Their mates, however, each donated a bit of bread to the punished men.[61]

The prisoners were not choosy about whose dog was devoured, so long as the meat was tender. Visitors were well advised not to bring their pets, as R. T. Bean discovered:

> A number of dogs lost their lives through their curiosity to see a live Reb. One case I recall to mind with clear remembrance. An aristocratic lady from Chicago drove in behind a pair of high-stepping Kentucky bays, and closely following the carriage was an aristocratic dog. While his mistress was talking and telling us unregenerate Rebs how wicked it was to be fighting against the best government in the world, the dog came in for his share of attention and was inveigled into the barracks, which he never left. His flesh was pronounced first-class, and sharp lookouts were kept for more of his kind.

Meat-hungry men occasionally trapped rats, and the flesh was said to be "good and palatable."[62]

It was tragic that some men were driven to such extreme measures to get food in the city that was the great food entrepot of the Union war effort. Many in the city were aware that some Confederates were in pathetic condition. Chicagoans occasionally made donations of food and clothing to the prisoners, although the government did not encourage such gifts. What irritated the prisoners was that they languished "within sound of the church bells, in the Christian city of Chicago."

Dwight Moody and the Christian Commission distributed thousands of New Testaments to the prisoners. How successful his efforts were is difficult to say, but John Copley ridiculed one minister as "a fine specimen of ugliness and ignorance" and claimed the real purpose of his visit was "the safe-keeping of our persons within the prison walls, and not the safety of our souls." Certainly, both those concerns were the duty of E. B. Tuttle, who acted as the camp's chaplain. His plans for a chapel seating six hundred men were approved by the government, and the prisoners supported the idea enough to construct it with volunteer labor. The chapel bell was cast from coins collected from guards and prisoners.

The Sisters of Mercy, whose efforts were directed toward caring for wounded Union soldiers also wished to give food to the rebels. Initially, Colonel Sweet denied them access to the camp. Perhaps he suspected the loyalty of the Irish-Catholic women. But the politically savvy soldier changed his mind when the nuns returned with a letter from the mayor requesting their admission to the stockade. The rebels eagerly accepted the food donated by indignant Chicagoans. It is not known if the nuns were able to repeat their visit to the camp or if rations were increased.[63]

Besides death, the only guaranteed ticket out of Camp Douglas was to take an oath of allegiance to the United States and join the Union Army. These "galvanized Yankees" were prisoners tired of camp life and disillusioned with the Confederacy. Their former comrades disdained them. John Copley described them as men as bad as "Israelites were in the wilderness of sin." The prisoners greeted defectors with physical abuse, so Union guards escorted them back to their barracks. "These fellows looked like they had stolen something and been caught with it; the ground had a special attraction for their eyes," wrote Copley. A galvanized Yankee quickly bundled up his belongings and was escorted to a special barracks for defectors. Here men waited for several weeks until their application was approved by Washington. Henry Stanley, who would later win fame as an explorer of Africa, was one prisoner who chose to wear a blue coat rather than face long confinement. As the war dragged on and hope of parole vanished, more and more men thought of taking the oath of allegiance.[64]

By spring of 1864 escape had become as much a chimera as the prospect of Confederate independence. With tunneling impossible and bribery difficult, men who were determined to break out took hopeless chances. One night a half-dozen Kentuckians rushed the camp wall with a heavy wooden mallet and succeeded in breaking a hole in it. They were easily captured by the guards, and the other men in the barracks were punished for not preventing the escape. Prisoners became less supportive of plans that meant freedom for one or two and increased hardship for the rest.[65]

Yet, hope for freedom is central to a prisoner's survival, and the rebels, in spite of the odds, were slow to give up the dream of escape and eventual Confederate victory. What they needed was a new strategy. That was provided by seven veterans of Morgan's Raiders who formed a new secret organization. Only the staunchest, most trustworthy rebels were allowed to join. "The character of every man proposed for membership was thoroughly investigated, and had to be unanimously approved by the committee, before one word was allowed to be said to him," recalled a Kentucky cavalryman. Slowly a camp-wide network was created. Prisoners began to post their own guards, thereby anticipating any raids by the Yankee jailers. When the guard was changed or the position of a guard beat was altered, the "committee of seven" knew within minutes.

By summer of 1864 caches of homemade weapons, such as sharpened bones, sticks, and stones, were hidden about the camp. The goal of this conspiracy was nothing less than, in the words of one of its members, "the surprise and capture of the garrison, the seizure of their arms and munitions, and escape to the Confederacy in a body."[66]

6

◇

"WONDER OF THE NINETEENTH CENTURY"

In the midst of a Civil War, Chicago continued to boom. "On every street and every avenue one sees new buildings going up," the *Chicago Tribune* enthusiastically declared in January 1864. "Warehouses, stores, and residences are moved into and occupied, in many instances before the buildings are completed, sidewalks laid before them—and some even before the roofs are on." The streets thronged with newcomers drawn to the city by its reputation for commercial opportunity and its open throttle attitude toward the future. During the Civil War Chicago grew from 110,000 inhabitants to a city of 190,000 who were sprawled over thirty-five square miles of soggy prairie. This remarkable expansion, building as it did upon the city's feverish growth in the generations after 1833, led one journalist to flatly declare that Chicago was "pre-eminently the wonder of the nineteenth century."[1]

The Civil War did not transform Chicago from a prairie town to one of America's greatest success stories. By the time the war began, Chicago was already widely heralded as a social phenomenon. For European travelers such as the Prince of Wales or William Howard Russell, caustic correspondent for the London *Times,* a trip to America that did not include Chicago was as unthinkable as omitting Niagara Falls. Readers in Europe, as well as the eastern United States, tired of hearing the statistics of Chicago's population growth and its preeminent position in the world's grain and lumber trades. One antebellum journalist described Chicago as "the type of that class of American towns which have made themselves conspicuous and almost ridiculous by their rapid growth." What the Civil War, more than any other event, did for Chicago was to rechannel its social and economic growth. During the war, Chicago laid the foundation for its emergence as an

159

————————◇————————

industrial center. The war intensified social problems as well. Economic growth and political division had a lasting impact on Chicago's development as a socially and ethnically diverse collection of communities. The Civil War's effect on Chicago was less revolutionary than it was evolutionary. Nonetheless, a new city would emerge in the generations after the Civil War. The city with big shoulders first flexed its muscles between 1861 and 1865. It earned for itself the title "hog-butcher of the world" and carved out an identity as the metropolis of mid-America.[2]

————————◇————————

When the Civil War began, southern journalists loudly declared that "grass would grow" in the streets of Chicago. They based their predictions on the enduring power of the Mississippi River as the Midwest's principal artery of commerce. St. Louis and New Orleans historically had dominated the Mississippi valley and they regarded its trade as their birthright. In 1861 the Confederacy believed that with New Orleans under their sway and St. Louis within their grasp, they could cripple the commerce of mid-America. But the economic logic of the rebels proved as flawed as their military strategy. During the 1850s Chicago made remarkable progress toward challenging St. Louis as the leading Midwest trade center. Fueled by New York capital and serviced by east coast railroads, Chicago forged a new east-west trade axis for the heartland. The region's prosperity and Chicago's remarkable growth during the war, proved the superiority of the eastern connection over the old Southern tie. In the process Chicago established its superiority over its rival, St. Louis.[3] Yet, when the war began in the spring of 1861, it initially looked as if southerners were right. Throughout the North panic ensued as rebel merchants repudiated their debts to Yankee businessmen.

Chicago was the hardest-hit city in the country because of Illinois' reliance on wild-cat currency. In Illinois virtually any scoundrel could open a bank, and many did. The state treasurer required neither deposits nor cash reserves. Any type of security, no matter how questionable, would satisfy the state. In 1860 alone, more than twenty new banks were established in Illinois. The most popular security offered by these banks was stock from Southern states such as Tennessee and Virginia—the junk bonds of their day. Historians have used such words as "cheap" and "trashy" to describe these stocks. Political events during 1860 clearly demonstrated that reliance upon these securities was folly. But mid-nineteenth-century banking practice compounded the folly by allowing insecure banks to issue currency. These notes circulated throughout the economy along with notes from hundreds of other banks in other states. All men of business preferred gold and silver coin, but particularly in the West specie was too rare to be used as a standard medium of exchange.[4]

A financial crisis was brewing by the time Lincoln was elected. As the value of Southern securities plummeted, people across the state became wary of currency. Nonetheless, it circulated freely, and a game of financial musical chairs ensued. "People were seized with a sudden desire to pay up," recalled one journalist. "The course of nature was reversed; debtors absolutely pursued their creditors, and creditors dodged them as swindlers dodged the sheriff." Consumers wanted to use dubious currency while it could still command something near its stated value. Merchants feared holding too much wild-cat money when devaluation inevitably occurred. By November 30, 1860, Chicago's dynamic wholesale business came to a virtual standstill. Some currencies were totally repudiated, and the issuing banks were forced to close. Whoever held their paper money was stuck with the loss. Bank failures became more common during the spring of 1861. In April, alone, thirty-seven Illinois banks collapsed.[5]

The economy limped through the crisis by using devalued currency. Some dollar bills were worth thirty cents, others sixty cents. A merchant might accept a Marine Bank note for eighty cents and wake up the next day to find it was devalued to seventy cents. Some people lost fortunes in a matter of weeks; others saw a week's wages erode in a single day. Frustration in the city was high. Laborers were sick of accepting paper money for their wages and huddled in impromptu street corner meetings. "Long John" Wentworth expressed their sentiment when he editorialized, "Wild cat bankers are worse than secessionists." He went on to predict that because "no man is safe sleeping overnight with one dollar of Illinois currency in his pockets, . . . there is a great danger of a mob in our city." But working men did not resort to violence in part because their anger was also directed at the Southern states. "The evils under which we are suffering are brought upon us," the *Tribune* argued, "in a great measure by the traitors of the South."[6]

The currency crisis cost Chicago much of its capital. Only $147,073 remained in its banks by the end of 1861. More than $12 million was lost in the state. Eighty-nine of Illinois's 110 banks failed. It was the city's last bitter lesson in wild-cat banking. When national banks were authorized by Congress in 1863, the Chicago Board of Trade led a movement to drive state currency from circulation by urging the acceptance of only federal notes.[7]

The havoc wreaked by the currency crisis was obscured by Chicago's rapid economic recovery. Merchants and manufacturers soon found themselves swamped with orders for military equipment. Although Chicago was the center for the Upper Midwest's wholesale business, it was initially unable to provide all the uniforms and accouterments needed for its own soldiers, let alone those of the wider region. Nor could these items be readily purchased from eastern manufacturers because of the sudden and overwhelming demand. The governor of Iowa sent representatives to Chicago to purchase cloth that the women of the state could use to make uniforms on their own. Some Chicago merchants and craftsmen responded to this type of frantic demand by beginning their own manufacturing operations. Facilitated by the introduction of the sewing machine and stimulated by government contracts, a new Chicago industry took root. Uniforms were sold for $7.35 each. The ready-made clothing business in the city grew from $2.5 million annually to $12 million in 1863. Quality cloth shot up in price and was in great demand. Iowa's purchasing agents left Chicago bearing material described as "very poor, thin, sleazy . . . only fit for summer wear." A few Chicago manufacturers thought nothing of sending troops to the front in uniforms made of "shoddy." This "villainous compound" was "the refuse stuff and sweepings of the shop, pounded, rolled, glued and smoothed to the . . . form of cloth." After a few weeks of rough use it broke apart, leaving a company of soldiers looking like a band of hobos. Fortunately, use of shoddy by Chicago manufacturers seems to have ended by 1862. The six largest uniform makers soon found themselves pressed by new competitors. In the wake of the war Chicago boasted eighty-five wholesale clothing firms.[8]

The Civil War soldier also required a vast amount of leather goods. Infantry men were outfitted with leather cartridge boxes, one for powder and another for percussion caps, a bayonet sheath, shoulder belt, waist belt, as well as leather shoes. Cavalry, of course, needed even more. Before the war Chicago had a handful of wholesale shoe makers and saddlers. For them 1861 was a boom year. By June, Turner and Sidway, the city's biggest saddle and harness makers, had executed more than $100,000 in army contracts. During the spring and summer, they employed more than three hundred fifty men, working in night and day shifts. So great was the demand for military material that Turner and Sidway completely abandoned their regular trade and focused solely on war work. Chicago's shoe and boot makers also expanded their operations. Before the war they could barely compete with New England–made products, but due to a flood of war orders their trade swelled from $2.5 million in 1860 to $14 million by 1864. Chicago shoe and boot makers supplied regiments from across the Midwest, while in their factories, they employed twenty-five hundred workers.[9]

Equipping infantry and cavalry during 1861 helped to sustain an economy reeling from the currency crisis. The $1.5 million in clothing and leather purchases made between April and December provided a much needed economic stimulus in the otherwise disastrous year. Nor were military purchases restricted to uniforms and personal equipment. As the year wore on Chicago merchants received an ever expanding range of supply requests.[10]

Among the more improbable businesses to thrive on war work was Gilbert Hubbard and Company, a ship chandler. The bulk of his trade was in rope for ship rigging and canvas for sails. The regimental quartermasters kept Hubbard's staff busy with requests to adapt sail designs to tent specifications. Hubbard became even better known as a flag maker. Before the war his chandlery made flags and banners for merchant vessels. Initially, unit battle flags were lovingly made by the wives of the soldiers, but by the summer of 1861 units in the field needed replacements much faster than women's nimble fingers could manage. Hubbard began to receive orders for national and regimental colors from numerous Wisconsin, Michigan, and Illinois units. The flags played an important role in coordinating a unit's actions in combat and were a great source of esprit de corps. Hubbard's flags were popular in part because his artists were not afraid to stray from rigid army specifications and produce a distinctive design. Hubbard flags were carried into most of the major battles of the war.[11]

One of the most visible of the businesses that were thriving was horse trading. Before the war Chicago had a large number of livery stables whose owners participated in the buying and selling of horses. The sudden creation of hundreds of companies of cavalry created an inordinate demand for horses. Chicago brokers fanned out into the countryside to purchase animals for sale to the army. The prospective mounts were often sold at open-air horse fairs where crowds would gather to argue about the merits of each animal. In the days before the automobile men prided themselves in their knowledge of horse flesh. To businessmen on lunch break or to street corner loafers, a horse fair was as interesting as a modern auto show. P. R. Morgan, one of the city's biggest horse dealers, always attracted a crowd to his sales. The Morgan stables, located behind the Tremont House, drew crowds of men who packed the sides of the alley. Each horse was brought out singly by a stable boy. Handsome, well-formed sorrels or bays won approving comment from the crowd, while tired nags were greeted with the derisive cry, "Crow-bait!" After close inspection by the army buyer, a horse was hastily put through its paces in the alley that led to LaSalle Street. The stable boy hung on for dear life as the charging horse was egged on by the crowd. "Hi, Hi," the men shouted, while others jabbed at the passing horse with canes or umbrellas. Occasionally an animal took umbrage, and instead of running faster, it crashed into the crowd, sending the bystanders "sprawling in all directions." Such incidents were part of the fun of a horse fair, although the brokers would not let the carnival atmosphere obscure the economic aspect of the inspection.[12]

------◇------

During 1861 Morgan sold twelve hundred horses to the army. His rival, the Phoenix Stable, sold twenty-nine hundred horses at an average price of $125. These transactions netted a healthy profit because the brokers purchased the horses for between $70 and $100. Such profits ensured the participation of a large number of horse brokers in the trade. By the end of 1861 twenty stables had entered into contracts with the army, and 8,332 horses had been sold in Chicago. Throughout the war the horse trade prospered. In 1864 railroads shipped 6,372 horses from the city. Most went to the western armies, although some were sent east to the Army of the Potomac. According to the *Prairie Farmer,* the peak year for the trade was 1865 when more than 15,000 horses were sold to the army in Chicago. That year the horse markets netted $2.4 million in military sales.[13]

Not until the summer of 1861 did the army appoint a quartermaster in Chicago to supervise the disbursement of federal funds. Captain Joseph A. Potter headed the office for most of the war. Prior to the conflict he worked with the Topographical Bureau making charts of the Great Lakes. He had some background in logistical administration but nothing on the scale he faced in Chicago. His appointment signaled the federal government's assumption of the job of feeding and equipping midwestern soldiers. Immediately on assuming his office Potter became one of the most influential men of business in the city. A contract from his office could make a small fortune for its owner. During his first three months as quartermaster, Potter purchased between $800,000 and $900,000 worth of military equipment. The prices he negotiated could save the government thousands of dollars or ensure an exorbitant profit for the contractor. The potential for corruption was manifest, but Potter discharged his responsibilities honestly and efficiently.

Potter's Northwestern Military Depot supplied all troops in Illinois, Iowa, and Minnesota. The Army of the Cumberland and the Department of the Mississippi also drew on Chicago for equipment, particularly wagons, horses, and harness. On one occasion Potter delivered, within six day's notice, a complete pontoon bridge to the front in Tennessee. Chicago business reaped the benefits of the depot's location in their city. Of $4.8 million spent by Potter in 1862, only $1,000 did not go into the pockets of Chicago merchants. The *Tribune,* which had long been frustrated by the slow development of industry in Chicago, praised the Quartermaster Department as a "stimulus to trade and manufacture in our midst."[14]

One essential element for an army that the Northwest Military Depot did not supply was weapons. Chicago manufacturers did produce lead bullets but no rifles. Eliphalet Blatchford, who later helped to found the Newberry Library, made a fortune manufacturing bullets. His Chicago

Lead Works produced miles of lead wire which was cut into Minié balls. The city had hopes of even more arms manufacturing. During the fall of 1861 Chicago lobbied mightily to secure a federal armory. The capture of the Harper's Ferry Armory in April 1861 forced Congress to consider a more secure location for one of its premier weapons factories. The huge military forces that were forming in the western states convinced many that an armory be built in that region. Chicago held several public meetings to build support for its bid as the location. William B. Ogden, Long John Wentworth, and the *Tribune*'s William Bross, the city's tireless boosters, rallied the business community to the armory plan. Businessmen were excited about the role an armory could play in stimulating heavy industry in the city. The armory, according to the *Tribune,* "will give us an impetus, a beginning, and will be felt for ages to come." Isaac Arnold, Chicago's congressman, tried to gain the armory by playing on Lincoln's association with the city. But Chicago lost out to another Illinois town, Rock Island, where the federal government owned land. Chicago's failure to secure the armory was a bitter blow to its industrial aspirations. Military procurement helped to build Chicago's clothing and leather goods manufacturing, but it did not play a direct role in the rise of heavy industry.[15]

Undetered by the loss of the armory, Chicago boosters tried to snare federal money for enlarging the Illinois and Michigan canal. When Congress failed to support the scheme, Chicagoans held a convention in June 1863 to demonstrate regional support for the project. Chicago claimed that a bigger canal was needed to transfer gunboats to the Great Lakes, but other Lake towns, like Milwaukee, saw the project for what it was—a pork barrel designed to get federal funds for one city.

It was the railroad that gave birth to Chicago's iron and steel industry. The Civil War shaped the city's industrial development indirectly through the iron horse. By the time the war broke out, Chicago was already the leading rail hub in America, with three main lines extending eastward and numerous tracks reaching out across the western prairie. In 1862 Lincoln rewarded Chicago by choosing the central route for the Pacific Railroad, thereby guaranteeing Chicago the trade of the Far West. However, it was Stephen Douglas's stepchild, the Illinois Central Railroad, which proved particularly important during the war. Its Lake Michigan to Gulf of Mexico right of way paralleled the thrust of Union forces down the Mississippi Valley. As early as 1862 William H. Osborn, president of the railroad, was able to truthfully boast that "the Illinois Central Railroad is second only to the Washington branch of the Baltimore and Ohio Railroad in relation to the military operations of the government." Without the Illinois Central, U.S. Grant's spectacular campaigns against Fort Donelson or Vicksburg would not have been possible. Because of such vital rail links, Chicago became the natural funnel through which Union forces in the West were provisioned.[16]

Chicago had become a great rail center before the Civil War because the city stood between the Northwest, rich in agricultural and natural resources, and the Eastern Seaboard cities. The war did nothing to disrupt this lucrative commerce. Because Chicago also stood between the Northwest and the seat of the war, it was able to add a new market for its products, the army. The same factors that made Chicago the primary market in the world for grain and lumber ensured that the city would add even more commerce because of the conflict. Rival cities such as St. Louis and Cincinnati were older and larger, but their reliance on Southern markets and their proximity to the fighting circumscribed their commerce, which also benefited Chicago.

Chicagoans were confident that their dominance of the grain market would ensure the city's prosperity throughout the war. In the midst of the currency crisis the *Tribune* predicted that there was not a city in America that would suffer less than Chicago because of the war. "The experience of all time demonstrates," an editorial proclaimed, "that in all countries engaged in war the tendencies of the price of food is upward."[17]

Symbolic of the city's economic reliance on the grain trade were the grain elevators along the Chicago River. Like the skyscrapers of the century to follow, the giant elevators dominated the skyline and were the object of great civic pride. No friend, relative, or dignitary visiting the city would be spared a trip to Chicago's vast vertical warehouses. They stood about 130 feet high and were composed of a series of long, narrow bins. The center of the structure housed a steam-powered belt equipped with buckets. This device scooped grain out of the rail cars and carried it up into the bins for storage. Later, the elevator would pour the grain into the hold of a ship for transport to the coast via the Great Lakes and Erie Canal. The elevators were an important Chicago innovation. Rival grain ports such as St. Louis and New Orleans required that grain be shipped in sacks or barrels, which had to be unloaded by hand and transported by dray to a warehouse where they would be kept until sold or forwarded elsewhere. Steep handling charges and tedious delays were unavoidable, because this method required the grain be loaded or unloaded at least four times. Chicago merchants with only a handful of men could unload more than one hundred rail cars per day or fill a schooner in a couple of hours. The city had eighteen giant elevators and a combined storage capacity of ten million bushels.[18]

The huge amounts of grain stored in the elevators was Chicago's true source of wealth and generally exceeded the value of the banks' deposits. Receipts from elevator operators were welcome collateral for eastern financiers. Because Chicago was the grain center of the Midwest, it became the financial center of the region. The Chicago Board of Trade rooms were the meeting grounds for grain markets.

While the sale of grain futures was engaged in during the early 1850s, it was not until 1856, when a system of grades and standards were introduced, that true speculation was possible. The ups and downs of the Civil War encouraged an orgy of grain speculation. For four years the "bulls" and "bears" were locked in a struggle only slightly less frantic than the war itself. The closing bell at the Board of Trade seldom brought an end to transactions. Traders spilled out into the street, quoting prices, making contracts, and risking fortunes as they made their way to the Tremont House saloon. There, glasses of Lill & Diversey ale soothed the anguish of the day's disheartened losers and fueled the winners to seek further transactions. Membership in the Board of Trade soared during the war from 665 to 1,462. Many were professional speculators. Unhindered by margins or other limitations, they preyed on the inexperienced like wolves on lambs. By 1865 the Chicago grain exchange was known throughout the financial world for its feverish activity and sharp trading practices—a reputation that has dulled but little since that time.[19]

The trade in grain futures was fueled by the flood of cereal channeled into Chicago by the war. St. Louis, which attempted to challenge Chicago's mastery of the grain trade, found itself cut off from its outlet to the South, while Chicago's eastern outlets demanded more grain. Farmers who usually sent their harvest down the Mississippi turned to Chicago and the Great Lakes route. During the first year of the war, the amount of grain exported by Chicago increased from 31 million to 50 million bushels. By 1862 the figure climbed to more than 65 million. As the war progressed it was proven to the benefit of Chicago that grain, not cotton, was king.[20]

On the West Side of the city, where the lumberyards sprawled over acres and acres of prairie, timber seemed to be king. Chicago had won the title of "the greatest primary lumber market in the United States" in 1856 when lumber receipts surpassed those of Albany, New York. But in the wake of the panic of 1857 the lumber trade stagnated. The Civil War only worsened matters until late in 1862 when the forest economy began to revive. By 1864 the lumber trade had reached the dizzy heights of the pre-panic years. As the flow of wood into Chicago increased, so too did the price of lumber. Boards that were being sold for $6.75 per thousand foot in 1861 now found eager buyers at $23 per thousand. This heavy demand stimulated the rise of new logging districts along the shores of Lake Michigan. Chicago was the natural distribution point for these new mills. Railroads that entered the city laden with grain returned to the treeless prairie with carloads of lumber. Before the Civil War most of the Mississippi Valley's need for forest products was met by the pineries of the upper river. Rock Island and St. Louis were principal distribution points. But problems with river transport, some environmental and some related to the war, made it impossible for towns along the Mississippi to meet the growing demand. Chicago's prominence as a grain market helped to create an opportunity for her lumber merchants to also secure new western markets, and once again St. Louis was the principal loser.[21]

Unparalleled prosperity in two of Chicago's basic industries created capital for investment in other sectors of the urban economy. Benjamin Peter Hutchinson, known among the grain speculators as the "Prince of the Scalpers," used some of his profits to found a meat-packing business. Banks were eager to loan money to established meat packers who wished to expand their operations. Albert and Sidney Kent were so bullish on the market for meat that in 1862 they invested $50,000 to build a new plant on the South Branch of the Chicago River. Their competitors rushed to do the same. So many new facilities were built by 1864 that the editor of the *Prairie Farmer* claimed that "packing houses now are among the wonders of this thriving city."[22]

During the 1850s Chicago emerged as an important market for livestock and meat packing. Indeed, in 1860 Chicago slaughterhouses led the nation in beef cattle killed, and the meat business overall accounted for nearly a third of the city's exports. Cincinnati, however, was the overwhelming leader of the pork-packing industry, and numerous other western towns vied with Chicago for a larger share in this trade. Terre Haute, Louisville, Milwaukee, and, of course, St. Louis all had hopes of expanding their meat-packing industries. Yet, by the close of the Civil War, Chicago had emerged as the unquestioned center of the meat industry.

Chicago's triumph in meat packing, like her wartime success in grain and lumber, was tied to the city's central location and superior railroad connections. Cincinnati, which proudly called herself "Porkopolis," was partly cut off from its supply of southern hogs. The Queen City lacked the rail network to expand its hinterland and, therefore, was unable to meet the growing demand of the Union armies. Chicago, on the other hand, easily increased its supply. Within the first three years of the war the number of hogs shipped to Chicago quadrupled, and cattle receipts tripled. Many Iowa and Illinois farmers, who before the war sent their grain to St. Louis, switched to breeding hogs and sold their corn-fed livestock in Chicago. One Chicagoan praised the efficiency of this cycle: "The hog eats the corn and Europe eats the hog. Corn thus became incarnate; for what is a hog but fifteen or twenty bushels of corn on four legs?" In April 1862, the *Chicago Tribune* chauvinistically claimed for the city the title "Porkopolis." By 1864 Chicago slaughtered three times the number of hogs as Cincinnati.[23]

The number of meat packers in Chicago quickly grew from thirty in 1860, mostly marginal operations, to fifty-eight, including several large-scale businesses in 1864. Packing-house operators from Michigan, Indiana, and Wisconsin moved their businesses to Chicago. Lads who a few years before cleaned dung in animal pens could rent a vacant building and bid on an army contract. One such young man was Nelson Morris, a German-Jewish immigrant who spent his first six years in Chicago in near poverty. Through the classic combination of frugality and hard work, he parlayed a few crushed and crippled hogs bought from other yards into a livestock commission firm. By 1862 he was purchasing thousands of quality beef cattle to fill a series of lucrative army contracts. The diminutive immigrant was a regular at the various stockyards. With his thick German accent, he ceaselessly worked to batter down the prices asked by livestock brokers. He was so successful that by the end of the war he was able to install his wife in a grand, new house a short ride away from the stock yards. With Philip Armour, Gustavus Swift, and Ben Hutchinson, he became one of the "big four" of the postwar meat packing industry.[24]

The sudden growth of the industry outstripped the facilities to handle the influx of animals. Each day herds of cattle were driven into the Chicago area by weary drovers anxious to corral the animals and arrange for their sale. Even more livestock entered the city by railroad. Frequently people found themselves driven off the public streets by herds of swine or cattle on their way from holding pens to slaughterhouses. Accidents were frequent. In November 1863 a herd of cattle destroyed the Rush Street Bridge. A drover, ignorant of the ways of Chicago's pivot bridges, herded his cattle onto the bridge as it began to open for a passing tug boat. The cattle stampeded to one end of the bridge, breaking the structure from its foundation and sending pedestrians, drovers, and animals tumbling into the river. A young girl and most of the cattle were killed, and the city lost a bridge worth $50,000.

Stockmen did not like the chaos any better than pedestrians. Because holding pens were located at various places in the city, it was difficult to compare and contrast the quality of livestock, thereby compounding the problem of accurately pricing beef or pork. Driving animals through the city streets injured their hooves, reducing their value. Railroads objected to the tedious and expensive task of switching cattle cars from one track to another in order to reach a different stockyard.[25]

Efficiency dictated a central corral where all cattle and hogs could be congregated before being slaughtered. In 1864 the Chicago Pork Packers Association discussed the possibility of building a large stockyard "somewhere out on the prairie, beyond the line ever to be reached by the expanding city" yet accessible to the numerous slaughterhouses along the South

Branch of the Chicago River and to all of the major railroads. This provision proved crucial to the project's success, because the railroads eventually provided $925,000 of the initial $1 million necessary to establish the stockyard.

Because no one had ever created a central stockyard before, the businessmen of the Union Stock Yard and Transit Company held a competition for the best engineering plan. The winner was a remarkable civil engineer named Octave Chanute. In later years he would help pioneer aviation along with the Wright brothers, but in 1864 he was an ambitious young railroad engineer. His design for the stockyard presaged the grand scale and ordering influence of Daniel Burnham a generation later. On 345 acres of wet prairie he laid out a rational and efficient commercial center. To keep the area dry, he provided thirty-one miles of sewers and drains. Seven miles of broad streets paved by smooth pine blocks ensured the easy movement of men and animals through the years. To promote orderly arrival, unloading, and exit of trains, Chanute divided the yards into four divisions, and each railroad company was assigned a specific division of the yard where it could unload livestock. An efficient shipping yard, complete with switching tracks, turntables, water tanks, and a steam pump, serviced all outgoing trains. The completed yard had a capacity of fourteen hundred cattle and fifty thousand hogs. Chanute's water system ensured that water delivered to animals awaiting slaughter was purer than that consumed by most Chicagoans. A reporter for the *Chicago Times* was so impressed with the entire delivery and drainage system that he claimed the "bovine city will be far ahead of the human city which it adjoins."[26]

By the time the stockyard opened on Christmas Day 1865, Chicago's meat-packing business was the biggest in the world. Meat packing was increasingly recognized as one of the pillars of the urban economy. The 1870 census revealed that the annual value of beef and pork packing was almost triple that of the giant lumber business. Packing-house by-products also expanded in Porkopolis during the war. Slaughtered animals yielded hides and lard. Tallow was used to make candles and soap; blood could be turned into clothing dye. The larger slaughterhouses made use of their own by-products, but there were plenty of small packers who regarded the material as mere waste and who were glad to provide it to the rendering plant.[27]

Chicago produced so many products so swiftly during the war that distribution problems inevitably arose. The most efficient way to reach the armies in Tennessee and Mississippi was by train. Throughout the war Quartermaster Joseph Potter grappled with the problem of an inadequate number of freight cars. Every week he shipped oats, bread, meat, lumber, or equipment to the Army of the Cumberland. Such shipments often required the use of an entire train. But the railroads were more interested in servicing their regular passengers and customers. This was particularly true of the Illinois Central, a land grant railroad that had an interest in seeing the grain trade thrive. In 1863 William Osborn of the Illinois Central complained that the army's "Quarter-master and commissaries are pulling and hauling at us at all points." But Potter did not let excuses or complaints get in his way when he had an order to fill. In January 1864, for example, he received an order for lumber to build barracks for the troops in Chattanooga. When shipment could not be arranged through ordinary channels, he seized a locomotive in Chicago and sent his assistants into Wisconsin to round up sixty freight cars. By the end of the war Chicago railroads had come to dread Potter's frequent "visitations" as much as they relished the profits they earned.[28]

The railroads struggled to keep up with the demand for locomotives and rolling stock. The Illinois Central, the Galena and Chicago Union, the Chicago and Northwestern, the Chicago and Rock Island, and the Chicago and Milwaukee all operated car shops in the city, which operated night and day. Between 1861 and 1865, the Illinois Central added more than two thousand cars, nearly tripling its rolling stock. Engines were difficult to construct; nevertheless, the Illinois Central added thirty-six during the war. Although more than half of these were purchased in the East, the Chicago shops built some new models and converted older engines from wood to coal power.[29]

Locomotive construction and repair fueled Chicago's infant iron and steel industry as foundries were established to make cast iron plates for steam engines. As early as 1852 the Union Car and Bridge Works provided structural members for iron railroad bridges. But the biggest single use of iron by railroads was for rails. The iron rails used by most American railroads during the 1850s and 1860s seldom lasted more than eight months. By that time the iron was so worn down that the rail had to be replaced. Rolling mills were specialized iron forges that recast worn rails and rolled them into new rails. Chicago's emergence as the nation's premier railroad center made it a natural location for a rolling mill. In 1857 Captain Eber Brock Ward, a Great Lakes shipping magnate, turned his attention from ships to railroads and established the North Chicago Rolling Mill on the bank of the Chicago River. Ward's enterprise was the real beginning of Chicago's iron industry.[30]

The war's heavy demands on the railroad system created an unprecedented need for iron rails. Some of this demand was met by importing rails from Great Britain, but most of the increase was provided by new American producers. In March 1862 the Union Rolling-Mill Company was established along the South Branch. By the Fourth of July the plant was producing fifty tons of rails per day. Captain Ward's North Chicago Rolling Mill built another plant in 1864 in order to double its production. Ward's plant also pioneered the production of steel rails in the United States.

Steel, an alloy of iron and carbon, is much stronger and more durable than iron. The famous Bessemer process for making steel economically and efficiently was not widely used in the United States until after the war. But Captain Ward's ironsmiths devised their own process during the war and experimented with manufacturing steel for railroad tracks. It was not until May 24, 1865, that the North Chicago Mill produced the first steel rails in the United States. Ironmakers from across the country, who were gathered in Chicago at the time, were impressed by the new steel rails. After several rails were cut up for souvenirs, the rest were laid along the Chicago and Northwestern's right-of-way and were monitored by railroad men for several years. When they failed to show any sign of wear after two years, even the cautious railroad executives were won over. Just a few years after the war, Ward's Chicago plant had contracts for steel rails with the leading western railroads. Chicago became the meeting ground for coal from Southern Illinois and Pennsylvania and iron ore from Michigan. The North Chicago Rolling Mill became the seed of a vast steel empire that eventually became the U.S. Steel Corporation.[31]

The economic boom of the Civil War also helped to nurture other industrial cornerstones of twentieth-century Chicago. In 1855 Richard Teller Crane was owner and sole employee of a small brass foundry. With the help of his brother and an avalanche of orders for steam engine parts, Crane built a prosperous business. Three times during the war they expanded their plant, and their business doubled. Their prosperous partnership eventually became a $100 million corporation and one of Chicago's largest employers.

John Crerar, who later endowed one of Chicago's finest libraries, came to the city in 1862 and in short order made a fortune manufacturing and supplying railroad supplies. After the war he used his profits to help bankroll the Pullman Palace Car Company.[32]

George Pullman also got his start in the railroad industry during the Civil War. Earlier he had won fame in Chicago when he engineered the raising of the Tremont House to the new grade level. His practical solution to that problem was attaching five thousand jackscrews to the foundation; with the help of twelve hundred men he jacked the building out of the mud. He next turned his pragmatic brain to the problem of passenger travel by rail. Sleeping accommodations on long-distance trains were abysmal. Yet railroads were loath to adopt his ideas for sleeper cars. In frustration he abandoned the city for the gold fields of Colorado, where he failed to find fortune either in the mountains or from behind the counter of a store. In

1863 he returned to Chicago eager to secure a place in the city's booming economy. Investment capital was abundant, and the railroads were making huge profits, so Pullman once more tried to sell his idea of sleeper cars. By this time there were competitors in the field. But what Pullman planned was like no other railroad car. He spent $20,000 on an elaborately decorated car with fold-down berths. The enormous cost and the size of the car led his critics to dub it "Pullman's Folly." It was a foot wider and several feet higher than other cars, making it impossible to clear many existing bridges and tunnels. Pullman called the car the *Pioneer* and predicted the railroads would change their right-of-way in order to use it. They did, and within two years after the war's end Pullman headed an industrial and service empire that lasted until 1983.[33]

Not the least of the war's effects on the Chicago economy was the introduction of a stable banking system. Industrialization required capital, a rare commodity in the chaotic financial district of ante-bellum Chicago. The Lincoln Administration brought a practical end to the multiplicity of currencies in the city when it empowered the creation of national banks which issued federal bank notes. These notes were backed by Washington, unlike most paper currency backed solely by the bank which issued it. The establishment of the First National Bank of Chicago in July 1863 ushered in a new era of financial confidence. Nowhere else in the country did national banking catch on as quickly as in Chicago. By the end of the war there were thirteen national banks in the city with deposits approaching $30 million. This was the beginning of the capital foundation necessary for industrialization. When the decade of the 1860s came to a close, census takers discovered that the number of factories in Chicago had tripled since the outbreak of the war.

Chicago's most prominent manufacturer, Cyrus Hall McCormick, did not especially thrive during the Civil War. Certainly the market for his product boomed. Wheat cultivation skyrocketed at the very time large numbers of men were joining the army. The use of such labor-saving machines as McCormick's reaper also soared. In 1863 the *Scientific American* declared, "This year the demand for reapers has been so great that manufacturers will not be able to fill their orders." Yet in that critical year, production at the McCormick Reaper Works actually declined by 16 percent.

Chicago historians are fond of quoting Edwin Stanton, Lincoln's Secretary of War, who once remarked, "Without McCormick's invention . . . the North could not win and . . . the Union would be dismembered." Stanton knew more about agricultural technology than anyone in the administration, and his statement was only a slight exaggeration. The reaper increased the production of farm labor tenfold. It insured abundant food for the army and a lively export trade with Europe. As long as the Union had armies in the field and wheat was king abroad, the Confederacy was doomed. What has been exaggerated, however, is McCormick's role as a manufacturer. During 1863, for example, his Chicago plant, reputed to be the largest reaper works in the world, accounted for only 12 percent of the forty thousand reapers made in the United States. While the rest of Chicago's manufacturers thrived, McCormick seemed to flounder.[34]

Cyrus Hall McCormick's attitude toward the Union war effort was ambivalent at best and in part explains his troubles. He and his brothers, Leander and William, had been born and reared in Virginia. Before the war they proudly stated, "Our heart still yields allegiance to the 'Old Dominion.' " Cyrus was also a great booster of Chicago and the Midwest, where his reaper business took root. He opposed secession, but he also opposed fighting the South. He wrote, "It would be unwise and impolitic to seek war to compel an unwilling Union." When war came Cyrus McCormick went to Europe and stayed there for two years. William McCormick, who managed the finances of the reaper works, accused him of "flee[ing] away from this land of blood and death—where we are trodden by abolitionism in the North—without liberty of speech—and with utter ruin in the South." At a time when American farmers were clamoring for reapers and offering to pay cash, Cyrus ordered his brothers in Chicago to prepare three hundred machines for sale in Europe. The European market was a chimera pursued by Cyrus to escape the difficult political choices brought by Civil War. His absence from the Chicago works and the diversion of resources abroad hurt production in a vital sector of the war economy.[35]

Production problems as well as political decisions hampered reaper manufacturing in Chicago. The McCormicks relied heavily upon skilled molders, machinists, and woodworkers, men who were in great demand during the war. Competition for labor was keen between the McCormicks and wagon makers filling army contracts, foundries building railroad engines, and other booming war-related industries. The use of specialized machine tools and interchangeable parts, well advanced in other industries, would have allowed greater production with fewer craftsmen, but the McCormick brothers lacked vision. They also were building a machine that was less reliable than those of their competitors. Attempts at altering the design repeatedly slowed production. While most Chicago businessmen were expanding their operations, the McCormicks, as late as autumn of 1863, were considering suspending manufacturing during the war. Throughout the war their operations were uncertain and off balance.[36]

The Civil War came at the peak of Chicago's first boom, when water and rail communications integrated the fertile heartland into the national economy. The Chicago of 1860 was the product of the east-west commerce established in the decades before. By the time the war began, Chicago was poised to begin the second stage of its urban development—manufacturing. The war did not create the opportunity for industry, but it did stimulate fledgling enterprises, many of which would have emerged even if the war had been avoided.[37]

Historians have long argued over the economic impact of the Civil War. Although the North experienced significant economic growth during the war, some scholars contend that the rate of growth experienced during the 1860s was severely retarded by the sectional conflict. However true this may be nationally, it does not reflect the Chicago experience. The war stimulated Chicago to greater economic activity, but the business and industry were natural outgrowths of its peacetime economy. The war did not build up an artificial armaments industry in Chicago, which would wither in time of peace. Instead, it stimulated the grain, lumber, and livestock trade Chicago sought to dominate before the war. The city's great rival as a transportation hub, St. Louis, found its communications crippled during the war, thereby allowing Chicago to cement its primacy as a rail center. The railroads, in turn, stimulated the growth of Chicago's nascent iron and steel industry. Cincinnati, the leader in manufacturing in the prewar West, lost dominance in pork packing, its largest industry. Chicago became the nation's butcher and fell heir to the scores of related industries allied to food processing. The ascendancy over St. Louis and Cincinnati might have occurred without the war, but the conflict sped the process and cemented the city's image as "the wonder of the nineteenth century."[38]

———◇———

"Our molders are going on their fourth strike for an advance of wages since last fall," lamented a clerk at the McCormick works in April 1864. "They now want 25 percent more!!! Manufacturers will have to shut up shop if things go much farther in this line." Throughout 1863 and 1864 the McCormicks complained about their workers. Many of the best men had either enlisted in the army or were attracted by higher wages at other facilities. Production problems were blamed on "green and obstreperous" hands, who lacked the experience necessary to build reapers and often quarreled with the shop foreman. To keep good workers, the McCormicks raised the pay of their men 20 percent between the summer of 1862 and autumn 1863. Yet the workers continued to demand more, causing William McCormick to complain, "Labor has the power and is on strike half the time."[39]

The problems of the McCormick Reaper works were not in the least bit unique. By the fall of 1862 Civil War Chicago's workforce became increasingly militant. Labor organizations were on the rise, and job actions often disrupted normal business operations. Inflation and high prices for such basic necessities as food, fuel, and clothing combined to drive up the cost of living. Workers, who had been forced to accept low wages since the panic of 1857, found themselves caught in the vise of the declining value of their salary and rising costs.

Currency inflation was the result of the introduction of $300 million in greenbacks into the economy. Certainly this new federal currency was an improvement over the numerous state bank notes that had caused havoc before the war, but all types of paper money were worth less than gold. An inflation rate of about 80 percent ensued. The cost of clothing in Chicago went up 100 percent, rent 66 percent, and the price of some food products more than doubled. "The price of *everything* is so high and increasing all the time," wrote one upper-middle-class matron, "that I don't see how it can hold out so. The poor must do without many of the necessaries of life." Fortunately, wages also increased. Chicago workers, in fact, did better than many of their counterparts nationwide. Bricklayers in the city, for example, earned twice as much as their counterparts in Massachusetts and Ohio. This kept a flow of new migrants into Chicago and allowed her industries to expand during the war.[40]

Wage increases, however, were by no means equal across the board. Workers on fixed salaries (such as teachers) or workers with low status and little leverage (such as women garment workers) suffered the high costs with little boost in pay. Men with skills and the ability to organize were the most successful at demanding raises. Strikes by iron molders, blacksmiths, coppersmiths, shoemakers, and carpenters were frequent. At a time when cost-of-living raises were unheard of, employers fought every wage increase. They organized industry associations to try to fight labor's demands with a common front. In March of 1863, for example, Chicago's iron manufacturers sought to restrain the upward spiral increase of wages by resolving to pay no molder more than $2 per day.[41]

The workers countered by establishing their own associations. Unions, which were then in their infancy, were given a significant boost during the war. More important was the General Trades Assembly, which was formed in Chicago in 1864. The assembly, modeled after similar organizations in eastern cities, was a representative body made up of delegates from each union and worker association in the city. Urging the assembly to action was the *Workingman's Advocate,* a new radical newspaper "devoted to the producing classes of the Northwest."

The spring and long hot summer of 1864 saw the labor situation come to a boil. In March the Brotherhood of Locomotive Engineers threatened to close down the city when it called for a general strike on all trains coming into Chicago. The Galena and Chicago Union Railroad had violated its agreement with the Brotherhood, and the engineers wanted immediate restitution. A minor panic ensued in Quartermaster Potter's office, which feared the flow of supplies to the front would be disrupted. The engineers tried to plan their strike in secrecy. Newspapers were labeled "unfriendly to the working man," and their reporters were barred from the strike meetings. Nonetheless, the railroad companies managed to break the strike on its first day by getting scabs to operate the engines. A second railroad strike in May for higher wages also floundered in the face of determined management action. Wildcat strikes by sailors, stevedores, and grain elevator operators—all for wage increases—further rocked the city.[42]

In an attempt to give direction to the dynamic labor movement, the General Trades Assembly announced a legislative program to reclaim the "dignity of labor against the grasping exactions of the capitalists of the country." Shorter hours, wages based on gold, and the need for an Illinois labor party were their cornerstones. The assembly, however, was distracted from this specific agenda by a blatant attempt to break the printers' union.[43]

The Typographical Union was one of the oldest labor organizations in the city. In September 1864 its members struck the *Chicago Times* for higher wages. The men could barely subsist on their wages, which were lower than printers in other cities were being paid. In striking the *Times* the printers were up against one of the most successful and determined publishers in the country, Wilbur F. Storey.

Storey got wind of the strike some weeks before, and he used his time well. In an empty loft on Randolph Street he installed a complete composing room. There, forty young women were trained to be printers. When the Union printers walked off the job, Storey did not miss a beat. He marched the women into the *Times* composing room and put them to work on the next morning's issue. The General Trades Assembly rallied to the printers union and called a mass meeting of labor. Only fifteen hundred "hardfisted workingmen" showed up, but the enthusiasm of those who were there made up for the small numbers. The labor gospel was cited chapter and verse: "As the capitalists are the aggressors let us meet them with a determined war, and God will help those that help themselves." Solidarity with the railroad workers was expressed through attacks on the management of the Illinois Central. The most bitter invectives were saved for Wilbur Storey, "a traitor to his country, to his God, and the Workingman."

Through his press Storey tried to paint the workers as being opposed to the introduction of women into skilled trades. The *Tribune,* which in this matter had an interest in supporting its rival, floated the same balloon. The Chicago Typographical Union strenuously fought this charge and at their mass meeting articulated an argument that exposed Storey's true mo-

———◇———

tivation. The union claimed it was the friend of the women workers, and "as their friends we demand that they receive the same wages that men receive for doing the same work." Storey paid them 25 percent less. Indignantly, the assembled workers vowed to boycott the *Times*. But the *Times* was one of the most influential newspapers in the country, and it was an official organ of the peace Democrats. In the midst of the 1864 election campaign, with voter interest high, the boycott was doomed to failure. The strike fizzled, the union men sought work with other papers, and the women printers were gradually replaced by nonunion males.[44]

Chicago women played a significant role in the workplace during the Civil War era. In industries such as garment making they were vital to the execution of army contracts. At military equipment manufacturers such as Turner & Sidway, between 10 and 15 percent of the workers who made saddles and haversacks were women. Labor-saving devices such as the Singer sewing machine improved the productivity of workers doing needle work. Civil War Chicago, however, did not witness the kind of wholesale employment of women in traditionally male occupations that happened during World War II. The city's growing population supplied most of the new workers needed for the expanding industry. Nor were women workers represented in the General Trades Assembly.[45]

The Civil War played an important role in developing labor consciousness in Chicago. Organizations such as the General Trades Assembly helped lay the groundwork for more successful workingmen's societies. The lessons learned in organizing job actions and coordinating the activities of several unions would later pay off during the fight for the eight-hour day. The frustration of repeatedly being outflanked by owners and replaced by scabs would help to fuel Chicago's violent reaction to the Great Strike of 1877. But as much as the inflation of the Civil War era drew laboring men together, the political passions excited by the war divided them. Labor leaders argued for solidarity among the laboring class, while the war demonstrated the sharp ethnic, racial, and political divisions that fractured unity.

———◇———

In July 1862, the Tenth Ward Workingmen's Society, a largely German group, held a picnic fund raiser near the banks of the Chicago River. It was a pleasant afternoon of music, lager beer, and talk of ethnic and labor unity. By seven o'clock in the evening most of the picnickers had left, and the organizing committees set to clearing the grounds and counting the donations. An Irish boatman came by and fell to quarreling with the Germans. The tired union men had no patience with the irascible boatman, whom they suspected of coveting their cash contributions, and they sent him packing. A few minutes later the Irishman was back with a mob

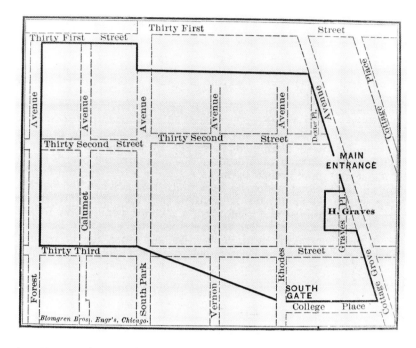

An 1885 map showing the location of Camp Douglas on the Chicago street grid. (A.T. Andreas, *History of Chicago,* vol. 2, 1885)

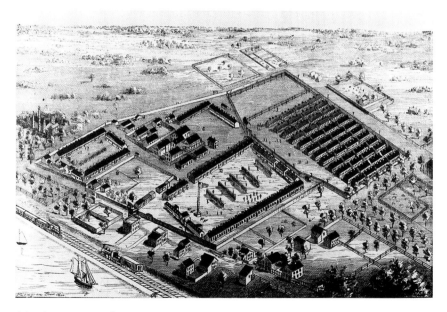

A bird's-eye view of Camp Douglas. In the upper right is the prisoner-of-war camp, while in the lower left are the Union barracks and parade ground. (A.T. Andreas, *History of Chicago,* vol. 2, 1885)

Rebel prisoners under close guard in Camp Douglas's dreary prison yard. This sketch and several of those that follow were drawn by Samuel B. Palmer, a Confederate prisoner from Knoxville, Tennessee. (*Our Young Folks Magazine,* 1865)

The Camp Douglas prison barracks after repeated escape tunnels forced the commandant to raise the barracks off the ground. (*Our Young Folks Magazine,* 1865)

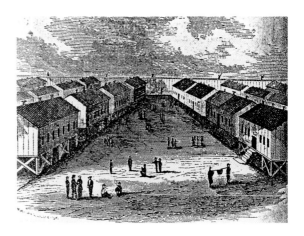

The interior of a POW barrack. When winter winds pierced the plank walls, the most popular place to gather was around the pot-bellied stove. (*Our Young Folks Magazine,* 1865)

(*Left*) Prisoners deeply resented the corporal punishments administered by their Union guards. Here, a man who was caught violating camp rules is attached to a ball-and-chain. Note how the prisoner attempts to strike a "nonchalant air" by smoking his pipe. (*Our Young Folks Magazine,* 1865)

(*Right*) Among the most common disciplinary actions was to assign wayward rebels a ride on "Morgan's Mule." After a half hour on the rail, men found it difficult to walk let alone run away. (*Our Young Folks Magazine,* 1865)

A dangerous but often successful way to escape from Camp Douglas was to build a ladder and clear the wall before being spotted by the sentry. (*Our Young Folks Magazine,* 1865)

(*Left*) Rebel prisoners tunnel their way out of Camp Douglas. (*Our Young Folks Magazine,* 1865)

The Rush Street bridge across the Chicago River marked the entrance to the Port of Chicago. The Civil War business boom helped make Chicago one of the busiest ports in North America. (Frederick F. Cook, *Bygone Days in Chicago*, 1910)

(*Below*) George Pullman profited from the wartime increase in rail traffic and cleverly exploited the Lincoln funeral train to promote his new sleeper car. (F.F. Cook, *Bygone Days in Chicago*, 1910)

(*Above*) Cyrus McCormick was Chicago's leading industrialist at the time of the Civil War. But his pro-Southern sympathies prevented him from taking economic advantage of the demand for labor-saving technologies such as his reaper. (A.T. Andreas, *History of Chicago*, 1885)

(*Below*) Colonel John A. Bross, Douglas Democrat, gave up a successful law practice to lead Illinois' only African-American regiment. (E.M. Eddy, *The Patriotism of Illinois,* 1865)

(*Above*) Father Dennis Dunne, pastor of St. Patrick's parish, championed the Union cause in the Irish community. In 1862 he helped raise the Irish Legion, the city's second Irish regiment. (A.T. Andreas, *History of Chicago,* 1885)

The McCormick Harvester Machine Company. (A.T. Andreas, *History of Chicago,* 1885)

(*Left*) Wilbur F. Storey, editor of the *Chicago Times* during and after the Civil War. Lincoln's bitterest critic and a race baiter of the worst sort, he was also one of Chicago's greatest journalists. (F.F. Cook, *Bygone Days in Chicago,* 1910)

(*Right*) Charles Walsh was a Bridgeport politico whose opposition to the war led him into a conspiracy with Confederate secret agents to attack Camp Douglas. (I. Winslow Ayer, *The Great North-Western Conspiracy,* 1865)

(*Left*) Colonel G. St. Leger Grenfell, British soldier-of-fortune, helped lead the Camp Douglas conspiracy. He was harshly punished—a life sentence at the federal prison in the Dry Tortugas. (I. Winslow Ayer, *The Great North-Western Conspiracy,* 1865)

(*Below*) Colonel Benjamin J. Sweet, the ambitious commandant of Camp Douglas, claimed credit for ruining the Confederate conspiracy against Chicago. (*Our Young Folks Magazine,* 1865)

(*Above*) Buckner S. Morris, a former mayor of Chicago. His personal enmity toward Abraham Lincoln and sympathy for Confederate prisoners-of-war combined to implicate him in the Camp Douglas conspiracy. (F.F. Cook, *Bygone Days in Chicago,* 1910)

Rebel prisoners in Camp Douglas. A secret organization of die-hard Confederates planned to coordinate a mass uprising against the guards with an attack from outside the camp by Southern agents. (*Harper's Weekly*)

Lincoln's body arrives in Chicago. (F.F. Cook, *Bygone Days in Chicago,* 1910)

The main hall of the 1865 Sanitary Fair. Many of Chicago's returning troops were formally received and thanked at the fair. (*Frank Leslies Illustrated Weekly*)

of fellow countrymen, all spoiling for a fight. A genuine donnybrook ensued. The outnumbered Germans got the worst of the fight, and several went home with broken arms and heads.[46]

The Tenth Ward riot was only one of a series of violent episodes between the city's two largest ethnic groups. Two days later another German-Irish fight took place. When the police tried to intervene two officers were beaten, and the rest took flight from an angry Kilgubbin mob. The Civil War exacerbated already hostile relations between the Germans, who made up 20 percent of Chicago's population, and the Irish, who made up 18 percent. The flash points of this conflict tended to be where the ethnic neighborhoods touched on the Near North Side and in Bridgeport to the south.[47]

The Irish and Germans had been political allies for many years. Both had been attracted to the Democratic party, which was perceived as more open to the foreign-born voters. The slavery issue in general, and the 1854 Kansas-Nebraska Act in particular, however, began to split the Germans from the Democrats. Nativist sentiment forced the Germans to cooperate with Irish Democrats until 1860, when the Germans of Chicago backed Lincoln. While the German community had a considerable number of unskilled workers, there were more skilled tradesmen and middle-class shopkeepers than in the Irish community. The Irish dominated the unskilled and semiskilled labor force of Chicago. They came to America largely for one reason, economic necessity. Many Germans left their homeland for idealistic political reasons. For the Germans, slavery was an insult to democratic ideals, while emancipation was perceived as a potential economic threat to the less well off Irish. The drift toward abolition as a federal policy in the summer of 1862 heightened tensions between the two groups.[48]

As the war progressed, the lines of division became more sharply drawn, although they never were hard and fast. Prominent Irish-Catholic clergy, such as the Reverend Mr. Denis Dunne, who organized the "Irish Legion" in 1862, and Bishop James Duggan, were vocal supporters of the war effort. Catholic Germans tended to be hostile to antislavery and became cooler toward the war when it appeared that the radical Republicans were in the ascendancy. Throughout the war the Democratic party sought to win back German voters by running German candidates. The Republicans, on the other hand, snubbed the Irish.

Partisan political journals, such as the *Tribune,* labored to widen the gulf between the two large immigrant groups. Germans were "frugal, peaceable, well-behaved, inoffensive: while the majority of the Irish are the very opposite, delighting in rows, drunken quarrels, whisky and ballot-box stuffing." An 1864 editorial laid the blame for the periodic violence between the two groups on the Irish, who were described as acting "with a determination worthy of their infamous compatriots" who caused the New York draft riots. When Irish Democrats made an effort of rapprochement with the German community, the *Tribune* accused the Irish of cunningly trying to "play their cards sharply and make as many 'points' as their 'hand' will afford."[49]

The Irish of Chicago were guilty of vicious and violent behavior toward the city's small black community. Clashes with the Germans were much less frequent than altercations between Irishmen and African-Americans. Most of these incidents were economically motivated, as blacks and Irish competed for many of the same unskilled labor jobs. Throughout the war black men tried to find employment along the extensive docks of the lumber district. Unloading lumber schooners was hot, heavy work. The burley lumbershovers formed informal work gangs and hired themselves out to schooner captains anxious to have their vessels unloaded. On a slow day when only a few ships entered the harbor, the workmen could only charge $10 or $15 for the job, but when the port was busy and many ships wanted to be unloaded at once, lumbershovers could command more than $50. The Irish rightly feared that rival gangs of black laborers would lower the fees they could command on busy days. To keep the riverfront all white they used intimidation and violence. Lumberyard managers and ship captains who hired blacks were met by a deputation of white workmen who demanded their rivals be fired. The black workers were often beaten-up as were white employers who failed to take the desired action.[50]

The Irish defended these actions by complaining that "it was degrading . . . to see blacks working upon an equality with themselves . . . while their brothers were out of employment." The insistence with which the Irish argued that black competition "degraded" Irish labor indicates that they feared something more than economic rivalry. The Irish were sensitive of their position at the bottom of Chicago's social ladder; only blacks occupied a lower rung. Discriminated against because of their religion and despised because of social problems in their ghettoes, the Irish resented radical Republican efforts to raise the Negro's status. Blacks were seen as political and social rivals as well as economic competitors.[51]

A second, more random type of violence against blacks reflected these social tensions. In November 1864 the *Chicago Times* reported that three to four hundred Irishmen gathered at the corner of Clark and Old streets to help in "drubbing an impudent negro who had dared insult an Irish citizen." The Irish were prominent, but not alone, in attacks on blacks accused of overstepping their "place." Such attacks occurred because blacks entered a "white" neighborhood or tavern, or because a black just happened to be nearby when a white was embarrassed. A drunken soldier who tripped on Dearborn Street, for example, started a riot that resulted in two blacks being beaten because he accused them of pushing him over. After the Emancipation Proclamation some Irish gangs in Bridgeport took to celebrating rebel victories. As one Chicago journalist later recalled, "These demonstrations generally took the form of hunting down any poor colored brother who might have strayed inadvertently within those delectable precincts."[52]

On December 31, 1862, a congregation of black Chicagoans gathered for an evening vigil. All night they prayed, read poems, and sat together in quiet reflection, patiently awaiting the dawn of freedom. At midnight the New Year began, and Abraham Lincoln's Emancipation Proclamation went into effect. A day of formal celebrations and speeches followed. At Quinn Chapel, one of the cornerstone institutions of black Chicago, Joseph Stanley optimistically declared, "In this age, bondage can never be an endless institution. The day of deliverance must come."[53]

Emancipation Day was greeted with enthusiasm by Chicago's black community more for its symbolic significance than its effect on their lives. Because it affected only the status of slaves whose masters were in rebellion, it had little bearing on the status of Chicagoans. It was viewed, however, as a promise of better times ahead. Such a promise was welcome because of the random racial violence of wartime Chicago and lingering persecution of the infamous black laws.

Illinois' black laws, a deeply resented symbol of racism, were modeled on the laws of slave states. Blacks were denied basic civil rights and forced to prove their status as freemen. Equally as insufferable was an 1863 change in the city charter which authorized the legal segregation of white and black students in Chicago schools. John Jones, the political father of black Chicago, led the fight to repeal the black laws and restore integrated schools. His tract *The Black Laws of Illinois and a Few Reasons Why They Should be Repealed* helped to rally Republican support in the state legislature. Jones pointed out that the black laws not only unfairly hindered black taxpayers but also were a dangerous precedent that could be used to justify codes restraining other minorities in the community. Through the winter of 1864–65 the black community was alive with fundraising festivities and petition drives to influence the state legislature. Finally, on February 7, 1864, the governor signed the repeal bill into law. Jones's victory was complete two months later when a new city charter ended de jure segregation in Chicago schools. In spite of considerable difficulties, Chicago blacks, with the help of their white Republican allies, demonstrated a willingness to fight for their civil rights.[54]

A powerful argument for the repeal of the black laws was the existence of black regiments under the Illinois banner. From the time the war began Chicago's black community wanted to strike a blow against the slave owners' Confederacy. In April 1861 black Chicago formed several companies of soldiers. For a time they drilled on their own and mustered in volunteers. The State of Illinois, however, refused to accept them into the ranks. It was through the unilateral and controversial action of Major General David Hunter (who was a Chicagoan) that the first black troops were brought into the Union Army in May 1862. The Emancipation Proclamation cleared the way for the more widespread use of black soldiers.

Quinn Chapel was the scene of the first black recruiting rally in April 1863. John Jones proclaimed to the excited crowd that he looked forward to the day when he might be able to point to the stars and stripes and say, "There is the flag for which I and my countrymen fought." The volunteers who surged forward were not enrolled in an Illinois unit. Democratic opposition in the state house temporarily prevented the governor from forming a black regiment. Massachusetts recruiting agents set up an office in the city and enrolled almost two hundred Chicago freemen. These soldiers served in the 54th Massachusetts Colored Infantry and contributed to the subjugation of South Carolina.[55]

The men of the 54th Massachusetts were not the first Chicago blacks to serve in the war. Light-skinned African-Americans had enrolled in white regiments at the outbreak of the conflict. H. Ford Douglas was perhaps the most remarkable of these men. He was born into slavery, but as a young man he escaped north and became an active advocate of abolition. He discarded his slave name and took the last name of the great Frederick Douglas. In Chicago he earned a reputation as one of the most eloquent critics of slavery and was in much demand as a speaker among abolition societies in northern Illinois. In 1862 he enlisted in the 95th Illinois Infantry, a McHenry County regiment, and fought with that unit throughout the Vicksburg campaign. A contemporary wrote, "His virtues, talents, and above all, his fiery eloquence, gave him welcome. He was fraternized with as if he were a white man. Everybody respected him." Douglas, however, did not forget that he was black. Contrary to the black laws, he used his position in the army to help reunite Southern slaves with their runaway relatives in Chicago. When separate black units were formed he was made a captain of a company of Indiana volunteers.[56]

Blacks also served with a wide variety of Chicago units in an unofficial capacity. When the 12th Illinois infantry fought its way through Georgia to the sea, its muster roll listed a group of "unassigned recruits of African descent." The 8th Illinois Cavalry, which served with the Army of the Potomac, had twenty-one "contrabands" (runaway slaves) living and working with the unit. When the 8th returned to Chicago on furlough in January 1864, the "contrabands" came with them and settled in the city.[57]

The unit most prominently identified with the Chicago black community was the 29th Regiment of U.S. Colored Infantry. It was made up almost entirely of Illinois men, although some recruits came from as far away as Ontario to serve in its ranks. Chicagoans were initially cool to joining the unit. The most eager volunteers had already enlisted in the Massachusetts colored regiments. Some of the city's most prominent black leaders were reputed to be paid recruiting agents for other states. They went to no great pains to fill the Illinois regiment, particularly when the state refused to offer an enlistment bounty. (White volunteers received a healthy bounty and a higher monthly pay allowance than blacks.) In vain, the *Tribune* pleaded for enlistments: "An opportunity is now open to you to shame into eternal silence the vile calumniators of your race." H. Ford Douglas returned to Chicago and took charge of the enlistment drive. His speeches and Cook County's willingness to offer a token bounty of $100 helped boost enthusiasm for the unit. By January 1864, the first company of Chicago Colored Infantry paraded down Clark Street. After "saluting the office of the *Tribune*" they boarded trains for Quincy, Illinois, where the regiment was getting organized.[58]

In May 1864, the 29th was ordered to join the Army of the Potomac in Virginia. A reception was held for the white officers and black soldiers at the Soldiers' Rest in Chicago. It was an emotional afternoon. A few weeks before, the soldiers and their families had learned of the massacre at Fort Pillow, where captured black soldiers were slaughtered by rebel troops. The long war, with no sign of ending in sight, had turned even uglier. For many of the men of the 29th, this was the last time they would see their friends and family.

Lieutenant Colonel John A. Bross, brother of a *Chicago Tribune* editor, commanded the 29th. Before the war he had been one of the most popular members of the Chicago bar. Although he was no abolitionist and was in line for a promotion in the 88th Illinois, "he felt God called him" to service with the colored infantry. When soldiers had made their tearful partings and the train was ready to depart, Bross delivered a brief farewell address. "When I lead these men into battle, we shall remember Fort Pillow," he said to an anxious crowd, "and shall not ask for quarter." Turning to his family he said, "I leave a home and friends as dear as can be found on earth, but if it is the will of Providence that I do not return, I ask no nobler epitaph than that I fell for my country at the head of this black and blue regiment."[59]

The 29th had a final taste of glory when they paraded before Abraham Lincoln in Washington. From there they entered the killing ground of northern Virginia. On the morning of July 30, 1864, they were ordered to take the rebel trenches guarding Petersburg. Only hours before a giant explosion had left a hole 150 feet wide in the Confederate line. Those defenders who were not blown sky high fled in panic. A coordinated Union attack might have won the Civil War at that moment. What happened instead was a hesitant, chaotic assault that lead to disaster. The opportunity for victory had already passed when the 29th charged. While they captured a rebel trench, their commanding general slipped off to a bombproof shelter where he drank rum with the other brass who were supposed to be leading the attack.

The battlefield was a confusion of smoke, shot, and the screams of wounded, bewildered men. From the rear came a succession of orders to continue the advance. Colonel Bross tried to keep the 29th together and advancing toward Cemetery Hill, the key to the rebel defenses. Their attack was at last broken in a field raked by canister. The 29th found itself hopelessly exposed and overextended in the heart of the rebel army. Bross grasped the regimental colors and ordered the men to retreat. Before he could take a step, however, a Minié ball smashed through his skull. He gasped, "O Lord!" and fell dead.

By this time the entire Union attack had been routed. The men of the 29th struggled with thousands of others to make their way back over the bodies of their comrades to the safety of their own lines. Many took up their position in the thirty-foot deep crater. Rebel soldiers were loath to take black prisoners, and some Illinois men died trying to surrender. Few of those who were captured survived the squalor of their imprisonment. Of the 450 men who made the charge, 124 were casualties. Company B, which had been raised in Chicago, was particularly hard hit.[60]

The disastrous Battle of the Crater was a severe blow to morale in Chicago. A minister noted,

> No failure of the war . . . had been more disastrous. In addition to the loss of life, the moral effect was intensely calamitous. It spread a gloom over all the land. It was widely felt, as a result, that we were making no progress in the war, and were likely to make none. All the friends of those who died in the undertaking felt that their lives had been sacrificed to the most stupid and criminal blundering.

Ministers and politicians assured the widows and their grieving families that the fallen were good men who died in a good cause. But by the summer of 1864 many in Chicago who believed the cause was good stopped believing that victory could be won or, if it could, that it was worth the price. With a presidential election only months away, a fire fueled by despair and defeatism smoldered behind the lines of the Union Army.[61]

7

$\diamond$

"A FIRE
IN THE REAR"

I n August 1864, Chicago hosted its second presidential convention.
Four years earlier, the first such gathering had forged a Republican victory and set the stage for civil war. The goal of the second convention was
to end that war. For a few brief days the attention of Americans in the
North as well as the South focused not on the battlefields but on Chicago.
The Democratic party gathered in the city while Grant was entrenched at
Petersburg and Sherman's troops were stalled before Atlanta. The victory
within the grasp of Union forces in the field could still have been lost behind the lines in Chicago.

To the confident delegates who flocked to the city it seemed as if the
time had come for the Democrats to have their chance at solving the crisis
of the Union. Like the Republican delegates of 1860, the Democrats of
1864 smelled electoral victory in the Chicago air. Two months earlier the
Republican party had begun to split apart. Its radical, antislavery wing,
disgusted with Lincoln's conservatism, met in a separate convention and
nominated for the presidency John C. Fremont, a general with a dubious
military record but impeccable abolitionist credentials. The main branch
of the party did not use the name Republican when it met in Baltimore a
few days later. Under the banner of the National Union party, it unenthusiastically nominated Abraham Lincoln. By August, Lincoln was so pessi-
mistic about his chances for reelection that he had his cabinet sign a statement agreeing to cooperate with the new president-elect between the
election and the inauguration.[1]

The Democrats counted on more than Republican divisions to win
the election. War weariness was apparent in the North. With every list of
casualties, with every inconclusive battle, despair of eventual victory deep-

ened and longing for peace rose. Peace was the tantalizing promise the Democrats could offer to millions of Northerners sick of the fratricidal slaughter and fearful of another draft. But peace was a difficult issue on which to build a consensus. Within the ranks of the party were many conflicting visions of how to end the bloody Civil War. On one extreme were such ultrapeace men as Cyrus Hall McCormick, who urged, "Stop the war, declare an armistice—call a convention, and consider terms of peace." Then there were those who believed that a complete military victory for the North was possible but only under Democratic leadership. The majority stood in the middle ground and maintained that military pressure needed to be balanced with a search for political solutions.[2]

The party was united in their grievances with the Lincoln Administration. On August 27, two days before the full convention, a group of Democrats calling themselves the National Union Democrats met in Chicago to review these complaints. Lincoln's policies were described as "destructive to the liberties of the people, the integrity of the states, and the rights reserved to them." The Emancipation Proclamation was abhorred as only stiffening Southern resolve and condemning the country to an "interminable war." Democrats became particularly incensed when they addressed the booming wartime economy. The short-term prosperity was based on fiscal irresponsibility and an "indifference" to the loss of life. "The idea is with everybody to go ahead," a Chicago Democrat observed, "and see how much you can *swindle* out of everybody while this thing lasts." A Democratic victory in the fall, they predicted, would lead to "immediate peace, with the restoration of the government."[3]

By August 28, the city was full of Democrats. Hotels were booked solid and only cots, rented by the night, were available to late arriving delegates. The Republican press noted ominously that the Richmond House was the first hotel to fill with Democrats, an indication of their support for Jefferson Davis and his government. The *Tribune* said nothing about the low rates at that hotel which attracted delegates from the "people's party." On the other hand, the Democrats might have been less pleased with their accommodations had they known that the hotel was named for Thomas Richmond, an abolitionist merchant and friend of Abraham Lincoln. In any event, they were in good spirits and were not ruffled by such trivialities. Arriving trains were greeted by booming cannons and marching bands. Even Republican observers had to admit that the convention brought in "great numbers" of people. Most of them "manifested a great deal of interest and excitement, particularly on the subject of 'Peace,' blindly and ignorantly bawling for 'Peace' without any comprehension or care, apparently, of how it is to come."[4]

Wearing white cotton dusters over their dark suits and carrying carpetbags, the delegates were tired and dirty from their journey but exhilarated to be at the convention. Although there were cynics in their ranks who agreed with the editor of the *New York Herald* that national conventions were "great congregations of unscrupulous politicians, among whom bargaining takes the place of principle and expediency is substituted for patriotism," most eagerly looked forward to the ninth national meeting of Democrats to revive their spirits. The party faithful needed this convention to remember their past triumphs, to identify new leaders, and to assure themselves that theirs was the party of the people. A Democrat is by definition an optimist, but four years as the opposition party in a country divided by civil war had worn down many of the party faithful. Since the defeat of the "Little Giant," both locally and nationally the Democrats had been through an unprecedented political ordeal.[5]

Politics during the mid-nineteenth century were extremely partisan. Most voters were committed to one political party and would back it no matter what. Allegiance to a political party was often transmitted like religious affiliation. Sons worshipped the god of their fathers and voted the same straight party ticket. An Ohioan remarked that during the 1860s, "it was natural to be a Republican; it was more than that, it was inevitable that one should be a Republican; it was not a matter of intellectual choice, it was a process of biological selection." Even more than the upstart Republicans, the Democrats, the party of Thomas Jefferson, were, by the Civil War, "a party of habits, prejudices, and traditions." The war challenged traditional party affiliation but did not break the bonds of partisanship.[6]

Partisan politics meant more than committed blocks of motivated voters. It also meant a bitter, jaundiced view of one's opponents. To Republicans, the Democratic party was composed of two groups of people: the rank and file, who were described as "the ragged infantines of steeves and brothels, the spawn of shipwreck taverns and dicing houses," and the leadership, who were dismissed as "weak-minded men of respectability." Democrats viewed their rivals as meddlesome autocrats intent on forcing "their harsh and uncongenial puritanical creed down the throats of other men, and compel them to digest it under pains and penalties." When war came, neither party was capable of restraining partisanship. Intemperate rhetoric and ill-advised actions were the contribution of partisan politicians to the war effort. An inner civil war between partisan Republicans and Democrats was waged throughout the conflict. Because the Republicans controlled the presidency, and through it the armed forces, the Democrats fought this war at a considerable disadvantage. Democratic opposition, although no less partisan than many of the actions of the Republicans, was frequently labeled treason.[7]

Wilbur F. Storey, editor of the *Chicago Times,* was one of the most prominent soldiers in the partisan war of words. He had come to Chicago in June 1861 from Detroit, where he had owned and edited the *Free Press.* The *Times* was a small, struggling Democratic newspaper when he bought it. As the voice of Douglas Democracy in the late 1850s, the *Times* had known success. But when Storey bought it from Cyrus McCormick in 1861, it had already turned against Douglas and was a poorly edited newspaper without an audience. Storey's goal was to once more make the *Times* the mouthpiece of the Little Giant. But the first issue Storey edited contained the obituary for Stephen Douglas. The editor and Chicago's Democratic party were leaderless.[8]

Initially, the *Times* took its editorial tone from Douglas's dying words, "Forget party—all—remember your country." Although Storey himself thought Lincoln was a man of mediocre ability led by those around him, he urged Democrats to follow the president's lead. From the summer of 1861 to the summer of 1862 Storey defended the president from attacks by the *Tribune,* which wanted a more aggressive, abolitionist war policy. During this year the *Times* improved its coverage of the war, increased its size, and changed its format. As a result, subscription sales increased, making it one of the city's most successful newspapers.[9]

Storey was a harsh, opinionated man with a caustic tongue and a purple pen. Although he was white haired at forty-four, the editor had a reputation as a carousing sexual athlete. An employee described him as "a Bacchus, a satyr, a Minotaur, all in one." When someone did something he disapproved of, the editor would launch into a tirade that made the transgressor's "hair stand up straight." One of his reporters boasted that Storey "could say meaner things in fewer words than any person I ever saw." His treatment of the Republican president seems to have been similar to the way he treated his employees. So long as Lincoln was in line with Storey's views, the president could be tolerated, even supported. Storey believed that a compact existed between Lincoln and Democratic stalwarts. While the president pursued the goal of reunion, they would eschew partisanship. When Lincoln issued the preliminary Emancipation Proclamation in September 1862, Storey reacted like a scorned suitor. First he sought to understand Lincoln's action as an effort to "shorten the war." Then he sought to dissuade the president with an editorial describing the Proclamation as "an act of national suicide." Only after he was convinced that Lincoln was in bed with the abolitionists did he let loose a torrent of vituperation.[10]

Lincoln was assailed as a "lank, nerveless, almost brainless and vacillating old man." "It is difficult to believe," Storey wrote on another occasion, "that so foolish an old joker can be President." After the Emancipation became law, Storey's headline shouted "The Awful Calamity of Abraham Lincoln." The administration was described as a "piratical crew" and the country a "hopeless wreck." The devastating defeat at Fredricksburg was declared "the most stupendous homicide of modern times," which left Lincoln's hands "dripping with gore."[11]

Storey's assault on "czar Abraham" rallied most Chicago Democrats to a bitter partisan opposition of the government. James Sheahan, editor of the city's other Democratic newspaper, the *Post,* had not been as shaken by the Emancipation Proclamation. He opposed the policy, but felt that Lincoln deserved support, at least until a Democratic president could be elected. This moderate policy, not quite in line with the War Democrats, who fully backed the administration, yet strongly in favor of the war, won few readers. The *Post* was gradually pushed to the fringe, and the *Times* became the mouthpiece for the Democrats of the Midwest.[12]

Chicago Democrats were staunchly conservative. Their opposition to the Lincoln Administration often became opposition to the war itself because of two related issues that were central to the party: the Constitution and white supremacy. Just as before the war, the Democrats remained the party of states' rights and a strict interpretation of the Constitution. According to their orthodoxy, slavery was guaranteed by the Constitution as a local institution. Therefore, Republican initiatives, such as the abolishment of slavery in the District of Columbia, the repeal of the Fugitive Slave Law, and most strikingly, the Emancipation Proclamation, were all unconstitutional actions. In their view, Lincoln was accumulating too much power at the federal level. The danger of this was seen in the arrest and detention of white dissidents simply because they spoke out too vigorously against the administration's questionable policies. Democrats were committed to the proposition that "the Constitution is as binding in war as in peace."[13]

Republicans were willing to trample on the sacred Constitution because, in the Democrats' view, they had "nothing except 'nigger on the brain.' " The war had become a mask for abolitionism. In December 1863, Storey proclaimed, "Every man . . . who is called into the field, goes not to fight for the Union, but to kill slavery. And every dollar of expenditure beyond what is necessary to preserve the *status quo* is not for the Union, but to kill slavery." Lincoln was accused of being "possessed of a mania for blood in the cause of negro emancipation." The Democrats saw themselves as defenders of "white men's lives" and white men's rights. Emancipation was a prelude to Negro equality, and eventually, the mixing of races. Storey saw resistance to the Republicans as "a case of life and death" for the white race.[14]

He was particularly unrelenting in his attacks on the black community of Chicago. Typical of the tone was his coverage of a black minister who seduced several women in his congregation. The story was headlined:

Negro Civilization

Its Bestiality and Degradation—
Incompetency of the Negro Race to Observe
the Laws of Society

Another story was titled "Shall Illinois Be Africanized?" Almost every issue contained brief items about "black wretches" who stalked the streets of the city "with insolent bravado." Invariably the "darkey," protected by an abolitionist or "negro sympathizer," would insult Union soldiers on the street or lust after respectable white women. The stories generally concluded with white men gaining the upper hand and physically beating the black men.[15]

What made Storey such a formidable opponent of Chicago Republicans and dangerous enemy of African-Americans was his talent as a journalist. For all his racism, Storey was the founder of the colorful, crusading style of progressive journalism that would make Chicago newspapers famous in the postwar period. Once he found an issue, he had the ability to milk it for all its public interest. As Lincoln discovered, Storey was also unafraid and unabashed in lampooning the great and powerful, particularly if they held elected office. The only time Storey ever beat a retreat was in August 1865, when he portrayed "the crime, brawls and drunkenness of the Irish in our midst." The exposé of the Kilgubbin ghetto touched the quick of the *Times*'s most loyal readership. The editor was abject in his apologies to the Irish and stemmed the tide of subscription cancellations by heaping unrestrained praise on the sons and daughters of Erin in the weeks that followed. On most occasions, however, he was unrepentant. British dancer Lydia Thompson horse-whipped Storey in the middle of Wabash Avenue after the *Times* portrayed her and her burlesque troupe as "Bawds." Unperturbed, the editor described his assailants less ambiguously as prostitutes in the next day's paper.[16]

It was this unrelenting quality that most aggravated Republicans. As early as August 1862, Governor Richard Yates wrote to the secretary of war recommending that the *Times* "be immediately suppressed." Indiana's Republican governor, Oliver P. Morton, also felt the *Times* was an "insidious" influence in his state. The *Tribune,* which since the beginning of the war had called the *Times* "the Jeff Davis organ," also called for the government to close down its rival. But these complaints were merely the croakings of highly partisan parties, and they fell on deaf ears in Washington.[17]

The government's ability to ignore the *Times* eroded by the beginning of 1863. Storey's editorials influenced thousands of disaffected Democrats in the Midwest. The Democratic legislators in Illinois and Indiana both called for an immediate end to the war. The *Times* went out of its way to highlight the failures of the war effort and to sow discontent among troops and citizens alike. In January Storey even raised the specter of disunion when he wrote that the midwestern states might need to "take their destiny into their own hands, and determine it according to their own interests and inclinations and desires."[18]

The political leader of the antiwar Democrats was Clement L. Vallandigham, a former Ohio congressman. The *Times* portrayed Vallandigham as a selfless crusader for "free speech and peace." To Republicans and War Democrats he was a foul traitor, and they had no compunction gerrymandering his Dayton, Ohio, district to remove him from Congress. Vallandigham was a handsome, almost charismatic, young politician. Opportunity, family connections, and his personal political philosophy thrust him to the forefront of the opposition. He was related to Virginia and Maryland planters and committed to the concept of limited government. His seductively simple recipe for ending the war was to "stop fighting. Make an armistice . . . withdraw your army from the seceded states." Once peace was in place, he believed, reunion could be easily negotiated.[19]

One man who had little patience with Democrats of Vallandigham and Storey's ilk was the former chief engineer of the Illinois Central Railroad, Ambrose E. Burnside. General Burnside had been transferred from command of the Army of the Potomac to the peaceful Department of the Ohio after the debacle at Fredricksburg in December 1862. After several months of listening to the Peace Democrats, he issued General Order No. 38, which subjected anyone who "expressed or implied" treason to military arrest, trial, and punishment. It was an impolitic, unilateral action on Burnside's part, and the Democrats did not wait long to challenge him.

Vallandigham openly flaunted the order in an effort to snare the Democratic nomination for governor. Following a standard antiwar speech, Burnside ordered his arrest. The incident could not have been more badly handled. The fiery politician was dragged from his house at 2:00 A.M. by a squad of soldiers who broke down the door. A military tribunal sentenced him to imprisonment until the war's end, although Lincoln commuted the sentence to banishment. On May 25 the Ohio Democrat was escorted to rebel lines and released into their hands.[20]

A storm of protest followed the Vallandigham arrest. In Dayton a mob burned the local Republican newspaper, and only the presence of Union troops prevented more trouble. Storey and the *Times* leaped to the attack. Burnside was thereafter dubbed "the Butcher of Fredricksburg." The arrest was described by the *Times* as the "funeral of civil liberty" in America. "If a terrible retribution does not fall upon the perpetrators of this foul wrong," the *Times* editorialized, "then is not God just." With Vallandigham banished, the *Times* became the rallying point of midwestern Democrats and the lightening rod of Republican wrath. It was a position Wilbur Storey relished.[21]

In Chicago, opinion concerning the *Times* had long since polarized. Circulation boomed among Democrats. The *Times* became the official organ of the Democratic mayor, Francis C. Sherman, and the Democratic-dominated city council. Among prowar forces, however, the *Times* was anathema. In January the Chicago Board of Trade banned the newspaper from the reading room and barred *Times* reporters from the building. The Galena and Chicago Union Railroad refused to allow the paper to be sold on its trains or at its stations. Even the Chicago YMCA voted to boycott the *Times*. The *Tribune*, meanwhile, called for the suppression of the *Times*.

Burnside himself had enough of being called a "butcher." On June 1, he telegraphed an order to the commandant of Camp Douglas to stop publication of the *Chicago Times*, and, if necessary, occupy the offices. Storey received a notice of the suppression and was ordered to cease operations. Defiantly, he set his staff to work immediately on a rush issue. A horseman was sent to wait outside Camp Douglas to warn when the troops left the post. By 2:00 A.M. the presses were running off the morning issue. Storey's messenger arrived to report that the troops left the camp. The *Times* had no more than an hour. As soon as an issue was printed Storey ordered it out of the building and into "safe quarters." At 4:00 A.M. two companies of federal troops stormed the Randolph Street building and ordered the presses stopped. The printers and editorial staff were herded from the offices, and the paper was closed. A caretaker was appointed to mind the building, and the troops returned to Camp Douglas.[22]

That morning, as the city awoke, everything began as usual. Republicans got their issues of the *Tribune* and most Democrats received the *Times*. But many people also received handbills announcing Burnside's order. Who printed them is a mystery, but it may well have been Wilbur Storey himself. The handbills called "upon the people to resent this military interference with the freedom of the press." A meeting was called at the courthouse square that evening. All day long the city debated the government's action. Radical Republicans were ecstatic, while dyed-in-the-wool Democrats were fighting mad. Outside the shuttered office of the *Times*, "great crowds were gathered." Randolph Street was "a solid pack of humanity." Several times during the afternoon the crowd chanted, "Storey, Storey," but he made no appearance.[23]

The editor remained remarkably calm during the day. He did not believe the people would let the suppression order stand. He took no chances, however, and filed for an injunction in U.S. Circuit Court. Judge Thomas Drummond scheduled a hearing for the following day and issued a restraining order to the army to prevent enforcement of the suppression until the legality of Burnside's order was established by the court. The troops, however, paid no attention to the court order.[24]

By nightfall a large crowd had gathered at the courthouse square. Democratic ward bosses had assiduously worked the riverfront all day long to ensure that a healthy number of Irish dock hands were present. Most people were so angry they needed little urging. One reporter estimated a crowd of twenty thousand people by 8 P.M. The prospect of mob violence was high. The suppression order had stoked the fires of partisanship in the city. Many wanted to immediately march on the *Tribune* and close that paper in retaliation. Republicans in their midst were lucky if they were only menaced by harsh words and "sullen" stares. Several were beaten, the Democratically inclined police joining in the effort.

Inside the courthouse some of the city's leading politicos gathered. Moderates of both parties were frantic to head off a riot. Among the most worried was Judge Van H. Higgens, a stockholder in the *Tribune* who feared that mob action might ruin his investment. Although Joseph Medill staunchly supported the suppression order, Higgins organized the meeting to try to find a way to have it revoked. Francis C. Sherman, the city's Democratic mayor, chaired the gathering. Senator Lyman Trumbull and Congressman Isaac Arnold were the ranking Republicans. None of the men in the room, no matter their opinion of the *Times,* felt that Burnside's order was legal; worse than that, it was impolitic. William B. Ogden, the city's first mayor, and head of the Chicago and Northwestern Railroad, proposed that a petition be sent to the president:

> Whereas, in the opinion of this meeting of citizens of all parties, the peace of this city and State, if not also the general welfare of the country, are likely to be promoted by the suspension or rescinding of the recent order of General Burnside for the suppression of *The Chicago Times*; therefore
>
> Resolved, that upon the the ground of expediency alone, such of our citizens as concur in this opinion, without regard to party, are hereby recommended to unite in a petition to the President, respectfully asking the suspension or rescinding of the order.

While it was not a stirring endorsement of the right of free speech, it was a document agreeable to all parties.[25]

Along with the petition, Trumbull and Arnold sent a telegram to Lincoln: "We respectfully ask for the above the serious and prompt consideration of the President." Radical Republicans, heedless of the dangerous situation, were appalled to find two of their most prominent party leaders involved in an effort to save the *Times*. A committee was sent to convince them to retract the telegram and to support suppression. Trumbull would not face reelection for several years, and he held his ground, citing the importance of free speech. Congressman Arnold, however, was more immediately accountable to the people. Long into the night he argued with Republican stalwarts that violence would result if the suppression were lifted. Finally, at 1 A.M. the weary representative telegraphed Lincoln that his earlier communication was not intended to "express an opinion that the order suppressing the *Chicago Times* should be abrogated."[26]

Attempts were made to quiet the crowd before the courthouse. E. W. McComas, a former *Times* editor and once lieutenant governor of Virginia, called for patience and trust in the power of the law. Other speakers followed the same course and the tension began to lift, until James W. Singleton began to speak. The downstate Southern sympathizer launched into a bitter attack on Lincoln that brought the meeting "close to the danger line." His idea of cooling down the mass of angry men was to suggest that there would be "time enough for violence" after the court made its decision on the legality of suppression. Fortunately, he was quickly followed by Wint Dexter, one of the city's most successful Republican lawyers. He assured the crowd that most men of his party opposed suppression, and he read them the resolution agreed on inside the courthouse. This speech and the prospect of presidential action against suppression "had an excellent effect on the assemblage." Although several attempts were made to organize a gang to attack the *Tribune,* most of the people went home peacefully.[27]

It was a good thing they did, because several blocks away at the offices of the Republican daily, "the loyal friends of the *Tribune* firm were stationed at various strategic points in the establishment, armed with muskets and prepared to resist attack." They even loosened hot water pipes from the boiler to send jets of steam at "the refuse and off scouring of the copperhead party." At the head of the defenders was Colonel Charles Jennison, one of the authors of "bleeding Kansas" and the leader of the Union guerrilla force known as the "Jayhawks," By asking him to "unholster his gun," the *Tribune* demonstrated how desperate they were. Fortunately, Jennison was given no occasion to fight that night.[28]

Lincoln was in a quandary. Although he was no friend of the *Times,* Lincoln did not approve of Burnside's action. He was politician enough to see that suppression of the *Times,* like the arrest of Vallandigham, was a blunder that played into the hands of the administration's foes. As soon as he heard of the order he suggested that Burnside "take an early opportunity" to revoke the suppression. Judge David Davis, Lincoln's rotund political advisor, wired from Springfield that the president needed to immediately end the suppression. Lincoln did not want to humiliate one of his best-known generals, but he was, as he later said, "embarrassed with the question . . . what was due the military service on one hand, and liberty of the press on the other." The president thought he found the proper course to follow when he received the bipartisan resolutions of the courthouse meeting and Trumbull and Arnold's note of endorsement. Since there seemed to be so little support for suppression in Illinois, Lincoln pragmatically asked Burnside to lift the ban on the *Times*.[29]

Now it was the Republicans' turn to howl. The *Tribune* had a giant pro-suppression rally planned for the evening of June 4. Only hours before the event, however, word was received that the *Times* was again free to (in Storey's words) "print the news and raise hell!" Chagrin that the administration had backed down soon turned to anger toward Storey and any who supported his right to free speech. This time the courthouse was crowded with Union men. They wanted to hear nothing from Trumbull or Arnold who had, in the *Tribune*'s words, "saddened and humiliated" them "by an exhibition of weakness, vacillation and timidity." Instead, the crowd chanted, "Give us Jennison the Jayhawker: Give us our man of blood." The colonel, who was as much a demagogue as he was a killer, was only to happy to come forward and make some incendiary remarks.[30]

"No man had a right to live a moment," the Jayhawker intoned, "who had a drop of traitorous blood in his veins." He was willing to grant Storey a trial first, but if he was guilty of publishing treason, Jennison said, he should be hung "until he is dead, dead, dead!" He went on to excite the crowd further by boasting of all of the traitors and slave owners whom he had hung in Kansas: "There is not one left now to hang—and if you will send us your traitors . . . we'll hang them for you." Amid great cheers he closed his address by advising, "When Old Abe thinks best to take this matter in hand in earnest, he will put this rebellion down by a war of extermination—by hanging traitors and confiscation of their prosperity." Fortunately, Jennison's fiery remarks were followed by several more speakers whose droning addresses combined with the late hour to defuse the crowd's emotions.[31]

For the second time in two days partisan passions in the city were raised to the boiling point. Another crisis over the *Times* nearly occurred when Lincoln reconsidered his revocation of the suppression order. Late on the afternoon of June 4 Lincoln received Congressman Arnold's second telegram, in which he supported suppressing the *Times*. Lincoln did not want to let down the Chicago Republicans who helped put him in the White House to begin with. If they were so against the *Times,* Lincoln was willing to limit Storey's constitutional rights a bit longer. He sent a second telegram to Burnside, advising him to hold off on lifting the suppression order. It was, fortunately, too late. Burnside's order that put Storey back in business had been received in Chicago at 6:30 P.M. Several hours later he got Lincoln's second message. The general then had a choice: reimpose suppression or let the revocation stand. Had he acted to reimpose, Chicago would have received the news in the midst of the Republican rally. It would have looked like the administration was now bowing to the threat of violence from Republicans. This could easily have led to a Democratic backlash and a full-scale riot. Burnside wisely pocketed the president's second order, and the suppression crisis quietly dissipated.[32]

For several days Colonel Jennison stalked the streets of Chicago "followed by a crowd of gaping admirers." But this was the Garden City, not Kansas, and he was gratified by no "showdowns" in the streets. The business that brought him to the city was finished, and when the threat of violence had clearly passed, he left. The big loser in the whole affair was Isaac Arnold, due for reelection in little more than a year. By initially advising Lincoln against suppression, he had angered the radical wing of his party. He was not reslated for the House of Representatives. Arnold had finished his days as a maker of history, and he contented himself with writing the history of others.

For Wilbur Storey the threat of violence did not end with suppression. Burnside's order had given official credence to the *Tribune's* often repeated charge that Storey was a traitor. As a result, a *Times* employee later wrote, "every loyal citizen believed he had a God-given right to attack Storey on sight, and kill him if he could." Soldiers on furlough often boasted that while passing through Chicago, they were going to "stop long enough to clear out that damned secesh sheet, the *Times.*" In May 1864, several men in blue acted on that boast. They swaggered into the counting room "brimming over with lofty patriotism and poor whiskey" and began to threaten the clerical staff. In the midst of their tirade, Wilbur Storey swept into the office. Briskly he walked toward his office, brushing against one of the soldiers as he passed them. "Who you a-pushin', you damned old secesh son of a _____?" shouted a corporal. As he did so he hurled a crumpled copy of the *Times* at the editor and knocked his hat off. "As quick as a flash of light," according to a *Times* reporter, "Storey turned, seized the corporal by the throat, and pushed him backward until they reached the window, through which the patriot went, head and shoulders, carrying a considerable portion of the sash and glass with him into the street. This done, Storey, without a glance at the other loyalists, who were rapidly falling back toward the sidewalk, went into the room, not having uttered a word during the occurrence."[33]

Storey was sometimes attacked right on the public street. George Trussell, a notorious gambler whose flexible morality allowed him also to be a staunch Republican, once knocked the editor on the head with a large cobblestone. The blow sent Storey to the ground, although he remained conscious enough to pull a Derringer from his pocket and fire a shot at Trussell. The bullet missed its mark but served notice that Storey was not a man to turn the other cheek. In the wake of the suppression he kept the *Times* office well stocked with muskets, pistols, and powder.

Storey relished the brief suppression, even though it made him and his reporters the occasional targets of attack. The feisty editor emerged as the only real winner of the suppression affair. Employees of the *Times* agreed that "the attempt at suppressing the *Times* was an immeasurable benefit to the financial interests of the journal." Burnside had unwittingly given the *Times* nationwide exposure, and subscriptions "bounded upward in unprecedented fashion." Storey and the *Times* became a national symbol of Democratic resistance to Lincoln's "tyranny."[34]

By the time the Democratic Convention met in Chicago in August 1864, political tensions within the city had intensified. A Union Army officer stationed in Chicago described the atmosphere as a "sleeping volcano" about to erupt. Storey noted that among the masses there was a "great popular fervor of anxiety." The peace delegates at the convention were looked to with hope by many a man in the street because Chicago, and most of the North, spent the summer of 1864 under the lengthening cloud of a draft.[35]

Unlike other areas of the Midwest, Chicago had avoided the draft calls of 1862 and 1863 because of high enlistments. But when Lincoln called for 500,000 more men in July 1864, few people thought the state could escape conscription. The War Department charged Illinois with raising 52,057 troops. Faced with such a heavy demand, the people braced themselves for the imposition of the Enrollment Act of 1863. In New York City the summer before the draft sparked a four day long riot, the worst in U.S. history, that left more than one hundred dead and much property destroyed. A year later Chicago exhibited many of the symptoms that had led to the New York riot. The city was divided politically, ethnically, and economically.

Draft registration in Chicago began just a few days after the *Times* suppression crisis in June 1863. It had been Storey's editorials on the draft that had helped lead to Burnside's order. He whipped up the city's Democrats by warning them that drafted men would be "carried away in chains." When the first enrolling officer entered the crowded neighborhoods that subscribed to the *Times,* he was not given a warm reception.

> Doors were barricaded upon his approach, and raw-boned, ferocious-looking curs, snapping furiously, jumped out from every direction to repel the invader. At the same time exasperated matrons flung open second story windows and, elongating their necks through the apertures, poured forth the most vile execrations. . . . Loving their husbands better than they did the law, they did not fail to make of this first enrolling officer a significant example to all who should come after. They beat their victim well, and rolled him in the mud, and then dismissed him with a half-dozen pails full of swill thrown lavishly over his body.

Nor was this treatment unique. Deputy Provost Marshall Carter fled from one woman's house when she produced a hatchet in response to his request for information about her husband.[36]

The clumsy process of conducting a door-to-door survey of eligible men in each of Chicago's wards exposed the provost marshall to a torrent of verbal and physical abuse. Some men merely lied to the enrolling officers, while others were blatantly obstructionist. Michael Caton, a defiant South Sider shouted to an officer "that he would not give . . . his name and would kick him into the wall unless he left the premises." In spite of such abuse, officers continued their unhappy task. When all other means of getting the names of men in a district failed, warrants of arrest were issued. Occasionally even this did not humble some draft dodgers. On June 25, 1863, enroller E. A. Carter, an assistant, and U.S. Marshall George C. Webb arrested four men who had refused to cooperate. As the prisoners were escorted through the street, a crowd of "infuriated Irish" began to form. At first they merely shouted words of encouragement to the arrested men. But in a short time the scene turned ugly as a hail of stones, bricks, and household garbage began to fall on the officers. By now a crowd of three hundred, many armed with clubs, began to close in on the lawmen. Desperate, they released the prisoners and tried to make a run for it. Carter was immediately felled by a violent blow to the head. The mob left him for dead and rushed the other officers. The other enrolling officer, J. B. Baily, was struck on the temple and fell to his knees, but with the help of the U.S. marshall he got to his feet and fled to safety.[37]

By the time draft registration was completed, conscription appeared inevitable. Perhaps because of this the draft laws and the war effort were openly questioned with greater frequency. Initially it was possible to buy one's way out of the draft by paying a commutation fee of $300. This led the German-born father of a Union soldier to complain, "We plebians have done our share. The patricians who live on Michigan Avenue need not think that only the sons of plebians are fit and worthy to be slaughtered and that the wealthy can sidestep their obligations as citizens of the United States and evade the rigors and hardships of military life." By the end of 1863 the commutation fee was widely criticized as the "barn-door of escape" for the rich. To quell accusations that the struggle for the Union was becoming "a rich man's war and a poor man's fight," Congress acted to repeal commutation in July 1864.[38]

The repeal was good public relations for the administration at a time when they desperately needed it. But the end of commutation did not worry the wealthy citizens of Chicago. Rich men of draft age, such as Marshall Field, Richard Crane, George Pullman, and scores of others who were fast on their way to becoming the city's business leaders, had little to fear from the draft. If their names were drawn, they could still purchase a substitute. Early in the year a substitute could be enrolled for a few hundred dollars. But by the summer of 1864, when Chicago began to confront the draft, the price had risen to about $1,200. At a time when the laboring man earned less than $1,000 annually, only the well-to-do could afford a substitute.

Early in the war a man interested in enlisting shopped around to find the right unit. His decision was generally based on who was raising the company and who were already in it. By 1864 it was the bounty system that determined when and where men enlisted. Money became a prime consideration. As early as May 1861, the federal government offered a bounty of $100 to every man who enlisted. Later this bounty was raised to $300. Local government, such as that of Cook County, also began to offer bounties to spur enlistments and to save Chicago from the "disgrace" of the draft. As the draft became imminent in the summer of 1864, even township and ward bounties were offered. It was possible for a recruit to march off to war with $1,000, which for many young men was two to three years' salary.

The bounty system and the need for substitutes spawned a new profession in Civil War Chicago: the enlistment broker. Like many middlemen, the brokers served almost no useful purpose. The federal government opened the door that led brokers into the enlistment process when it promised $2 to anyone who brought in an acceptable recruit. The bounty system greatly increased the amount of money involved and stimulated the growth of brokerage. The fixed federal bounty was paid to soldiers only after they had served in the army or navy, but local bounties were paid at the time of enlistment, and they fluctuated in amount. In the summer of 1864 Chicago wards agreed to offer no more than $100, but after only three days this agreement broke down as each ward sought to avoid the draft and meet its quota by enticing more volunteers. Brokers promised naive young men that only they could find recruits the highest possible bounty. Because some local draft districts worked closely with brokers, they appeared to have a certain "official" status. One of Chicago's largest brokers established his office across from the provost marshall's headquarters, thereby reinforcing that impression. In reality, brokers swindled large numbers of volunteers out of part of the bonus money while ensuring that men in the market for a substitute paid the highest possible price.[39]

Chicago was flooded with brokers in the summer of 1864. They crowded the entrances to recruiting stations and patrolled the train stations and wharves hoping to entice country boys visiting the city or immigrants just off the boat. But mostly they preyed on patrons of saloons. There working men in their cups might be seduced into enlisting or occasionally even be shanghaied into the service. The saloons on Wells Street were notorious rendezvous for rings of bounty "jumpers." Unscrupulous brokers would form groups of jumpers that were transported from place to place. After enlisting the men and collecting their bounties, the broker would go to a prearranged meeting spot. The jumpers would desert as soon as they could, usually within twenty-four hours, and gather at the rendezvous to split the profits. The process would then be repeated, often as many as ten to twelve times.[40]

Some brokers were themselves bounty jumpers. Edward Jones and his wife, Ida, ran a profitable ring; they pocketed the bounties from Jones's eight enlistments as well as their cut of bounties from others whom they induced to jump. Their greed, however, got the better of them, and they began to cheat jumpers out of their share of the loot. These disgruntled jumpers then joined with the police to arrest Jones in a Canal Street hotel. He finished the war at the Camp Douglas dungeon in irons.

No irons could hold Joe Harper. He enlisted in the navy in October 1864, but before leaving the city, he took his bounty and deserted. Three times the Navy recaptured Harper and three times he escaped. Finally he fled to Cincinnati. A private detective was assigned to the case, and Harper was recaptured and returned to the navy recruiting center in Chicago. But the navy could not hold him. In spite of iron manacles on his hands and feet, Harper escaped from a train that was taking him to join the gunboat fleet at Cairo. Harper was an irrepressible rogue; wearing a disguise on the train back to Chicago, he had dinner with the naval captain who had been his guard. As it was, the Navy recaptured Harper by staking out his home and nabbing him when he returned to visit his wife. This time the jumper was locked in solitary confinement in the city's central station. After two days, Harper overpowered a guard, locked him in the cell, and strolled freely out of the jail. He was not retaken, nor did he serve in the Navy.[41]

The acclaimed "prince of the bounty-jumpers" was the barroom brawler, "horse-thief, and all-around bad man," Con Brown. Between 1861 and 1864 Brown enlisted in more than twenty separate military units and was reputed to have collected $8,000 in bounties. But by the summer of 1864 his reputation caught up with him. Brown was confined in the city's Bridewell lock-up, from which he escaped five times and managed to enlist in three more regiments. In 1865 he was sent to the state prison near Joliet, from which he escaped six times in less than three years. His habit of frequenting seedy saloons and brothels led to his repeated recapture, but after one escape, he was murdered in a drunken brawl.[42]

Provost Marshall William James had his hands full watching the numerous saloons and railroad stations jumpers inevitably frequented. His men had an easier time identifying AWOL soldiers enjoying a spree than the practiced bounty jumper. In February 1865, James seized twenty-nine men, many of whom were jumpers, in a raid on a single saloon.[43]

The Democratic press and politicians took full advantage of the city's growing hysteria over the draft. Throughout the long, hot summer they hammered away at what they viewed as the failed policies of Lincoln, which they believed were prolonging the war. The *Times,* in particular, tried to use the draft to drive a wedge between the northwestern states and New England. Chicago's initial quota of 4,128 was "required to make up the delinquencies of Massachusetts and other abolition states" which, according to Storey, "never had furnished and never will furnish, their quotas." Congressman Isaac Arnold, already on the run because of his waffling position on the *Times* suppression, was mercilessly lampooned by Storey. The *Times* referred to him at all times as "Mrs. Nancy Arnold." Its editor even went so far as to allege that Arnold had personally requested a higher quota for Chicago as a way to ingratiate himself with Lincoln.[44]

The draft crisis played into the hands of the peace Democrats. The crowds of ordinary citizens who flocked to the nightly parades and rallies that preceded the convention thirsted for words of relief. "Peace was the cry of every man, woman, and child to be encountered on the streets," the *Times* reported, "Peace was the watchword of every orator." After one postponement, the Democrats finally gathered in Chicago on August 29. It was the latest a national convention had ever been held, but the wait seemed worth it. The stalemate at the front, civil repression, and the impending draft at home all made it seem that events were conspiring to bring to power a party willing to put peace above all else.[45]

The focal point of the convention was an impressive, round, wooden amphitheater. Republicans might joke that the building looked like a railroad roundhouse, but it was a structure as imposing as the Wigwam of

1860 had been. Like the earlier Republican convention center, it was built with funds raised by the local party faithful. The location they chose—in Lake Park near the site of the Art Institute today—was admirable, although not without controversy. The Democratic mayor and city council allowed the use of public park land, arguing that the "Democratic Coliseum" was a temporary structure. The elite residents of Park Row, whose townhouses faced the convention hall, were incensed. But even a temporary injunction failed to stop the Democrats from building on one of the city's most beautiful locations. The completed structure was one and a half stories with windows along the top of each of its curved walls. Atop the structure was an oval cupola and a large flagpole bearing the banner of the beleaguered Union.[46]

On the morning of August 29 the amphitheater began to fill with anxious observers and expectant party stalwarts. The building, only recently completed, smelled of fresh wood and reverberated with denunciations of Lincoln and disputations over who could unseat him. So many spectators packed the gallery that it collapsed, sending hundreds of people tumbling fifteen feet to the ground. Surprisingly no one was hurt. In the streets outside the hall a tremendous crowd milled about. Women and boys hawked red, white, and blue badges and print portraits of the candidates. According to the *Times,* "Michigan Avenue presented during the whole forenoon such a spectacle as was never witnessed on the avenue before." The city's Democrats turned out in such large numbers that it was almost impossible for some delegates to push their way down Michigan to the hall. Pickpockets had a field day, and cab drivers fumed as their carriages were barred from approaching the amphitheater.[47]

Heedless of the spectacle outside, August Belmont raised his gavel precisely at noon and called the convention to order. Belmont was the chairman of the Democratic National Committee and an influential banker. He was not a "peace Democrat," but he was highly partisan. His job was to set the tone for the convention. "Four years of misrule, by a sectional, fanatical and corrupt party, have brought our country to the very verge of ruin," he began. "The past and present are sufficient warnings," he continued, "of the disastrous consequences which would befall us if Mr. Lincoln's re-election should be made possible by our want of patriotism and unity." But just in case anyone was unclear about the "inevitable results of such a calamity," Belmont went on to predict "the utter disintegration of our whole political and social system amidst bloodshed and anarchy." He made it clear that the Democrats were going to come out of Chicago swinging for a knock-out blow against Lincoln.[48]

What was unclear was whether they could come up with either a candidate or platform that could assure a united party. General George B.

McClellan was the front runner going into the convention. For more than a year conservative Democrats saw the heroic image of "Little Mac," in spite of his indifferent military record, as the natural rallying point for the party. His candidacy was seen as the perfect way to criticize Lincoln's handling of the war. The general's commitment to victory by military means, however, left the peace faction cold. Nor was he a good candidate to attack the administration's record on civil liberties, because earlier in the war Little Mac had arbitrarily arrested his share of civilians. Unfortunately, no viable candidate came forward.

Clement L. Vallandigham, the darling of the peace men, was viewed as an extremist by the much stronger conservative wing of the party. They saw Vallandigham's dramatic duel with the administration not as martyrdom but as wrongheaded vainglory which played into the Republican party's charges of treason. He was also blamed for the party's defeats in the 1863 congressional races. Vallandigham came to Chicago a powerful party leader, but without a chance of securing the nomination.[49]

The general's only real rival was the governor of New York, Horatio Seymour, a supporter of the war who crossed swords with Lincoln over emancipation, the suspension of habeas corpus, and the draft. As governor of a populous state and as a politician acceptable to both conservatives and radicals, Seymour had much to recommend his candidacy. Added to that he had a certain popular appeal. In front of a crowd he had a "stately, almost a picturesque bearing, while a strikingly intelligent face changed its expression with the ease and swiftness of an actor's." The trouble with Seymour was, as one supporter decried, he tended to get "carried away by his own subtlety." Because McClellan's early candidacy had secured the support of many party leaders, Seymour was as loath to openly declare his availability as he was to step out of the race. He was a sort of twilight candidate, in part above the fray and in part hopelessly struck by "presidential fever."[50]

Just prior to the convention Seymour clearly stated he was not a candidate, and he announced his intention to attend the gathering, which supported the sincerity of that announcement. Anti-McClellan Democrats, desperate for a champion, for a time lighted upon Thomas Seymour, Horatio's brother and the former governor of Connecticut. But because in all other ways Horatio continued to act the part of a candidate—accepting ovations, honors, and salvos, while saying not a word in favor of McClellan—the opposition continued to hope for his candidacy.

McClellan's supporters, on the other hand, anguished over Seymour's ambiguous course. If Seymour was a candidate, his merits could be openly challenged and his blemishes exposed. If not, he was a powerful politician to be courted. Caught between the two extremes, they needed to

match Seymour's subtlety with their own strategems. This was made difficult because McClellan's campaign manager, New York lawyer Samuel
Barlow, adamantly refused to attend the Chicago convention. Little Mac
had powerful friends at the convention, among them August Belmont and
Samuel J. Tilden, but there was no coordination of their efforts.[51]

Shortly after the convention came to order, Belmont and Tilden cannily arranged to have Seymour chosen as permanent president of the convention. While this gave Seymour a chance to directly address the convention, it also thrust him into an honorary position that made even a twilight
candidacy untenable. Seymour, for his part, saw that a first ballot McClellan victory was likely, and he all but gave up hope of the nomination. His
ambitions, however, had distracted the McClellan forces from the fight
over the party platform.

The peace faction may have lacked a popular candidate at the convention, but their simple solution to America's bloodiest war was enthusiastically embraced by many delegates, including most of Chicago's Democratic faithful. Vallandigham was greeted by Chicagoans as the heroic
defender of "Democratic principles and the rights and liberties of the people." He was frequently called from private caucuses to address impromptu audiences who clamored for his presence. Crowds of well-
wishers followed him wherever he went. At a preconvention rally he held
five thousand people spellbound for an hour with a long verbal assault on
the Lincoln administration. Vallandigham used his popularity to increase
his leverage in the committee meetings that would hammer out the actual
platform.[52]

The first show of strength came on the evening of August 29. The
peace faction pushed Vallandigham for the powerful position of chairman
of the Committee on Resolutions, which had charge of the platform. It
was an obvious test of strength, and the McClellan men, led by Samuel J.
Tilden, were ready for it. Vallandigham was defeated by a thirteen-to-
eleven vote. Nonetheless he persisted in his vigorous insistence on a peace
platform. Through the evening the committee wrangled over wording as
well as principles. The closed-door meetings finally came down to the
question of how the party would achieve peace. Vallandigham demanded
that the party commit itself to an immediate armistice if it was victorious,
while Tilden and the McClellan men held out for a military solution. The
committee finally adjourned at 1:00 A.M. with no agreement.

When the convention went back into session Horatio Seymour assumed its chairmanship. He immediately launched into a long speech that
emphasized the sins of the Republicans and the need for democratic unity.
It drew loud cheers but lacked the heat to ignite a pro-Seymour movement.
The governor himself began to realize his chances of being a successful

dark horse were remote. As he gaveled the convention back to order, he called for the report of the resolutions committee.

A chagrined James Guthrie, the McClellan loyalist, who had defeated Vallandigham as committee chairman, reported that the committee had failed to agree on a platform, and a debate ensued as to when the platform would be ready. Tilden asked for an adjournment until 4:00 P.M. Panicked, Vallandigham immediately pressed his objections. He knew he was outnumbered on the committee and wanted at least another day to build support. A vote was taken, and the McClellan men were supported by the convention. Vallandigham was defeated once again.

The committee had only a brief recess to hammer out the platform. The McClellan supporters had twice demonstrated they had the votes to defeat the peace plank, yet during the afternoon, Vallandigham managed to win the committee to his point of view. It is likely that he played his trump card—a divided party—to win a peace plank. The Democrats feared a repeat of their disastrous 1860 convention. The McClellan men would rather give the devil his due than risk a bolt by the peace men.[53]

When the convention reassembled at 4:00 P.M., the platform was read. Vallandigham supporters were thrilled when they heard the second resolution declare the war a "failure" and "demand that immediate efforts be made for a cessation of hostilities." Tilden and Belmont were aghast when a thunderous ovation followed. The doctrine of "peace at any price" had triumphed, and for a few minutes it looked as if the peace faction might steal the presidential nomination as well. While the McClellan supporters were still "a picture of despair," the convention moved immediately into the nominations for president.

The peace faction threw their support behind Thomas Seymour, more in an effort to block McClellan than to elect the former governor of Connecticut. Seymour's nomination was seconded by short-tempered Benjamin A. Harris from Maryland. Only the day before he nearly caused a riot when he struck a McClellan supporter on the convention floor. On this occasion he also launched into Little Mac himself and, in a bitter diatribe, denounced him as an "assassin of states rights, the usurper of liberties" because of the general's 1861 arrest of the Maryland state legislature. Did they really think Antietam was a "victory"? he asked. "As a military man, he has been defeated everywhere." A chorus of hisses mixed with cheers threatened to drown out the speaker. Horatio Seymour several times restored order so Harris could be heard. The wild scene buoyed his hopes of yet being called forward as a compromise selection. An Ohio delegate followed Harris with a plea not to nominate McClellan. "I beg of you," he concluded, "give us another candidate." A chorus of "Seymour of New York!" swept across the amphitheater.

While the ballots were being prepared the McClellan supporters were forced to endure Horatio Seymour's continued "ogling with the ultra peace men" and the antics of a professional mimic who entertained the crowd of fifteen thousand onlookers with clownish imitations of the general. This was not the atmosphere they had envisioned. Even in the twilight of a cool Chicago afternoon it was clear they were losing their grip on the convention. Fortunately, there were no gas lamps in the amphitheater, and as the sun began to set the hall grew dark. Motions for adjournment were shouted from the floor, and after heated argument, the convention adjourned.[54]

The delay allowed Belmont and Tilden to regroup McClellan's shaken supporters. Hasty efforts by the peace faction to unite on a candidate who could seriously challenge McClellan failed. The next morning was the moderates' moment of triumph. The same convention that the day before voted for peace at any price overwhelmingly endorsed a war candidate for president. On the first ballot McClellan captured the nomination. Yesterday's object of laughter was transformed into today's man of the hour.

A giant banner bearing McClellan's portrait was unveiled to the tune of "Hail to the Chief." Men swung their hats and women waved white handkerchiefs, while the crowd outside the amphitheater shook the rafters with "thunders of applause."[55]

In a final gesture of party unity and ideological incoherence, the Democrats nominated George H. Pendleton, an Ohio congressman only slightly less radical than Vallandigham, as their vice-president. The conventioneers congratulated themselves that they had avoided the danger of party disunity. Instead of choosing between war and peace, they "saddled two horses" and asked McClellan to ride both at the same time. "Little Mac" was enough of a showman to attempt this feat. McClellan formally accepted the nomination after several days of consultation with his advisors. His letter of acceptance equivocated on the peace plank but in the end still held an olive branch to the American people, North and South.[56]

The Chicago Convention ended with a "monster" torchlight parade through the city. In an era of grand parades this was one of the most elaborate. Military bands, marching clubs, and horsemen were out in force, with abundant fireworks lighting the sky. The highlight of the parade was a series of floats that drew howls of delight from the "dymmicrats" who lined the street. Each was a caricature of Lincoln. The final one was the most popular. It was done up in a hearse with a black coffin and a sign that read, "Abe in 1865."[57]

———◇———

"I am now very anxious to hear from the Chicago Convention," wrote Alexander Stephens, vice-president of the Confederacy. "When I see what has been done there I can form some more rational conjecture as to the probable general prospect before us." All across the South people anxiously awaited the results of the Democratic convention. A Confederate War Department clerk noted in his diary, "Our people take a lively interest in the proceedings of the Chicago Convention, hoping for a speedy termination of the war." When the results were published, the clerk was delighted. He recognized the platform was "a defiance of Lincoln" which he hoped would "inaugurate civil war" in the North.[58]

The Chicago Convention and the presidential election were vital to the interests of the South. The growing war weariness and political division in the North gave the Confederacy an opportunity to launch clandestine operations designed to foment discontent and disrupt the war effort. Among the many delegates attracted to Chicago by the convention were a group of Confederate secret agents. What they intended to do in the city and what support they received have been highly controversial aspects of Civil War Chicago.[59]

The leader of the rebel agents was Thomas Henry Hines, a handsome former cavalry officer. In Oldham County, Kentucky, he had been known as a classical scholar. At Masonic University he was a popular teacher who took a dozen members of the senior class with him into the Confederate Army. He had gone to war in the wake of Fort Sumter, a thin, pale lad of twenty. Hines' war service was dramatic. He led numerous raids behind Union lines, sometimes crossing the Ohio River. By 1862 he commanded a company in General John Hunt Morgan's Kentucky cavalry. Following Morgan's spectacular ride across Indiana and Ohio, Hines was imprisoned with the general. For several months they cooled their heels in the Ohio Penitentiary, brooding over their harsh treatment and reading romantic novels. After reading of Jean Valjean's numerous escapes in *Les Miserables,* Hines devised a plan to tunnel out of their cells. On November 20, 1863, Hines, Morgan, and four other officers successfully made their escape. This remarkable coup, and Hines's demonstrated skill for behind-the-lines operations, persuaded Confederate Secretary of War James A. Seddon to assign him to special service in Canada.[60]

Hines's mission was threefold. He was to organize the return to the South of Confederate prisoners of war who had escaped to Canada and to "confer with the leading persons friendly or attached to the cause of the Confederacy, or who may be advocates of Peace." The Kentucky captain was further given the "liberty to employ such of our soldiers as you may collect, in any hostile operation." After several months in Canada Hines narrowed this broad mandate into an ambitious plan to liberate some, if not all, of the thousands of rebel soldiers confined in Illinois and Indiana prison camps.[61]

Hines arrived in Chicago on the morning of August 28, 1864, and checked into the Richmond Hotel. The small group of men who accompanied him were part of a force that may have numbered as many as seventy-four, all of whom arrived in small groups of four or five men. Amid the thousands of people drawn to the city by the convention, the renegade rebels went unnoticed. Hines expected that his men would form the leadership cadre for the released prisoners. To make the actual assault on Camp Douglas, he relied on discontented Democrats drawn to the city by the convention. All day Hines went over his plan of attack. That evening he met with the leaders of the rebellious midwesterners on whom so much depended. It was supposed to be a final meeting to arrange the last-minute details of the attack. When the would-be revolutionaries arrived, frightened and nervous, Hines knew something was wrong.[62]

The men who met that evening with the Confederate agents were copperheads, named after a poisonous snake that hides in the grass. All favored peace. Lifelong Democrats, many avowed a distinct bias toward the Confederacy. They were members of a select secret society known as the Sons of Liberty, formed in February 1864 to protect free elections and Democratic newspapers, and to aid the election of Democratic candidates. Clement L. Vallandigham was its "supreme commander," and it was made up solely of peace advocates. Yet even this faction of the party was divided. In April 1864, the organization had its first leadership council meeting in Windsor, Ontario—where Vallandigham was living in exile. The meeting became acrimonious after the state representatives quarreled over whether the organization would endorse secession. From that point on leading Democratic politicians, including Vallandigham himself, had little to do with the Sons of Liberty. The organization continued to exist, however, as a clandestine political action club, complete with secret oaths, handshakes, and passwords.[63]

The Sons of Liberty was only the most notable of a number of "dark lantern" organizations that Democrats founded to build political opposition to Lincoln. Earlier organizations, such as the Order of American Knights and the Knights of the Golden Circle, had fallen apart because of Republican opposition and a lack of support from rank-and-file Democrats. Wilbur Storey of the *Times* warned Democrats not to join secret societies. He argued that "when personal liberty in this country can only be protected by the intervention of secret organizations, it may as well be surrendered altogether." Yet the very existence of such groups, no matter how weak, fostered a Republican reaction. By the middle of 1862 the Republicans built on the foundation of the Wide Awakes campaign club and formed a series of local political clubs known as the Union League, also a secret club boasting its own passwords, grips, and signals. In Illinois the

Union League and the Sons of Liberty were partisan responses to the extraordinary crisis that divided the nation. Their existence helped to polarize politics even further as each side claimed it needed a secret society to protect its interests from the machinations of the other.[64]

The Union League in Chicago organized some of its members into a Home Guard. Following the crisis over the suppression of the *Times,* the League requested arms from Governor Yates. Democrats were appalled by the suggestion and warned that they would retaliate by forming their own militia units. Such a prospect frightened moderates, and even fire eater Wilbur Storey was alarmed. "Will not organizations on one side beget organizations on the other," he wrote, "and when the parties face each other, armed and organized, how much of a spark will be required to produce an explosion?"[65]

The Sons of Liberty, however, were much more dangerous than the Union League. The republican organization was largely controlled by such responsible, experienced, if partisan, leaders as the *Tribune*'s Joseph Medill. The Sons of Liberty fell into the hands of a series of inept, petty politicos, each of whom nursed delusions of grandeur well beyond the grasp of their organization. By summer 1864 these men were deeply involved in negotiations for financial aid from the Confederate government.

The Confederate commissioners in Canada and the Sons of Liberty became entangled in a web of deception and self-delusion. The Sons of Liberty wanted, above all else, peace. They saw a Democratic victory at the polls as the fastest road to that goal. That would remove Lincoln's administration and, they believed, pave the way for quick reunion. Thomas Hines was careful not to disabuse the midwesterners of the notion that peace would bring reunion, even though Confederate policy was clearly independence. What the Confederacy wanted was to subvert the Union war effort. If this could be done by helping to elect a peace candidate, so much the better. If it meant sparking civil war in the Midwest or releasing Southern prisoners of war, that, too, was fine. The men who led the Sons of Liberty (we do not know the names of most of them) must have known at the time they conspired with the Confederacy that they lacked the strength to lead a revolution. Nonetheless, they took large amounts of money from the rebels and continually planned military operations against the government. Perhaps they felt that they were on the verge of winning widespread support. They did not blanch when they told Captain Hines that they had eighty-five thousand supporters in Illinois and enough for two regiments in Chicago alone. Hines and the Confederate commissioners in Canada were overly eager to accept the exaggerated claims of the Sons of Liberty. They, as much as the copperheads, wanted to believe the North was on the verge of revolution.[66]

The meeting at the Richmond House on the eve of the Democratic convention produced a collision between expectation and reality. Charles Walsh, leader of the Sons of Liberty in Chicago, reported that his men were not ready for action. Although he had spent $2,000 "to get the boys organized," his alleged force of several thousand men was unavailable, nor had downstate copperhead leaders raised the men they were supposed to bring to Chicago. Hines and his Confederate colleagues were enraged and frustrated. This was not the first time the Sons of Liberty had fallen back from the brink of revolution. The original uprising had been planned for July 4, then July 20, 1864; on each occasion the copperheads asked for a postponement. Now Captain Hines was beginning to see the Sons of Liberty for the humbugs they were.[67]

For their part the Sons of Liberty could offer two strong arguments for yet another postponement. The Camp Douglas garrison had been raised from nine hundred men to a force of twenty-one hundred. This allowed Colonel Benjamin Sweet, the post commandant, to send patrols through the streets of the city. Some copperheads claimed that Lincoln intended to use the patrols to disrupt the convention, but their rabblerousing failed. The reinforcements doubled the odds against a successful attack on Camp Douglas. The Sons of Liberty were also shaken by the news of the arrest of their counterparts in Indiana and the discovery by federal troops of an arms cache. The *Indianapolis Journal* announced that a vast conspiracy had been discovered. Illinois copperheads were inclined to keep a low profile, apprehensive that they might be caught in the same net.[68]

Revolutionary action seemed unpropitious at best, and the political front appeared to favor the peace faction. Vallandigham's great popularity in Chicago and the fact that he was lionized by the delegates held out the promise that the party would adopt a peace-at-any-price program. The Sons of Liberty were not anxious to risk their lives in August to discredit a government that they might be able to expel through the ballot box in two months. Yet they wanted the Confederate gold to continue to flow to their candidates and to keep the possibility of armed action alive. From their view, the best thing to do was to string Hines along until November.[69]

When the copperheads left his room, Captain Hines consulted other leaders of the Confederate force. John Castleman, Hines's second in command, was loath to leave Chicago without trying something. The son of a Bluegrass squire who rode to war with Morgan's cavalry, he favored gathering several hundred copperheads and attacking the lightly defended prisoner of war camp at Rock Island, Illinois. This plan was supported by Colonel George St. Leger Grenfell, a fifty-six-year-old British soldier of fortune. The Englishman had a devil-may-care attitude toward life. His quasi-military career included service in France, North Africa, India, and the Crimea. Out of a sense of adventure he served for two years with Morgan's Raiders, and he did not shirk from the impossible odds faced in Chicago. Hines shared the desire for action. He hoped that once the shooting started, the copperheads would realize that the time for fence sitting was over and rally to his side. The men agreed to request five hundred volunteers from Walsh's Sons of Liberty.

Another meeting was held on the evening of August 29. Hines planned to seize the 9:00 P.M. train to Rock Island. He proposed to cut all telegraph lines, liberate the prisoners there, and take them by train to Springfield, where another camp would be attacked. Railroad employees had already been bribed to allow them access to the train. Yet the plan fell apart when Brigadier General Walsh arrived. He had been able to muster only twenty-five men. Within a space of twenty-four hours his two regiments had shrunk first to five hundred men and then to a mere two dozen. The only thing to do was cancel the plan and get the Confederates out of town as quickly as possible.[70]

Hines had spent $13,600 to spark a revolt in Chicago and had not even a civil disturbance to show for it. Yet the copperheads were bold enough to ask for more money to finance Democratic candidates and to plan for future uprisings. Two things the Confederate agents had was money and hope. They gave the former in exchange for the latter. Before the rebels fled the city, Walsh and Hines agreed to yet another plan. A copperhead uprising and assault on Camp Douglas would occur on November 8, 1864, Election Day.

Most of Captain Hines's men quietly returned to Canada or continued south to the Confederacy. Colonel Grenfell assumed the role of the sporting gentleman and took a train to Carlyle, Illinois, where he spent the interm hunting prairie chickens. Hines and Castleman went into hiding in southern Illinois. The grandiose Northwest Conspiracy had proven to be more comic opera than high drama. Yet the Confederate agents could console themselves that their script had one last act to be played out. A bravura performance on their part might still prevent the curtain from crashing down on the Confederate States of America.

———◇———

On September 2, 1864, the day after the Democratic party declared the war a failure, committed itself to peace, and adjourned its convention, General William Tecumseh Sherman sent a telegram to Abraham Lincoln: "Atlanta is ours, and fairly won."

The Republicans of Chicago used the victory as a call to action. Throughout the summer they had seen the peace movement rise in popularity and power. They had endured the Democratic Convention, which had attracted to the city, in the words of the *Tribune*'s Deacon Bross, "a horde of cutthroats, and bloated, beastly wretches, spoiling for free whiskey and free fights." The popularity enjoyed by the peace advocates seemed a clear indication that the city was sickening of war. The Republicans had been off balance and dispirited. Although they tried to put up a brave front in public, they were uncertain of the course of the war, tired of defending every action of an unpopular administration, and fearful of an impending draft. Sherman's telegram was a much needed tonic.

Coming on the heels of the convention, the fall of Atlanta seemed like the army's reply to the contention that the war had been "four years of failure." Atlanta combined with David Farragut's naval triumph at Mobile Bay seemed a vindication of the administration's grand strategy. "Sherman and Farragut," contended Secretary of State William Seward, "have knocked the bottom out of the Chicago platform."[71]

At the top of the local Republican ticket was Long John Wentworth, a fitting phoenix-like symbol of political rebirth. After his antics during the 1860 election, Wentworth was relegated to the ash heap of Chicago politics. By 1862 he lost his newspaper, as well as the mayor's office. He shrank from the physical challenges of military service and seemed out of step with war politics. In an attempt to keep a hand in public affairs, he blundered into participation in the 1862 Illinois constitutional convention. Republicans made opposition to the "copperhead" convention a test of party loyalty. Long John flunked and fell further from grace. His only public responsibility, a seat on the Chicago Board of Police, came as a gift from the Democratic mayor, Francis Sherman. Long John had another Democrat to thank for transforming him from a party exile to a Republican champion.

For Clement Vallandigham the Democratic Convention was a personal triumph, save for one incident on August 26. At a preconvention rally the peace advocate delivered a speech that held a crowd of citizens spellbound for an hour. Among the crowd was Long John, allegedly there to see that the police maintained order. When Vallandigham came to his fiery conclusion, he was cheered enthusiastically. Republicans in the crowd called for a rejoinder. Wentworth seized the moment and stepped forward.

Standing on the courthouse steps, the former congressman looked the perfect image of faded glory. A French traveler described him as "a large gross figure, a true colossus, a sort of barrel perched on long legs, with a little, bald pink head, two gray gimlet eyes, a thick square jaw, a voice harsh and unsteady from drink, the full-fledged type of the demagogue." In a brief three-minute reply to Vallandigham, Long John did what demagogues do best—he wrapped himself in the flag of patriotism. "If we want peace then let us conquer," he cried out. "If the South want peace let them lay down their arms and cease war. . . . Then I will try to forget the rivers of Northern blood they had shed in their unholy struggle for slavery." He concluded by reminding the mostly Democratic audience how "that glorious old war horse of Democracy"—Andrew Jackson—felt about secession. "Will you stand for Vallandigham and against General Jackson?"[72]

The mighty ovation that followed clearly indicated that Long John, in the eyes of the Chicago mob, had defeated the prophet of peace at any price. The luster of this victory was hardly dimmed five days later when the Republicans met to choose a candidate for Congress. The party leadership was divided between Lincoln's friend Isaac Arnold, the incumbent who was disgraced by the *Times* suppression, and John Scripps, one of the founders of the *Tribune*. The rank and file, however, had other ideas. Spontaneously, they gave three cheers for "John Wentworth, our next congressman, and the political crucifier of the infamous Vallandigham." Wentworth was nominated on the same day Sherman took Atlanta.[73]

The Democratic party regulars in Chicago were undeterred by news of Sherman's victory. They remained staunchly pro-peace. Their candidate for governor, James C. Robinson, was so antiwar he was given a $40,000 subsidy from Confederate agents in Canada. To run against Wentworth, they nominated Cyrus Hall McCormick for the First District of Illinois. Throughout the campaign, the politically inept "Reaper King" insisted on proclaiming that the South would never be defeated militarily. While he spoke to half-empty halls, amid catcalls and insults, Union forces continued to divide and conquer the Confederacy.[74]

Events were unkind to the peacemakers of 1864. The victories at Mobile and Atlanta were followed by General Philip Sheridan's crushing defeat of Confederate forces in the Shenandoah Valley. Even John C. Fremont's splinter candidacy was ended, ensuring a solid Republican front going into the election. "Union men, the dark days are over," the *Tribune* proclaimed. "We see our way out. The gallant boys in blue had given the keynote. Now is the time to strike. Close up the ranks. Forward march. Thanks be to God the Republic is safe."[75]

Only the draft darkened the bright prospects of the Republican party. The possibility of conscription should have buoyed McCormick's peace candidacy. But because he was a millionaire, McCormick was unable to capitalize on the growing resentment of the working class toward the draft. Alderman John Comiskey (father of the founder of the Chicago White Sox baseball club) was in tune with the anxieties of the laboring man. He feared the consequences of a draft and pragmatically reasoned that if his Irish constituents had to fight, they might as well receive a substantial bounty. He worked hard to raise bounty money through the Cook

County War Fund. He had no compunction criticizing both Wentworth and McCormick for doing "little for the war fund." The *Tribune* jumped on this and claimed McCormick made more than $2,000 per day and that he could afford to loan Cook County all of the money needed to avoid a draft.[76]

On September 29, 1864, Comiskey called a mass meeting of working men. Because the circular for the meeting was headlined "the rich man's gold and the poor man's blood," it is not surprising that few businessmen showed up at the rally. Comiskey delighted the "rough laboring men" by launching into a tirade against the business class. "The capitalists want the war carried on so they can make more money," he said, "and when the draft comes they don't care, for they can purchase substitutes; but the poor man must give his life." With loud cheers the meeting resolved: "That while the poor man has to do the fighting it is but fair and just that the rich man should be generous and liberal in his expenditure of money to carry on the war."[77]

McCormick tried to square himself with labor by currying favor with the publishers of the *Workingman's Advocate*. In an interview published in that newspaper he claimed that, as a businessman, he understood the working man, and reasoned that, after all, "money and work were equally necessary to each other." When the *Workingman's Advocate* endorsed the Reaper King over a rival War Democrat, Charles Walker, the *Tribune* charged its support had been bought for $4,000. Walker accepted the party's decision to nominate McCormick, and remained active in county war work. When Walker was the only capitalist to show up at Comiskey's rally, he received a loud ovation. His donations to the fund showed more solidarity with the working man than McCormick's empty words.[78]

By late September the draft lottery began in some of the wards of the city. Cards with eligible men's names on them were placed in a large drum and spun around. One by one names were pulled out, until the quota for the ward was filled. While some wards tensely waited their turn, others held wild celebrations as word was received that they met their enlistment quota. The Republicans were again fortunate that Chicago's share of the draft was reduced from over 4,000 men to only 1,816. This meant that by October 22, several weeks before the election, the draft was over. Eighty-eight Chicagoans purchased substitutes, while only 59 were forced into the army.[79]

After months of anxiety about widespread draft resistance, the handful of men selected, combined with the parade of Union victories, tended to deflate the draft as an election issue. Little wonder the Union men of Chicago entered November confident of a Lincoln victory.

In Camp Douglas, Confederate prisoners were also confident. They did not follow the presidential contest with much interest. What preoccupied them was escape. Since spring of 1864 that had been a difficult task even for a determined group of men. Frustrated by the stronger security at the camp, the prisoners largely abandoned individual escape efforts and began to plan a massive breakout.

Behind the scheme were seven veterans of Morgan's cavalry. They developed in the camp a secret organization designed to frustrate federal stool-pigeons and spies. "The character of every man proposed for membership was thoroughly investigated," recalled one of the conspirators, "and had to be unanimously approved by the committee, before one word was allowed to be said to him." To bind the organization together, each man swore an oath of obedience. When Kentuckian R. T. Bean joined the conspiracy, he was led underneath his barracks out of the sight of the guards, "and, with my hand grasping a Bible, I repeated . . . the most terrible, blood-curdling oath ever concocted by the brain of man." Eventually, between one thousand and fifteen hundred prisoners took the oath.[80]

These men formed the leadership cadre for a breakout attempt that would involve virtually every barracks in the camp. The plan was to make three simultaneous attacks on the garrison. One group would rush the guardhouse and seize the weapons stored there, while another contingent would drive the guards from the parapet and a third force would break through the stockade and secure the artillery park. Every item that could conceivably serve as a weapon, including beef bones, lumps of coal, and sticks, as well as several axes, were cached for the day of the grand assault. Their most valuable weapons, however, were their numbers and audacity. The prisoners outnumbered the guards of Camp Douglas ten to one. The leaders of the conspiracy were confident that on their own, without any aid, they could seize the camp.

The prisoners were not without friends on the outside. By the summer of 1864 Captain Thomas Hines had established communications with the Camp Douglas escape organization. Through the exchange of coded messages he coordinated their plans with the activities of his agents in the North and the Sons of Liberty in Illinois. When Hines was forced to cancel the August 31 attack on Camp Douglas, it was an occasion of great despair for the men in prison. However, they saw the reinforcements at the camp and understood the need for a delay. Two months later they were again prepared to strike.[81]

By November 5, Hines's rebel agents began once again to gather in Chicago. St. Leger Grenfell checked in at the Richmond House after two months hunting in central Illinois. The British adventurer was apprehensive and perhaps a bit wistful. He wrote to his daughter, "What difference will it make whether I lived in London or Illinois? And whether I died in a four-posted bed with a nurse and phials on the bed table jar, or whether I died in a ditch?"[82]

The soldier of fortune's apprehensiveness was prophetic. Federal agents were slowly closing in on the band of confederate conspirators. John Castleman, who had been Hines's second in command in August, was arrested by Union troops in Indiana. Hines suspected that Castleman was betrayed by a turncoat. Certainly the Chicago conspiracy had been shared by too many people, over too long a time, to remain a secret.

Already the Lincoln administration knew the broad outlines of what the Confederacy hoped to achieve in the northwestern states. A bungled phase of the grandiose plan of which Camp Douglas was part had made headlines. In September 1864, a handful of Canadian-based rebels seized a Lake Erie merchant vessel, pirated a second ship, and made an abortive attempt to seize the U.S.S. *Michigan,* the only armed vessel on the lakes. Republican newspapers claimed the incident as proof of a rebel attempt to liberate the Johnson Island POW camp and to bombard the defenseless ports of the Great Lakes. A month later, further proof of rebel skullduggery was seen in Vermont, where confederates looted the town of St. Albans and safely recrossed the Canadian border with more than $200,000. As the election drew near, civil and military authorities across the North were on the alert for any sign of Confederate covert operations.[83]

Hines had been trailed by Thomas H. Keefe, a federal detective. But by the time Keefe got to Chicago, the rebel captain had vanished. A second detective gained the confidence of Vincent Marmaduke, a young Missourian who was thought to be part of Hines's cadre of Confederates. The Chicago chapter of the Sons of Liberty had also been thoroughly infiltrated. Dr. Isaiah Winslow Ayer, a seller of patent medicines, had somehow gotten wind of the indiscretions of the more radical Democrats in Chicago. Sensing a profit in this new form of deception, he played the part of a double agent. He joined the conspirators but revealed what little he heard to Colonel Sweet, the Camp Douglas commandant. Eventually Sweet had five detectives involved in the Sons of Liberty. Considering that the organization had no more than twenty active members, its potential for causing trouble was easily checked.[84]

For some reason Charles Walsh, the "brigader general" of the Chicago copperheads, continued to pretend that he could raise more than a thousand armed revolutionaries. Having taken Hines's money for so long, he may have had no recourse but to press ahead with the plot. The "general" did have legitimate military experience, first against the Seminoles and later in the Mexican War. Since moving to Chicago, the Irish-born immigrant had established a successful dray business and sired ten children. Early in the war he helped to raise the Irish Legion, but after Emancipation he became a bitter foe of the administration. Walsh had been on the fringe of Chicago politics for many years, and once was candidate for sheriff of Cook County. (A generation later he might have made an effective precinct boss for "Bathhouse John" Coughlin or Hinky Dink Kenna, and would have done nothing worse than stuff a few ballots or extort political "contributions.") In the midst of the Civil War, Walsh's partisanship and personal ambition led him into dangerous waters.

Walsh was a sloppy conspirator. He left piles of weapons lying about his house and was careless in his speech. When a neighbor complained about the problems of living next to Camp Douglas, Walsh cryptically remarked, "You will soon be rid of that." Even the handful of men he was able to muster for action against the administration were dispirited and confused. When one young man demanded to know what was being planned, Walsh laughed at him and said he was "too junior to know."[85]

The front for Walsh's activities was the Invincible Club, an old and respectable Democratic organization. Meetings, however, were not held in the Invincible Club hall, but on the fifth floor of the McCormick building. The most prominent member of the group was Buckner S. Morris, the second mayor of Chicago. He had known Lincoln during his days as a judge of the circuit court and nursed a strong dislike for the backwoods lawyer who rose to be president. In bitter and personal terms he denounced Lincoln in speeches before the radical group. He was later described as the "treasurer" of the conspiracy, which probably meant that when Confederate gold was unavailable, he footed some of the costs of the Sons of Liberty. There is no proof that Morris was involved in the Camp Douglas plot: in fact, he always counseled obedience to the law. To whom Walsh confided the details of the conspiracy plan is unclear. At one meeting, L. A. Doolittle, son of one of the city's oldest settlers, delivered a speech which threatened that if the Republicans interferred with the polls, Democrats should counter by liberating the prisoners from Camp Douglas. But the extent to which the young lawyer was involved in the conspiracy is unknown. Walsh may have been discreet enough to separate the political from the military aspects of the Sons of Liberty.[86]

Captain Hines must have known that the chance of a successful attack on the camp was slim. He was not stupid. But he knew that with a Republican victory imminent, the South's position would soon be grave. It is likely that he put more faith in the abilities of the rebels in Camp Douglas than he did in the copperheads of Chicago. Even a slight diversion might allow a mass breakout to succeed, and with eight thousand Confederate soldiers free in the North, anything might happen.

Hines never had a chance to make his desperate gamble. He was betrayed by one of his own men. On the afternoon of November 5, 1864, Maurice Langhorne visited the Union Army headquarters in downtown Chicago. There he had a long interview with Colonel Benjamin Sweet and revealed the plan of attack. Langhorne was another veteran of Morgan's raiders, although it is likely that he was a deserter, not an escaped prisoner like most of Hines's men. For several months he had lived in Canada and participated with other Confederates in schemes to undo the North. His motivation, however, was money, not patriotism. At one point he concocted a phoney rebel raid on Detroit and then tried to sell the secret plan to Union authorities in that city. The cynical con game failed, and Langhorne joined the force of rebel soldiers sent to Chicago at the time of the convention. Although he was badly frightened by the prospect of attacking Camp Douglas, he was prepared to participate. When the attack was postponed, Langhorne must have decided to look to his own interests. Hines later described him as an "infamous traitor who sold his comrades for 'blood money.' " Just how much money he received is open to question, although he told some people it was $6,000—a handsome fee for betrayal.[87]

Colonel Sweet now knew the place and the date of the rebel attack. He could have made a show of force at this point and arrested those whom he suspected of being involved. This would have stopped the conspiracy dead in its tracks. But the colonel was after bigger game: he wanted to net the entire force of rebels and copperheads involved in the plan. Not only would this earn him personal distinction, but on the eve of the election, it would strengthen the Republican claim that copperheads were traitors.

Benjamin J. Sweet was an ambitious and shrewd man. Although brave, he was not an especially astute soldier. His brief active career came to an end during the Battle of Perryville, when he led his regiment into a deadly crossfire. In a matter of minutes, 179 men were casualties, including Sweet himself, who was wounded twice. He was then assigned to the Veterans Reserve Corps. While commandant of Camp Douglas he gloried in politicking with such Republican luminaries as Deacon Bross and Joseph Medill of the *Tribune*. At one point he had to be ordered to remove his office from the center city to the prison camp, where his principal responsibilities lay. Sweet knew how to use his position to build a base for a postwar political career. The colonel could be counted on to take maximum advantage of the conspiracy.[88]

Sweet picked John T. Shanks, a young Texan, to effect his plan. One historian has described Shanks as "a forger, thief, traitor, spy, liar, perjurer, and a coward." Hines wrote of him: "A blacker-hearted villain never lived." Captured during Morgan's Ohio raid, he was sent to Camp

Douglas. He quickly curried favor with the camp command and was given a job as clerk. Other prisoners were repelled by his behavior; in the words of one, "[I] dropped him as I would an adder." Sweet found Shanks to be a dependable stool-pigeon, well suited to the task of infiltrating Hines's rapidly disintegrating conspiracy.[89]

On November 3, Sweet ordered Shanks to see what he could discover about the activities of the Sons of Liberty. Shanks made his way to the home of Buckner S. Morris and posed as an escaped Confederate prisoner. The prudent Judge Morris said "he did not wish to compromise himself" and refused to answer Shanks's questions about where escaped prisoners were hidden in Chicago. The judge's wife, however was less discreet. She was a native Kentuckian who, in the face of public scorn, tried to help the many Kentucky prisoners at Camp Douglas. She often visited the camp, distributing coats, blankets, and gifts of food. In keeping with this generosity she could not turn Shanks out into the night empty-handed. She gave him an old suit and $30 and admonished him to take the next train out of town.[90]

Shanks learned nothing about the conspiracy from the Morrises. But three days later, on November 6, he again played the role of the escaped prisoner and this time he was more successful. Shanks was sent to the Richmond House, where Sweet suspected some of the Confederate conspirators were staying. The Texan slowly signed the guest register, careful to look over the names of the other guests. Recognizing the name "G. St. Leger Grenfell, Great Britain," he sought out the fellow veteran of Morgan's cavalry. At first Grenfell did not recognize Shanks and was guarded in his responses to the spy. But when Shanks said he had recently escaped from Camp Douglas, Grenfell must have seen a perfect opportunity to get accurate information on the current disposition of the Camp's defenses. He told Shank he would try to get him funds with which to leave the city and to visit his room later that night.[91]

Long after the war Hines claimed that both he and Grenfell knew Shanks was a Union spy. This, however, is unlikely, because the conspirators continued to communicate with Shanks and in the end revealed valuable information to him.

When Shanks returned to Grenfell's room at 9:15 P.M., he found two other conspirators there. One was identified simply as "Mr. Ware" and the other as "J. B. Fielding," the alias of Kentucky lieutenant J. J. Bettersworth. They wanted detailed information about the prisoner-of-war camp, while Shanks wanted details about the conspiracy. Bettersworth and Shanks, seated at a table, did most of the talking. During the conversation, Shanks later reported, "something was said about effecting the release of the prisoners." Bettersworth asked numerous questions about the camp and its defenses. Grenfell paced the room listening but seldom joining in save to redirect Shanks's questions from the conspiracy. It is likely that he became increasingly suspicious of Shanks. Bettersworth later wrote that at one point Grenfell said, "I have, as you know, been in the CSA but am now out of it, and do not wish the conversation to continue relative to an attack on C[amp] D[ouglas]." A short time later, Grenfell broke off the meeting, complaining that he was feeling ill.[92]

Shanks gained valuable information on what the rebels planned, but he still did not know all the actors or their hiding places. This he gained over a bottle of brandy with Lieutenant Bettersworth. Drink after drink broke down the caution of the lonely young officer. Within a few hours Shanks knew more about the plot than many members of the conspiracy. It was not until 1:00 A.M. that the groggy Bettersworth left Shanks's room. The spy was on his way to Colonel Sweet's office a few moments later.

Sweet was delighted with Shanks's discoveries. He had already decided to arrest all suspected conspirators, and Shanks's evidence allowed him to cast his net broader and with great accuracy. Three squads were sent out into the night. The first to the home of Charles Walsh, the second to the Richmond House, and the third to the business district to preserve order and to arrest potential conspirators.

Colonel Lewis C. Skinner and the fifty soldiers sent to arrest "Brigadier General" Walsh behaved a bit like the Keystone cops. Their first problem was finding Walsh's house. Although he lived only a quarter-mile from the camp, none of the men knew the house. Frantically Colonel Sweet and Skinner polled the garrison, but no one knew where the copperhead lived. Fortunately Maurice Langhorne was still on the payroll. He had made cartridges at Walsh's house two months earlier and provided a description of its location.[93]

Skinner had his men surround the large frame house before knocking on the door. In the early hours of the morning, Skinner did not expect an immediate answer, so he waited patiently at the door. Gradually, the house was roused, and a woman came to the door. Without opening she asked who was there. The Union soldiers identified themselves and demanded immediate access. What followed was a war of words between the soldiers and the daughters of Charles Walsh that lasted a full fifteen minutes. The copperhead was given precious time to prepare himself and to destroy or hide incriminating evidence. Finally, the frustrated Skinner ordered his men to kick in the door.

Walsh was waiting for them, and after putting on his hat and coat, he made a show of going with the troops peacefully. Skinner was through being deceived, however, and ordered his men to make a thorough search. In the kitchen they found bullet molds and percussion caps. In the front bedroom was a store of double-barreled shotguns, cartridges, and two barrels of gun powder. The real harvest was on the second floor. As the troops mounted the stairs, the rear windows flew open and two men scrambled out and over the roof. In the room they fled were bags of buckshot and a pile of loaded weapons. The men were quickly apprehended and, with the arms, taken to Camp Douglas. Sweet was delighted when he discovered that the men were Charles T. Daniel and Captain George Cantrill, both late of Morgan's Kentucky Cavalry.[94]

Grenfell was next to fall into the federal net. At just before 3:00 A.M. federal officers knocked on his hotel room door. The adventurer was awake and fully dressed. Sometime before he had received a note from Lieutenant Bettersworth. It read, "Colonel—you must leave tonight. Go to the Briggs House." Grenfell may have been in the process of acting on it when the knock sounded. His biographer speculates that Grenfell may have decided to simply "brazen it out" and play the role of the wronged British sportsman to the hilt. But whatever was on his mind, he was captured and dragged to Trinity Church at Wabash and Jackson Street, where Colonel Sweet had established a temporary lock-up for his late night sweep.[95]

The church quickly filled with an assortment of bleary-eyed Democrats, vagabonds, and Confederates. Judge Buckner Morris was dragged from his bed, as were a number of people whose only crime was being southern born. Vincent Maramduke was arrested because he was the brother of a Confederate general. The Missourian had been banished by Union authorities from his native state because of his pro-secessionist sympathies. Richard T. Semmes, a young attorney from Cumberland, Maryland, was arrested because of his participation in the Sons of Liberty. At the Fort Donelson Hotel, twenty-seven men were arrested and accused of being copperhead "bushwackers" from southern Illinois. Army patrols working their way through the saloons of North Water Street found scores of other suspicious characters. Colonel Sweet was disinclined to restrain his men. He advised them that rebels and their sympathizers could be identified by a "general kind of wolfish aspect." When this approach was later criticized, Sweet confidently asserted, "I can tell a man's character pretty well when I see him."

More than 150 people were arrested that night, most of whom were innocent. Sweet's tactics succeeded in capturing only one other member of the conspiracy, Colonel Benjamin M. Anderson of the 2nd Kentucky Cavalry. Anderson was another veteran adventurer, serving in "irregular actions" before the war with William Walker in Nicaragua. By 1865, however, his nerve had been shattered. During the time he was in the North, he was hesitant and fearful and not trusted by his colleagues.[96]

Most of the Confederates involved in the conspiracy got away, including the ringleader, Captain Thomas Hines. Union soldiers searched the house he was staying in but failed to detect him hiding in a box spring. His bold plans had failed. Bitter and frustrated, he made his way home to Kentucky where he abandoned any further thoughts of conquering Chicago. In a matter of days on a rainy November evening, he married his young fiance and gave up the life of a secret agent.

———◇———

Chicagoans awoke on the morning of November 7 to the shocking story of the Confederate conspiracy. The *Tribune* played the story to the hilt, declaring that the liberated prisoners would have plundered and burned the city. At the office of the *Evening Journal* an assortment of weapons seized from the conspirators were on display, including a large rusty knife. A placard identified it as having been found "under the shirt of a man who, when asked what it was for, replied that 'it is to cut the throat of the abolitionists.' " Down the street the Sanitary Commission accepted twenty-five-cent donations for a view of "Grenfell's bloodhound," a harmless hunting dog that imaginative Republicans claimed "could 'do a man up' in no time."[97]

The city's Home Guard was called out by Mayor Sherman, and the militia was mustered for three days' service. A citizen's mounted patrol paraded up and down the streets for two days. Fortunately, the militia did not have weapons. After being organized in a Lake Street warehouse, several "companies" of men marched to State Street and seized control of the horse-car line. They then rode to Camp Douglas, where they expected to be armed and assigned to duty. Benjamin Sweet had no intention of arming this mob of boys and old men, but he was politician enough to flatter their civic pride. He had the men fall into parade formation and gave them a hearty speech. They were ordered to go home and to report at their warehouse each morning at 8:00 A.M. until further orders. Those orders never came.[98]

Sweet could not have timed his sweep any better. The breaking of the conspiracy story had a major impact on the election. "Republicans are furious," wrote a French traveler, "the Democrats, surprised or pretending to be, respond that they are the victims of an odious trick . . . a pretext for making arrests and troop movements to intimidate people." The story further discredited the copperheads and rallied the Republicans to a high voter turnout.[99]

"Vote early and often!" was the battle cry when the election finally began on November 8. After all the talk of violence, the day was surprisingly peaceful. In spite of rain the turnout was heavy, and all day there were long lines at most polling places. A wait of three hours was not uncommon. A foreign visitor was surprised that the voters spent the time "talking to one another in a friendly way, calmly discussing the merits of their respective candidates." Occasionally, he noted

> one hears quips, profanity and the whole charming collection of epithets and exclamation with which the Americans embellish their thoughts; sometimes two opponents will give one another a shove or a belligerent glare, but these quarrels are soon pacified by a handshake.

Waiting voters amused themselves discussing the odds on each candidate with bookmakers, who operated "open-air gambling houses" outside each polling place.[100]

The election results were not known until the next morning. Republicans enjoyed a clean sweep of all the important races. Wentworth was sent to Congress, the *Tribune*'s Deacon Bross became lieutenant governor, and Richard Oglesby was elected governor. Lincoln carried Chicago by less than two thousand of the twenty-seven thousand votes cast (Lincoln 14,388; McClellan 12,691). By a narrow margin Chicago endorsed the Republican war policy and favored the continuation of the conflict.[101]

"This is an event that does the greatest honor to the good sense and patriotism of America," proclaimed Duvergier de Hauranne, a Frenchman who witnessed the election in Chicago. He was greatly impressed that in spite of rebel plots, America successfully held an election in the middle of a bloody civil war. "This turbulent democracy, which had seemed on the point of tearing itself to pieces, spontaneously felt the need to impose self-discipline and to invest the choice of a new government with gravity and order."[102]

For Wilbur Storey and the peace Democrats the future looked grim. The reelection of Lincoln proved to Storey "that our republican system is a failure" and that the "Last remnants of American liberty" had been extinguished. The "imbecilic and unfaithful" Lincoln was destined to be a "perpetual dictator," while America was condemned to "carnage."[103]

8

◇

A CITY
IN SABLE

O n the afternoon of February 23, 1865, Abraham Lincoln had a
meeting with some old friends from Illinois. Across from the president sat Samuel S. Hayes, Roselle M. Hough, and Joseph Medill. Hough
was a veteran soldier and a wealthy meat packer; Hayes, a Chicago attorney, was an old rival from prewar political campaigns. Although a few
jokes and pleasantries were exchanged as the meeting began, Lincoln expected a serious, difficult afternoon. The mere fact that Joseph Medill, the
Midwest's arch Republican and one of the party's strongest supporters of
the war, was accompanying the two well-known Chicago Democrats indicated an exceptional set of circumstances.[1]

A month earlier Lincoln had issued a call for 300,000 more soldiers.
Cook County's share, according to the War Department and the State of
Illinois, was set at 5,200 men. Even the most optimistic Union men regarded this figure as unattainable through recruiting. Only eight weeks after Chicago's first draft had been suspended, the city was faced with the
certainty of another conscription crisis.

As the date of the draft approached, Chicagoans protested with
greater and greater frequency that the county's assessment was unjustly
high. Joseph Medill complained that Cook County was being unfairly
"salted" by downstate politicians. Others blamed the War Department for
not crediting Chicago for all the troops the city had raised in the past. In a
speech to ward draft committees, Medill contended that Chicago's draft
enrollment, which was conducted in the face of great opposition in 1863,
was grossly overestimated. The adjutant general's list failed to consider
the large number of aliens in Chicago, who were not eligible for the draft.
"There was but one thing to be done," Medill concluded, "to send an influ-

ential committee to Washington to lay the case before Father Abraham and get the order for a new enrollment."[2]

The president was disinclined to order new draft enrollments. The process would take months, and he needed men that spring. The rebellion had been battered to the brink of defeat by Sherman's March to the Sea and Grant's incessant pressure on Robert E. Lee. But the cost of the offensive operations was high casualty rates. The Army of the Potomac lost fifty-five thousand men during the first month of Grant's campaign. The long siege of Petersburg further sapped its strength. The conflict had come down to a war of attribution, and Lincoln would not let his armies diminish when victory was within their grasp. Washington was filled with delegations from other states, all asking for their enrollments to be revised, and their quotas reduced. To give the Chicagoans what they wanted would threaten the entire draft system.[3]

Lincoln knew from the outset he would have to refuse the Chicago delegation, but he was too good a politician to reject them out of hand. The men Chicago sent to see him were extremely influential. Medill had played an important role in nominating Lincoln in 1860 and had supported him throughout the war. The editor's brother died at Gettysburg. Moreover, the Chicagoans firmly believed they were in the right, and it is likely that Lincoln privately agreed with them. What he wanted to do was to make them see their local problem from a national perspective.

For two and a half hours they discussed the city's request that its draft enrollment be completely revised. Lincoln agreed that the city's allotment seemed excessive, observing that across the country "the enrollment of the cities was too high." He told them that he thought something might be done, but he did not want to do so without further consultation. "I cannot do it, but I will go with you to Stanton and hear the argument of both sides," he said.[4]

Four days later the Chicago delegation, flanked by several congressmen and Abraham Lincoln, "marched down to the office of the Secretary of War." Edwin M. Stanton was Lincoln's ace in the hole. He was a hard man to out argue, and he had no compunction in refusing requests from influential people. The Chicagoans made their case. They concluded with the observation that Cook County had "already furnished more men" than any district in the Union, save for one in southern Illinois. Stanton then took over. In a carefully worded, thirty-minute reply, he calmly pointed out that with the city's rapidly growing population, it was very unlikely that a new enrollment would lead to a reduced draft for Chicago and might very likely give them a higher total. In any event, granting Chicago a recount would effectively destroy the draft for 1865 and "keep 100,000 men out of the field when most needed."[5]

When Stanton finished administering his bitter medicine, Lincoln stepped in with a sugar coating. The current draft would continue, he decided, but when it was done, Chicago would have its recount of eligible men. For every man enrolled in excess of the recount, Chicago would receive a triple credit toward any future draft. In return for helping with the current draft, Lincoln held out the hope of freedom from any further call for troops. This was not enough for the Chicagoans, however. First meat packer Hough (who was profiting handsomely from the war) and then Medill, the abolitionist, quibbled with the president's decision.[6]

Lincoln, who had been both patient and diplomatic, smelled the faint odor of hypocrisy in their attitude, and he lost his temper. "I shall never forget," Medill later recalled, "how he suddenly lifted his head and turned on us a black frowning face."

> "Gentlemen," he said in a voice full of bitterness, "after Boston, Chicago had been the chief instrument in bringing this war on the country. The Northwest had opposed the South as the Northeast has opposed the South. It is you who are largely responsible for making blood flow as it has. You called for war until we had it. You called for emancipation and I have given it to you. Whatever you have asked for you have had. Now you come here begging to be let off from the call for men which I have made to carry out the war you have demanded. You ought to be ashamed of yourselves. I have a right to expect better things of you. Go home and raise your 6,000 extra men.
>
> "And Medill, you are acting like a coward. You and your *Tribune* have had more influence than any other paper in the Northwest, in making this war. You can influence great masses and yet you cry to be spared at a moment when your cause is suffering. Go home and send us those men."

In stunned silence the Chicagoans sat upright in their chairs, their ears ringing with Lincoln's rebuke. "I couldn't say anything," Medill remembered. "It was the first time I was ever whipped and I didn't have an answer." Quietly, they rose from their seats and left the room.

They stood in the hall a moment, still shaken by Lincoln's anger. "Well, gentlemen," one of them finally said, "the old man is right. We ought to be ashamed of ourselves. Let us never say anything about this but go home and raise the men."[7]

On their return, a final, half-hearted attempt was made in the spring of 1865 to rally the war spirit. A few mass meetings were held. Speakers from across the country were brought in to fire the emotions of men eligible for service. Recruiting offices were set up all over the city (fifty, according to one report). Yet, save for a few youths who had come of age during

————◇————

the war, enthusiasm had been replaced by calculation. Men inclined to join the ranks had a dizzying array of bonus options from which to choose. Money, not patriotism, spurred enlistments.

In the courthouse square brokers erected a shanty town of temporary offices from which they barked out the various cash bounties offered to recruits. Packaging cannon fodder had become a full-fledged business. And like most other fields of business, cities and towns from across the country competed with each other. Because of its rapidly growing population, Chicago was a mecca for recruiting agents from across the country. Uniformed bounty agents from New York or Massachusetts sometimes pretended to be federal soldiers to disguise the fact that they were enrolling Chicagoans to the credit of another state. The small towns of northern Illinois also sent agents to the city. When the *Tribune* complained that a recruiter from Marengo, Illinois, was leaving the city with twenty-five men, the provost marshall's office said that it was powerless to stop such raids. Even the various wards of the city began to raid each other for potential soldiers.[8]

Several wards formed "insurance" societies in which men contributed $10 to $20 to pay for a substitute for any man selected by the draft. The Seventh Ward Society lost some of its funds to an embezzling treasurer. Others found that even honest bookkeeping did not prevent the escalating cost of hiring a substitute from bankrupting the society and leaving men vulnerable to the draft. A safer but more costly investment was commercial draft insurance. In January 1865 the Chicago Draft Insurance Company was formed. It was capitalized at $100,000 and headed by experienced bankers. For $200 the company promised to provide a drafted man with a substitute. Its promotional flyer asked: "Is it not cheaper to pay a fair but reasonable price now, and be certain of having a SUBSTITUTE AT CALL, than to pay an exhorbitant price (from $900 to $1200) after you are drafted, and be compelled to take your chances of getting one at all?"[9]

Men who were induced to enlist were mustered into service at Camp Fry, a training camp located in Lakeview, far from the prisoners at Camp Douglas. There the young men were drilled and disciplined by veteran noncommissioned officers. They jokingly referred to their weeks of marching as being "Fry's on the gridiron of torture." Yet, each day of drill was a day away from the front, a day to count their lavish bounty money, plan for the future, and hope the war ended soon.[10]

————◇————

It was during the final years of the Civil War that Chicago first earned the title it held for many years as "the wickedest city in the United States." Prostitution and gambling flourished in wartime Chicago. The lack of an effective police force, the booming war economy, and the migration to the city of scores of "blackleg" Southern riverboat gamblers combined to create an atmosphere of lawlessness that delighted furloughed soldiers as much as it outraged middle-class society.[11]

"The swarthy, long-haired blackleg of the Lower Mississippi . . . affecting the manners of his favorite old-time victim, the high-rolling, slave-owning planter—invaded Chicago at the outbreak of hostilities," recalled Frederick Cook, *Chicago Times* reporter. They were "Rebel to the core" but uninterested in the hardships of army life. When war shut down commerce on the Mississippi, they abandoned New Orleans and Nachez and moved where the money was, to the booming capital of the Midwest. According to Cook, "This element, so numerous, and so offensively in evidence by its blatant secession talk, not only worked up a good deal of Southern sympathy among the unthinking younger generation about town, but it went far in giving the impression that Chicago was a hotbed of disaffection."[12]

Their loud talk, however, was only that. As Captain Thomas Hines discovered, they were in no way willing to risk their lives for the Confederate cause. The only action they were interested in seeing was at the gambling tables. Some specialized in poker, others in bunko or faro. All relished the collection of turf and blood sports that made up the city's sports scene during the Civil War. Betting was lively at cockfights, prize fights, and rattings. (The latter was a grotesque spectacle where a hunting dog was placed in a pit with a hundred rats, and the gamblers wagered on how long it would take the hound to kill all the rodents.) Dog fights were also popular.[13]

Most of these events took place in saloons or were sponsored by saloon owners. With no television, movies, or mass spectator sports, there was little entertainment available during the evening. The growth of the city's businesses attracted thousands of young men to jobs as clerks. Those without family ties lived near the business district in apartments located in commercial buildings. They were the first young urban professionals in Chicago's history, and saloons were one of their few recreational outlets. "It was this state of things that gave such an air of liveliness to 'downtown' at night," recalled one of the young men. "It made all of us, that were footfree, literally 'Johnnies-on-the-spot' all the time; and it was this intimate and peculiar community life, unmodified by anything like home influences, that gave the gambler his opportunity to play a dominant role."[14]

Some saloons specialized in sports and sponsored boxing matches or foot races. Others adopted more sophisticated gambling activities and often had separate rooms for faro and keno tables. Gambling was illegal, but a proper pay-off to the police generally assured the saloon owner freedom from harassment.

Women were another attraction for the sporting set of the city. Some saloon keepers operated "dance houses" where young women, paid twenty-five cents an evening, were available for dancing and drinking. Many of the girls were housemaids out for a good time and anxious to meet some boys. Others were prostitutes who used the dance house to solicit customers. Brothels were often maintained upstairs or adjacent to a saloon. The commercialization of sex was fairly common in downtown Chicago during the 1860s and 1870s.[15] By 1865 there may have been as many as six thousand prostitutes in Chicago. Many were impoverished immigrant women laid low by circumstances. The social code of middle-class society made few allowances for a "good girl" guilty of even a single indiscretion; such a woman was often considered as "ruined." Frederick Cook recalled that "a single false step precipitated the victim straight into the depths." The increase in the ranks of prostitutes that occurred during the conflict led some wags to describe streetwalkers as "war widows." Originally this referred to married women who took advantage of their husbands' service at the front to enjoy the night life of the "fancy" sporting set. But the term was soon applied to any women who "went obtrusively forth to seek her prey under the gaslight."[16]

Behind the smug jokes about "the bereaved" was the harsh reality that many soldiers' wives were forced into poverty, and many poor women resorted to prostitution. Jobs for women were not abundant and those available were hard for mothers of children to manage. The Sanitary Commission often received pleas for assistance from destitute wives of soldiers. Mary Livermore made weekly rounds to visit some of these women. Others were too proud to accept charity or were frightened of the moral condemnation that might accompany a plea for help. The well-meaning sanitary workers were always worried about the possibility of "imposition" on their services, so they made a point of learning a woman's circumstances intimately. Women with a weakness for drink or who had been guilty of "indiscretions" may have feared facing the middle-class matrons of the Sanitary Commission. The gambling houses and brothels were a growth industry in search of more labor.[17]

During the 1850s vice in Chicago had been largely restricted to an area north of the Chicago River (near the present *Sun-Times* building), in the notorious "Sands," a collection of shanties that housed an assortment of gambling dens, brothels, and flophouses. In 1857 Mayor "Long John" Wentworth led a police raid on the Sands to forever destroy the vice district. It succeeded—the rookeries of sin were torn down and burned—but their denizens were only dispersed, and they set up shop elsewhere in the city. By the Civil War Chicago had a number of different nodes of underworld activity. The high-toned gambling houses were situated on Randolph Street between Clark and State, on what was known as the "Hairtrigger Block." Around the corner, Clark Street from Randolph to Monroe was Gambler's Row. The seediest establishments were congregated south of Madison Street accessible to wharves of the riverfront. In 1862 one block on Clark between Van Buren and Harrison Street boasted no fewer than fourteen brothels. "After nightfall the street was thronged with cyprians," the *Tribune* complained. "They stood in the doorways, bedizened in tawdry fineries and dressed to a degree of indecency which disgusted every respectable person."[18]

The most notorious dive was "Under the Willow" at the corner of Wells and Monroe. It was, according to Frederick Cook, "the very core of corruption." Not content with raking in profits from gambling, liquor sales, and whore mongering, its owner harbored a band of pugs who would strong-arm the drunks who staggered out of the saloons. The *Tribune* charged that "there were undoubtedly more robberies committed there than at all other places combined." Cook maintained that "the place was a refuge for the very nether-most strata of the Underworld—the refuse of the bridewell [the city lock-up]. Only by seeking the bottom of the malodorous river could its inmates go lower—as they sometimes did." Nonetheless, Under the Willow hosted a throng of customers. The infamy of its reputation served as a magnet to soldiers on leave and sailors newly arrived in port. The potential patron who hesitated outside the dive was lured by the sound of music and laughter and a series of gaudy, blue window shades, whose gilt letters spelled out "Why Not?"[19]

The leading figures of the Chicago underworld were Cap Hyman and George Trussell. A tall, handsome Yankee from Vermont, Trussell owned one of the swankest gambling parlors in the Hairtrigger Block. He was known as "top-sawyer among the 'highest rollers,' " and he had "a record of many broken 'banks' to his credit." His arch enemy was Cap Hyman, a pleasant bon vivant when sober or on a winning streak, but an "excitable, emotional jack-in-the-box" when he was in his cups or down on his luck. While neither man lost very often, they both drank too much. Whenever shots were fired on the Hairtrigger Block, the press men in the offices of the *Times*, which was located on that block, would look up from their copy and remark, "Guess Cap Hyman is out for practice. . . ." Frequently, Trussell or Hyman would go gunning for the other. Drunk or sober, both men were terrible shots, and nothing came of these fights.[20]

These crown princes of the underworld were barred from participating in the polite society of the city, and so it was natural that they formed liaisons with Chicago's leading madams. George Trussell's mistress was a handsome young Irish girl named Mollie Cossgriff. She had come to Chicago to work as a chambermaid in one of the downtown hotels and became a prostitute. Trussell took an interest in her, gave her gifts of hand-some clothing and gaudy jewelry, and installed her as the madam of one of his bordellos. Their relationship was anything but normal. She genuinely loved him, and endured his violent rages whenever he was drunk. One Sunday afternoon he assaulted her in public. Scores of people watched in shock while he "battered and bruised her until she was insensible" and left her lying, near death, in the mud of Randolph Street. When the *Times* published an account of the brutal assault, Trussell and several compan-ions waylaid that paper's city editor. Mollie herself had a violent streak. In September 1866 she shot the gambler dead because he stood her up for a date. Cap Hyman learned his lesson from Trussell's fate. A few weeks later he married his paramour, "Gentle Annie" Stafford, a notable madam and a mean lady with a whip.[21]

The rapid increase in vice and related crime Chicago experienced dur-ing the Civil War led to considerable public outcry. "Why does nearly every man walk the streets of Chicago armed?" asked the *Times*. Because "the monster, crime, had been abroad and with its red, right hand, the demon has dealt death and destruction." The *Tribune* took the position that South-ern gamblers were to blame for much of the trouble. "Quite half the crime of this city originates in the holes of infamy kept by professional blacklegs." The *Times* countered that the crime wave "and a thousand other equally lamentable conditions in society today can be traced to the influence of the war, and the reign of atheists, miscegenationists, free-lovers and fanatics who now control the country and its destinies." Closer to the mark, Storey editorialized, "Human life has everywhere depreciated in value."[22]

By the spring of 1865 the temper of the city had been greatly affected by the conflicting emotions released by four years of Civil War. In 1862, Chicagoans pitied the suffering prisoners of Camp Douglas and held ral-lies to raise funds for their relief. Three years later, they planned ways to make the rebels' lives more miserable. Stories of Andersonville and years of casualty reports prompted the Chicago Board of Trade to urge Lincoln to subject rebel prisoners to the same horrible conditions that cost thou-sands of Union soldiers their lives. To consciously adopt war crimes as a matter of policy was explained as "a matter of necessity." "We are aware," they wrote the president, "that this, our petition savors of cruelty," but the time had come for "retaliatory measures."[23]

While some sought to make the South pay in kind for every ounce of suffering brought by the war, others simply turned their back on the war and any thought of obligation toward those involved. A Chicago business-man who promised to provide a soldier's family with winter fuel ignored the woman and children when inflation drove up the cost of fuel. When the shivering woman reminded him of the promise, he rudely denied her. The cries of the poor woman's hungry and cold children forced her to beg for charity, although she "longed to die" because of the misery and humiliation. Some landlords had no compunction about evicting soldiers' families in midwinter if they fell behind in their rent. The infant son of a soldier in the colored 54th Massachusetts died after the man's family was evicted on a cold, rainy day. Because the government was late in paying the African-American unit, the mother did not even have money to bury the boy.[24]

The Soldiers' Home near Camp Douglas was crowded with disabled men that most Chicagoans would simply have liked to forget. When the weather was mild, the men would assemble on the porch and look out over the lake. A blinded trooper often played the accordion, and the men would join in singing old camp songs. Among the most pathetic cases was a soldier whose body, arms, legs, and head continually twitched and twisted beyond his control. "I tell you it is hard to look at him," wrote a comrade, who had himself lost a leg, "without tears coming into one's eyes." Many soldiers were sent to the home after being discharged from hospital, and they stayed in the city to be fitted out with artificial limbs. A portion of the harvest from the world's busiest lumber port was channeled into replacing the shattered arms and legs lost in the war.[25]

News from the front was scarce during the first months of 1865. Chicagoans trying to forget about the war could focus on "The Street Railway Swindle," a scandal so typical of Illinois politics that it may have made some war-weary citizens almost nostalgic for the days of peace when such events could be thoroughly enjoyed. The immensely prosperous companies that ran the city's horse-drawn street railway franchises combined to introduce a bill in the state legislature extending their grants for ninety-nine years. Chicago press railed against the proposal, and public meetings appealed to the governor to veto any such legislation. But the streetcar magnates knew the language of the legislature, and they distributed enough "gifts" to override Governor Richard Oglesby's veto. The *Tribune* righteously intoned, "The public knows that a given sum in greenbacks will pass any bill at Springfield."[26]

The episode strengthened Chicagoans' desire to see the state capital moved from the dreary prairie town to their city. They argued that rail connections now made Chicago easier to reach than any other part of the state, and that in the "Garden City" the state government would be closer to the people. The legislators were interested in leaving what was described as a "one-horse town," but they could not agree on where to move. Peoria and Decatur lobbied for the honor. The Chicago City Council offered the state an excellent site in Union Park, which at that time was the city's biggest park. The city also offered $500,000 to help pay for new state government buildings. In the end, legislators found it easier to make no decision at all, and the capital, by default, remained in Springfield. State authorities frustrated logic and Chicago boosters further when they located the Illinois Industrial and Agricultural University (the future University of Illinois) in Urbana instead of in the metropolis.[27]

No less intriguing was the newspaper coverage of the trial of the Camp Douglas conspirators. The eight rebel agents were tried in Cincinnati by a military commission. Their defense attorneys tried to discredit the federal agents who broke up the pathetic conspiracy. But even after the agents were shown to be untrustworthy scoundrels, the fact remained that several of the conspirators were guilty of treason. During the trial, Charles T. Daniel, a Confederate soldier, escaped from prison and successfully eluded recapture. Benjamin Anderson, a former rebel officer whose nerve had been shattered by combat and cloak-and-dagger operations, committed suicide in prison. Vincent Marmaduke, who some Chicagoans thought was the ringleader of the conspiracy, was acquitted; so, too, was Judge Morris. The former mayor returned to Chicago a broken man. The cost of defending himself exhausted his savings, and during the trial his daughter had died. In Chicago, the politically indiscreet copperhead was a pariah. His wife, who also had been arrested, was filled with bitterness toward the city. She abandoned the old man and returned to Kentucky, where she lived with her rebel brothers.[28]

Charles Walsh was found guilty but was given only a five-year prison sentence. George Cantrill, a Confederate soldier, suffered a mental breakdown and was never brought to trial. Richard T. Semmes, a young lawyer with dubious connections to the conspiracy, was sentenced to three years hard labor, but the sentence was remitted two months later. Walsh also was later pardoned. The only man punished for the bungled plot against Chicago was the English adventurer, George T. St. Leger Grenfell. While the court was disposed to show mercy to those guilty of disloyalty, it was stone-faced toward the foreigner. Of 150 people arrested, only Grenfell was sentenced to be hung.[29]

Even that rogue was not without friends, however. British officials and American acquaintances begged for clemency. After the war was over, his sentence was commuted to a life of hard labor in the Dry Tortugas, America's Devil's Island. Efforts to have Grenfell freed were blocked in Congress, ironically, by "Long John" Wentworth, whose reelection had been cinched when the conspiracy was discovered. Grenfell grew tired of waiting for help, so on the night of March 6, 1868 he made a daring escape from the island fortress. His boat capsized in the Gulf of Mexico, and although rumors circulated for years that he managed to survive, it is likely that the man who plotted Chicago's ruin drowned.[30]

"All over the city, south, west, and north . . . flames lighted up the evening sky, presenting a truly magnificent spectacle," wrote a *Chicago Tribune* reporter. From the courthouse cupola he could see the entire city in a vast panorama. "Tongues of flame shot towards heaven, and the fireworks burst around us in rich profusion, while from hundreds of windows streamed forth the flood of light from thickly set candles." Richmond, "the modern Babylon," had fallen, and Chicago celebrated with its usual unchecked enthusiasm. Watching the revelry, which lasted until morning, the young reporter recognized that it was a moment that comes "once in a century." Like most Chicagoans he wanted to savor every minute of it.[31]

About nine o'clock on the morning of April 3, 1865, Chicago received word that Grant's army had at last forced Lee to retreat from Petersburg, leaving Richmond to fall into Union hands. The first troops into the rebel capital were General A. M. Weitzel's Colored Infantry. The news spread through the city "as if by magic"; within an hour every business, save the saloons, was closed. People rushed into the streets, shouting, cheering, and singing patriotic songs. The African-American community took special pride because of the role played by blacks in the campaign. A Chicago minister who encountered a black man rushing down Dearborn Street swinging a battered hat asked, "What's the matter?" The man blurted out, "Richmond's took, and Weitzel's niggers is in it!" The confused clergyman failed to grasp his meaning. "But don't you know such proceedings are unconstitutional, that the local laws of Richmond forbid free negroes coming in without a pass?" "I 'spect sir," the black man joked, "they's not enforcen' such laws as much as they used to be."[32]

Throughout the city American flags were unfurled and impromptu parades were arranged. Artillery from Camp Douglas boomed out a salute to Grant, while numerous old pistols and carbines were taken from closets and fired into the air. The saloons "were all crowded from morning till night." Patriotic barmen set up open barrels of beer or ale so that everyone could enjoy, on the house, a toast to victory. The churches were also crowded as ministers led prayer meetings in honor of "the God of Battles."[33]

The capture of Richmond brought a Niagara of good news to the city. In the days that followed, Chicagoans read of Lincoln's emotional visit to the rebel capital and Grant's pursuit of Lee's haggard army. On April 6 the army of the free captured six thousand rebels, almost one-quarter of Lee's total force. Jefferson Davis and his cabinet took flight. The Confederate Army was checked again at Appomattox, and dispatches promised, "The war is closing—is virtually closed."

The people of Chicago were filled with anxiety. Victory had seemed at hand before; now "the delay of even a few hours was an excruciating agony for tens of thousands," the *Tribune* wrote. "Who shall tell the numbers whose nights were sleepless, whose days open heavily, till the tale of victory should be completed, and the news come that the rebellion was finally crushed!"

That news was received in Chicago late on Palm Sunday evening. Those who were already asleep in their beds were roused by a hundred-gun salute. Long before the cannons were stilled, the streets of the town were filled. News that the war was over had a different effect on Chicago than had the fall of Richmond. The end of the war brought to the surface more complex emotions. People alternately laughed and cried. Many could not help but recall the faces of those who had fallen during the war. No public meetings were held so that politicians could give long-winded speeches. The people of the city needed no one to interpret the meaning of this event. They went out into the streets to talk, shout, laugh, and weep with their neighbors.[34]

The doorways of many Chicago homes were draped with black crepe to signify the loss of a loved one. "It was hard for the mothers," Joseph Medill later recalled; it seemed that "every family had lost a son or a husband." Cook County sent 22,436 men to fight, of which about 15,000 came from Chicago. This was a large percentage of the male population, especially considering that Chicago polled only 18,791 voters in the 1860 election. Of those who marched away, nearly four thousand died on Southern battlefields or in Union camps. The end of the war was a time not only to celebrate but also to reflect.[35]

Some of the city's notables met at the Tremont House to organize a parade, but the plain folk of Chicago were way ahead of them. A "people's procession" composed of thousands of citizens formed spontaneously. Beer wagons, fire engines, and units of soldiers joined in the procession as it moved through the downtown.

> On they came—the blue coated soldiers stepping proudly to glorious music—and shouts rent the air, and white handkerchiefs floated from the windows, and gentle hands waved them welcome. Then followed the brazen-mouthed cannon, drawn by noble horses, that arched their necks and stepped loftily, as if conscious they had the "peace-makers" in their train. On they came—men on horseback, men a-foot, six abreast, led by the Veteran Reserve Corps Band, thrilling the air with the triumphant strain, "Glory, Glory Hallelujah!" The great multitude—tens of thousands of men, women and children—caught up the refrain, and joined in the glorious chorus, singing, with heart and soul and might, "Glory, Glory, Hallelujah!"

Fathers held their children on their shoulders and admonished them to look and remember the great day so they might tell their offspring. People were so "frenzied with gladness" that it seemed to an observer that there were "no men and women in Chicago—only crazy, grown-up boys and girls." A Northwestern University student wrote in his diary that the sights of that day "will truly be remembered generation after generation. I am thankful that I live in such a time."[36]

The vast peoples' parade, said to stretch for four miles, was the first of many parades in the months that followed. Almost every train brought regiments home to Chicago or through the city on their way to Wisconsin, Iowa, or Michigan. The troops would be stationed at Camp Fry on the north side or Camp Douglas for a week or two while they turned in their weapons, received their pay, and were formally discharged from service. Chicago had more soldiers in the city between April and July of 1865 than at any time during the war. Some Chicagoans took pride in treating the veterans as conquering heroes. The Union Defense Committee and the women of the Sanitary Commission tried to meet each unit on its arrival, parade the men to the Soldiers Home, and provide them with a welcome-home dinner. The newspapers delighted in describing the soldiers' appearance as "bronzed and battletore . . . tough and hardened by thousands of miles of marching." Friends and loved ones, however, grieved at the sight of them "reduced in strength . . . war-torn with faded uniform, tattered flags, sometimes with an empty coat-sleeve, sometimes swinging on crutches." Some still quaked with swamp fever; all were anxious "to hear the voices of wives and children, parents and friends."[37]

The welcome-home festivities took place in conjunction with the second Northwest Sanitary Fair. For three weeks in June 1865 the Sanitary Commission and the Christian Commission combined to put on a giant spectacle that was part shopping mall, part-carnival, and part museum. It dwarfed the fair of 1863. It was held in Dearborn Park near Lake Michigan, and one of the buildings, Union Hall, enclosed more than an acre of ground. The fair was the last act of war-related philanthropy. Proceeds went to the care of soldiers' families, to pay the debts of the aid societies, and to support the Chicago Soldiers' Home. One afternoon the fair staged a reenactment of the battle between the *Monitor* and the *Merrimac* with eight-foot-long scale models. The crowd pleaser of the fair, however, was "old Abe," the bald eagle mascot of the 8th Wisconsin. His record in battle and high-pitched screech made him the darling of every schoolchild.[38]

The returning troops became another attraction at the fair. When the 88th Illinois ("Second Board of Trade Regiment") the 89th Illinois ("Railroad Regiment"), and the 90th Illinois ("Irish Legion") returned, they were honored on the fairgrounds. That day served as Chicago's "grand review." The 88th and 89th arrived in Chicago the night before and were bunked at Camp Douglas. In the morning they lined up in marching order and moved up Cottage Grove Avenue to the city. By the time they reached the start of Michigan Avenue, the men had acquired an honor guard of small boys, who ran alongside their ranks cheering. The streets became densely packed with people, and the "gallant boys were saluted by waving handkerchiefs and flags, clapping of hands and loud huzzahs."[39]

At Park Row, the units were met by their sponsors, the Board of Trade and the city's leading railroad men. Along with a marching band they led the parade to the fairgrounds. A thirty-six-gun salute announced their approach, but the cannons' roar was not louder than the cheers of the crowd for the tattered regimental colors as they passed beneath the welcome banners. When the regiments were drawn up on the grounds, surrounded by clapping, shouting, crying friends and family, their officers finally allowed them to break ranks. "Mothers, sisters, fathers, brothers, aye, and sweethearts, rushed forward," the *Tribune* wrote, "to embrace and welcome back the heroes of a hundred battles."[40]

The elite of Chicago society turned out to meet the soldiers. Former mayor Francis C. Sherman proudly shook hands with his son, William, who returned as the commanding general of the 88th. Charles N. Holden, the Republican Sherman had beaten for mayor, ran forward to embrace his son, Major Levi Holden, who had been Will Sherman's comrade for three years. Gurdon S. Hubbard, the sixty-five-year-old former fur trader who had helped to found Chicago, congratulated the remaining men of the company he raised and briefly led as their captain. The faces of many onlookers were solemn and their eyes swollen and red. Deacon Bross, part owner of the *Tribune* and lieutenant governor of the state, could not forget that his slain brother had marched to war with the 88th before volunteering for service with the colored infantry. John B. Rice, the recently elected mayor, tried to carry out his civic duty and warmly greet each man, but he was overcome by the memory of his son, William H. Rice, captain of Company A, 89th Illinois Infantry, who was killed on the bloody field of Chickamauga.[41]

When the troops formed their ranks, it became painfully clear how depleted their numbers were. The 88th had left Chicago with 900 soldiers; on the fair grounds only 209 stood at attention. The Railroad Regiment whose battle cry was "Clear the track!" had been reduced from 900 to a mere 300. General Charles T. Hotchkiss, a contractor turned regimental commander, told the crowd, "Our history is written on the headboards of rudely made graves, from Stone River to Atlanta. Such a record we feel proud of." As he spoke the troops remembered their comrades killed or wounded at Perryville, Chickamauga, Resaca, and the last bloody battle at Nashville. They thought of the many more who spent their last hours wasted by dysentery or racked with swamp fever. The crowd stood less than a hundred feet from the veterans, but the soldiers were separated from their friends and families by more than distance. The experience of combat, the intimate association with death, random and agonizing, had given the men a conception of war that bore little relationship to the heroic platitudes offered by Chicago's politicians.[42]

Four abreast, the soldiers marched into cavernous Union Hall. The good-hearted Thomas Bryan led a waiting audience in "three cheers for the glorious 88th and 89th regiments." William Tecumseh Sherman, who was serving as the honorary vice-president of the fair, came forward to address the soldiers. He had warm feelings for the men who made the miraculous assault on Missionary Ridge and whom he led during the Atlanta campaign. In an affable soldier-to-soldier speech, he complimented them. He won applause and not a few snickers when he quipped, "I see before me men more capable of leading armies than the majority of the batch of Major Generals appointed at the beginning of the war." He drew an even bigger laugh when he noted, "I believe there is no one more gratified to see you and welcome you home to your wives, children, and sweethearts than I am. If you have no sweethearts where you live, you will find plenty of them here." When the General finished, a band struck-up the "Star Spangled Banner," and the troops were led on a tour of the fair and its "hundred thousand curiosities." The Board of Trade Regiment marched to Metropolitan Hall, where the commodity traders had prepared a banquet. The Railroad Regiment was entertained in similar fashion by the rail magnates of Chicago.[43]

The Irish Legion passed the other two regiments as they left the fair grounds. Although it had rained and the streets were muddy, the troops were in good spirits and joked with one another as they passed. Welcoming speeches by Senator Richard Yates and General Sherman were prelude of a tour of the fair. The Irishman liked the Horticultural Hall best of all, although not because of a love of botany. An elaborate reproduction of "Jacob's Well" presided over by "a lovely Rebecca" stood in the center of the exotic hall. From the well Rebecca withdrew buckets of lemonade, which was distributed to the soldiers by a "bevy of handsome maidens" dressed "in brilliant oriental costumes."[44]

After sampling the pleasures of the well, the Irish Legion reassembled for its long-awaited return to the old neighborhood. First they marched to South Des Plaines Street, where they stopped in front of the home of Father Dennis Dunne, pastor of St. Patrick's parish, and the colonel called for "Three cheers for the Father of the Regiment." In 1862

Dunne had spearheaded the drive to raise a second Chicago Irish regiment. As he looked out of the rectory window at the 250 cheering soldiers—41 of whom were too disabled to even carry a gun—he may have thought back on the 300 men who had died in the fighting. The proud pastor led the remnants of his regiment into St. Pat's school hall, where the soldiers "were then regaled with a choice repast," while the school band serenaded them. It was not as splendid as a Board of Trade reception, but it was the sounds and tastes of home and it brought tears to many soldiers' eyes.[45]

Much later, the regiment marched back to Camp Fry, where they were to wait until the army bureaucracy was ready to discharge them. But after marching through Georgia, South Carolina, and North Carolina, and participating in Washington's "Grand Review," the men of the Irish Legion had no more patience with military procedure. Within a day or so, most had returned to the homes they had left three years before, vowing not to be seen at Camp Fry until payday.[46]

Not all returning soldiers were received so warmly. In fact, many regiments got a cold shoulder from Chicago, and they resented it greatly. The 105th Illinois Infantry, organized in downstate Dixon and mustered in at Camp Douglas, returned to Chicago on the evening of June 11, 1865. After participating in the Grand Review in Washington, they were sent west by train. When the train stopped in Pittsburgh, the men were met by a reception committee that congratulated them and provided coffee, crackers, and meat. All the way across Ohio and Indiana the men talked about the warm reception they would receive in Chicago, "the metropolis of our own beloved state." Unfortunately, their train pulled into the city after midnight. They were met by "not a breath of welcome; not even a cup of cold water." The officers were less concerned about a heroes' welcome than they were about getting their men some dinner. So they marched them several blocks through the rain to the Soldiers Rest, which they found dark and shuttered. The 460 tired, wet, and disappointed men were then marched to the city's central depot, where there was room to improvise a bivouac for the regiment. For supper they tried to eat some moldy bread and spoiled meat that had been issued days before. One wag shouted "Three cheers for the ladies of Pittsburgh" in memory of "the last pleasant thing they had to remember," and they settled down on the floor, grumbling about "their first night in dear old Illinois."[47]

The next morning, when the men were marched to Camp Fry where barracks awaited them, a policeman ordered the regiment off the sidewalk and into the muddy street. "Could a greater insult have been offered us?" plaintively asked Corporal James A. Congleton. Fortunately, most of the men did not realize what had happened when their officers led them into the street. Corporal Congleton still smarted from the incident years later and mused in his memoirs, "We had our guns and quite a good supply of cartridges, also our bayonets, and it is safe to add that the whole police force of Chicago would not have forced us from the walk."[48]

Many of the men returning to Chicago harbored bitter feelings toward the civilians who had enjoyed the prosperity, not the pain, of four years of war. One infantryman described Chicago as "a city that has grown rich while our families and every interest dear has been suffering." Sometimes this resentment would burst forth in violence. One evening the men of the 105th avenged the shabby treatment they received when they arrived in Chicago by terrorizing the patrons of a North Side beer garden. A group of soldiers scattered the crowd of drinkers with a bayonet charge. One of the men noted with satisfaction, "It was fun to see them run from those bayonets." When the mayor appealed to General Joseph Hooker, senior officer in the city, "Fighting Joe" warned city authorities to back off or the soldiers might "burn down your city." For some soldiers Chicago was seen as a copperhead bastion that was too cowardly to openly declare itself during the conflict and took pleasure in depreciating the soldier now that it was over.[49]

Fear of violence from the returning veterans was a persistent, if sublimated, theme in the months following the war. Major General Sherman, who was in Chicago during the peak of the demobilization, personally bade farewell to many of the units in his army. They had made Georgia "howl" by living off the land and destroying personal property; no one wanted a repetition in Illinois. Sherman invariably concluded his farewells with an admonishment. "Go to your homes and behave yourselves. Illinois is proud of you" or "I place myself as a hostage to Illinois for the good behavior of Sherman's army—I know you will not betray me."[50]

Major General Richard J. Oglesby, who in 1864 was elected governor of Illinois, made the same plea to veterans. He told a group of soldiers at Camp Fry, "I do not want you to leave Chicago, and break up your military organization and go back into society, feeling bad. It makes me feel sad to meet a soldier who thinks he had been treated unkindly when he came back home." He tried to assure the men that "there is nobody [who] feels unkindly to you. That is not the feeling of our citizens at home now. If you have been neglected, I only want to say you have not been intentionally treated so." As a former soldier he could defuse their anxiety by joking. "You must not expect to be taken and wrapped up in a gay cloak and put upon beds of down, and soup given to you in a silver spoon." Oglesby asked the veterans for patience during the discharge procedure and promised them "the admiration of your friends . . . and the combined respect of your neighbors and fellow citizens."[51]

Chicago's uneven reception of the returning soldiers in part reflected the emotional roller coaster that had exhausted the city's patriots during the months following the fall of Richmond. The Sanitary Fair further strained their resources. Others simply did not want to be bothered. An appeal by the *Evening Journal* for a volunteer committee to arrange appropriate greetings for veteran troops largely fell on deaf ears. Throngs of enthusiastic Chicagoans followed General Grant and General Sherman during their visits to the city. With such heroes about, it was easy to ignore the common soldier. Besides, some businessmen harbored the sentiment that many soldiers spent the bulk of the war "loafing" about camp, far from work as well as battle.[52]

The alienation of the returning soldier was naturally strongest among the men of downstate units, who had few bonds of affection with Chicago under any circumstances. A soldier writing to the *Evening Journal* claimed that "among the five thousand men of this camp [Camp Fry], not one speaks a word of praise of Chicago; but everyone is anxious to get his pay and leave the city." The camp was overcrowded and unpleasant during the wet June of 1865. It is little wonder that a considerable number of soldiers sought relief in the saloons, gambling parlors, and brothels of Chicago's thriving underworld.

At the end of the war "the city was alive with suckers," according to the leading historian of the nineteenth-century underworld. The gamblers and thiefs had a field day preying on returning soldiers. The standard procedure was to find a soldier who had been drinking, lure him to a brothel (which could not have been too difficult), and there relieve him of his money. It happened so often that the *Tribune* soon called for a "Soldier Protective Society" that would hold the discharge pay of veterans until they received jobs or returned home. But the idea flew in the face of human nature. The soldiers wanted no further controls on their freedom. They flocked to Under the Willow and with comrades raised their glasses in a farewell toast. Morning invariably found one or more of the men poorer, sorer, and more anxious than ever to leave Chicago.[53]

The gulf between soldiers and civilians was only in part the product of combat experience. The city had changed as well. Since 1861 Chicagoans had experienced unprecedented social growth and economic expansion. Chicago returned to the optimism of the pre-1857 period but with the vigor and energy befitting a city that had nearly tripled in population since that business panic. By war's end Chicago was filied with thousands of newcomers. Theodore Dreiser described them as "gauche, green ignorant. But how ambitious and courageous! Such bumtiousness! Such assurance!" They were part of the new Chicago. The soldiers remembered the old town where everyone lived within the sound of the courthouse bell. Chicago had leaped ahead while they were at war, and most veterans were anxious to catch up with their booming town.[54]

In some ways peace took the lid off Chicago's bubbling caldron of energy. While the war lasted, Chicagoans had two goals: preserve the Union (not that they were united about how to do that) and make money. The victory of federal forces left them unfettered to pursue fortune. True, there was a minor downturn in the economy early in 1865 in anticipation of Appomattox. The price of gold tumbled, and wheat lost half its value, but few businessmen were surprised by these events. The large wartime profits helped them weather the storm. During the first twelve months after the war, business was brisk but profits were low due to a fall in prices. In the years that followed, the business climate in Chicago was described by one journalist as "almost magical," a period of unprecedented growth. The unchecked allegiance to business values left some men millionaires and thousands of others anxious and unsatisfied. Clergymen complained, "Chicago people are money and pleasure mad." It was during the years after the Civil War that Chicagoans first learned to ask the question that in time became the city's unofficial motto—"What's in it for me?"[55]

Returning soldiers embraced these values because the "boys in blue" wanted something more of life than to return to their old jobs. After years of sacrifice, they wanted a share of the good life. Many privates who left manual labor jobs enrolled in commercial colleges in an effort to enter the ranks of the downtown business clerks. Although few commercial colleges provided quality training, they enjoyed a thriving business after the war. Many veterans, particularly officers, entered the insurance business. The fire and life insurance industry in Chicago was poised for expansion in the wake of the Civil War boom. The growth of heavy manufacturing necessitated new measures to protect capital investment. Brevet generals and regimental colonels filled the top positions in many of the new companies created after 1865. Lower-rank officers swarmed into the growing number of agent positions. By 1870 the ranks of insurance agents in Chicago had doubled, and the number of companies grew almost fourfold.[56]

With new opportunities within their grasp, veterans looked to the future, not the past. Although two chapters of the Grand Army of the Republic were established in Chicago by 1866, the veterans' clubs failed to thrive and within a few years were defunct. Former soldiers did vote for veterans at election time, as the Republicans found out in 1867 when they were swept into office with a slate that was nearly half veterans. But most men did not flaunt their status as veterans. Some were so eager to put the army experience behind them that they did not even wear their uniforms home from the front. Mary Livermore recalled that people "turned with relief to the employments of peaceful life, eager to forget the fearful years of battle and carnage." She wrote, "[I] put away all mementos of the exceptional life I had led, and re-entered with gladness upon the duties connected with my home and family. . . . I expected this quiet and happy order of things would continue to the end."[57]

It took many years for veterans to put their experience in perspective. Softened by the glow of nostalgia, military service became a pleasant memory of brotherhood that extended not only to comrades-in-arms but also to Confederate veterans. By the late 1870s the ranks of the Grand Army of the Republic, the largest veteran group, began to swell; ten posts were established in the city by 1882. A host of other organizations were established as well. The Cairo Survivors Association was founded by veterans of the first troops Chicago sent to the front. The Chicago Union Veteran Club and the Veteran Union League flourished, as did the Loyal Legion, which was limited to former officers. Regimental veterans' clubs became popular, as did tours of former battlefields.[58]

The celebrations of Memorial Day became more elaborate over time. Chicago first celebrated the day in 1867 when General Philip Sheridan led a group of bereaved families to the city's principal cemeteries to decorate soldiers' graves. In 1868 the Grand Army of the Republic proclaimed May 30 "a day for the decoration of soldiers' graves." By 1888 Chicago-area school children visited eighty-seven area cemeteries and over sixteen thousand graves. In 1896 Confederate and Union veterans joined to dedicate a monument in Oakwood Cemetery to the 4,457 prisoners who died in Camp Douglas. Not a word was said about treason or the appalling conditions of the camp. It was instead an occasion to honor those on both sides who "made the name of the American soldier a synonym for bravery, fortitude, and honor."[59]

More than nostalgia motivated veterans to call attention to the sacrifices of the war. Memorial ceremonies and soldiers' reunions served to remind the veterans, and the public, of the ideals for which the war was fought. The Veterans Union League admitted it was a social club "so far as cultivating, promoting and strengthening the soldierly and brotherly instincts which banded together comrades . . . during the late war." Yet its 1880 charter also declared that "the League was formed to encourage the spirit of universal liberty, equal rights, and justice to all men, regardless of nationality or color." These men, like hundreds of others who fought in the war, remained true to the idealism behind the conflict. For a generation after the war many Chicagoans tried to keep faith with the vision of a society based upon compassion, individualism, idealism, and social responsibility, a vision historian Ray Ginger described as "the Lincoln ideal."[60]

Like the bronze soldiers erected in Chicago's parks and cemeteries, the image of Father Abraham endured as a source of inspiration to the graying generation of the Civil War. Lincoln was the martyr to all that was good in American life, a powerful symbol of idealism triumphant. In a city increasingly given over to the "tooth and claw" capitalism of the robber barons, Lincoln's legacy of sacrifice was a powerful counterforce. The legacy of Lincoln and the experience of war prodded veterans to keep faith with the ideals of their youth.

Military service had given Chicago blacks their first opportunity to participate in any sort of community activity. During the postwar era, they used this service to successfully fight for equal rights. Veterans organized the Hannibal Guards to keep alive black military service. The organization became a social and political rallying point in the postwar African-American community as well as the basis for the 8th Illinois Volunteer Infantry, the only black-led unit to fight in the Spanish-American War. In 1870, John Jones, who spearheaded the fight against the Black Laws, led a parade of blacks through downtown Chicago in celebration of winning the battle for black suffrage. A year later he was elected Cook County commissioner by a two-to-one margin over his white opponent. Black political emergence was further recognized in 1870 when W. H. Thomas, a black veteran who lost an arm during the war, was named state commissioner of deeds. Political gains continued in 1875 when Chicago sent its first black representative to Springfield. However, by then the mood of the country as a whole was changing—away from a commitment to Negro rights. A National Reunion of Anti-Slavery Veterans held in Chicago in 1874 was an almost entirely all-white affair. Not only was the meeting cool to a resolution supporting civil rights, but many of its most distinguished speakers held out the olive branch to the white people of the South.[61]

For others the legacy of commitment and service fostered by the national emergency persevered long after the war. This was particularly true for Sanitary Commission veterans, who formed an important network of progressive political activists. Ezra McCagg, a leader of the Northwestern Branch, played a formative role in the creation of Lincoln and Jackson parks. It was also at his insistence that Frederick Law Olmstead, a fellow Sanitary Commission veteran, was retained to design Jackson Park. Mary Livermore and Myra Bradwell moved immediately from caring for wounded soldiers to working for women's rights. Bradwell was also among those most responsible for securing the Columbian Exposition for Chicago. Supporting the cause of women's rights was John Peter Altgeld. He was sixteen when he volunteered for service and had matured into a crusading lawyer. Eventually, he became governor of Illinois.[62]

The notion of the "Lincoln ideal" reached into the next generation. Lincoln was a political and moral presence in the homes of young Jane Addams and Florence Kelley. Their fathers had been friends of Lincoln, and the women brought his compassion for the downtrodden to the wretched immigrant neighborhoods of turn-of-the-century Chicago. Jane Addams was born the year Abe Lincoln was elected president and left Illinois. She developed at a young age an idealistic image of the president and recalled, "Through all my vivid sensations there persisted the image of . . . Lincoln himself as an epitome of all that was great and good. I dimly caught the notion of the martyred President as the standard bearer to the conscience of his countrymen." In later years, when Addams had become a world-famous settlement-house worker, "the memory, the mention of his name" often served to revitalize her spirits "like a refreshing breeze from off the prairie."

Of course, in 1865 Jane Addams was only a girl of five and thought little about the war and its meaning. But forever etched in her memory was an April afternoon when she found her home decorated with American flags and black crepe. In the parlor sat her father, his eyes swollen and cheeks streaked with tears. Gently he put his arm around her and said, "The greatest man in the world has died."[63]

———◇———

Abraham Lincoln returned to Chicago on May 1, 1865. The funeral train stopped at the southern edge of Lake Park where a special depot had been constructed. A cold, wet rain had fallen all morning, but as the train came to a halt, the clouds parted and the sun began to shine. Lake Michigan, whose waves had been crashing against the railroad embankment, became calm. The only sound was the tolling of the courthouse bell, telling the thousands of mourners gathered in the streets that the martyred leader had arrived. A battery of cannon took up the salute, filling the park with the all-too-familiar smell of gunpowder.

The shock of Lincoln's death, coming on the heels of victory celebrations, stunned Chicago as it did the nation. The news swept across Illinois on Saturday morning, April 15. "Men refuse to believe that it is possible. But every dispatch confirms it," wrote a Joliet man. "Men of all parties are struck dumb with grief and consternation." At the Soldiers' Home, many a wounded veteran openly "cried like a child." The *Tribune* reported, "Sorrow and indignation struggled for the mastery in thousands of breasts."[64]

Some in the city feared that angry citizens might lash out at any symbol of the Confederacy—prisoners, alleged copperhead politicians, or private citizens. The shop of a copperhead merchant was nearly wrecked when the man's wife took down a black drape "and tried to do normal business." "I am constantly reminded of the bloody scenes of the French

Revolution," wrote Judge David Davis, a close friend of Lincoln, "and feel we are again plunged in a sea of darkness just as we thought the day was breaking." He choked back his grief and called a meeting of Chicago's lawyers and judges. "It is our duty to calm the public mind," he admonished them, "not to excite it." With his leadership the legal profession resolved to make "every effort to maintain order."[65]

The identification of the assassin as actor John Wilkes Booth brought reminiscences of his triumphant performances in Chicago. His debut on the Chicago stage in January 1862 had been the theater event of that season. It was remembered that Booth was so absorbed in the role of the murderous Richard III that during a sword fight he broke his rival's weapon, "and for a moment one half of the audience supposed he would kill the actor himself." A *Tribune* critic once pronounced Booth "a genius" and predicted "he might become a popular and worthy artist." After the actor's performance in Washington's Ford Theater, however, Chicagoans agreed with the soldier who described Booth as a "cold black hearted villain," and predicted, "Hell awaits him with open mouth."[66]

The assassination came on the eve of the mayoral election. Democrat Francis C. Sherman, running for his third consecutive term, withdrew his candidacy, and Republicans reported that Sherman did so because he "could not stand with the copperheads who had murdered the President." More likely he knew that the chances of a Democrat winning were nil. Unopposed Republican nominee John B. Rice was swept into office. Left unstated was the fact that Rice, a theater manager, knew rather well the entire Booth family.[67]

Even Wilbur Storey suspended partisanship. The *Times* of April 16, 1865, was bordered in black. An editorial claimed, "There are not on this day mourners more sincere than the democracy of the northern states." Yet there was not a hint of regret for Storey's vicious and personal attacks on Lincoln while he was alive. Only five weeks before, Storey had pointedly asked the country, "How will you shake off [a president who had become a] noisome stench?"[68]

The president's coffin was taken from the railroad car and placed on a black dias that had been built in the park. Three black-draped gothic arches covered the platform. In bold lettering, each bore a sentiment: "Our Union Cemented in Patriot Blood Shall Stand Forever," "The Poor Man's Captain— The People Mourn Him," " We Honor Him Dead Who Honored Us While Living." Thirty-six high school girls, dressed in white gowns and black headbands, stepped forward and placed wreaths, one for each state, about the casket.

There were no speeches and none of the interminable panegyrics in which nineteenth-century Chicagoans usually delighted. The assassination was such a grievous and shocking incident that it quieted all the city's puffed-up politicians. Their sorrow was genuine and deeply felt. No words could assuage the sense of loss; no words were spoken. The city's posture, hushed and reverent, made her Lincoln observance the most moving and dignified during the cortege's long journey to Springfield.[69]

The procession from Lake Park to the courthouse, where the president would lie in state, was one of the largest ever seen in Chicago. At its head was a band playing a dirge written for the occasion and a squad of mounted horsemen; most were generals, with a scattering of regimental colonels. The casket was born by a black hearse pulled by ten black horses. Alongside walked the official pallbearers, twelve of the city's most outstanding men of each party. The procession that followed was divided into five divisions and was composed of 37,000 citizens. Walking somberly together in the same division were the United Sons of Erin, a deputation of "Colored citizens," the Chicago Board of Trade, and the Laborer's Benevolent Association. It was a display of unity that did justice to Lincoln's memory. The entire procession took four hours in passing.[70]

Along the route sidewalks were packed solid with onlookers, as was every doorway, window, and rooftop. For three hours before the procession began, at least 150,000 people had quietly stood in the rain. (Some reporters claimed the crowd was 500,000 strong.) They were convinced that the funeral was "one of the most important days in the history of Chicago."[71]

The tremendous outpouring of sentiment Lincoln inspired in Chicago was in part a response to his past associations with the city. Many Chicagoans had looked upon him as an adopted son. He had friends in the legal and business community. The Chicago press took credit for boosting him to national prominence, and it was in the Garden City five years earlier that Lincoln had been nominated for the White House. He had promised to return to the city in May to open the Sanitary Fair, and instead he came back in a hearse. Friends of the president tearfully contended that he even told them that when his second term was over, he intended to retire to Chicago. (If Mary Todd Lincoln had had her way, Lincoln would have been buried in the city.) The funeral was also a formal occasion for recognizing the terrible cost that had been exacted by the war. Many of the tears shed as the Lincoln cortege passed were for boys who would never return and young men crippled and made old by war. Lincoln, the symbol of what they had fought for, became the symbol for what Chicago—and the nation—had lost.[72]

Somber adornments were displayed on the buildings along the procession route. The wealthy residents of Michigan Avenue's Park Row hung giant black flags with a single white star or the initials "A. L." from roofs, while every window and door was decorated with black crepe. One of the few buildings not draped in black was the Wigwam, which by then was a store. Most of the thousands along the street were also dressed in mourning.

Only the muddy streets spoiled the dignity of the somber scene. The Board of Public Works had tried to scrape the mud off the wet roadway, but when rain fell in Chicago, there was no avoiding a quagmire. The feet of those in the procession became caked with mud. While it was an embarrassment to the leaders of Chicago, the good-natured president, who knew well Illinois' bottomless roads from his circuit riding days, would have acknowledged how appropriate the mud was. In that respect, Chicago still looked like the frontier city Lincoln had known as a young man.[73]

The president laid in state in the courthouse rotunda, and from the second-floor balcony choirs sang a succession of dirges. George Frederick Root, who had inspired thousands of enlistments with his "Battle-Cry of Freedom," composed a requiem, "Farewell, Father, Friend and Guardian." While the mournful strains drifted over the casket, an endless stream of Chicagoans filed past to pay their last respects. Newspapers estimated that at least 125,000 people viewed the remains. The long lines continued through the night of May 1 and the afternoon of May 2. A *Times* reporter who waited until three o'clock in the morning to see the president still had to wait in line for an hour and a half. Many women, according to the *Tribune*, fainted while waiting. Those who persevered were struck by the "restful" appearance of Lincoln's face but were shocked by the darkness of his complexion. (Veterans recognized the color as the natural result of a bullet wound to the head.[74])

On the evening of May 2, 1865, after a day and a half in Chicago, the people of the city escorted the cortege to the railroad depot for the trip to Springfield. By the eerie light of thousands of torches, the symbol of a nation preserved, the Union triumphant, was borne away like a hero in a mythic tale. At the station the emotional scene was marred by a unseemly display of the commercialism that postwar Chicago so eagerly embraced. Among the cars of the special Chicago, Alton and St. Louis Railway train was the "Pioneer," the first of George Pullman's palace cars. Its splendid appointments were a clear indication of how much the heartland had changed since Abe Lincoln split his last rail. Because the palace car was so wide, every depot and tunnel between Chicago and Springfield had to be modified. This logistical nightmare was deemed worthwhile because the Pioneer was the best Chicago had to offer. Lincoln's funeral was an unparalleled opportunity to promote one of the most important products of Chicago's emerging industrial workshops.[75]

It was sadly fitting that Chicago bade farewell to Abraham Lincoln and ended its involvement in the Civil War by looking both to the past and to the future with a mixture of youthful idealism and crass commercialism. As the funeral train made its way across the dark prairie, passing blazing tar barrels and tearful farmers, Chicagoans turned away from war, some scarred by its fire, others shaped by its brilliance or made wealthy by its waste—all forever changed by the four years of Civil War.

Notes

◇

Introduction

1. Theodore Dreiser, *Dawn* (New York: World Pub. Co., 1931), 159–60; Lloyd Lewis and Henry Justin Smith, *Chicago: The History of Its Reputation* (New York: Harcourt, Brace and Co., 1929), 113.

2. S. Matthew Gallman, *Mastering Wartime: A Social History of Philadelphia During the Civil War*. (New York: Cambridge University Press, 1990).

3. Bruce Catton, *A Stillness at Appomattox* (New York: Doubleday, 1953, 311–12.

4. Gerald F. Linderman, *Embattled Courage: The Experience of Combat in the American Civil War* (New York: Free Press, 1987), 218–25.

Chapter 1

1. *New York Times*, 18 May 1860.

2. Ibid.

3. Ibid.

4. *Chicago Tribune*, 14 May 1860; Frederick Cook, *Bygone Days in Chicago: Recollections of the "Garden City" of the Sixties* (Chicago: A. C. McClurg, 1910), 341–43.

5. *Chicago Tribune*, 14 May 1860.

6. Franc Wilkie, *The Gambler* (Chicago: T. S. Denison, 1888); Carl Abbott, "Civic Pride in Chicago, 1844–1860," *Illinois State Historical Society Journal*, 63, no. 4 (Winter 1970), 399–421.

7. Harold M. Mayer and Richard C. Wade, *Chicago: Growth of a Metropolis* (Chicago: University of Chicago Press, 1969), 44.

8. Ibid., 45–48; Abbott, "Civic Pride in Chicago," 409; William J. Cronon, "To Be the Central City: Chicago, 1848–1857," *Chicago History* 10 (Fall 1981), 130–40; U.S. Bureau of Census, *Manufacturers of the United States in 1860* (Washington, D.C.: U.S. Government Printing Office, 1865), 87.

9. Cook, *Bygone Days in Chicago*, 172–77.

10. Ibid., 339–41; Franc Wilkie, *Walks About Chicago, 1871–1881* (Chicago: Belford, Clarke & Co., 1880), 14–17.

11. Wilkie, *Walks About Chicago*, 10–13; Dominic A. Pacyga and Ellen Skerrett, *Chicago: City of Neighborhoods* (Chicago: Loyola University Press, 1986), 38.

12. Cook, *Bygone Days in Chicago*, 205–10; Richard Sennett, *Families Against the City: Middle Class Homes of Industrial Chicago, 1872–1890* (New York: Vintage Books, 1974), 14–17; Pacyga and Skerrett, *Chicago: A City of Neighborhoods*, 205–7.

13. The *Chicago Daily Journal*, 21 May 1860, wrote, "The number of strangers in the town last week is variously estimated at from fifty to one hundred thousand: fifty thousand will, we think, come nearest the mark." However in P. Orman Ray's *The Convention That Nominated Lincoln* (Chicago: University of Chicago Press, 1916), 15, the figure is placed between 75,000 and 125,000. The *New York Tribune* on the day of the nomination estimated the throng at only 10,000, while the *New York Times* thought the number was at least 40,000 on the day before. Clearly, there was no accurate method of estimating crowds at this time.

14. *Chicago Tribune*, 30 March 1860, 16–17 May 1860.

15. Glydon G. Van Deusen, *Thurlow Weed: Wizard of the Lobby* (Boston: Little Brown, 1947), 238–44.

16. Ray, *The Convention That Nominated Lincoln*, 15.

17. Ibid., 12; Chester L. Barrows, *William M. Evarts: Lawyer, Diplomat, Statesman* (Chapel Hill: University of North Carolina Press, 1941), 90–91; Van Deusen, *Thurlow Weed*, 250–51.

18. Van Deusen, *Thurlow Weed*, 246.

19. Addison G. Procter, *Lincoln and the Convention of 1860* (Chicago: Chicago Historical Society, 1918), 3–7.

20. Carl Schurz, *The Reminiscenses of Carl Schurz*, vol. 2. (New York: Doubleday, 1908), 174–79.

21. *New York Times*, 16 May 1860.

22. Procter, *Lincoln and the Convention of 1860*, 8.

23. Jeser Allen Isely, *Horace Greeley and the Republican Party, 1853–1861* (Princeton, N.J. Princeton University Press, 1947). 280–85; Van Deusen, *Thurlow Weed*, 200–203.

24. Allan Nevins, *The Emergence of Lincoln*, vol. 2 (New York: Scribner's, 1950), 237.

25. William Baringer, *Lincoln's Rise to Power* (Boston: Little, Brown, 1937), 184–88; 205–7.

26. Nevins, *The Emergence of Lincoln*, 2: 243–45.

27. Willard L. King, *Lincoln's Manager: David Davis* (Cambridge, Mass.: Harvard University Press, 1960), 134–35.

28. Ibid., xi, 128, 135.

29. Ibid.; Baringer, *Lincoln's Rise to Power*, 212–13.

30. King, *Lincoln's Manager*, 136–37.

31. Ray, *The Convention That Nominated Lincoln*, 5–6; *Chicago Tribune*, 17 April 1860, 16 May 1860; *Chicago Daily Journal*, 16 May 1860.

32. Baringer, *Lincoln's Rise to Power*, 218–20.

33. Ray, *The Convention That Nominated Lincoln*, 5–6, 16–7; *Chicago Tribune*, 17 April 1860, 16 May 1860; *Chicago Daily Journal*, 16 May 1860.

34. Murat Halstead, *Three Against Lincoln: Murat Halstead Reports the Caucuses of 1860*, ed. William B. Hesseltine (Baton Rouge: Louisiana State Press, 1960), 145–47; *Chicago Tribune*, 16 May 1860; *Chicago Daily Journal*, 16 May 1860.

35. Halstead, *Three Against Lincoln*, 143; A. K. McClure, *Abraham Lincoln and Men of War-Times* (Philadelphia, Penn.: Times Pub. Co., 1892), 30–31.

36. Halstead, *Three Against Lincoln*, 149.

37. Ibid., 150–53; Baringer, *Lincoln's Rise to Power*, 250–63.

38. Don E. Fehrenbacher, "The Republican Decision at Chicago," *Politics and the Crisis of 1860*," ed. Norman A. Graebner (Urbana: University of Illinois Press, 1961), 49–51.

39. Halstead, *Three Against Lincoln*, 155–59; *New York Times* 18 May 1860; *Chicago Tribune*, 17 May 1860; Baringer, *Lincoln's Rise to Power*, 261–63.

40. Baringer, *Lincoln's Rise to Power*, 267.

41. Halstead, *Three Against Lincoln*, 142; *New York Herald Tribune*, 23 May 1860.

42. Baringer, *Lincoln's Rise to Power*, 270–71.

43. Halstead, *Three Against Lincoln*, 142; *New York Herald Tribune*, 18 May 1860.

44. Halstead, *Three Against Lincoln*, 161; *New York Times*, 18 May 1860.

45. William Harlan Hale, *Horace Greeley: Voice of the People* (New York: Harper and Bros., 1950), 221–23.

46. Henry C. Whitney, *Lincoln the Citizen* (New York: Lincoln Centenary Assn., 1907), 289.

47. Baringer, *Lincoln's Rise to Power*, 271–74; Halstead, *Three Against Lincoln*, 161–62.

48. Ibid.; Ray, *The Convention That Nominated Lincoln*, 26–28.

49. Tracy E. Strevey, "Joseph Medill and the Chicago Tribune During the Civil War Period," Ph.D. dissertation, University of Chicago, 1930, 80–83.

50. Mary A. Livermore, *My Story of the War: A Woman's Narrative of Four Years' Personal Experience* (Hartford, Conn.: A. D. Worthington, 1889), 550–51.

51. Halstead, *Three Against Lincoln*, 164–66; Baringer, *Lincoln's Rise to Power*, 281–83.

52. Strevey, *Joseph Medill and the Tribune*, 83.

53. *Chicago Tribune*, 19 May 1860; Halstead, *Three Against Lincoln*, 167–68.

54. Van Duesen, *Thurlow Weed*, 252–53; William Ernest Smith, *The Francis Preston Blair Family in Politics* (New York: Macmillan, 1933), 481–83.

55. Strevey, *Joseph Medill and the Tribune*, 83.

56, Halstead, *Three Against Lincoln*, 165–67.

57. Ibid.; Edwin O. Gale, *Reminiscenses of Early Chicago and Vicinity* (Chicago: Fleming H. Revell, 1902), 400–402.

58. Van Deusen, *Thurlow Weed*, 253–54; Halstead, *Three Against Lincoln*, 172.

59. Halstead, *Three Against Lincoln* 173–74; *Chicago Tribune*, 19 May 1865.

60. Halstead, *Three Against Lincoln,* 173–74.

Chapter 2

1. *New York Times*, 19 May 1860; Halstead, *Three Against Lincoln*, 176–77.

2. *Chicago Tribune*, 19 May 1860, 22 May 1860, 23 May 1860; *New York Tribune*, 19 May 1860.

3. Ibid.

4. *Chicago Tribune*, 19 May 1860.

5. Robert W. Johannsen, *Stephen A. Douglas* (New York: Oxford University Press, 1973), 5–7, 16–17, 65–67, 210–11.

6. Ibid., 451.

7. Ibid., 765–73.

8. *Chicago Tribune*, 25 June 1860; *Chicago Times*, 24 June 1860.

9. Ibid.

10. Damon Wells, *Stephen A. Douglas: The Last Years, 1857–61* (Austin: University of Texas Press, 1971), 238–42; Johannsen, *Stephen A. Douglas*, 778–79.

11. Johannsen, *Stephen A. Douglas*, 790.

12. *Chicago Daily Journal*, 29 June 1860.

13. *Chicago Times*, 7 November 1860.

14. *Chicago Daily Journal*, 2 October 1860.

15. Don E. Fehrenbacher, *Chicago Giant: A Biography of "Long John" Wentworth* (Madison, Wis.: American History Research Center, 1957), 2–3, 17–18; Stephen Longstreet, *Chicago 1860–1919* (New York: David McKay Co., 1973), 4; *Chicago Daily Journal*, 2 October 1860.

16. *Chicago Daily Journal*, 2 October 1860.

17. St. Clair Drake and Horace R. Cayton, *Black Metropolis: A Study of Negro Life in a Northern City* (New York: Harcourt, Brace and World, 1945), 32–36; *Chicago Inter-Ocean*, 28 June 1891.

18. *Chicago Tribune*, 2 October 1860.

19. *Chicago Daily Journal*, 2 October 1860.

20. *Chicago Tribune* and *Chicago Daily Journal*, 5 October 1860.

21. *Chicago Tribune*, 6 October 1860; Johannsen, *Stephen A. Douglas*, 795–96.

22. Ibid.

23. Fehrenbacher, *Chicago Giant*, 180–82; Anonymous, *In Memoria, John Hossack* (Ottawa, Ill.: Republican Times, 1892), 3–7.

24. *Chicago Tribune*, 8 October 1860.

25. Ibid., 18 October 1860.

26. Ibid.

27. Strevey, *Joseph Medill and the Chicago Tribune*, 87; *Chicago Tribune*, 18 October 1860.

28. *Chicago Tribune*, 18 October 1860.

29. Ibid., 3 November 1860.

30. Ibid., 6 November 1860.

31. Mary O. Gallery, ed., "A Civil War Diary," *Mid-America*, 4, no. 1 (July 1931), 66.

32. *Chicago Daily Journal*, 17 November 1860; Johannsen, *Stephen A. Douglas*, 803.

33. William E. Baringer, "Campaign Technique in Illinois—1860," *Transactions of the Illinois State Historical Society* (1932), 273–75; *Chicago Tribune*, 29 September 1860; 7 November 1860.

34. *Chicago Tribune*, 7 November 1860; *Chicago Daily Journal*, 8 November 1860.

35. *Chicago Tribune*, 7, 13 November 1860; Bessie L. Pierce, *A History of Chicago*, vol. 2 (New York: Knopf, 1940), 248; *Chicago Daily Journal*, 7 November 1860.

36. *Chicago Daily Journal*, 7 November 1860; *Chicago Tribune*, 8 November 1860; *Chicago Times*, 7 November 1860.

37. *Chicago Daily Journal*, 21, 22 November 1860.

38. Ibid.; Charles E. Hamlin, *The Life and Times of Hannibal Hamlin* (Cambridge, Mass.: Riverside Press, 1899), 367.

39. *Chicago Daily Journal*, 23 November 1860; Pierce, *History of Chicago*, vol. 2, 253.

40. *Chicago Tribune*, 24 November 1860; H. Draper Hunt, *Hannibal Hamlin of Maine: Lincoln's First Vice President* (Syracuse, N.Y.: Syracuse University Press, 1969), 128.

41. *New York Herald*, 24 November 1860.

42. Hunt, *Hannibal Hamlin*, 128; Hamlin, *Life and Times of Hannibal Hamlin*, 368.

43. Ibid.

44. Allan Nevins, *The Emergence of Lincoln*, vol. 2 (New York: Scribner's 1950), 355; William E. Baringer, *A House Dividing: Lincoln as President Elect* (Springfield, Ill.: Abraham Lincoln Association, 1945), 63–71.

45. Hamlin, *Life and Times of Hannibal Hamlin*, 368; Don Piatt, *Memories of the Men Who Saved the Union* (New York: Frank F. Lovell, 1887), 32–34.

46. Nevins, *Emergence of Lincoln,* 355; Baringer, *A House Dividing*, 33.

47. *Chicago Tribune* 13, 14, 16 November 1860.

48. *Chicago Daily Journal* 8 April 1861; Drake and Cayton, *Black Metropolis*, 35–37.

49. *Chicago Tribune* 4 April 1861; "Slavery in Chicago: A Scrapbook," Chicago Historical Society, n.d., n.p.

50. Paul M. Angle, ed., *New Letters and Papers of Lincoln* (Boston, Mass.: Houghton, Mifflin, 1930), 257–88; Baringer, *A House Dividing*, 89.

51. *Chicago Tribune* 27 November 1860; Rima L. Schultz, *The Church and the City: A Social History of 150 Years at Saint James, Chicago* (Chicago: Cathedral of St. James, 1986), 57; Richard K. Curtis, *They Call Him Mister Moody* (Grand Rapids, Mich.: William Eerdmans, 1962), 83.

52. Curtis, *They Call Him Mister Moody,* 83; James L. Findlay, *Dwight L. Moody: American Evangelist, 1837–1899* (Chicago: University of Chicago Press, 1969), 76–80; *Chicago Tribune,* 27 November 1860; Cook, *Bygone Days in Chicago,* 304–8.

53. Baringer, *A House Dividing*, 84.

54. Ibid., 90; *Chicago Tribune,* 27 November 1860.

55. Fehrenbacher, *Chicago Giant*, 183; *Chicago Tribune*, 12 November 1860; 9 January 1860.

56. James M. McPherson, *Battle Cry of Freedom: The Civil War Era* (New York: Oxford University Press, 1988); Pierce, *History of Chicago*, vol. 2, 251; *Chicago Tribune*, 9 January 1861.

57. *Chicago Tribune*, 9 January 1861.

58. Johannsen, *Stephen A. Douglas,* 809–19.

59. Frank Morn, *"The Eye That Never Sleeps": A History of the Pinkerton National Detective Agency* (Bloomington: Indiana University Press, 1982), 39–41; Fehrenbacher, *Chicago Giant*, 188.

60. Johannsen, *Stephen A. Douglas,* 848–54; Thomas Church, Jr., Memoir, Illinois State Archives, Springfield, n.d.

61. Johannsen, *Stephen A. Douglas,* 814, 848–49; Pierce, *History of Chicago*, vol. 2, 250.

62. *Chicago Tribune*, 15 April 1861.

63. George F. Root, *The Story of a Musical Life: An Autobiography* (Cincinnati, Ohio: John Church Co., 1891); Garry Freshman, "Chicago in the Civil War," *Reader,* 27 August 1982, 1, 18.

64. Johannsen, *Stephen A. Douglas*, 861–62; *Chicago Times*, 15 April 1861.

65. Thomas W. Goodspeed, "The Deaths of Lincoln and Douglas," *Journal of Illinois State Historical Society*, 26, no.3 (October 1933), 199; Johannsen, *Stephen A. Douglas*, 867; *Illinois State Journal*, 26 April 1861.

66. *Chicago Daily Journal*, 2 May 1861; *Chicago Tribune*, 2 May 1861.

67. Johannsen, *Stephen A. Douglas*, 871–72; *Chicago Tribune* 26 May 1861, 4 June 1861, 6 June 1861.

Chapter 3

1. *Chicago Tribune*, 28 May 1861.

2. Meredith M. Dytch, " 'Remember Ellsworth!' Chicago's First Hero of the American Civil War," *Chicago History*, 11, no. 1 (Spring 1982); 15–6; Ruth P. Randall, *Colonel Elmer Ellsworth: A Biography of Lincoln's Friend and First Hero of the Civil War* (Boston: Little, Brown, 1960), 36–37.

3. Randall, *Colonel Ellsworth*, 36–40.

4. Ibid., 95–101; Marcus Cunliffe, *Soldiers and Civilians: The Martial Spirit in America, 1775–1865* (Boston, Mass.: Little, Brown, 1968), 230–35, 400.

5. Dytch, "Remember Ellsworth," 17–18.

6. Ibid., p. 20; Randall, *Colonel Ellsworth*, 168–72.

7. Henry H. Miller, Story of Ellsworth and His Zouaves by a Member of "Ellsworth Zouaves," 1896, manuscript in Ellsworth Collection, Chicago Historical Society.

8. *New York Tribune*, 18 July 1860; Randall, *Colonel Ellsworth*, 182–88.

9. Ibid., 94.

10. *Chicago Tribune*, 15 August 1860.

11. Cunliffe, *Soldiers and Citizens*, 358, 402, 404.

12. Randall, *Colonel Ellsworth*, 264–65; Cunliffe, *Soldiers and Civilians*, 246–47; *Chicago Tribune*, 26 May 1861.

13. Alfred T. Andreas, *History of Chicago*, vol. 2 (Chicago: A. T. Andreas Pub. Co., 1885), 161–62.

14. Ibid., pp. 162–63; John A. Page, "A University Volunteer," *Reminiscenses of Chicago During the Civil War*, ed. Mabel McIlvaine (New York: Citadel Press, 1967), 84–85.

15. Augustus H. Burley, "The Cairo Expedition," *Reminiscenses of Chicago During the Civil War*, ed. McIlvaine, 52–55; William Christian, Memoir, 29 May 1911, Chicago Historical Society, 4; M. Brayman, Narrative of the Seizure of Cairo, n.d., Chicago Historical Society, 6.

16. Christian, Memoir, 5.

17. Ibid.; Burley, "Cairo Expedition," 55.

18. Christian, Memoir, 6; Burley, "Cairo Expedition," 56.

19. Ibid.

20. Burley, "Cairo Expedition," 57; T. M. Eddy, *The Patriotism of Illinois: A Record of the Civil and Military History of the State in the War for the Union*, vol. 1 (Chicago: Clark and Co., 1865), 103–4.

21. Ibid.

22. *Chicago Tribune*, 24 April 1861, 1 May 1861.

23. McPherson, *Battle Cry of Freedom*, 322–33; Eddy, *Patriotism of Illinois*, vol. 1, 108–9.

24. *Chicago Tribune* 15 May 1861, 21 May 1861, 23 April 1861; Eddy, *Patriotism of Illinois*, vol. 1, 579–84.

25. Alexander C. McClurg, "American Volunteer Soldier," *Reminiscences of Chicago During the Civil War*, ed. Mabel McIlvaine (New York: Citadel Press, 1967), 108–9.

26. Ibid.

27. *Chicago Tribune*, 24 April 1861; Eddy, *Patriotism of Illinois*, vol. 2, 567–88; Andreas, *History of Chicago*, vol. 2, 190–91.

28. *Chicago Tribune*, 15 June 1861; *Chicago Daily Journal*, 12 June 1861; Andreas, *History of Chicago*, vol. 2, 191.

29. *Chicago Tribune*, 12 June 1861, 15 June 1861, 9 October 1861, 17 October 1861.

30. *Chicago Tribune*, 23 April 1961; William Kennedy to wife, 23 August 1861; William Kennedy Papers, Illinois State Historical Library, Springfield; William Scripps to brother, 18 June 1861, William H. B. Scripps Papers, Illinois State Historical Library.

31. *Chicago Tribune*, 13 May 1860, 3 July 1861, 25, 29 April 1861; McClurg, "American Volunteer Soldier," 121–33. The McClurg incident took place during the summer of 1862 at a training camp outside Chicago.

32. *Chicago Tribune*, 29 April 1861, 25 June 1861; *Chicago Times*, 23 June 1861.

◇

33. *Chicago Tribune*, 29 April 1861, 29 May 1861; *Chicago Times*, 15 June 1861.

34. *Chicago Tribune*, 16 July 1861; Andreas, *History of Chicago*, vol. 2, 191.

35. Harold F. Smith, "Mulligan and the Irish Brigade," *Journal of Illinois State Historical Society*, 53, no. 1 (Sept. 1960), 166–71; Andreas, *History of Chicago*, vol. 2, 192; Eddy, *Patriotism of Illinois*, vol. 1, 163.

36. Mary O. Gallery, ed., "A Civil War Diary," *Mid-America* 14, no. 1 (July 1931), 71–72; *Chicago Times*, 22 September 1861, 26 September 1861; *Chicago Tribune*, 11 November 1861.

37. *Chicago Tribune*, 2 October 1861, 8 October 1861.

38. *Chicago Tribune*, 22 July 1861; Eddy, *Patriotism of Illinois*, vol. 1, 110–11.

39. Andreas, *History of Chicago*, vol. 2, 301.

40. Ibid.; Howard K. Story, "Camp Douglas, 1861–1865," Master's thesis, Northwestern University, 1942, 1–3.

41. *Chicago Tribune*, 9 October 1861, 30 January 1861.

42. *Chicago Tribune*, 6 February 1862.

43. *Chicago Tribune*, 11 November 1861.

44. *Chicago Tribune*, 23 January 1862; *Chicago Times*, 16 June 1861.

45. Story, "Camp Douglas," 6, 9; *Chicago Tribune*, 22 August 1861, 12 June 1862.

46. McPherson, *Battle Cry of Freedom*, 398–403.

47. *Chicago Tribune*, 18 February 1862; Mary A. Livermore, *My Story of the War: A Woman's Narrative of Four Years of Personal Experience* (Hartford, Conn.: Worthington & Co., 1889), 176–77.

48. Ibid.

49. Karl E. De Jonge, "The History of Camp Douglas, 1861–1865," Master's thesis, University of Illinois, Urbana, 1961, 7–9.

50. Livermore, *My Story of the War*, 182; Story, "Camp Douglas," 13–15; *Chicago Tribune*, 22 February, 1862.

51. McPherson, *Battle Cry of Freedom*, 404–7; Robert Tarrant, Diary, 1862, Chicago Historical Society; Gallery, "A Civil War Diary, 155–66.

52. Victor Hicken, *Illinois in the Civil War* (Urbana: University of Illinois Press, 1966), 52–70; Andreas, *History of Chicago*, vol. 2, 219; Eddy, *Patriotism of Illinois*, vol. 1, 246.

53. *Chicago Tribune*, 18 April 1862.

54. Ibid.

55. Ibid.; Hicken, *Illinois in the Civil War*, 74–80.

56. *Chicago Tribune*, 16 and 17 April 1862.

57. Ibid.

58. *Chicago Times*, 15 April 1862.

59. Hicken, *Illinois in the Civil War*, 79; *Chicago Tribune*, 11 April 1862.

60. Gerald F. Linderman, *Embattled Courage: The Experience of Combat in the American Civil War* (New York: Free Press, 1987), 218–25.

Chapter 4

1. *Chicago Tribune*, 16, 18 April 1862.

2. Ibid.

3. Ibid.

4. Ibid.; Ellen R. Jolly, *Nuns of the Battlefield* (Providence, R.I.: Providence Visitor Press, 1927), 45, 235.

5. *Chicago Tribune*, 16, 18 April 1862; Agatha Young, *The Women and The Crisis: Women of the North in the Civil War* (New York: McDowell, Obolensky, 1959), 170–71.

6. *Chicago Tribune*, 18 April 1862.

7. James M. McPherson, *Battle Cry of Freedom: The Civil War Era* (New York: Oxford University Press, 1988), 480–81.

8. *Chicago Tribune*, 24 April 1861, 21, 22 May 1861; Mary A. Livermore, *My Story of the War: A Woman's Narrative of Four Year's Personal Experience* (Hartford, Conn.: A. D. Worthington, 1889), 121, 126.

9. *Chicago Tribune*, 13, 21, 22 May 1861, 29 April 1861; Livermore, *My Story of the War*, 122.

10. Alfred T. Andreas, *History of Chicago*, vol. 2, (Chicago: A. T. Andreas Pub. Co., 1885), 314; *Chicago Tribune*, 1 May 1861.

11. Andreas, *History of Chicago*, vol. 2, 315; Jolly, *Nuns of the Battlefield*, 136–37, 225–36.

12. Livermore, *My Story of the War*, 112, 224.

13. Ibid.

14. Ibid., 121; Young, *Women and the Crisis*, 69; *Chicago Tribune*, 24 April 1861.

15. *Chicago Tribune*, 24, 25 April 1861; Livermore, *My Story of the War*, 121.

16. Andreas, *History of Chicago*, vol. 2, 165; *Chicago Tribune*, 24 April 1861, 12 December 1861.

17. *Chicago Tribune*, 29 August 1861.

18. Andreas, *History of Chicago*, vol. 2, 314–15; Frederick Cook, *Bygone Days in Chicago: Recollections of the "Garden City" in the Sixties* (Chicago: A.C. McClurg, 1910), 96–97.

19. Andreas, *History of Chicago,* vol. 2, 315; Kathleen D. McCarthy, *Noblesse Oblige: Charity and Cultural Philanthropy in Chicago 1849–1929* (Chicago: University of Chicago Press, 1982), 57.

20. McCarthy, *Noblesse Oblige*, 17–24.

21. Andreas, *History of Chicago*, vol. 2, 315–16; L. P. Brockett and Mary C. Vaughan, *Women's Work in the Civil War: A Record of Heroism, Patriotism, and Patience* (Philadelphia, Penn.: Zeigler, McCurdy, 1867), 161–65, 560–61.

22. *Chicago Tribune*, 28 December 1861; Andreas, *History of Chicago*, vol. 2, 315; Brockett and Vaughan, *Women's Work in the Civil War*, 562–63.

23. Brockett and Vaughan, *Women's Work in the Civil War*, 562–64.

24. Mary A. Livermore, *The Story of My Life, or the Sunshine and Shadows of Seventy Years* (Hartford, Conn.: A. D. Worthington, 1899) 70, 74–75, 126, 145, 217, 396.

25. Livermore, *My Story of the War*, 187–88.

26. Brockett and Vaughan, *Women's Work in the Civil War*, 563–65.

27. Livermore, *My Story of the War*, 228; Andreas, *History of Chicago*, vol. 2, 316–17; *Chicago Tribune*, 10, 14, 23 April 1862, 12 August 1862.

28. Andreas, *History of Chicago*, vol. 2, 317.

29. Tracy E. Strevey, *Joseph Medill and the Chicago Tribune During the Civil War Period*, Ph.D. dissertation, University of Chicago, 1930, 114–17.

30. Cecil Clyde Blair, *The Chicago Democratic Press and the Civil War*, Ph.D. dissertation, University of Chicago, 1947, 60–63.

31. Arthur C. Cole, *The Era of the Civil War, 1848–1870* (Springfield: Illinois Centennial Commission, 1969), 269–71; Bessie L. Pierce, *A History of Chicago*, vol. 2 (New York: Knopf, 1940), 264–65.

32. *Chicago Tribune*, 8 October 1862.

33. Ibid., 15, 17, 20 July 1862.

34. Ibid.

35. Ibid., 11 August 1862.

36. McPherson, *Battle Cry of Freedom*, 491; T. M. Eddy, *The Patriotism of Illinois*, vol. 1 (Chicago: Clark and Co., 1865), 125.

37. *Chicago Tribune*, 21 July 1862.

38. Ibid., 2 August 1862.

39. Ibid., 28 July 1862; Cook, *Bygone Days in Chicago*, 118–20; Dena J. Epstein, "The Battle Cry of Freedom," *Civil War History* (Sept. 1958), 307–18; George F. Root, *The Story of a Musical Life* (Cincinnati: John Church Co., 1891), 132–34.

40. Epstein, "Battle Cry of Freedom," 307–18; Cook, *Bygone Days in Chicago*, 121.

41. Epstein, "Battle Cry of Freedom," 307–18; George F. Root, *The Story of a Musical Life: An Autobiography* (Cincinnati, Ohio: John Church Co., 1891), 137–39. William St. Clair, *Chicago Jokes and Anecdotes for Railroad Travelers and Funlovers* (Chicago: John R. Walsh, 1866), 13.

42. J. Henry Haynie, *The Nineteenth Illinois: A Memoir of a Regiment of Volunteer Infantry* (Chicago: M. A. Donahue, 1912), 131, 166, 177–78; Eddy, *Patriotism of Illinois*, vol. 1, 336–37.

43. Ibid.; Livermore, *My Story of the War*, 114–15.

44. *Chicago Tribune*, 20 August 1862.

45. Ibid., 8, 9, 11, 15, 16 August 1862.

46. Andreas, *History of Chicago*, vol. 2, 346–47.

47. *Chicago Tribune*, 8 August 1862.

48. Ellias Colbert, "Chicago in 1862" (a scrapbook of clippings from the *Chicago Tribune*, n.d.), Chicago Historical Society.

49. Robert E. Sterling, "Civil War Draft Resistance in the Middle West," Ph.D. dissertation, Northern Illinois University, 1974, 90–91; *Chicago Times*, 9 August 1862.

50. Sterling, "Civil War Draft Resistance," 92–93.

51. McPherson, *Battle Cry of Freedom*, 493, 557; *Chicago Times*, 12 October 1862, 22 September 1862.

◇

52. Andreas, *History of Chicago*, vol. 2, 318; Frederick Law Olmstead, *An Accounted of the Executive Organization of the Sanitary Commission* (Washington, D.C.: McGill and Witherow, 1862), 1–6.

53. Livermore, *My Story of the War*, 232–33; William Y. Thompson, "The U.S. Sanitary Commission," *Civil War History*, 2, no. 2 (June 1956), 51–52.

54. Livermore, *My Story of the War*, 157–88.

55. Jane C. Hoge, *The Boys in Blue* (Chicago: C. W. Lilley, 1867), 241–45.

56. Andreas, *History of Chicago*, vol. 2, 319.

57. Ibid.; Ezra B. McCagg, "The United States Sanitary Commission," *Military Essays and Recollections: Papers Read Before the Commandery of the State of Illinois* (Chicago: A. C. McClurg, 1891), 492–93.

58. Andreas, *History of Chicago*, vol. 2, 311.

59. Gardiner H. Shattuck, *A Shield and Hiding Place: The Religious Life of Civil War Armies* (Macon, Ga.: Mercer University Press, 1987), 25–26.

60. Gerald F. Linderman, *Embattled Courage: The Experience of Combat in the American Civil War* (New York: Free Press, 1987), 83; Livermore, *My Story of the War*, 192–94.

61. J. C. Pollock, *Moody Without Sankey: A New Biographical Portrait* (London: Hodder & Stoughton, 1963), 51; Albert D. Richardson, *The Secret Service, the Field, the Dungeon, and the Escape* (Hartford, Conn.: American Publishing Co., 1865), 235–36; John Haynes Holmes, *The Life and Letters of Robert Collyer* (New York: Dodd Mead, 1917), 271. This clash between Collyer and Moody left a vivid impression on each man. Both were young Protestants who rose to great prominence during the war and after the conflict they established national reputations. Yet, after Shiloh they did not again meet for thirty-six years. When they did, by chance on a Chicago El platform, the first thing Moody said was, "You were all wrong that day in the saloon." Collyer, equally righteous, replied, "Old friend, if I was ever all right in my life, it was on that afternoon on the steamer" (Holmes, *Life and Letters of Robert Collyer*, 273).

62. Andreas, *History of Chicago*, vol. 2, 323–24; F. Roger Dunn, "The Formative Years of the Chicago Y.M.C.A.," *Journal of the Illinois State Historical Society*, 27 (December 1944), 343–45; Lemuel Moss, *Annals of the United States Christian Commission* (Philadelphia, Penn.: Lipincott, 1868), 76.

63. Paul Gericke, *Crucial Experiences in the Life of D. L. Moody* (New Orleans, La.: Insight Press, 1978), 25; Dunn, "Formative Years of the Chicago Y.M.C.A.," 346.

64. Gericke, *Crucial Experiences of D. L. Moody*, 26–28.

65. Pollock, *Moody Without Sankey*, 47–49.

66. Livermore, *My Story of the War*, 331–32.

67. *Zouave Gazette*, 30 October 1861, quoted in Andreas *History of Chicago*, vol. 2, 183.

68. Shattuck, *A Shield and Hiding Place*, 11, 32, 81–82; Haynie, *The Nineteenth Illinois* 255–66.

69. James Lee McDonough, *Chattanooga—A Death Grip on the Confederacy* (Knoxville: University of Tennessee Press, 1984), 142, 205–6; Moss, *Annals of the Christian Commission*, 467–70.

70. United States Sanitary Commission, *The Sanitary Commission of the United States Army: A Narrative of Its Works and Purposes* (New York: U.S. Sanitary Commission, 1864), 114–15; Andreas, *History of Chicago*, vol. 2, 320; *Chicago Tribune*, 5 July 1863.

71. Livermore, *My Story of the War*, 409–11.

72. Ibid., 414–15.

73. Ibid.

74. Ibid.; Bruce Catton, *Glory Road* (New York: Doubleday, 1952), 1.

75. Livermore, *My Story of the War*, 430.

76. J. Christopher Schnell, Mary Livermore and the Great Northwestern Fair," *Chicago History* (Spring 1975), 43.

77. Livermore, *My Story of the War*, 417–21.

78. Ibid., 428; Richard H. Zeitlin, "Beyond the Battle: The Flags of the Iron Brigade, 1863–1918," *Wisconsin Magazine of History* 69, no. 1 (Autumn 1985), 36–39; *Chicago Tribune*, 28–30 October 1863.

79. Livermore, *My Story of the War*, 446–47; Young, *Women and the Crisis*, 310, 370.

80. Ibid.

81. Livermore, *My Story of the War*, 428–34.

82. *Chicago Tribune*, 28 October 1863; *Chicago Times, 5–6* November 1863.

83. *Chicago Times*, 4, 10 November 1863; *Chicago Tribune*, 23–24 September 1863.

84. Andreas, *The History of Chicago*, vol. 2, 321; William Y. Thompson, "Sanitary Fairs of the Civil War," *Civil War History* 4, no. 1 (March 1958), 52, 64–65; Livermore, *My Story of the War*, 419; *Chicago Tribune*, 28 October 1863.

85. Livermore, *My Story of the War*, 436–37; Steven M. Buecher, *The Transformation of the Women's Suffrage Movement, The Case of Illinois: 1850–1920* (New Brunswick, N.J.: Rutgers University Press, 1986), 64–67, 76–79.

86. *Chicago Tribune*, 9 November 1863; Livermore, *My Story of the War*, 452–54.

87. Ibid.

Chapter 5

1. James M. McPherson, *Battle Cry of Freedom: The Civil War Era* (New York: Oxford University Press, 1988), 796; *War of Rebellion: A Compilation of the Official Records of the Union and Confederate Armies*, Series 2, vol. 8 (Washington, D.C.: U.S. Government Printing Office, 1880–1901), 986; Thomas Livermore, *Numbers and Losses in the Civil War in America, 1861–1865* (Boston: Houghton, Mifflin, 1901), 79–80.

2. *Chicago Tribune*, 14 February 1862.

3. William B. Hesseltine, *Civil War Prisons: A Study in War Psychology* (Columbus: Ohio State University Press, 1930), 42.

4. Howard K. Story, "Camp Douglas, 1861–1865," master's thesis, Northwestern University, Evanston, IL, 1942, 14–15.

5. *Chicago Tribune*, 25 February 1862.

6. Ibid.

7. Karl E. De Jonge, "The History of Camp Douglas, 1861–1865," master's thesis, University of Illinois, Urbana, IL, 1961, 10; Alfred T. Andreas, *History of Chicago*, vol. 2, (Chicago: A. T. Andreas Pub. Co., 1885), 301; Story, "Camp Douglas," 16; *Chicago Times*, 6 March 1862.

8. Story, "Camp Douglas," 17a; *Chicago Times*, 22 April 1862.

9. Henry M. Stanley, *The Autobiography of Sir Henry Morton Stanley* (London: Sampson Low, 1909), 210.

10. *Chicago Tribune*, 9, 17, 29 March 1862; Story, "Camp Douglas," 26.

11. Story, "Camp Douglas," 25; *Chicago Tribune*, 5 April 1862.

12. *Chicago Tribune*, 25 February 1862, 29 March 1862; De Jonge, "History of Camp Douglas," 15.

13. *Chicago Tribune*, 23 May 1862; Story, "Camp Douglas," 26–27.

14. *Chicago Tribune*, 5 February 1862, 15 June 1862, 9 May 1862.

15. Story, "Camp Douglas," 17–18; James J. McGovern, ed., *The Life and Letters of Eliza Allen Starr* (Chicago: Lakeside Press, 1904), 154; Stanley, *Autobiography,* 213.

16. Story, "Camp Douglas," 31–32.

17. *Chicago Tribune,* 30 March 1862; 4 August 1862.

18. *Chicago Times,* 22 April 1862; De Jonge, "History of Camp Douglas," 17–18.

19. Andreas, *History of Chicago,* vol. 2, 194; *Chicago Tribune,* 30 July 1864, 3 August 1864.

20. Frederick Cook, *Bygone Days in Chicago: Recollections of the "Garden City" of the Sixties* (Chicago: A. C. McClurg, 1910), 38; *Chicago Tribune,* 13 May 1862.

21. Andreas, *History of Chicago,* vol. 2, 300; Edmund Kirke, "Three Days at Camp Douglas," *Our Young Folks,* 1 (April–June 1865), 255–57.

22. Story, "Camp Douglas," 32; De Jonge, "History of Camp Douglas," 16–17.

23. McPherson, *Battle Cry of Freedom,* 791; Hesseltine, *Civil War Prisons,* 80–81.

24. Ibid.

25. Hesseltine, *Civil War Prisons,* 79–80; *Chicago Tribune,* 10 October 1862.

26. *Chicago Tribune* 1, 2, 4, October 1862.

27. Otto Eisenschiml, ed., *Vermont General: The Unusual War Experiences of Edward Hastings Ripley, 1862–1865* (New York: Devin-Adair, 1960), 55–56: Story, "Camp Douglas," 37–39.

28. Story, "Camp Douglas," 41; Eisenschiml, *Vermont General,* 60–72.

29. *Chicago Tribune* 28–31 January 1863.

30. Story, "Camp Douglas," 45; Eisenschiml, *Vermont General,* 73.

31. *Chicago Tribune,* 12, 16, 20, March 1863; Story, "Camp Douglas," 48–49; Eisenschiml, *Vermont General,* 73.

32. William E. Wilson, "Thunderbolt of the Confederacy or 'King of the Horse Thieves' (General John H. Morgan)," *Indiana Magazine of History,* 56 (1958), 119–30; *Chicago Tribune,* 19, 27 August 1863.

33. *Chicago Tribune,* 9 September 1863, 19 October 1863.

34. *Chicago Tribune,* 19 October 1863.

35. *Chicago Tribune*, 4 November 1863; Griffin Frost, *Camp and Prison Journal, Embracing Scenes in Camp, on the March, and in Prison* (Quincy, Ill.: Privately printed, 1867), 272.

36. *Chicago Tribune*, 4 November 1863; *Chicago Times*, 4 December 1863.

37. *Chicago Tribune*, 18 December 1863.

38. Ibid.

39. Ibid., 26 October, 1863; 13, 21 November 1863.

40. Story, "Camp Douglas," 56–60.

41. Ibid., 68–72.

42. Hesseltine, *Civil War Prisons*, 195–96; McPherson, *Battle Cry of Freedom*, 796–99.

43. R. T. Bean, "Seventeen Months in Camp Douglas," *Civil War Quarterly*, 10 (Sept. 1987), 12–14; McPherson, *Battle Cry of Freedom*, 794–95.

44. Frank L. Klement, *Dark Lanterns: Secret Political Societies, Conspiracies, and Treason Trials in the Civil War* (Baton Rouge: Louisiana State University Press, 1984), 191–92.

45. Cook, *Bygone Days in Chicago*, 49; Bean, "Seventeen Months in Camp Douglas," 16; John M. Copley, *A Sketch of the Battle of Franklin, Tennessee, with Reminiscences of Camp Douglas* (Austin, Tex.: Privately printed, 1893), 143–44.

46. Frost, *Camp and Prison Journal*, 270; Bean, "Seventeen Months in Camp Douglas," 20.

47. Copley, *Battle of Franklin*, 135–36.

48. Andreas, *History of Chicago*, vol. 2, 303; Bruce Catton, *A Stillness at Appomattox* (New York: Pocket Books, 1958), 162.

49. Bean, "Seventeen Months in Camp Douglas," 17; Copley, *Battle of Franklin*, 103–6, 188–89; J. J. Moore, "Camp Douglas," *Confederate Veteran* 2, no. 5 (May 1903), 270.

50. Bean, "Seventeen Months in Camp Douglas," 17.

51. Ibid.; Copley, *Battle of Franklin*, 142.

52. Ibid., 172–73; *Chicago Tribune*, 19 October 1863.

53. *Chicago Tribune*, 19 October 1863; Kirke, "Three Days at Camp Douglas," 257–59.

54. Copley, *Battle of Franklin*, 162–63; *Prisoner Vidette*, Manuscript edition in Special Collections, Chicago Public Library, n.d.

55. Story, "Camp Douglas," 77–80.

56. Copley, *Battle of Franklin*, 158–61.

57. Story, "Camp Douglas," 75–76; Bean, "Seventeen Months in Camp Douglas," 16; Moore, "Camp Douglas, 270.

58. Bean, "Seventeen Months at Camp Douglas," 16–17.

59. Ibid.

60. Frost, *Camp and Prison Journal*, 267; Moore, "Camp Douglas," 270; Copley, *Battle of Franklin*, 121–25.

61. Copley, *Battle of Franklin*, 175–76.

62. Bean, "Seventeen Months in Camp Douglas," 15–16.

63. Frost, *Camp and Prison Journal*, 276; John V. Farwell, *Early Recollections of Dwight L. Moody* (Chicago, Ill.: Winona Pub., 1907), 43–45; "The Historic Bell of St. Mark's," *The Diocese of Chicago* 34, no. 9 (Nov. 1921), 14, 18; Ellen R. Jolly, *Nuns of the Battlefield* (Providence, R.I.: Providence Visitor Press, 1927), 235–36.

64. David T. Maul, "Five Butternut Yankees," *Journal of the Illinois State Historical Society*, 53, no.1 (Spring 1960), 177–80; Copley, *Battle of Franklin*, 149–58.

65. Bean, "Seventeen Months in Camp Douglas," 15; Bradfute N. Otaway, "Organized Prisoners in Camp Douglas," *Confederate Veteran* 11, no. 4 (April 1903), 168–69.

66. Ibid., 169.

Chapter 6

1. Paul M. Angle, "War-Time Chicago, 1863," *Chicago History* 2, no.4 (Fall 1963), 2; *Chicago Tribune*, 1 January 1864; Carl J. Abbott, "The Divergent Development of Cincinnati, Indianapolis, Chicago, and Galena, 1840–1860: Economic Thought and Economic Growth," Ph.D. dissertation, University of Chicago, 1971, 298.

2. Bessie L. Pierce, ed., *As Others See Chicago: Impressions of Visitors, 1673–1933* (Chicago: University of Chicago Press, 1933), 172; "Chicago in 1856," *Putnam's Monthly Magazine* 7 (June 1856), 606.

3. Chicago Tribune, *Chicago in 1864: Annual Review of the Trade, Business and Growth of Chicago and the Northwest* (Chicago: Chicago Daily Tribune, 1865), 1; Wyatt W. Belcher, *The Economic Rivalry Between St. Louis and Chicago, 1850–1880* (New York: Columbia University Press, 1947), 96–97.

───────◇───────

4. Emerson D. Fite, *Social and Industrial Conditions in the North During the Civil War* (New York: Frederick Ungar Pub. Co., 1909), 110–11.

5. Ibid.; Albert D. Richardson, *The Secret Service: The Field, the Dungeon, and the Escape* (Hartford, Conn.: American Pub. Co., 1865), 158; Alfred T. Andreas, *History of Chicago*, vol. 2 (Chicago: A. T. Andreas Pub. Co., 1885), 623.

6. *Chicago Democrat*, 18 May 1861; *Chicago Tribune*, 29 June 1861.

7. Fite, *Social and Industrial Conditions*, 111–12; Andreas, *History of Chicago*, vol. 2, 624.

8. Bessie L. Pierce, *A History of Chicago*, vol. 2 (New York: Knopf, 1940), 109–10; *Chicago Tribune*, 15 June 1861; Fred A. Shannon, *The Organization and Administration of the Union Army, 1861–1865* (Cleveland, Ohio: Arthur Clark Co., 1928), 85–86, 94.

9. *Chicago Tribune*, 30 January 1862; Chicago Tribune, *Eighth Annual Review of the Trade and Commerce of the City of Chicago* (Chicago: Daily Press and Tribune, 1860), 32–33; Chicago Tribune, *Chicago in 1864*, 22.

10. *Chicago Tribune*, 30 January 1862.

11. *Chicago Tribune*, 3 April 1861; W. Thorn, *Chicago in 1860: A Glance at Its Business Houses, Its Manufacturers and Commerce* (Chicago: Thompson & Day, 1860); Howard M. Madaus, "Into the Fray: The Flags of the Iron Brigade, 1861–65," *Wisconsin Magazine of History* (Autumn 1985), 4–9.

12. *Chicago Tribune*, 8 May 1861, 14 January 1862.

13. Ibid.; *Prairie Farmer*, 20 May 1865; Pierce, *History of Chicago*, vol. 2, 90.

14. *Chicago Tribune*, 12 December 1861; 26 February 1863; 19 March 1863.

15. *Chicago Tribune*, 1 May 1861; Charles H. Blatchford, *Eliphalet Blatchford and Mary E. W. Blatchford* (Chicago: Privately printed, 1962), 15; *Chicago Tribune*, 25 September 1861, 5 October 1861, 11 November 1861.

16. Wyatt W. Belcher, *The Economic Rivalry Between St. Louis and Chicago, 1850–1880* (New York: Columbia University Press, 1947), 68–71; Robert M. Sutton, "The Illinois Central; Thoroughfare for Freedom," *Civil War History* 7, no. 3 (Sept. 1961), 273.

17. *Chicago Tribune*, 1 June 1861, 11 August 1861; Guy A. Lee, "The Historical Significance of the Chicago Grain Elevator System," *Agricultural History*, no. 4 (Jan. 1937), 16–23.

18. Ibid.; Belcher, *Economic Rivalry*, 102–3; Andreas, *History of Chicago*, vol. 1, 580–81; Auguste Laugel, *The United States During the Civil War*, Allan Nevins, ed. (Bloomington: Indiana University Press, 1961), 113.

19. Pierce, *History of Chicago*, vol. 2, 77–80; Lee, "Significance of the Chicago Grain Elevator System," 23–28.

20. Belcher, *Economic Rivalry*, 150–51; Lloyd Lewis and Henry J. Smith, *Chicago: The History of Its Reputation* (New York: Harcourt, Brace, & Co., 1929), 92.

21. Belcher, *Economic Rivalry*, 154–56; Frederick Merk, *Economic History of Wisconsin During the Civil War Decade* (Madison: State Historical Society of Wisconsin, 1916), 61–65; *Chicago Tribune*, 14 January 1864.

22. Andreas, *History of Chicago*, vol. 2, 331; Louise C. Wade, *Chicago's Pride: The Stockyards, Packingtown and Environs in the Nineteenth Century* (Urbana: University of Illinois Press, 1987), 33–34.

23. Wade, *Chicago's Pride*, 22–23; *Chicago Tribune*, 10 April 1862.

24. Rima L. Schultz, "The Businessman's Role in Western Settlement: The Entrepreneurial Frontier, Chicago, 1833–1872," Ph.D. dissertation, Boston University, 1985, 250; Wade, *Chicago's Pride*, 27, 221.

25. Pierce, *History of Chicago*, vol. 2, 92–93; Wade, *Chicago's Pride*, 49–50; *Chicago Tribune*, 4, 7 November 1863.

26. Wade, *Chicago's Pride*, 50–35; Lewis and Smith, *Chicago*, 94; *Chicago Times*, 12 December 1965.

27. Wade, *Chicago's Pride*, 61.

28. Sutton, "The Illinois Central," 286; *Chicago Tribune*, 13 January 1864.

29. *Chicago Tribune*, 15 June 1863; Sutton, "The Illinois Central," 284–85.

30. Andreas, *History of Chicago*, vol. 2, 674–76; Bernard C. Korn, "Eber, Brock Ward: Pathfinder of American Industry," Ph.D. dissertation, Marquette University, 1942, 184.

31. Ibid.

32. John M. Glenn, "The Industrial Development of Illinois," *Transactions of the Illinois State Historical Society*, 28 (1921); 68–69; Andreas, *History of Chicago*, vol. 2, 674–82.

33. Ray Ginger, *Altgeld's America: The Lincoln Ideal Versus Changing Realities* (New York: New Viewpoints, 1973), 143–45.

34. Fite, *Social and Industrial Conditions*, 6–8; David A. Hounshell, *From the American System to Mass Production, 1800–1932: The Development of Manufacturing Technology in the United States* (Baltimore, Md.: Johns Hopkins University Press, 1984), 161; Stephen Longstreet, *Chicago: 1860–1919* (New York: David McKay, 1973), 39.

35. William T. Hutchinson, *Cyrus Hall McCormick: Harvest, 1866–1884* (New York: Appleton-Century, 1935), 52–57; Hounshell, *From the American System to Mass Production*, 166–67.

36. Hutchinson, *McCormick*, 86–89.

37. Abbott, "The Divergent Development of Cincinnati, Chicago and Galena," 327–28.

38. Thomas C. Cochran, "Did the Civil War Retard Industrialization?" *Mississippi Valley Historical Review*, 48 (1961), 197–209.

39. Hutchinson, *McCormick*, 89; Hounshell, *From the American System to Mass Production*, 166–67.

40. James M. McPherson, *Battle Cry of Freedom: The Civil War Era* (New York: Oxford University Press, 1989), 447–50; Pierce, History of Chicago, vol. 2, 157–60; Esther E. Espenshade, "The Economic Development and History of Chicago, 1860–65," Master's thesis, University of Chicago, 1931, 134; Hutchinson, *McCormick*, 89.

41. Pierce, *History of Chicago*, vol. 2, 164–65; Hutchinson, *McCormick*, 89.

42. Pierce, *History of Chicago*, vol. 2, 165–66; *Chicago Tribune*, 15 March 1864, 9 May 1864, 17 May 1864.

43. *Workingman's Advocate*, 17 September 1864.

44. Ibid.; Pierce, *History of Chicago*, vol. 2, 161–64; Arthur S. White, "Historical Notes," *Michigan History*, 11, no. 1 (1927), 145–46; Franc B. Wilkie, *Personal Reminiscences of Thirty-Five Years of Journalism* (Chicago: F. J. Schulte & Co., 1891), 154–55.

45. *Chicago Tribune*, 30 January 1862; *Workingman's Advocate*, 17 September 1864.

46. *Chicago Tribune*, 23 July 1862.

47. Ibid., 22 July 1862.

48. Mark Wyman, *Immigrants in the Valley: Irish, Germans and Americans in the Upper Mississippi Country, 1830–1860* (Chicago: Nelson-Hall, 1984), 222–27; Bruce C. Levine, "Free Soil, Free Labor, and Freimaner: German Chicago in the Civil War Era," *German Workers in Industrial Chicago, 1850–1910: A Comparative Perspective* (Dekalb: Northern Illinois University Press, 1983), 172–78.

49. *Chicago Tribune*, 18 January 1864, 16 March 1864, 13 July 1864; *Illinois Staats Zeitung*, 15 July 1863.

50. *Chicago Tribune*, 15–16, 30 July 1864; 11 August 1862; *Chicago Times*, 13 July 1864.

51. *Chicago Tribune*, 15 July 1864.

52. *Chicago Times*, 10 November 1864; *Chicago Evening Journal*, 11 November 1864; *Chicago Tribune*, 1 February 1862, 14 January 1864, 13 July 1864, 12 April 1865; Frederick Cook, *Bygone Days in Chicago: Recollections of the Garden City in the Sixties* (Chicago: A. C. McClurg, 1910), 10.

53. *Chicago Tribune*, 5 January 1863; Miles M. Fisher, "Negro Churches in Illinois: A Fragmentary History with an Emphasis on Chicago," *Journal of the Illinois State Historical Society*, 56, no. 3 (Autumn 1963), 558.

54. Robert L. McCaul, *The Black Struggle for Public Schooling in Nineteenth Century Illinois* (Carbondale: Southern Illinois University Press, 1987), 42–43, 55–72; *Chicago Tribune*, 8, 14 February 1865.

55. *Chicago Tribune*, 15 April 1863; *Chicago Evening Journal*, 30 April 1863.

56. Vicker Hicken, "The Record of Illinois Negro Soldiers in the Civil War," *Journal of the Illinois State Historical Society* 56, no. 3 (Autumn 1963), 533; Mary A. Livermore, *My Story of the War: A Woman's Narrative of Four Year's Personal Experience* (Hartford, Conn.: A. D. Worthington, 1889), 351–53.

57. Hicken, "Illinois Negro Soldiers," 533; *Chicago Times*, 19 January 1864.

58. *Chicago Tribune*, 31 October 1863, 13 November 1863, 28–29 December 1863, 6, 13 January 1864.

59. T. M. Eddy, *The Patriotism of Illinois*, vol. 1, (Chicago: Clark and Co., 1865), 590.

60. Ibid., 590–95; Bruce Catton, *A Stillness at Appomattox* (New York: Pocket Books, 1958), 273–86; William F. Fox, *Regimental Losses in the American Civil War* (Albany, N.Y., Albany Pub. Co., 1889), 55; H. W. Rokker, *Report of the Adjutant General of the State of Illinois*, 8 (Springfield, Ill.: H. W. Rokker, 1886), 777–805.

61. Eddy, *Patriotism of Illinois*, vol. 1, 592.

Chapter 7

1. Paul Angle, "Chicago's Second National Convention," *Chicago History* 7, no. 4 (Summer 1964), 104–5; Bruce Catton, *A Stillness at Appomattox* (New York: Doubleday, 1953), 324–25.

2. Joel H. Silbey, *A Respectable Minority: The Democratic Party in the Civil War Era, 1860–1868* (New York: W. W. Norton, 1977), 124–27; William

T. Hutchinson, Cyrus Hall *McCormick: Harvest, 1866-1884* (New York: Appleton-Century, 1935), 58.

3. Angle, "Chicago's Second Convention," 105; Hutchinson, *McCormick*, 122.

4. Frederick Cook, *Bygone Days in Chicago: Recollections of the Garden City in the Sixties* (Chicago: A. C. McClurg, 1910), 85-88; Angle, "Chicago's Second Convention," 107.

5. Silbey, *Respectable Minority*, 126-27.

6. Ibid., 9-11.

7. Ibid., 11-25.

8. Justin E. Walsh, *To Print the News and Raise Hell!: A Biography of Wilbur F. Storey* (Chapel Hill: University of North Carolina Press, 1968), 150; Cook, *Bygone Days in Chicago*, 331.

9. Walsh, *To Print the News*, 154-57.

10. Ibid., 118-21; Franc B. Wilkie, *Personal Reminiscences of Thirty-Five Years of Journalism* (Chicago: F. J. Schulte & Co., 1891), 140-45; *Chicago Times*, 23, 24, 25 September 1862.

11. Walsh, *To Print the News,* 162-66; Cecil C. Blair, "The Chicago Democratic Press and the Civil War," Ph.D. dissertation, University of Chicago, 1947, 56-57; *Chicago Times* 12, 14 January 1863.

12. Blair, "Chicago Democratic Press," 76-77; Alfred T. Andreas, *History of Chicago*, vol. 2 (Chicago: A. T. Andreas Pub. Co., 1885), 493.

13. Silbey, *Respectable Minority*, 69-78; Blair, "Chicago Democratic Press, 162-66.

14. *Chicago Times*, 22 July 1864, 21 September 1863, 12 December 1863; Silbey, *Respectable Minority*, 82-83.

15. Walsh, *To Print the News*, 164-66; *Chicago Times*, 23 July 1862, 8 January 1864.

16. Walsh, *To Print the News*, 181-90; *Chicago Times*, 15, 26 February 1870; 7 August 1865.

17. Walsh, *To Print the News*, 159-62.

18. *Chicago Times*, 28 January 1863.

19. Frank L. Klement, *The Limits of Dissent: Clement L. Vallandigham and the Civil War* (Lexington: University of Kentucky Press, 1970), 90-113; James M. McPherson, *Battle Cry of Freedom: The Civil War Era* (New York: Oxford University Press, 1988), 591-93.

20. McPherson, *Battle Cry of Freedom*, 596–97.

21. Walsh, *To Print the News*, 173–75; *Chicago Times*, 27–30 May 1863.

22. Craig D. Tenney, "To Suppress or Not to Suppress; Abraham Lincoln and the Chicago *Times*," *Civil War History*, 27, no.3 (Sept. 1981), 248–51; Cook, *Bygone Days in Chicago*, 52–53; *Chicago's Evening Journal*, 2 June 1863.

23. Ibid.

24. *Chicago Evening Journal* 2, 3 June 1863.

25. Ibid., 4 June 1863; Cook, *Bygone Days in Chicago*, 53–56; Tenny, "To Suppress or Not to Suppress," 254–55; Mark Krug, *Lyman Trumbull: Conservative Radical* (New York: Barnes, 1965), 208–9.

26. Ibid.

27. *Chicago Evening Journal*, 4 June 1863; Cook, *Bygone Days in Chicago*, 54–55.

28. *Chicago Tribune*, 4, 7 June 1863; Cook, *Bygone Days in Chicago*, 57.

29. Tenny, "To Suppress or Not To Suppress," 255–57; Willard L. King, *Lincoln's Manager: David Davis* (Cambridge, Mass.: Harvard University Press, 1960), 211.

30. Cook, *Bygone Days in Chicago*, 57–58; Jay Monaghan, *Civil War on the Western Border, 1854–1865* (Boston, Mass.: Little Brown, 1959), 289; Tenney, "To Suppress or Not to Suppress," 252.

31. *Chicago Tribune*, 5 June 1865.

32. Tenney, "To Suppress or Not to Suppress," 256–59.

33. Cook, *Bygone Days in Chicago*, 57–58; Wilkie, *Personal Reminiscences*, 101, 116–17.

34. Ibid.

35. Robert E. Sterling, "Civil War Draft Resistance in Illinois," *Illinois State Historical Society Journal*, 64, no. 3 (Autumn 1971), 260–79.

36. Robert E. Sterling, "Civil War Draft Resistance in the Middle West," Ph.D. dissertation, Northern Illinois University, 1974, 223–24.

37. Ibid., 224–25; *Chicago Tribune*, 2 July 1863.

38. Bruce C. Levine, "Free Soil, Free Labor, and Freimaner: German Chicago in the Civil War Era," *German Workers in Industrial Chicago 1850–1910: A Comparative Perspective* (DeKalb. Northern Illinois University Press, 1983), 176–77; McPherson, *Battle Cry of Freedom*, 603–5.

———◇———

39. Eugene C. Murdock, *One Million Men: The Civil War Draft in the North* (Madison: State Historical Society of Wisconsin, 1971), 171–76; Eugene C. Murdock, *Patriotism Limited, 1862–1865: The Civil War Draft and the Bounty System* (Kent, Ohio: Kent State University Press, 1967), 18–22.

40. Herbert Asbury, *Gem of the Prairie: An Informal History of the Chicago Underworld* (De Kalb: Northern Illinois University Press, 1986), 66.

41. Murdock, *One Million Men*, 229–36.

42. Asbury, *Gem of the Prairie*, 66.

43. Murdock, *One Million Men*, 233; *Chicago Tribune*, 24 February 1865.

44. *Chicago Times*, 15, 16, 17 August 1864, 7 September 1864.

45. Ibid., 30 August 1864.

46. Bessie L. Pierce, *A History of Chicago*, vol. 2 (New York: Knopf, 1940), 277; *Chicago Tribune*, 29, 31 May 1864.

47. *Chicago Times*, 30 August 1864.

48. Ibid.

49. Silbey, *Respectful Minority*, 118–19.

50. Stewart Mitchell, *Horatio Seymour of New York* (Cambridge, Mass.: Harvard University Press, 1938), 364–65.

51. William F. Zornow, "McClellan and Seymour in the Chicago Convention of 1864," *Journal of the Illinois State Historical Society*, 63, (Winter 1950), 283–87.

52. *New York Times*, 30 August 1864; Don E. Fehrenbacher, *Chicago Giant: A Biography of "Long John" Wentworth* (Madison, Wis.: American History Research Center, 1957), 198–99.

53. *New York Times*, 31 August 1864; Stephan Sears, *George B. McClellan: The Young Napoleon* (New York: Ticknon and Fields, 1988), 372; Alexander C. Flick, *Samuel Jones Tilden: A Study in Political Sagacity* (Port Washington, N.Y.: Kennikat Press, 1939), 148–49; Irving Katz, *August Belmont: Political Biography* (New York: Columbia University Press, 1968), 130–31.

54. Ibid.

55. Angle, "Chicago's Second National Convention," 110–11; *New York Times*, 2 September 1864.

56. Sears, *Young Napoleon*, 375–78.

57. *Chicago Times*, 1 September 1864.

58. Larry E. Nelson, *Bullets, Ballots, and Rhetoric: Confederate Policy for the United States Presidential Contests of 1864* (Tuscaloosa: University of Alabama Press, 1980), 112–13.

59. The controversy over the "Chicago Conspiracy" yielded two principle schools of thought. The traditional view sees it as one of several attempts made by the Confederacy and midwestern Democrats to pull the states of Ohio, Indiana, and Illinois out of the war. Traditional historians view the support received by rebel agents and copperhead insurrectionists to have been considerable but poorly coordinated. For more on this view see Wood Gray, *The Hidden Civil War: The Story of the Copperheads* (New York: Viking Press, 1942); George Fort Milton, *Abraham Lincoln and the Fifth Column* (New York: Collier, 1942); Mayo Fesler, "Secret Political Societies in the North During the Civil War," *Indiana Magazine of History* 14 (1918), 183–286; and Stephen Z. Starr, "Was There a Northwest Conspiracy?" *Filson Club Historical Quarterly* 38 (1964); 328–41. Revisionist historians view the conspiracy as largely the product of Republican partisans who were anxious to paint all Democrats with the brush of treason. The revisionists do not deny that rebel agents operated in the North, but they greatly discount the extent of their activities and their level of support in the Midwest. The leading historian of this subject, Frank L. Klement, regards the story of the conspiracy as a "myth." For more on his work, see *Dark Lanterns: Secret Political Societies, Conspiracies, and Treason Trials in the Civil War* (Baton Rouge: Louisiana State University Press, 1984), and *The Copperheads in the Middle West* (Chicago: University of Chicago Press, 1960). One reason for such sharp disagreement is the number of unreliable and sensationalist accounts written in the immediate wake of the Chicago Conspiracy, especially Thomas H. Keefe, "How the Northwest Was Saved," *Everybody's Magazine* (Jan. 1900), 82–91; James Gilmore, "The Great Chicago Conspiracy," *Atlantic Monthly*, 16 (1865), 108–20; and I. Winslow Ayer, *The Great North-West Conspiracy* (Chicago: Rounds and James 1863). The truth of the Chicago Conspiracy is neither as colorful as Gilmore and Keefe described nor as harmless as some revisionists contend.

60. James D. Horan, *Confederate Agent: A Discovery in History* (New York: Crown, 1954), 3–5, 36–46; Klement, *Dark Lanterns*, 208–9.

61. Thomas H. Hines and John B. Castleman, "The Northwest Conspiracy," *Southern Bivouac*, N.S. 2 (June 1886–March 1887), 442–43.

62. Maurice Langhorn, testimony before Military Commission, Cincinnati, Ohio, Records of the Judge Advocate General, National Archives, Washington, D.C., R.G. 153, Box 1109, 284–308; Stephen Z. Starr, *Colonel Grenfell's Wars: The Life of a Soldier of Fortune* (Baton Rouge: Louisiana State University Press, 1971), 172–73.

63. Klement, *Dark Lanterns*, 100–104.

64. Ibid., 37–51, 68; McPherson, *Battle Cry of Freedom*, 599; Walsh, *To Print the News*, 188–89; Guy J. Gibson, "The Union League Movement in Illinois

During the Civil War," Master's thesis, University of Illinois, Urbana, 1953, 14–30.

65. Gibson, "Union League Movement," 170–78.

66. Hines and Castleman, "Northwest Conspiracy," 503–6.

67. Horan, *Confederate Agent*, 129–30; Klement, *Dark Lanterns*, 167–69.

68. Ibid.

69. Charles W. Merrifield, "The Chicago Conspiracy: A Study of the Insurrectionary Phase of the Civil War Peace Movement in the Old Northwest," Master's thesis, University of Chicago, 1935, 41–46.

70. Hines and Castleman, "Northwest Conspiracy," 574.

71. McPherson, *Battle Cry of Freedom*, 774–75; *Chicago Tribune*, 4 September 1864.

72. Fehrenbacher, *Chicago Giant*, 197–98.

73. Ibid.

74. Hutchinson, *McCormick*, 56–60; *Chicago Tribune*, 18, 19 September 1864.

75. *Chicago Tribune*, 5 September 1864.

76. Ibid., 29 September 1864.

77. Ibid., 30 September 1864.

78. Ibid.; Bessie L. Pierce, *A History of Chicago*, vol. 2 (New York: Knopf, 1940), 282; *Workingman's Advocate*, 13 September 1864.

79. Pierce, *History of Chicago*, vol. 2, 274; *Chicago Tribune*, 13 October 1864.

80. Bradfute N. Otaway, "Organized Prisoners at Camp Douglas," *Confederate Veteran*, 2, no. 4 (April 1903), 169–71; R. T. Bean, "Seventeen Months in Camp Douglas," *Civil War Quarterly*, 10 (Sept. 1987), 21.

81. Ibid.

82. Horan, Confederate Agent, 140.

83. Ibid.; *Chicago Tribune*, 21 September 1864; Klement, *Dark Lanterns*, 188–90.

84. Klement, *Dark Lanterns*, 196–97; Horan, *Confederate Agents*, 189–94; Robert Alexander, testimony before Military Commission, Cincinnati,

Ohio, Records of Judge Advocate General, National Archives, Washington, D.C., R. B. 153, Box 1109, 475–78.

85. William C. Walsh and William P. Comstock, testimony before Military Commission, Cincinnati, Ohio, 374, 383.

86. Klement, *Dark Lanterns*, 214; I. Winslow Ayer, *The Great Northwestern Conspiracy* (Chicago: Walsh, Baldwin & Samford, 1865), 38–39.

87. Maurice Langhorne, testimony before Military Commission, Cincinnati, Ohio, 346–53.

88. Klement, *Dark Lanterns*, 191–92; William Bross, "Biographical Sketch of the Late General B. J. Sweet, History of Camp Douglas: A Paper Read Before the Chicago Historical Society, June 18, 1878," Chicago Historical Society, 1878, 18–27.

89. Starr, *Colonel Grenfells' Wars*, 189–98; Bean, "Seventeen Months in Camp Douglas," 21.

90. John T. Shanks, testimony before Military Commission, Cincinnati, Ohio, 18–26.

91. Ibid., 30–38.

92. Ibid.; Starr, *Colonel Grenfells' Wars*, 196–99.

93. Lewis C. Skinner, testimony before the Military Commission, Cincinnati, Ohio, 566.

94. Ibid.

95. Starr, *Colonel Grenfells' Wars*, 201–4.

96. Ibid.; Horan, *Confederate Agent*, 181; Langhorne, testimony Before the Military Commission, Cincinnati, Ohio, 314–15; Benjamin Sweet, Testimony before the Military Commission, Cincinnati, Ohio, 703–4.

97. Starr, *Colonel Grenfells' Wars*, 201–3; *Chicago Evening Journal*, 7 November 1864; Ernest Duvergier de Hauranne, *A Frenchman in Lincoln's America* (Chicago: Lakeside Press, 1975), 18.

98. A. F. Scharf, "Camp Douglas Conspiracy," unpublished memorandum dated 1911 in the A. F. Scharf Collection, Chicago Historical Society.

99. de Hauranne, *A Frenchman in Lincoln's America*, 19.

100. Ibid., 19–25.

101. Pierce, *History of Chicago*, vol. 2, 280.

102. de Hauranne, *A Frenchman in Lincoln's America*, 31.

103. *Chicago Times*, 8, 11, 28 November 1864.

———◇———

Chapter 8

1. Ida M. Tarbell, *The Life of Abraham Lincoln*, vol. 2 (New York: Harper & Brothers, 1909), 148–49.

2. *Chicago Tribune*, 14 February 1865.

3. Ibid., 28 February 1865; Gene Smith, *Lee and Grant: A Dual Biography* (New York: New American Library, 1984), 218.

4. *Chicago Tribune*, 8 March 1865; Tarbell, *Life of Lincoln*, vol. 2, 148.

5. Ibid.; *Chicago Tribune*, 28 February 1865.

6. *Chicago Tribune*, 8 March 1865.

7. Tarbell, *Life of Lincoln*, vol. 2, 149.

8. Frederick Cook, *Bygone Days in Chicago: Recollections of the "Garden City" of the Sixties* (Chicago: A. C. McClurg, 1910), 29–30; *Chicago Tribune*, 4 March 1865; Eugene C. Murdock, *One Million Men: The Civil War Draft in the North* (Madison: State Historical Society of Wisconsin, 1971), 276–78.

9. Robert E. Sterling, "Civil War Draft Resistance in the Middle West," Ph.D. dissertation, Northern Illinois University, 1974, 498.

10. *Chicago Tribune*, 14 April 1865.

11. Herbert Asbury, *Gem of the Prairie: An Informal History of the Chicago Underworld* (DeKalb: Northern Illinois University Press, 1986), 61.

12. Cook, *Bygone Days in Chicago*, 139–40.

13. *Chicago Tribune*, 2 June 1861; 16 September 1862; 23 March 1865.

14. Cook, *Bygone Days in Chicago*, 131.

15. Asbury, *Gem of the Prairie*, 67–70; Perry R. Duis, *The Saloon: Public Drinking in Chicago and Boston, 1880–1970* (Urbana: University of Illinois Press, 1983), 235–39; *Chicago Tribune*, 2 July 1861; 23 March 1865.

16. Cook, *Bygone Days in Chicago*, 134–35.

17. Mary A. Livermore, *My Story of the War: A Woman's Narrative of Four Years' Personal Experience* (Hartford, Conn.: A. D. Worthington, 1889), 587–99.

18. Asbury, *Gem of the Prairie*, 62, 71; *Chicago Tribune*, 29 September 1862.

19. Cook, *Bygone Days in Chicago*, 159–60; *Chicago Tribune*, 1 March 1864.

20. Cook, *Bygone Days in Chicago*, 139–40.

21. Ibid., 143; *Chicago Tribune*, 15 June 1864; Asbury, *Gem of the Prairie*, 75–77.

22. *Chicago Times*, 16 August 1864; *Chicago Tribune*, 8 February 1865.

23. Bruce Catton, *A Stillness at Appomattox* (New York: Doubleday, 1953), 311–12.

24. Livermore, *My Story of the War*, 588–89.

25. Philip M. Coder to Emily Coder, 7 February 1865, Philip M. Coder Collection, Illinois Historical Library, Springfield.

26. Philip Kinsley, *The Chicago Tribune: Its First Hundred Years*, vol. 1 (New York: Knopf, 1943), 364.

27. Ibid., 359; *Chicago Tribune*, 22 January 1865, 1 February 1865; Arthur C. Cole, *The Era of the Civil War 1848–1870* (Springfield: Illinois Centennial Commission, 1919), 389.

28. Frank L. Klement, *Dark Lanterns: Secret Political Societies, Conspiracies, and Treason Trials in the Civil War* (Baton Rouge: Louisiana State University Press, 1984), 213–17. Cook, *Bygone Days in Chicago*, 50.

29. Steven Z. Starr, *Colonel Grenfell's Wars: The Life of a Soldier of Fortune* (Baton Rouge: Louisiana State University Press, 1971), 246–48.

30. Ibid., 325–30.

31. *Chicago Tribune*, 4 April 1865.

32. Ibid.

33. Ibid.

34. *Chicago Tribune*, 11 April 1865.

35. Bessie L. Pierce, *History of Chicago*, vol. 2, (New York: Knopf, 1940), 276; Elias Colbert, *Chicago: Historical and Statistical Sketch of the Garden City* (Chicago: P. T. Sherlock, 1868), 96–97; Cook, *Bygone Days in Chicago*, 30; State of Illinois, *Report of the Adjutant General 1861–1866*, vol. 1, 198–205.

36. Livermore, *My Story of the War*, 468–71; Merritt C. Bragdon, Diary, April 16, 1865, Illinois State Historical Library, Springfield.

37. *Chicago Tribune*, 12 June 1865; Livermore, *My Story of the War*, 472.

38. Sarah E. Henshaw, *Our Branch and Its Tributaries: A History of the Work of the Northwestern Sanitary Commission* (Chicago: Alfred L. Sewell, 1868), 297–99.

39. *Chicago Evening Journal*, 3 June 1865; *Chicago Tribune*, 16 June 1865.

40. Ibid.

41. Ibid.; Alfred T. Andreas, *History of Chicago*, vol. 2 (Chicago: A. T. Andreas Pub. Co., 1885), 242–9.

42. Ibid.; Gerald F. Linderman, *Embattled Courage: The Experience of Combat in the American Civil War* (New York: Free Press, 1987), 220–26.

43. *Chicago Evening Journal*, 13 June 1865; Henshaw, *Our Branch and Its Tributaries*, 296.

44. *Chicago Evening Journal*, 13 June 1865; Henshaw, *Our Branch and Its Tributaries*, 296.

45. *Chicago Evening Journal*, 12 June 1865.

46. Ibid., 14 June 1865.

47. *Chicago Evening Journal*, 13 June 1865.

48. Reid Mitchell, *Civil War Soldiers* (New York: Viking, 1988), 207.

49. *Chicago Evening Journal*, 12 June 1865; Linderman, *Embattled Courage*, 224; Mitchell, *Civil War Soldiers*, 207.

50. *Chicago Evening Journal*, 12 June 1865; *Chicago Tribune*, 15 June 1865.

51. *Chicago Tribune*, 14 June 1865.

52. *Chicago Evening Journal*, 15 June 1865; *Chicago Tribune*, 14 August 1864.

53. Asbury, *Gem of the Prairie*, 70; *Chicago Tribune*, 2, 10, 12, 13, 16 June 1865.

54. Theodore Dreiser, *Dawn* (New York: World Pub. Co., 1931), 159–60.

55. Elias Colbert and Everett Chamberlain, *Chicago and the Great Conflagration* (Chicago: J. S. Goodman, 1872), 122; Ray Ginger, *Altgeld's America: The Lincoln Ideal Versus Changing Realities* (New York: New Viewpoints, 1973), 9.

56. Colbert and Chamberlain, *Chicago and the Great Conflagration*, 123.

57. Alfred T. Andreas, *History of Chicago*, vol. 2 (Chicago: A. T. Andreas Pub. Co., 1885), 590; Pierce, *History of Chicago*, vol. 2, 289; *Chicago Evening Journal*, 12 June 1865; Livermore, *My Story of the War*, 7.

58. Andreas, *History of Chicago*, vol. 2, 590–91; J. Henry Haynie, *The Nineteenth Illinois: A Memoir of a Regiment of Volunteer Infantry* (Chicago: M. A. Donahue, 1912), 14, 60.

59. E. R. Lewis, *The Roll of Honor* (Chicago: Cook County Commissioners, 1922), 25–28; John C. Underwood, *Report of Proceedings . . . of the Confederate Monuments* (Chicago: Johnston Printing Co., 1896), 5–9.

60. Andreas, *History of Chicago*, vol. 3, 590; Ginger, *Altgeld's America*, 1–16.

61. Willard B. Gatewood, "An Experiment in Color: The Eight Volunteers, 1898–99," *Journal of the Illinois State Historical Society* 65, no. 3 (Autumn 1972), 293–95; McCaul, *Struggle for Black Public's Schooling*, 90–91, 96; Larry Gara, "A Glorious Time: The 1874 Abolitionist Reunion in Chicago," *Journal of the Illinois State Historical Society* 65, no. 3 (Autumn 1972), 280–87.

62. Herman Kogan, "Myra Bradwell, Crusader at Law," *Chicago History*, 3, no. 3 (Winter 1974), 132–35; Glenn Holt, "Private Plans for Public Spaces: The Origins of Chicago's Park System, 1850–1875," *Chicago History*, 8, no. 3 (Fall 1979), 173–79.

63. Ginger, *Altgeld's America*, 124–25; Jane Addams, *Twenty Years at Hull House* (New York: Signet Classic, 1961), 37, 45.

64. *Chicago Tribune*, 2 May 1865; James Goodspeed, *Fifteen Years Ago or the Patriotism of Will County* (Joliet, Ill.: Joliet Republican, 1876), 76–77, Philip Coder to Emily Coder, April 15, 1865, Coder Letters, Illinois State Historical Library; *Chicago Tribune*, 17 April 1865.

65. *Chicago Tribune*, 17 March 1865; King, *Lincoln's Manager*, 226–27.

66. *Chicago Tribune*, 21 January 1862; Philip Coder to Emily Coder, April 15, 1865. Coder Letters, Illinois State Historical Library.

67. *Chicago Tribune*, 17 April 1865.

68. Justin E. Walsh, *To Print the News and Raise Hell: A Biography of Wilbur F. Storey* (Chapel Hill: University of North Carolina Press, 1968), 196–98.

69. *Chicago Tribune*, 2 May 1865; Victor Searcher, *The Farewell to Lincoln* (New York: Abingdon Press, 1965), 236–37.

70. Ibid.; "Reception of the Remains of President Lincoln, at Chicago, May 1, 1865," Lincoln Collection, Chicago Historical Society.

71. *Chicago Tribune*, 2 May 1865; William H. Hutton to Friend Ida, April 3, 1865, Hutton Collection, Chicago Historical Society.

72. *Chicago Tribune*, 2 May 1865.

73. Ibid.

74. Ibid.: Merrit C. Bragdon, Diary, April 16, 1865, Bragdon Collection, Illinois State Historical Society, Springfield; Frederick Cook, *Bygone Days in Chicago: Recollection of the "Garden City" of the Sixties* (Chicago: A. C. McClurg, 1910), 317–20.

75. *Chicago Tribune*, 3 May 1865; Almont Lindsey, *The Pullman Strike: The Story of a Unique Experiment and of a Great Labor Upheaval* (Chicago: University of Chicago Press, 1942), 22.

Index

Gallman, James M., xii, xiii
General Trades Assembly, 176–78
Germans, 4–5, 11, 23–25, 33, 49,
   60, 71–73, 77–78, 178–80, 199
Gibson, Charles, 29
Giddings, Joshua, 20, 29
Grand Army of the Republic, ix,
   242–43
Grant, Ulysses S., 85–88, 90–91,
   105, 119, 123–24, 133, 185,
   225, 234, 241
Grayson, Eliza, 55–56
Greeley, Horace, 12–13, 20, 22–24,
   31
Grenfell, George St. Leger, 210–11,
   215, 219–21
Guthrie, James, 57

Halleck, Henry, 134
Halstead, Murat, 19
Hamlin, Hannibal, 32–33, 51–56
Hardee, William J., 67, 70
Harding, Frederick, 71
Harper, Joseph, 200
Hauranne, Duvergier de, 223
Havelock, Henry, 98
Hay, John, 68
Hayes, Samuel S., 224
Hecker, Frederick, 113
Higgins, Van H., 193
Hines, Thomas Henry, 207–11,
   215–22, 228
Hoffman, William H., 139
Hoge, Jane C., 102–5, 117–20,
   125–32
Holden, Charles N., 237
Holden, Levi, 237
Home for the Friendless, 101, 103
Hooker, Joseph, 240
Hossack, John, 46–48, 55
Hotchkiss, Charles T., 237
Hough, Roselle, M., 224, 226
Hoyne, Thomas, 53
Hubbard, Gurdon, 57, 237
Hugunin, James, 72

Hunter, David, 182
Hutchinson, Benjamin Peter,
   168–69
Hyer, Tommy, 9
Hyman, Cap, 230–31

Illinois and Michigan Canal, 34, 165
Illinois Central Railroad, 34, 73,
   111, 165–66, 171, 177, 191
Illinois 8th Cavalry, 182
Illinois 12th Cavalry, 121
Illinois 8th Infantry, 111
Illinois 12th Infantry, 183
Illinois 19th Infantry, 96, 98,
   111–13, 122–24, 128
Illinois 23rd Infantry, 77–83, 85,
   97, 99, 134–41
Illinois 57th Infantry, 89
Illinois 67th Infantry, 138
Illinois 88th Infantry, 183, 236–38
Illinois 89th Infantry, 113, 236–37
Illinois 90th Infantry, 113, 236, 238
Illinois 93rd Infantry, 144
Illinois 95th Infantry, 182
Illinois 105th Infantry, 239–40
Illinois State Register, 47
Indianapolis Journal, 210
Irish, 4–5, 37, 44, 49, 77–76, 85,
   97, 111, 113, 157, 178–81,
   198, 213–14
Irish Brigade. *See* Illinois 23rd
   Infantry
Irish Legion. *See* Illinois 90th
   Infantry
Island No. 10, 88, 136, 141

Jacksonville, Ill., 33
Jacobs, Benjamin F., 121
Jefferson Barracks, 73, 75
Jennison, Charles, 194–96
Jews, 113–14, 107, 125, 169
Johnson, Herschel V., 38
Joliet, Ill., 77, 201, 245
Jones, John, 181–82, 244
Judd, Norman B., 16, 27, 30